KLEZMER AMERICA

KLEZMER AMERICA

Jewishness, Ethnicity, Modernity

JONATHAN FREEDMAN

COLUMBIA UNIVERSITY PRESS NEW YORK

Columbia University Press
Publishers Since 1893
New York   Chichester, West Sussex

The author and the Press are grateful to the University of Michigan Office of the Vice-President for Research, the School of Literature, Arts and Sciences, and the Department of English for generous support in the publication of this volume.

Portions of chapter 1 appeared as "Angels, Monsters, and Jews: Crossings Between Jewish and Queer Identities in Kushner's *Angels in America*," *PMLA* 113 (1998): 90–113; portions of chapters 6 and 7 appeared as "Transgressions of a Model Minority," *Shofar* 23 (2005): 69–97; portions of chapter 7 appeared as "Who's Jewish? Some Asian American Writers and the Jewish American Literary Canon," *Michigan Quarterly Review* 41 (2003): 230–254. The author is grateful to all for permission to reprint.

Copyright © 2008 Columbia University Press
Paperback edition, 2010
All rights reserved

Library of Congress Cataloging-in-Publication Data
Freedman, Jonathan, 1954–
  Klezmer America : Jewishness, ethnicity, modernity / Jonathan Freedman.
    p. cm.
  Includes bibliographical references and index.
  ISBN 978-0-231-14278-6 (cloth)—ISBN 978-0-231-14279-3 (pbk.)—
  ISBN 978-0-231-51234-3 (ebook)
    1. Jews—United States—Intellectual life—20th century. 2. United States—Intellectual life—20th century. 3. United States—Popular culture—History—20th century. 4. Jews—United States—Identity. 5. Jews—Cultural assimilation—United States. I. Title.

E184.36.I58F74 2007
973'.04924—dc22   2007026326

For Sara

CONTENTS

ix   ACKNOWLEDGMENTS

1   **Introduction**

39   **1. Angels, Monsters and Jews**
    From Kushner to Klezmer

94   **2. Arthur Miller, Marilyn Monroe, and the Making of Ethnic Masculinity**

140   **3. Antisemitism Without Jews**
    Left Behind in the American Heartland

164   **4. The Human Stain of Race**
    Roth, Sirk, and Shaw in Black, White, and Jewish

209   **5. Conversos, Marranos, and Crypto-Latinos**
    Jewish-Hispanic Crossings and the Uses of Ethnicity

251   **6. Transgressions of a Model Minority**

283   **7. Asians and Jews in Theory and Practice**

322   **Conclusion**
    The Klezmering of America

333   NOTES
371   INDEX

ACKNOWLEDGMENTS

AM I THE ONLY PERSON who turns first to the acknowledgments page when opening an academic book? Perhaps, but the experience nevertheless reminds me just how impossible is the task of recognizing the numerous people and institutions whose contributions of time, money, and, most important, intellectual stimulation and moral support have gone into the making of this book. Nevertheless, I must try. As far as the institutions concerned, I need to thank the John Simon Guggenheim Foundation; it was during my Guggenheim year, when I was supposed to be doing something else, that several of the projects that made their way into this book were conceived. Thanks are due as well to Oxford University, and especially Ron Bush, for inviting me to serve as a Drue Heinz Visiting Professor; during my time at Oxford, more crucial thinking got done, usually, in the best donnish tradition, while walking in the University Parks. And one more such thanks: during a term spent at Williams College as the Scott Visiting Professor, arranged by the indefatigable Karen Swann, I was able to finish the manuscript in the beauty of the Berkshires, surrounded by friends old and new.

This book is also, it should be said, shaped by two remarkable—and remarkably different—institutions. One is the University of Michigan, whose commitment to interdisciplinarity is as stimulating as it is exhausting. I live here in two different and equally capacious academic units, the English Department and the Program in American Culture, and spend much of my time walking up and down stairs between their offices; the reader will perhaps note the methodological consequences of this perambulation in what follows. I've also been sustained intellectually by my extraordinary colleagues at the Frankel Center for Judaic Studies, and again there's much evidence of their knowledge and wisdom in the pages that follow. I've received help of a more material nature from the university; many thanks are due to the Office for the Vice-President for Research and the College of Literature, Arts, and Sciences for research and publication support. I want to thank with particular fervor all-powerful Donna Johnston, mistress of the mysteries of HBFI, for guiding me through the thickets of Michigan bureaucracy, to the wellsprings of its financial generosity.

Second, this book is shaped by my experience at the Bread Loaf School of English. Bread Loaf's mountain campus has been a home for me and my family on and off for twenty years, and I think now that I know every tree and rivulet between Ripton and the Middlebury Gap; certainly, I know them all on my beloved running path up into the mountains and then back down again, where much good thinking (and I fear, endorphins being somewhat indiscriminate in their effects, some bad) has taken place. More to the point, it's been persistently inspiring to be a member of a community of people united in the odd belief that talking about ideas and books is the best thing one can do with one's life, as well as one's summers. I've been truly honored over the years by my colleagues at Bread Loaf in the broadest sense of the word—my fellow faculty members, too numerous to name here, all know how important they have been to me. But Jim Maddox, the master of ceremonies who keeps inviting me back, deserves special mention. So, above all, do my remarkable Bread Loaf students/fellow teachers, the people who put themselves on the line in high schools of every description across the country with a dedication and a persistence that embarrasses me by comparison.

I need to recognize here a number of fellow scholars whose conversations, suggestions, questions, and examples have nourished me in the course of this project: Joanna Brooks, Ron Bush, David Hollinger, Amy Hungerford, Hermione Lee, Jeffrey Melnick, George Sanchez, Starry Schor, Maaera Schreiber, Michael Szalay, and Eric Sundquist, to name just a few. Ellen McLaughlin, the original Angel in America, and director/impresario Oskar Eustis were particularly generous with time and information with respect to the *Angels* material. Conversations with Bryan Cheyette in Washington, D.C. and on the Chelsea soccer pitch have catalyzed much of my thinking here; his and Susan Cooklin's numerous acts of hospitality have also made much here possible. Hana Wirth-Nesher deserves special thanks for her persistent questioning as well as bringing me face to face with lively audiences at Tel Aviv University; I need also to thank Bob Griffin, for his inspired chauffeuring and tour-guiding while in Israel, where I learned that no one is particularly interested in the dynamics of American ethnicity, since they have their own things to worry about. I've been lucky, too, to have as colleagues and friends Paul Anderson, David Halperin, Kristen Hass, June Howard, Julian Levinson, Josh Miller, Anita Norich, David Scobey, Bill Worthen, Patsy Yaeger, the indefatigable Alan Wald, and the amazingly cool Gregg Crane, each of whom has contributed in ways specific to this project as well as through making life richly pleasurable at the University of Systemic Overwork. Sidonie Smith taught me that one can write and administer at the same time; Phil Deloria taught me the art of staying sane while doing so. Colleagues here and throughout the profession—Tamar Barzel, Amy Carroll, Maria Cotera, Tom Ferraro, Kirsten Silva Gruesz, Dan Itzkovitz, Maria Montoya, Deborah Dash Moore, MacDonald Moore, Ross Posnock, Marina Rustow, Cindy Weinstein—have commented on specific portions of the manuscript or answered frantic research questions in ways that have made it substantially better. Other friends—Pearl Abraham, Sarah Beckwith, Monica Feinberg Cohen, Dan Hack, Marvin Krislov, Anita Sokolsky, Sam Tanenhaus, Steve Tifft, Blakey Vermeule—have nourished me (often on email) in ways they might not always recognize, but for which I am grateful. My astonishing research assistant, Josh Lambert, has chased down Chinese restaurant menus in Yiddish and ballet photographs in the archive with an efficiency matched only by his cheerfulness. Susan Pensak was more than an amazingly accomplished copyeditor; interlocutor and perhaps even coconspirator would more fully describe her role. Jennifer Crewe shepherded the book through the editorial process with admirable efficiency and grace; two wonderful anonymous reader's reports, from which it has much profited, helped as well. Needless but necessary to say, none of the above bears the slightest hint of responsibility for the aberrations and inaccuracies of the author.

These people have all made my life and work better in incalculable ways. Ben and Miriam, delightful combinations of seriousness and scampiness, make it meaningful. So does the person to whom this book is dedicated. Sara Blair has read every single word of the manuscript of this book, multiply, approving of most of them; encouraged me when I felt too strongly the inadequacies of my argument; pushed me to think harder and write more clearly. More important, she's offered me her love as well as her intelligence. I don't know which is the rarer gift; I remain grateful for both more than words can say.

KLEZMER AMERICA

INTRODUCTION

IN 1874 Oliver Wendell Holmes—doctor, essayist, Autocrat of the Breakfast Table, Boston Brahmin par excellence (indeed, the very figure who first gave that caste its name)—penned a poem that, among its many attributes, announces some of the key themes and variations of this book. Entitled *At the Pantomime*, the poem describes a proper Bostonian very much like Holmes himself attending a popular theatrical event in Boston. Already grumpy when he arrives, further irritated by the crowd in which he finds himself, he is particularly troubled by the arrival of "Hebrews, not a few" whom he then describes in classically stereotyped terms: "Black-bearded, swarthy,—at their side / Dark, jewelled women, orient-eyed." As the poem continues, the speaker's ire augments, and he launches into a rant whose intensity seems to catch even the poet himself by surprise:

> Next on my left a breathing form
> Wedged up against me, close and warm;
> The beak that crowned the bistred face
> Betrayed the mould of Abraham's race,—
> That coal-black hair, that smoke-brown hue,—
> Ah, cursèd, unbelieving Jew!
> I started, shuddering, to the right,
> And squeezed—a second Israelite!
>
> ... The hook-nosed kite of carrion clothes,
> The snaky usurer, him that crawls
> And cheats beneath the golden balls.
> Moses and Levi, all the horde,
> Spawn of the race that slew its Lord.

But midway through this catalogue of aspersions, the speaker quite literally takes another look. He refocuses his attention "full on the younger of the twain" and notices neither an egregious nose nor visible signs of usurious instincts but rather the visage of a biblical hero: "a fresh young cheek whose olive hue / The mantling blood shows faintly through; / Locks dark as midnight, that divide / And shade the neck on either side; soft, gentle, loving eyes that gleam / Clear as a starlit mountain stream." And more: the poet also notes that this young David's "peerless blood . . . flows unmingled from the Flood"—and contrasts it with the mixed, mingled status of Anglo-Saxons like himself, whose "scutcheon [is] spotted with the stains / Of Norman thieves and pirate Danes!" Following this bout of self-deprecating irony, Holmes reconciles himself to the Hebrews among whom he finds himself and ends first with a phantasmagoric vision, then something of a benediction:

> A sudden mist, a watery screen,
> Dropped like a veil before the scene;
> The shadow floated from my soul,
> And to my lips a whisper stole,—
> "Thy prophets caught the Spirit's flame,
> From thee the Son of Mary came,
> With thee the Father deigned to dwell,—
> Peace be upon thee, Israel!"

Although written (or, properly, rewritten) three years before the banning of Jewish businessman Joseph Seligman from the Saratoga Resorts, an incident generally considered to kick off the rise of fin de siècle anti-semitism in the U.S; seven years before the attempted assassination of Czar Alexander I, which sparked first a wave of pogroms and repressive legislation and then the massive emigration of Russian Jews to America; and exactly fifty years before the passage of the Immigration Restriction Act of 1924, which effectively choked that immigration off, the poem presciently traces some of the major patterns of response to the presence of Jews in the American scene. It suggests that despite their relatively small numbers, Jews played a disproportionately prominent role in the U.S. literary and cultural imagination; it also implies that they disrupted its theater as thoroughly as they did Holmes's pantomime house. Throughout the poem a large amount of symbolic capital is invested in these irritating Hebrews.[1] At its opening they stand in for what *really* seems to be troubling Holmes, the audience itself. Like the Dantean crowd ("heads piled on heads at every door"), the Hebrews "not a few" supply the mass that makes mass culture, squeezing the representative of genteel high culture between their "close and warm" foreign bodies. But their presence in the crowd has a more complicated, indeed complicating, dimension. Not only do they represent the audience of the mass cultural event; as the ambiguous title of the poem suggests, they also comprise an essential part of the spectacle itself. At the pantomime it is the Jews who are the silent objects of representation rather than being—or in addition to being—spectators of the performance they and the slumming speaker are there to witness.

Equally complicating is the variety of terms with which the poet seeks to catalogue these nettlesome Hebrews. Notably, these include not only the standard physiognomic markers of Jewish identity—hook-nosed men, "orient-eyed" women—but also that classic American marker of identity, skin color. Here, too, his identifications are labile, confused, all over the place. The Hebrews are variously described as possessing a "smoke-brown hue," as bearing "olive skin," and as being "bistered" in color—the last of these a yellowish-brown pigment, which, to jump ahead in by two generations, also names the sallow greasepaint minstrel performers applied to their face when playing Jews.[2] The Hebrews' brown/olive/yellow bisteredness can't be placed in either of the culturally loaded categories that define American racial ideology, black and white; instead, it exists in a liminal state, a place somewhere in-between.

Similarly, Holmes proposes multiple, contradictory gender identifications for these Jews, especially these Jewish men. In the first stanzas they are identified in the familiar terms of medieval and early modern antisemitism. Snaky and hook-nosed, these "Hebrews" are not only duskyhued Satans but also marked by facial accoutrements that makes them seem more like rampant monsters—"spawn"—than full humans. But the second Jew to whom he turns is described in strikingly different language. Quite other than a biblical David, he is limned as a heroine of historical romance. His dark visage can't obscure his rosy-hued cheeks (a mark of the romance heroine dating back at least to the *Roman de la Rose*), and his deep, soulful eyes resemble those of the orient-eyed Jewish women described a few stanzas earlier or, perhaps more tellingly, of a character like Rebecca in Sir Walter Scott's *Ivanhoe*. Indeed, Holmes's description of this young man's delicate hair, fine neck, and chiseled nose quite closely tracks Scott's panegyric to the young Jewess:

> Her turban of yellow silk suited well with the darkness of her complexion. The brilliancy of her eyes, the superb arch of her eyebrows, her well-formed aquiline nose, her teeth as white as pearl, and the profusion of her sable tresses, which, each arranged in its own little spiral of twisted curls, fell down upon as much of a lovely neck and bosom as a simarre of the richest Persian silk, exhibiting flowers in their natural colours embossed upon a purple ground, permitted to be visible—all these constituted a combination of loveliness, which yielded not to the most beautiful of the maidens who surrounded her.³

The Jewish man, according to the poem, alternates between threatening hyperphallicism and ravishing, radiant femininity; insofar as that figure is to be seen as fully human, it is in the latter capacity that he is included in the species. And here the poet's words call into question not only the specifics of his subjects' identity but also of his own. What does it mean, exactly, for this aggressively normative speaker, one made so acutely uncomfortable by the phallic Jewish men surrounding him, to paint a detailed portrait of a beautiful, androgynous Jewish youth?

Last but not least in the poem's parade of complexities is its theology. On this ground in particular, Holmes undergoes a striking metamorphosis. He begins by articulating the classic slurs of Christian anti-Judaism, the claim that Jews were "cursed" for "unbelieving," that they turned deaf ears on Christ's revelation. He goes further, invoking the yet more loaded slur of the Jew as Christ killers, as a people bearing collective responsibility for Christ's hideous death itself. And he goes further still. This "horde" is "spawn of the race that slew its Lord!": the very language reduces Jews, as is so common in the slurring imagery of antisemitism, to a subhuman status. But, as the poem continues, the poet explores the flip side of this claim—the recognition that Mary and Christ (much less the unmentioned Joseph) were themselves Jews. The result is what can only be described as ambivalence not only about the ontological status of the Jew but of the Christian as well. If Jews are indeed so vile, then how can Christ and Mary have been, well, Jewish? And if Christianity really is the fulfillment of the Jewish prototype, doesn't this mean that the Jews got there first—and that

Christians are uniquely dependent on their covenant for their own dispensation?*

I've spent so much time on this lyric because it either registers or anticipates many of the imaginative developments with which I shall be concerned here, both with respect to the figure of the Jew and to that figure's effect on the culture into which Jews were entering in such great numbers at precisely this time. The wildly overwrought symbolic power invested in these newly arriving Jews (indeed, "not a few" collapses, over the course of the poem, into just one or two); the labile and wildly disproportionate affect, ranging from disgust to identification and passing at just about every point in between; the persistent identification of Jews with mass culture, either as spectacles, producers, or audiences; most importantly of all, the play of overdeterminations and ambivalences on a variety of planes—ethnic, racial, gendered, as well as theological: these, as we shall see, define the shifting backdrop of the theater of the West in general and America in particular that Jews entered with such disruptive force—as both subjects and objects—in the late nineteenth century.

But merely to put the matter this way is to understate its complexity. Americanizing Jews underwent comparable discursive contortions as they started to find their place in the playhouse that was U.S. culture and society in the later years of the nineteenth and first years of the twentieth

---

*This poem represents something of a departure in American representations of the figures it attempts to name. It takes conspicuous exception to its precursor text, Henry Longfellow's 1852 "The Jewish Cemetery in Newport." For Longfellow, as so much of the Christian culture for which he speaks, Jews are to be construed as victims of history, eternal wandering exiles ("the Ishmaels and Hagars of mankind") who have been annihilated by the passage of time:

> The mystic volume of the world they read,
> Spelling it backward, like a Hebrew book,
> Till life became a Legend of the Dead.
>
> But ah! what once has been shall be no more!
> The groaning earth in travail and in pain
> Brings forth its races, but does not restore,
> And the dead nations never rise again.

As I have been arguing, Holmes's poem, by contrast, locates Jews as an altogether too-alive presence in the culture and society at large—an uncomfortably multiplying addition to the theater and the speaker's consciousness into which they are so painfully intruding.

century. Beginning in the decades after Holmes's poem, Jewish Americans of many varieties and cultural positions responded to their social construction with a virtually unparalleled set of imaginative productions in a number of media: newspapers, theater, novels, poetry, music, and—beginning in the 1910s—social and cultural criticism in the academy as well as in Lower East Side feuilletons or the *Forward*. Indeed, the shifting tides of twentieth-century Jewish American imaginative production in the broadest sense of the word—from the fictions of Cahan and Yezierska and Henry Roth through those of Bernard Malamud, Saul Bellow, Grace Paley, Philip Roth, and Tony Kushner; from the schema of pioneering sociologists like Horace Kallen, Franz Boas, and Lewis Harth to those of the more established generation of Seymour Martin Lipset, Daniel Bell, or Milton Gordon; from the music of Irving Berlin, George Gershwin, and Artie Shaw to that of Leonard Bernstein and beyond to that of John Zorn or the Klezmatics—can be read as a dynamic, shifting set of responses to the ambivalences and overdeterminations announced in Holmes's poem. Sometimes Jewish intellectuals and culture makers contested the images with which they were confronted and by which they were construed. At others, they internalized these constructions—or perhaps apotropaically externalized by embodying them, as in the classic Jewish jokes of the classic Jewish comedians, which mingle stereotype with aggression.[4] Often they did both—as in Philip Roth or Tony Kushner's triumphant transformation of the culturally loaded figure of the Jewish pervert into a culture hero. At still other times, they projected these images outward onto other racial and ethnic groups, whom they either consciously or unwittingly viewed as successful or failed versions of their images of themselves. But they also did more. In their manifold forms of cultural production Jewish writers, artists, and intellectuals helped transform the ways in which Americans imagined Otherness itself—the concept in the abstract, to be sure, but—of equal or even greater importance—the specific contours that other Others took in the unfolding ethnoracial drama of the twentieth-century U.S. Indeed, I argue that the series of representations created by gentiles and Jews alike, on the fly, out of their mutually constitutive and destabilizing encounters with each other, helped crucially to shape the stories and the metastories U.S. culture tells about race, ethnicity, and gender and their shifting relation to normative and counternormative identities in a rapidly changing America.

INTRODUCTION   7

To cite but the most obvious example: the cultural narrative of the immigrant in America—one in the headlines even as I write—is unimaginable without Jews. Although Jews constituted a decided minority of the remarkable immigration to the U.S. between 1880 and 1924 (roughly four out of the twenty million or so who made their way to the U.S. during this period), Jewish-specific images, sites, experiences have become broadly representative of that social moment itself—a culturally validated synecdoche, to put it in rhetorical terms, for the experience undergone by all immigrants to America between 1880 and 1924. It's a poem by Jewish American Emma Lazarus that gives articulate speech to the mute Statue of Liberty; it's the host of Jewish-authored novels about experience on the Lower East Side that have helped define not just that space but immigrant experience tout court; it's a set of tropes associated with Jewish culture at its most stereotypical—the hardworking entrepreneur with the pushcart or the small candy store, the rapid ascent from the overcrowded tenements to the soulless suburbs, the all-sacrificing or all-devouring mother wringing her hands over her Americanizing children, etc., etc., etc.—that have built a normative narrative for immigrants across the board.* But, as that last development in

---

* To be clear about my argument here: the claim isn't that there aren't important forms of social experience among so-called ethnics that are counter to the Jewish norm or for that matter, to that of the European immigrants who flooded into the United States in this period that Jews have come to symbolize: to the contrary, these are precisely what I'm trying to emphasize. Nor is it that there aren't other crucial forms of imaginative expression from or about this era by writers of other immigrant groups—see the excellent fictions of Sui Sin Far or, later, John Fante—but these are sporadic in comparison with Jewish cultural production, at least insofar as that cultural production served to define the urban immigrant experience for the white, Anglo, mainstream audience. With respect to Italian Americans, for example, Thomas Ferraro writes, not without ruefulness: "Although the Italian sections of the Lower East Side always attracted notice in the slumming narratives of the late Gilded Age . . . and although a couple of autobiographies were published by successful Italian immigrants in the 1920s . . . there is almost nothing by way of fiction proper in English between a short story, 'Peppino,' which Luigi Venture translated from his own French in 1886, and the first accomplished novel, Garibaldi M. Lapolla's *The Grand Gennaro* (1934), both of which are entirely forgotten except by a handful of Italian-American literature specialists. Ghetto literature in its myriad incarnations, at least from the 1890s through the 1930s, was primarily and therefore iconically about Russian-Polish Jews." *Feeling Italian: The Art of Ethnicity in America* (New York: New York University Press, 2005), pp. 214–215. Similarly, Irish American literature of the period (and before) is wonderfully treated by Ron Ebest's *Private Histories: The Writing of Irish Americans, 1900–1935* (South Bend: University of Notre Dame Press, 2005), but here too one senses the (perhaps

particular suggests, what seems to be synecdoche, a part standing for a larger whole, rapidly transformed itself into a set of metonymies—of substitutions that work by the fuzzy logic of association—in such a way as to project these narratives onto other ethnic groups, conflating their quite diverse histories with Jewish American norms and expectations, images and shadows, frequently eliding their own distinctive trajectories and experiences in favor of Jewish ones.

Sometimes these overlapping and mutually reinforcing processes worked in such a way as to Jewify a mass of heterogeneous cultural material; at others they worked to do the reverse, to replace a Jewish-centered discursive context with something quite different. Consider, as an example of the first, the nature and properties of that place, at once real and symbolic, we call "the Lower East Side." Even though, as Hasia Diner has powerfully argued, Jews were just one of the many groups who lived in that now hallowed ground (an ill-defined entity at the time whose actual lineaments extended broadly throughout downtown New York) and were the first to abandon it for Brownsville, the Bronx, and Westchester, "the Jewish Lower East Side" has served as a metonym not only for Jewish American experience but for that of turn-of-the-century immigrants at large, uniting the very different races, cultures, and experiences that jostled there in one associational admixture in which the Jewish ingredient came to define the entire concoction.⁵

As an example of the opposite tendency, consider that equally resonant trope, "the ghetto." Born of the Jewish experience in medieval Europe (the word originates in fourteenth-century Venice, originally referencing the slag from the iron foundries in the quarter in which Jews were confined), the term became attached to Jewish quarters of London by Israel Zangwill's *Children of the Ghetto* (1892). A theatrical version of Zangwill's play toured America with great fanfare in 1901, leading to a widespread adoption of the term in the following years by such gentry intellectuals as Hutchins Hapgood (*The Spirit of the Ghetto*, 1902) and Lincoln Steffens (*The Shame of the Cities*, 1904). In 1929 Chicago-school sociologist Lewis

---

undue, certainly problematic) priority of the Jewish literary tradition as a paradigm for ethnic writing across the board. Ebest has much to say about James Farrell in the context of urban writing, for example, but it's telling that far more ink has been spilled in the past decades on Farrell's contemporary Henry Roth, completely reversing the priorities of the 1930s and 1940s.

Wirth entitled his path-breaking study of the pathologies and possibilities of the Jewish neighborhoods of Chicago *The Ghetto*—a book, as Edna Nashon has observed, that quotes substantially from Zangwill.[6] In the 1930s and 1940s, however, the term broadened out, via Langston Hughes and James Baldwin as well as sociologists like Kenneth Clark (*Dark Ghetto*) and Gunnar Myrdal, to designate a specifically black experience of immiseration and segregation in the urban metropolis. This is how the term got used broadly throughout culture in the 1960s and 1970s—who can forget Elvis Presley's warbling, in his late-career baritone, "On a cold and gray Chicago mornin' / A poor little baby child is born / *In the ghetto*"? Now the term has no historical memory at all (for example, Beverly Hills is called the "Gucci ghetto")—a process that again began early with Jews (there are references to the Bronx or the suburbs as a "gilded ghetto" as early as 1927) but that lost any such identification over time.[7]

The most powerful deployments of the discourse of Jewishness combine these principles of remembering and forgetting, projection and erasure, to create new ideological and imaginative structures, amalgams that have done crucial cultural work. Thus, as Zygmunt Bauman and, following in his footsteps, Jon Stratton have reminded us, although the hallowed notion of assimilation was first defined by Robert Park and E. W. Burgess in the 1920s, its ensemble of normative implications was constructed and then installed in the center of the study of U.S. ethnic experience by Jewish American social scientists with the model of the quite anomalous Jewish experience in mind.[8] So too, even more powerfully, the very idea of ethnicity as it got built in the 1920s was crucially shaped by the Jewish experience. Indeed, this had been the case from the very origins of the idea of ethnicity tout court. The construction—or as Werner Sollors would put it, the invention*—of a category of group identity shaped around national

---

* Sollors's stress, especially in his work of the 1980s, on ethnicity as a construct, and on its relation to modernist culture making, have been quite important to my privileging of the ethnic as a space of category confusion and hybridizing reinvention. His work has been crucial to the field at large, even though I think it would be fair to say that that field has been increasingly dominated by a greater awareness of the intransigencies of race, an awareness with which this book is quarreling. Sollors's work has since moved on to the equally fascinating question of multilinguality in America. I might take the occasion to add here that Sollors may well have influenced Harvard-trained Gish Jen, whose *Mona in the Promised Land*, discussed in chapter 7, is a virtual illustration of the consent-and-descent thesis of ethnic identity formation. See Werner Sollors, *Beyond Ethncity: Consent and Descent in*

or regional origin, culture, language rather than religion (the prime vector of registering difference until the Enlightenment) or race (the master category that was to replace it) was itself a possibility largely negotiated through the figure of the assimilating Jew from at least the fifteenth century forward. I'll be arguing later that the complex responses to the Iberian conversion and persecution of the Jews culminating in their expulsion in the *annus horriblis* of 1492 saw the first emergence of this new category of identification, challenging both the religious-based norms of established Jewish communities and the proto-racialism of the Spanish crown who insisted on *limpieza de sangre*—purity of blood—as a sine qua non for social acceptance and privilege. But the notion roils through the career of Jews in Europe thereafter. The notion of culture, religion, and language as crucial determinants of group identity was specifically developed in German Romantic philosophy, especially in Hegel and Herder, with constant nervous reference to the Jew, who might prove to be either an example of such a category—this is a possibility that Herder, whose discursive nexus between language, mores, and group identity was to prove crucial to the construction of ethnic identity, was to assert—or an example of its failure—as in Hegel, where Jews are seen as atavistic, tribal pursuers of a degraded and superseded faith.[9] Such a notion grows, too, in nineteenth-century German sociology in which, as Sander Gilman suggests, the Jew is positioned as the archetypal "ethnic" Other: as the stranger within the nation-state (as German Jewish sociologist Georg Simmel argued, with interesting resonances in such diverse scholars as Park and Burgess, who translated Simmel's *The Stranger* in 1921, and Ronald Takaki, who alluded to Simmel in the very title of his survey of Asian American history, *Strangers from a Different Shore*) or as the self-willed "pariah caste" (as Max Weber suggested, with equally powerful ramifications in the work of Hannah Arendt). In all these cases the question of the Jewish presence within the new nation-states of Europe, brought to a fever pitch by massive immigration from eastern and southern Europe in the later portion of the nineteenth century, got caught up in a contest over national, racial, and cultural belonging in which the Jew-as-archetypal insider-outsider "comes to be the litmus test for cultural ... difference" itself.[10]

American Culture (New York: Oxford University Press, 1986), and "Introduction: The Invention of Ethnicity," in *The Invention of Ethnicity* (New York: Oxford, 1989), pp. ix–xx.

I've gone into this European context because it provides a crucial backdrop to the American adaptation of the notion of the ethnic (one rarely noted by even the most attentive students of the American invention of ethnicity); in the U.S. as in Europe, a demographic change led to a challenge to the national narrative, and the construction of a category that would recognize difference without falling into the language of racial or religious essentialism became caught up with the dialectics of Jewish entry into the American ethnosphere. Thus, as Victoria Hattam has recently argued, the concept of ethnicity in the sense in which we understand the term was constructed by Jewish intellectuals like Horace Kallen, Maurice Fishberg, Julius Draschler, and Isaac Berkson in the 1920s and 1930s, who crafted the notion of ethnic identity in venues like the *Menorah Journal* in large measure as a response to their experience as racialized others in a particularly reactionary America. Having been put into academic play in the 1940s by scholars W. Lloyd Warner and Paul Lunt, the notion was consolidated in the 1950s by Jewish social scientists like Nathan Glazer, Daniel Bell, and Seymour Martin Lipset, responding implicitly and at times explicitly not only to U.S. racial politics but also to the Nazi discourse of Aryan superiority. The idiom of ethnicity was persistently shaped, in other words, by Jewish intellectuals of various persuasions, backgrounds, and ideological dispositions working at various times and in different ways in dialogue with, and dissent from, gentile colleagues (Kallen's colleagues at the University of Wisconsin included Robert Park and Thorsten Veblen, whom he quite consciously sought to counter; Bell's included Talcott Parsons; Glazer of course coauthored with Daniel Patrick Moynihan). More consequentially, the idea of ethnicity itself was produced under the shadow of the anti-immigrant movement of the 1920s and the Holocaust and was designed to contest those two explosions of antisemitic sentiment in twentieth-century history.*

---

*This is not the time or place to go into an elaborate discussion of the idea of ethnicity and its complex and fallible negotiations between the idioms of "culture" and "race" as determinants of identity—for Hattam the attempts to break out of the idiom of race via a discourse of ethnicity fail, felled by the persistence of the very race thinking its theorists tried to escape. (The argument is similar to the one that Walter Michaels makes about race and culture in the same period.) What I'm pointing to here are two things: first that this problematic was built into both the idioms of race and ethnicity itself from the moment Herder conflated racial identity with language, nation, family et al.—the things we have come to

Since the notion of ethnicity will be my one of my central concerns over the course of this book, I have devoted perhaps too much time to the unstable but powerful role played Jews and by the shifting figure of the Jew in its construction. But, before moving on, I need to note that the same metonymizing role is played by the Jew in more specific debates. I am thinking here of—and in later chapters will devote more attention to—the construction at the crossroads of the discourses of ethnicity and assimilation of the "the model minority," a notion built on the Jewish American success story that frequently places Asian Americans in the category of the "new Jews" and critiques other ethnic and racial groups for not following this model of success through educational achievement and inspired bootstrapping.[11] Such too is the case with other, darker, fictions originating in the American encounter with Jews that still linger on: in the identification of the Jew with forms of sexual pleasure and/or perversion, for example, that rears its ugly but seductive head not only in Holmes's poem but throughout the twentieth century: the discursive slide from the stereotypical lascivious Jew to the "homosexual," for example. Similar, and even more consequential, has been the continuing force of the overdetermined relation of Jews to Christianity that shapes contemporary Christian right fictions and politics alike.

But—as that last example suggests—the Jewish precedent doesn't just remain a shadowy subtext in the making of the American racial and ethnic imaginary; rather, Jews served and serve as a powerful but ambiguous signifier, one whose meaning is as much up for grabs in the ethnoracial hurly-burly of contemporary America as it was for Holmes and the WASP

---

name by both the terms *ethnicity* and *culture;* so it's no surprise to see that discursive conflation at work a century and a half later. Second, and perhaps more important, a largely ignored subtext in all these writers is the specificities of the Jewish (as opposed to the Jewish American) experience that these writers bring to the conceptual table. "Cultural pluralism," after all, has not only a Deweyan provenance but a specific application for peoples of a diaspora, peoples, in other words, whose own experience was plurally constructed out of a centuries-long dialogue with the peoples among whom they lived. So, I am suggesting, did "ethnicity," which, mutatis mutandis, projects the experience of diasporic identity formation into a cultural universal. What these writers, thinkers, and social scientists did, for better or worse, in other words, was to project their own experience as Jews in a racist and/or post-Holocaust world into a set of intellectual principles that helped reshape the ways in which their culture envisioned human difference itself. That they failed the test of consistency is not unimportant—but it's not the whole story either.

intellectuals who followed in his footsteps. To cite but one, particularly resonant, example: as I was revising this introduction for what seemed to be the millionth time, my mandatory Web scanning for the day took me to the *Los Angeles Times*, where I encountered a story entitled "Latinos Give New Voice to Neil Diamond Anthem."[12] It portrays the uses of Diamond's song "America," from the remake of *The Jazz Singer*, in the remarkable (and, to this critic, totally inspiring) mass rallies being staged by immigrants in 2006, largely but not exclusively Latino, across the United States in protest of punitive anti-immigration legislation. Like "We Shall Overcome," Neil Diamond's song is poised to become the theme song of a radically transformative social movement, according to the piece's author, Ann Powers. But "America" is a self-reflexively kitschy amalgam: it's "rooted in the Yiddish music of Diamond's Brooklyn youth ... on to Broadway and the Borscht Belt and lands on the edge of disco—a border-crossing trek unto itself." According to Powers, the tune resonates not through *The Jazz Singer*, or the ethnic revival of the 1980s (it did service as background music for Michael Dukakis's ill-fated presidential campaign of 1988), but as it got routed through Cheech and Chong's 1987 film, *Born in East L.A.*, where it serves as an ironic musical counterpoint to a comic scene portraying a mad rush of Mexicans across the border. "In this light," Powers continues, "the Latino resurrection of Diamond's 'America' makes delicious sense. It's a joke that's not a joke, an embrace of something seemingly 'other' that ends up an invocation of ethnic pride."

Many activists find the use of this song problematic, preferring instead to foreground the work of performers who conjoin political engagement with an organic relation to the community in the service of whom their music is being deployed: Los Tigres del Norte, Ricardo Arjona, and the Jornaleros del Norte, who helped lead the Wilshire Boulevard march. (As Powers also reminds us, Arjona's "Mojado" can serve as a compelling alternative to the bootstrapping optimism of "America"; it's a haunting ballad about the lives and plights of undocumented workers.) Others in the Latino community see the citation of "America" as a benign, even praiseworthy phenomenon. My point here is not to take a position in the controversy but to point to how it suggests both the continuing *loadedness* of Jewish cultural production to the politics of our current moment. And on all sides: the activists who critique the appropriation of Diamond's "America" are objecting not so much to its *shlocky* tonalities as to the implicit claim that their experience in America can be charted in terms of those of previous ones. They stand for the position that the dynamics of racialized difference, globalization, post-NAFTA outsourcing and the persistent process of immigrant proletarianization, as well as the specific dynamics of Latino subcultural production, should not be conflated with the experience of turn-of-the century whites incarnated not only by Diamond's song but also by the film versions of *The Jazz Singer*, both of which center on the Jewish experience and one of which (the 1927 version) notoriously suggests that the path to popular success for Jews lay through the adoption of blackface. Those who seek to deploy the song—by and large, it would seem, the rank and file rather than the leaders of this new political movement—have no less serious political work in mind. Vis-à-vis the larger Latino audience, they suggest that the sacralized model of immigration ought to apply to this ethnoracialized group as much as it has come to do for their predecessors: to play "America" the song at an immigrants' rights rally is to claim that America the nation is the marchers' as well as Neil Diamond's (a sentiment with which Diamond enthusiastically concurs). And vis-à-vis the white audience for whom the notion of immigrant had, in the 1970s and 1980s become either sacralized or routinized, they remind us that the complaints that circulate about the "new immigrants"—that they're foreign-language speaking, culturally alien, unassimilable outsiders owing allegiance to other countries; that they're dirty, disease-ridden undercutters of the labor market for working-class Americans—were made quite explicitly about "old" immigrants as well. The marchers' use of Diamond's song deconstructs the divide between the rhetoric of new and old itself, suggesting that a politics of immigrant rights can plausibly call upon the *mythoi* of a previous generation while pushing toward a quite different set of predications about race, citizenship, and identity.*

---

*In Diamond's version of the film, young Jack Robin is asked to fill in for a friend in an all-black group at a crucial black nightclub gig; in order to make the masquerade work, he goes onstage in blackface. But, halfway through the performance, audience members, noticing that his hands haven't been blacked up, hiss him offstage, causing a riot that lands him in jail. The scene offers a comic reversal of the blackface tradition: in the post–civil rights era, it suggests, the Jewish performer *can't* make his racial masquerade work. The scene may also contain a ironic reference to the song "Dirty Hands, Dirty Face" performed by Jolson in the 1927 *The Jazz Singer:* which, after all, is "dirtier" in this context, a black face or white hands?

And the means by which they do so are significant as well. The song is perhaps best envisioned through a no doubt overfamiliar trope Freud used to describe the unconscious, as a "mystic writing pad"—a palimpsest onto which is inscribed a variety of texts and contexts that in turn overwrite each other without effacing traces of previous inscriptions. What the marchers are doing, after all, is alluding not just to one song but to a whole chain of cultural remakings: they adopt and transform Cheech and Chong's ironical redeployment of Neil Diamond's reverent reworking of the Warner Brothers's overwrought revision of Samson Raphelson's stage adaptation, *The Day of Atonement*, of his original short story, *The Jazz Singer*, each of which leaves its traces behind even as it gets overwritten by a successor text. Adding their own contribution to this chain of transmission, these marchers remind us that the process of culture making at its most elemental and dynamic proceeds through virtually innumerable such acts of appropriation, revision, counterrevision, and outright theft, ones whose ends are never wholly predictable from their origins. After all, the Broadway production added blackface to Raphelson's story; the Warner Brothers extended the blackface from one scene to several when they made *Day of Atonement* into *The Jazz Singer*; Diamond's *Jazz Singer* alludes ironically to the blackface tradition in its opening scenes, then cites it no more. Similarly, Diamond added the "America" topos to the Warner Brothers version of the narrative; Cheech and Chong made that topos signify something quite different. But, even through their revisionary adaptation of a revisionary adaptation of a revisionary adaptation, the Diamond-deploying marchers remind us that Jews, Judaism, and/or Jewishness, however occulted and resignified by such cultural reworkings, remain central to the process of ethnocultural rechurning.

Hence the occasion for this book. It's the central thesis of my project that dealing with the collective fictions that accrete around the example of Jews, Jewishness, and Judaism can unsettle even the most seemingly secure of the seemingly calcified categories by which our culture parses otherness—and, to the immigrant and ethnic othernesses I have inventoried above, I would add racial alterity, gender difference, sexual dissidence. Perhaps more important, they can do this in such a way as to reveal what was at stake in the making of those categories in the first place. When we place the Jew and all the things associated with that figure into such culturally powerful if resolutely multiple conceptual contexts, the things we "know" about all of these categories become less certain—and this allows us to know, or at least guess, other things about them as well. Think of this process—the process this book attempts to anatomize—as a series of swirling Venn diagrams in which the conceptual circles rotate into each other's gravitational field, creating as they go new centers of meaning, which in turn swirl into new, and different circles of significance. Or think of it—as I suggested above—as a kind of postmodern mystic writing pad in which new and previous inscriptions combine to making an intricate, if constantly shifting, lacework of designs.

Tracing—and frequently celebrating—these designs will be my goal in the pages that follow. I range up and down the ladder of cultural hierarchy, treating popular films, jazz, classical music, middlebrow and high cultural fiction alike, engaging as I do so critical work from film studies and musicology, although I return to the central field of my expertise and interest, the study of literary texts. I have framed this inquire in interdisciplinary terms for a number of reasons—for one thing, it gives me a chance to write about works I adore from a number of different media—but with a frankly utopian—or at least a persistently forward-looking—bias in mind. It is, I have come to believe, in the dynamic interplay between individual and collective imaginations, new technologies and the social and cultural institutions they spawned, and the enlarging but reshaping reading, listening, and viewing publics that new configurations of social life are scouted out, tested, and shaped well before they enter into political consciousness. In this sense, I hope that this book will not only be a study of the cultural and social work done in and through Jews, Judaism, and Jewishness from, say, Holmes's time to that of postwar suburbia (the usual time span of important studies with which this book is in dialogue, most of which tellingly end their ethnocultural histories with the cultural and social dispensations of the 1950s). I also aim to provide an account of the newer cultural formations that continue to swirl around the figure of the Jew, formations that point toward changing ethnoracial and ethnocultural dispensations with enormous implications for the future of the U.S. in years to come.

For in recent years Jewish and non-Jewish writers, musicians, and culture makers have, in remarkable collaborative efforts, been seeking to forge a poetics and politics of representation that would negotiate new relations to the social and new predications of gender, race, and ethnicity; chart out new structures of imaginative experience; and create new institutions in which to express them. Indeed, it seems to me that, from the perspective of the *longue durée* of Jewish culture in the United States, this is less of a novelty than a return to an earlier dispensation: to the febrile and complex experimentation of the early modernist era, for example, when Jews and gentiles, whether on Tin Pan Alley, in Greenwich Village, or around Hollywood, were engaged, in various ways at all ends of the cultural spectrum, with modalities of artistic creation that bent and reshaped received aesthetic forms and practices. We could call this distinctive quality of the Jewish interface with a distinctively American modernity many things, and associate it with many different kinds of cultural practice: the movies, novels, social science, and so on. The artistic form I want to use both as an organizing trope and as a compelling practice in its own right to gloss and illuminate the Jewish/modernity complex is a form that has itself undergone a rapid and remarkable transformation in the past decades: the kind of music Americans have come to call *klezmer*.

Originating among eastern European Jewry as an intimate part of everyday life, klezmer (from *kley zemer*, or "musical instrument" in Yiddish, the word morphed into "musician" itself, with a slightly derogatory connotation) was transported to the United States and flourished in traditional neighborhoods like the Lower East Side and Brooklyn. (The Brooklyn crime syndicate in the 1920s, for example—largely drawn from the criminal underclass of Odessa—virtually adopted the great klezmer virtuoso Naftule Brandwein, who played regularly at their all-night bacchanalias in addition to his regular gigs with various Lower East Side orchestras and the usual performances at ceremonial events.) By the 1940s and 1950s, however, klezmer receded in communal prominence; the nostalgic property of an older generation, it appeared to be superannuated in the face of the rise of a postwar Jewish culture focused on such newer formations as stand-up comedy, jazz music, and New Left politics. But in the 1980s klezmer staged a remarkable revival. Led by an unlikely assortment of figures—scholars, musicians from the New England Conservatory of Music, jazz musicians from the "downtown scene" of the Lower East Side— klezmer revivalists brought this seemingly discarded music back into popular currency and cultural vibrancy.

The klezmer revival has itself been the source of much historical and critical excavation-work in recent years by both scholars inside the academy like musicologist Mark Slobin or Tamar Barzel and those without, like Henry Sapoznik; and it has also been theorized wonderfully by Barbara Kirschenblatt-Gimblett, for whom the transformation of klezmer from an example of nostalgic roots nurturing into a wide-ranging set of cultural practices betokens the variable, shifting uses of traditional culture itself.[13] But, in the intervening years, the klezmer revival has to a certain extent receded—or to be more precise, split in two. On the one hand, it has mainstreamed itself, become a part of official Jewish culture: a staple of programming at local Jewish Community Centers and synagogues as well as weddings and bar mitzvahs. On the other, it continues to ramify within the world of avant-garde musical praxis, where it has entered into dialogue with other musical forms and idioms (jazz, hip-hop, Balkans music, classical) through the offices of a number of very talented and versatile musicians. We are, that is to say, in a postklezmer moment, at least in the sense in which klezmer first burst on the American cultural scene: a moment at which klezmer has become an acknowledged—at times, almost a routine—part of the musical soundscape while klezmer-inflected experimentation continues to transform even as it is transformed by the manifold musics of America.

Like Kirschenblatt-Gimblett, if with a different spin, I accord klezmer central importance as both a practice and a metaphor. Two qualities of the klezmer revival and the postklezmer moment alike make them especially salient to the larger arguments of this book: their relentless and even definitional hybridity and their ceaseless and even foundational revisionism— the revisionism, indeed, that has pushed klezmer beyond klezmer. Both, I will be suggesting, are valuable not only as ways of theorizing Jewish difference in twentieth-century America but also as ways of better understanding (and valuing) the nature and properties of ethnic culture-making itself.

For Klezmer music, like the Yiddish language whose revival is so intimately tied to it, is a resolutely impure cultural form. It conjoins sacred and secular Jewish melodies and harmonies with those of the peoples who surrounded the *klezmorim*—the gentiles at whose weddings they frequently played, and at whose taverns and inns they frequently drank and caroused. It's no surprise, then, that Gypsy, Greek, Bulgar, and Russian folk musics are prominent components of the klezmer harmonies and melodies, and the other way around (indeed, ethnomusicologists tend to think of klezmer as a subset of these musics rather than as a distinct musical practice in its own right).[14] This program of systematic outreach within klezmer continued once it entered the United States, especially in its later phases, in which it has been brought into dialogue by some of the klezmer

INTRODUCTION

revivalists not only with the African American traditions I have gestured toward but also with Appalachian folk music (as is the case with clarinetist Margot Leverett) and Latino musical traditions (the last of these often entering into dialogue with the other wing of Diaspora musical traditions, that of the Sephardim).[15] And, as the above catalogue suggests, what makes klezmer music a fascinating cultural form with which to work is that it has both retained its connection to the historical experience of eastern European Jews and has revised, while it has been revised by, its circumambient musical traditions.

As for my second point, klezmer is revisionist in a different way as well. In recent years klezmer served as a political as well as a "heritage" music, especially as it has entered into contact with the avant-garde, a transaction brilliantly traced by musicologist Tamar Barzel, to whose analysis I am much indebted.[16] To cite but one of many examples, the fusion of avant-garde and klezmer produced a band, the Klezmatics, that conspicuously combines radical musical innovation with radical cultural and social politics. Defiantly queer and leftist, the Klezmatics actively sought to unify these two political impulses within the context of Jewish American culture. Their first album was entitled *Shvaygn = Toyt,* or "Silence = Death" in Yiddish—an attempt to unify 1980s AIDS activism with the movement to revive the almost-murdered Yiddish language. On their CD *Rise Up!* they include a 1920s Yiddish song, "Barikaydn," written as an anthem for the Bund, the Yiddish socialist movement, but included there with obvious implications for the current international antiglobalization movement. Their attempt, in other words, is consistently to stress the continuities between the Marxist-socialist tradition of the 1920s and 1930s and the identity-based politics of our own moment—to heal the gap, or at least mediate the differences, between Old and New Left by regrounding each in a specifically Jewish tradition of activism that has so powerfully shaped both.* The same, on the other side of the coin, is true of the Klezmatics's

---

*And their synthesizing endeavors aren't restricted to the Jewish side of the coin: the group has recently recorded two albums of songs written by Woody Guthrie on Jewish themes, inspired by the mother of Guthrie's second wife, Martha Mazur: Alicia Rozenblatt, a Yiddish poet and socialist activist who lived across the street and helped raise their children. Leftist gentiles and Jews, the Klezmatics remind us, worked together to create a genuinely progressive culture that could unite the experience of even Okies and eastern European immigrants.

persistent engagement with the gender and queer issues that Old and New Left alike tended to downplay or ignore.

The Klezmatics and the new wave of musical expression they represent, then, are searching to create a new form of radical Jewish culture (to allude to the name of one of avant-garde jazz saxophonist, composer, impresario, and recent MacArthur winner John Zorn's projects, about which more below) that wants to reestablish continuity with the tradition of political and artistic vanguardism within Jewish culture while rebelling defiantly against the politics and the culture of nostalgia to which Jews turned in the postassimilation era of the 1970s and 1980s. And a second, salient character of the klezmer revival is worthy of note. Just as klezmer music was formed by and further developed through hybridizing encounters with the musics of other people, so too the klezmer "scene" has been open to non-Jewish as well as Jewish musicians. The classic case here—the one most often cited, to his irritation—is that of Don Byron, an African American clarinetist whose career began with the Klezmer Conservatory Orchestra and received a mighty boost with his 1990 reanimation/cover of the music of antic klezmer clarinetist *cum* performance artist Mickey Katz.[17] But this is hardly the only instance. John Zorn's Great Jewish Music series, which includes reanimations of the oeuvre of Bert Bacharach and Serge Gainsbourgh persistently draws on an array of musicians who are not Jewish (very much like those who originally "covered" Gainsbourgh and Bacharach, including Gainsbourgh's wife, Jane Birkin, and Bacharach's muse, Dionne Warwick): figures like Julian Lennon, the great jazz guitarist Bill Frisell and Blonde Redhead, a New York downtown band consisting of Kazu Makino, Maki Takahashi, and Simone and Amedeo Pace. (After the Zorn collaboration, Blonde Redhead added a song to their repertoire called "Gainsbourgh Jewish Music.")

Zorn's point in creating these collaborative collections is not the humanistic banality that Great Jewish Music is a cultural universal—or even "hey, Jews can make great music, too!"—but rather that Jewish music, and by extension the art, literature, and social thought created by Jews in the Diaspora, has reshaped the culture and consciousness of Jews and non-Jews alike. He makes his case brilliantly via his versions of Bacharach (whose extremely sophisticated yet artless-sounding melodies have redefined the possibilities of popular song as fully as did the chromaticism of Gershwin or, in a slightly artier vein, the sophistication of Sondheim) or Gainsbourgh (a boundary-challenging *chanteur* who wore the yellow star as a child in Vichy France and who grew up to bring sophisticated, punning play to his lyrics, transcultural experimentation to his music, and scandalous self-representation to his public persona). In their ceaseless experimentalism, artists like Gainsbourgh and Bacharach made a new amalgam, Zorn claims (his tongue not entirely out of cheek): composite, cross-cultural, but nevertheless recognizably Jewish. And in so doing, they're also part of a larger cultural formation:

> It is arguable that the history of the Jews in this century has produced one of the most richly rewarding periods of culture in Jewish history. Yet, this fact is somehow kept neatly hidden. WHAT? Compare Philip Roth to Sholem Aleichem? Kafka to Moses de Leon? Walty Benjamin to Rashi? Wittgenstein to Spinoza? Steve Reich to Felix Mendelssohn? Allen Ginsberg to Yehuda Helevi? Einstein to Nostradamus? Lenny Bruce to Hillel? Burt Bacharach is such a name.[18]

Aware of and even delighting in the incongruity of his examples, Zorn places all these figures together—comics and converts, pop tunesmiths and composers of holy *piyyutim* (or sacred poems), secular philosophers and Talmudic sages—and in so doing radically expands the notion of what Jewish culture is and can be. What unites them is not an essentialist "Jewishness" (Nostradamus? "Walty" Benjamin?) but rather a tendency to push to the limits the intellectual or artistic terrain they're occupying, with powerfully transformative effects on Jewish culture, on the culture at large, or both. And vice versa: not just the modern half of his pairings, but all of these figures, Zorn is suggesting, are as fully shaped by their circumambient cultures as the other way around (Halevy wrote in both Arabic and Hebrew; Spinoza oscillated between Judaism and rationalism; Sholem Aleichem parodied the conventions of European fiction, and so on). What better way to enact these understandings than to bring together Jewish revisionists and avant-garde musicians of all racial and ethnic and religious backgrounds?

The klezmer revival, in short, keyed but has also metamorphosed into a larger cultural project, one that expands the notion of Jewish otherness into a cultural politics of alterity that contests both the assimilationist, acculturated notion of Jewish identity and the cultural institutions of the society into which Jews have entered—but that does so in the name of something older, or at least other, than that which the modern discovers to be perpetually new. ("Thank you," writes Zorn to Bert Bacharach on his liner notes, "for not changing your name.") Not for nothing does Zorn's record label Tzadik (in Hebrew, a "righteous person") issue most of its work under the name I mentioned above, that of Radical Jewish Culture—although, as I suggest more fully in chapter 1, the paradox imparted by the word *radical*, which stems from the Latin for "root," implies that this form of Jewish culture stages itself as a return rather than as a revolution. Jewish culture is radical, Zorn insists, because the very presence of Jews among the cultures of the West challenges the establishment of norms and boundaries, fixities and reifications; it is rooted, however, in precisely the heterogeneity, the multiplicity, the hybridity (to use the somewhat overused term) that has arguably defined Jewish culture from its inception. (In this context, of course, the phrase *radical Jewish culture*, with the Latinate root of the first word complementing/clashing with the diasporic histories embedded in the second, exemplifies the particular hybrid I am trying to name.) And the terms by which Zorn defines his endeavor apply to that of his contemporaries as well. Precisely by returning to the syncretic, heterogeneous practices that characterized Jewish cultures in the Diaspora from the assimilating project that marked American Jewish culture of the past forty years, klezmer revivalists and postklezmer Radical Jewish Culture makers alike have not only redefined "Jewishness"; they have created new configurations from categories (black/white, Jewish/gentile, Western/Eastern) that have long seemed perdurable, fixed. In their knowing and self-conscious art—these musicians are, by and large, intensely aware of the factitiousness of their gestures of cultural hybridization, of their belatedness in Harold Bloom's sense of the word—they proudly enter into the spirit of mutually generative remaking that shapes the Jewish encounter with innumerable other Others since the beginning of Jewish history.

It is this latter aspect of the klezmer and postklezmer phenomenon that I'm invoking here as an organizing trope: a tradition of dynamic innovation wrought in the encounter between Jewish and gentile cultures that has the property of reanimating both, creating in this interplay new configurations of ethnic belonging, new aesthetic forms in which to express them, and ultimately new vessels for delineating and interrogating the experience of a multiracial, multiethnic modernity at large. In this, my argument is closest in form, although perhaps not in substance, to that of Paul Gilroy's now classic *Black Atlantic* (1994), in which the interposition of the slave subject both disrupts traditional European ideas of modernity and hazards a new model that exists within and alongside it: a modernity that is frankly diasporic and resistant to, rather than affirmative of, entrenched structures of cultural hierarchy. This is no coincidence, for a number of reasons: Gilroy's emphasis on music as a maker of social meaning has been crucial for me, as has his persistent linkage between intellectual praxis and other forms of social life. Most important of all however has been the example provided by the powerful conclusion of Gilroy's book, its open invitation to rethink the nature of Jewish and African diasporas through the lens of each other's visions and histories, and especially through the narratives of exile and return that shape both, for it focuses in productive ways one of the challenges to the work I'm trying to do here-the challenge of race. The interchange Gilroy asks us to reconceptualize—between in the broadest sense of the terms *Jewishness* and *blackness*—is of course the most powerful and the most contested engagement between Jews and other historically oppressed peoples, and Gilroy's sane yet critical take on the interplay is one I've found consistently inspiring. The invitation, however, is hitherto one that has not been fully reciprocated by Jewish studies scholars or by those of the African Diaspora as it might have been, although, as I shall be suggesting in what follows (especially in chapter 5), musicians and other culture makers in the last two decades have begun this process of mutual recognition, of call-and-response, across a racial divide.[19] Indeed, if this book has one point to underline, it is that, for all their tensions and antagonisms, culture makers often show far more respect for each other's creative and imaginative traditions than do the critics who write about their intertwinings, and, in a very real sense, what I want to do here (I am tempted to write: all I want to do here) is follow in my own venue the paths that musicians, artists, and writers have blazed.

To say this, however, is not to suggest that either Gilroy's own endeavor or the effort to respond to it is unproblematic; as numerous critics have argued—and Eric Sundquist has demonstrated in the opening chapters of his recent, encyclopedic treatment of the fraught relations between blacks and Jews in America, *Strangers in the Land* (2005)—many of the grounds of Gilroy's suggested linkages between the Jewish and the African experiences have long served, at least in the U.S., as irritants or impediments to the full concord between African Americans and Jews.[20] Precisely because African Americans share with Jews the experience of exile, disempowerment, oppression; precisely because the Old Testament metaphors of freedom from slavery and escape to the Promised Land applied so powerfully to the black experience in America; precisely because Jews played such a prominent part in the civil rights movement: for all these reasons and more, the relative ease with which Jews became fully credentialed members of American polity served as a justifiable irritant for African Americans. And as Jews have, by and large, prospered in America and increasingly seen themselves less as an oppressed minority and more as spectacularly successful stakeholders in U.S. culture, the imaginary as well as the political linkages forged in the popular front of the 1930s and tested in the civil rights movement of the 1960s seem to have come wholly undone.

Sundquist's narrative is a powerful and probing one, fair to each side in this ongoing and tragic story of affinity and distrust. And his nuanced account can help explain why Gilroy's more optimistic take on the Jewish/African dialogue at large has not, to date, panned out. Sundquist may, I think, profitably be read as suggesting the ways in which an older metanarrative—that of Jewish/black affinity and their mutual political work—has come to a regrettable end. But if this is true—and I think it is a slight exaggeration—even such a sad outcome presents opportunity as well as closure. It suggests that we can move to other inscriptions and understandings of difference, ones to which the Jewish example can make a less (but not un-) fraught contribution than it has in the articulations of relations colored black and white. Those understandings are particularly crucial at the current moment, when Latinos and Asian immigrants (as well as many others,, including those of African and Middle Eastern descent) are augmenting in power and social prominence, supplementing (in the Derridean sense of the word) the picture of difference in this country in ways that are challenging not only the political order, but also the epistemic one.

At such a moment, I'll be arguing, the example of Jews and Jewishness remains crucial, if overdetermined: serving both as a model and an irritant, a guide and a goad, not only for the Latino demonstrators I described above, but for a host of ethnic others—including, to cite an example to which I will devote a chapter, contemporary Asian American novelists and playwrights struggling with their ascription as "New Jews," the model minority following the example of these predecessors by attempting to gain social success via education and entrepreneurial bootstrapping. Both the Jewish example and the responses to that example, however, prove to be more complex—rooted in far richer histories of encounter—than even these accounts suggest, and I'll be devoting considerable work in what follows to tracing the imaginative work done with those histories, whether those of crypto-Jews in the U.S. Southwest, Mexico, or Cuba, of that of the longstanding encounter of Jews and East Asians under the shared experience of Orientalization. In doing this, I want to explore the process of ethnic making and remaking not as a contest between two separate generations of immigrants—new and old—but rather as the latest juncture in an interweaving of experiences and traditions sustained among peoples who have been encountering each other for centuries, in the U.S., to be sure, but also throughout the world.

This is what I mean by suggesting that bringing the Jewish experience into the ongoing national conversation about race and ethnicity makes the very terms of that conversation richer, more complex. The same effect is created by another, no less crucial, form of otherness: the dimension of gender. As we've seen in Holmes's poem, the play of antisemitic and philosemitic representations always already swirling around the figure of the Jew churned with particular intensity with respect to gender and sexuality, creating not only the classically stereotypical figures of the Orientalized Jewish woman, and that of the sexually ambiguous Jewish male. It is the latter to which I will be devoting some attention in my first chapters, for within the defiles of Jewish masculinity were generated not only hypernormative images but also the most powerful transgressive ones: as I'll argue more extensively below, what was lynching victim Leo Frank but a stereotypical queer Jewish man? Or serial killers Leopold and Loeb? Or McCarthyite bullies Roy Cohn and David Schine? And this process continued through the sixties to the present day: one could add fictional characters like Alexander Portnoy to this roster and, for that matter, incest-tainted Woody Allen.

Again, the Jewish example is not unique—a good deal of excellent recent work on gendered identity, masculinity, and queer or alternative sexualities has emerged focusing on African Americans (as one fine example among many, that of Marlon Ross), Latinos (Tomás Almaguer), and Asian Americans (David Eng).[21] But I think it is accurate to say the Jewish example is uniquely *charged*: the point of foregrounding Jewish difference in the context of masculinity is that it was itself foregrounded by the dominant culture as a prime instance of—indeed frequently as a symbol of— forms of gendered and sexual identity outside the norm. I argue in chapters

1 and 2 that Jewish men have had to wrestle with these ascriptions, alternating between defensively insisting on their normativeness or accepting—and reveling in—their culturally contumacious queerness. Bringing these constructions into dialogue with other racialized inscriptions of masculinity can show unexpected affinities (e.g., the too-masculine-not-enough-masculine dilemma that afflicts Asian American men) as well as divergences (as I point out in chapter 2, Joe DiMaggio and Arthur Miller have much in common as images of male potency—they were both lovers, after all, of the most desired woman in America—but pose starkly different models of white ethnic maleness that complicate our understanding of these categories and their interplay.)

In all of these cases—in my emphasis of the complex interweave between a host of alterities and the social and cultural experience of Jewish Americans—I see this work as being continuous with the efforts of critics affiliated with what two of them called Jewish cultural studies: that powerful impulse I associate with Daniel and Jonathan Boyarin, Sander Gilman, and a host of others to bring the discourse on Jews and Jewishness into contact with contemporary theory (that of postcoloniality, race, and gender in particular). I've learned much from these critics: but my concern here is less with the theory than the practice of difference-making: with the actual cultural production of Jews and those who identify themselves as members of different (if sometimes overlapping) communities—Asian Americans, African Americans, queers, and so on—rather than, or perhaps it would be better to say in addition to, the conceptual machinery that produces such categories of identity. Indeed, if I have any contribution to make to this discourse, it's to suggest that we may now be at a posttheoretical moment, a moment, in other words, where we can let the sheer heterogeneity of texts or experiences that define Jews' mutually modifying encounter with other Others produce richer, but less resolute, accounts of the multiple cultural interactions between American Jews and their fellow citizens and hence, I would also hope, of the new combinations and possibilities opening up in a U.S. (and global) culture at large.

The polemical endeavors of this book, however, are also focused elsewhere and it might be best to end this introduction by being forthright about them. My quarrels, questions, or quibbles are directed in two directions: vis-à-vis U.S. literary and cultural studies at large and vis-à-vis certain trends in Jewish American culture and politics.

To begin with the first: I write here in dialogue with a broad range of American and ethnic studies critics who have made the production of race, ethnicity, gender, and sexuality crucial to their enterprise. But I do so with the intention of endeavoring to correct a problematic tendency pervading those discourses: one that includes Jews, Judaism, and Jewishness as part of their master narratives of U.S. culture making only by invoking the putative whiteness of the Jew. To be sure, this has not been the case in American literary studies, although here, too, the addition of Jewish difference to the interpretive palette has come relatively late. Although it is a noteworthy fact that many of the finest Americanists of the 1950s through the 1980s were Jewish, their energies frequently took them in directions that ignored the imaginative challenges posed by Jewishness or treated Jewish American literature as a separate subcultural tradition, a canon beginning with Cahan and Yezierska and ending in Bellow, Roth, Ozick. (A splendid exception to this rule was Leslie Fiedler, whose book *The Jew in the American Novel*, 1959 (first published as essays in *Midstream*), anticipates and has shaped my emphasis on the reciprocal qualities of the Jewish-gentile cultural interchange in the U.S.)[22] Moreover, a new generation of younger critics has emerged interested not just in tracing the Jewish presence in American letters but in parsing the intersection of the central themes and writers of U.S. literature with Jews, Judaism, and Jewishness. Their work continues the process that Fiedler began by offering readings of works ranging from Poe's "The Facts in the Case of M. de Valdemar" (given a brilliant reading in the context of discourses of Jewish genius by Gustavus Stadler), the sensation novel's obsession with the figure of the Jew (the object of excellent work by David Anthony), through Emerson's interlocking relation with Emma Lazarus (the subject of compelling work by Julian Levinson and Maaera Schreiber), to Alain Locke's intertwining with Horace Kallen (the subject of some equally fine work by Daniel Itzkovitz) to Nathaniel West's encounter with tropes of American Indians (the subject of a powerful argument by Rachel Rubenstein).[23] Cognate to their endeavors has been work focused on the literary interplay between Jewish writers and blackness (in addition to Sundquist's, I would cite important studies by Emily Budick, Ethan Goffman, and Adam Newton); between Jews and the idiom of multiculturalism (here I would cite in particular the work of Andrew Furman and Dean Franco) and between Jewish writers and gender, with particular emphasis on the extraordinary imaginative contributions of Jewish women.[24] Meanwhile, a revival of scholarship centering around the powerful tradition of Yiddish (and more recently Ladino) writing and culture in the U.S. emerged through the efforts of critics like David Roskies, Ruth Wisse, Anita Norich, Ilan Stavans; what's powerful and important about this work is its implicit understanding that Yiddish or Ladino are crucial components of *American* literary expression construed under the sign of multilingualism rather than products of an exoticized "foreign" culture or a long-past "world of our fathers" à la Irving Howe.[25] And, more recently, Hana Wirth-Nesher has brought this sense of the power of Yiddish and Hebrew as linguistic and imaginative resources to bear on the writing of (American) English literary texts in her extraordinary *Call It English*.

But, sadly, a similar dialectical abundance, a mutual de- and reconstruction of the discursive terrain, has not been evident in the linked terrains of American and U.S. ethnic studies, where such an interplay was first bruited and where one might expect to find it flourishing. Instead, however, one finds, on the one hand, the silence or marginalization that once obtained throughout the literary field and, on the other, an odd replay of the very narrative of assimilation younger critics and culture makers alike are seeking to contest, here flipping that narrative around to reread that process in racializing terms. Indeed, after the publication of such works as Michael Rogin's *Blackface/White Noise* (1996), Karen Brodkin's *How the Jews Became White Folks* (1998), Matthew Frye Jacobson's *Whiteness of a Different Color* (1998), and Jeffrey Melnick's *The Right to Sing the Blues* (1998), extended in more recent works by David Roediger (*Working to Whiteness*, 2005) and Eric Goldstein (*The Price of Whiteness*, 2006), the reframing of the hoary issue of Jewish assimilation in the idiom of whiteness has become canonical in American studies discourses (even as it has been highly contested within Jewish studies). *Pace* the excellent work of George Sanchez and Josh Kun the state of play in current American studies discourse may be best put in David Roediger's words: Jews, like other European-born ethnics, were, in the crucial period between 1880 and 1924 (or even up until 1939), "not-yet-white."[26] And in the period thereafter, it would seem, Jews were no longer anything but.

I'm frankly ambivalent about this narrative, because it seems to me on the one hand incontestable (at least with respect to broad categories of racial typing) and on the other inadequate. Many of the chapters below are devoted to exploring this double sense, and attempting to provide suppler accounts of the interplay between Jewish Americans and the process of racialization than those on offer in American and ethnic studies. But because the argument has become so forceful within these fields, I need to devote some time here to responding on a metalevel as well as with the more specific engagements that follow. I should begin by saying that my real discomfort with the Jews-as-white-folks argument lies not so much with the argument per se. I accept, with qualifications, the major axioms underlying it—DuBois's recognition that the white "race" can be anatomized as such as well as the other races whom white people have themselves spent much time invigilating; the understanding that whiteness works by rendering invisible its own privileged condition; the narrative that Jews, like many ethnics now viewed as white, were initially deemed to be non- or off-white and now, whatever their actual "hue," are enfolded into the ontological and socially contumacious status of white—although here in particular I think things remain more complicated than whiteness critics assume, for a number of reasons I'll detail. I have also been persuaded by the historical work of Jacobson, Roediger, and Goldstein in tracing the ways that Jewish middle-class assimilation frequently involved not only the acceptance of whiteness but also the active rejection of blackness—and, often, of African Americans themselves. But, in my experience, this set of axioms and the conclusions that are drawn from them are all too often used to close down further conversation: whiteness is all too frequently posited as the end-point of analysis—the white rabbit pulled out of the interpretive hat, the white whale of interpretive monomania—rather than the beginning of a more nuanced and complex set of narratives not only about the past but about the present and ultimately the future. Like the Whiggish celebration of the Jew's assimilation it is designed to contest, the argument to whiteness imports an inevitability to a process that was variable, fragile, and contingent; the historian's resonant phrase "not-yet-white" imposes an ex post facto certitude to a process that could have turned out much differently. More problematically still, as a result, whiteness critics have effaced the many alternative narratives of Jewish identity formation that not only grew but continue to grow out of these multiple identifications.

I'll be dealing with several of these possibilities in what follows. Here, however, I want briefly to foreground another one of these earlier narratives, to give a sense of the range of cultural work that got done through these alternative constructions: the widespread notion of the essentially Oriental quality of Jewish difference, at least in the sense of Oriental that

Edward Said has so influentially charted: one in which the Oriental is associated with the Near East, exoticism, feminization, the multiple pleasures of ambiguous sexuality, etc.* For, as I'll show in more detail in chapter 6, the description of the Jew as an Oriental is all over the discourse of the prewhiteness period—indeed, it is a virtual commonplace in that period—and its implications ranged broadly and powerfully. Such a description has, however, been shunted to the historical background. To be sure, in *Blackface, White Noise*, Michael Rogin pauses in his influential reading of *The Jazz Singer* to note that the Jew in the 1920s was frequently envisaged as Oriental, but he then rapidly conflates Jews' putative Orientalism with racialized blackness: "orientalism . . . signified racially alien, primitivist qualities, embraced by Jewish and black musicians, that would revify American life."[27] There's warrant for him to do so: this ascription was not uncommon, particularly in accounts of the Jewish role in mainstreaming black music via jazz, as Melnick (whose work, like Jacobson's, is at once critical and nuanced) notes, middlebrow factotum and would-be Gershwin collaborator Isaac Goldberg discussed the "common Oriental ancestry in both Negro and Jew" (via Al Jolson, no less) in a biography of Gershwin as late as 1936, and, as MacDonald Moore has shown, high-culture critics routinely wrote of a putative Jewish affinity for jazz as being influenced by both figures's "Oriental" identity.[28] (So did contributors to the explicitly antisemitic *The International Jew* (1930), published by no less a figure than Henry Ford.) But there are many moments when the so-called Oriental qualities of the Jew disarticulated that figure from the African, placing contemporary Jews in a direct line of descent to the biblical

---

*A significant caveat: as a number of recent critics have shown—and as David Roediger in particular has argued—the notion of the "Oriental" quality of ethnic otherness was applied to a number of non-Jewish groups at this time, particularly Italian Americans. But there seem to me to be three significant differences to the Orientalization of the Jewish and that of the Italian or other southern European American: first, a greater degree of gender ambiguity, particularly although not exclusively with the (frequently feminized) Jewish man; second, a connection to the "Holy Land" and its culture, which also leads to a certain degree of ambivalence; and third, a presumptive racially (and perhaps religiously mandated) melancholia or "sadness" that is identified in the writing of the era as an intrinsic, essential part of the Jew's Oriental character. To be sure, there are numerous points of overlap between these aspects of Jewish Orientalism and that ascribed to people of Italian descent: Ancient Rome often stands to Mulberry Street as Jerusalem does to Hester Street, for example. But the differences I am marking out here are significant enough to form the hub of my analysis here and in chapter 5, where I go into them in greater depth.

Jews of the Near East (indeed, we have spent much time with one of these in the reading of Holmes's poem that began this chapter) and in which the Jew gets loaded with the full weight of the contradictory ascriptions that were generated by the supple and contradictory discourse of Orientalism.

Sidelining this genealogy in favor of one grounded in the black/white dichotomy has had a number of problematic consequences. First, it effaces the *religious* anxieties that surround Protestant-dominated culture's experience of Jews in this period—and that resonate well into our own.[29] When, to cite another example from the pre- or proto-whiteness era, William Dean Howells wanders the Lower East Side, he begins by noting the "debasement" of the people among whom he finds himself, but then starts describing those people in terms that mix Orientalist stereotypes with a recognition of the Christian example:

> Everywhere I saw splendid types of that old Hebrew world which had the sense if not the knowledge of God when the rest of us lay sunk in heathen darkness. There were women with oval faces and olive tints, and clear, dark eyes, relucent as evening pools, and men with long beards of jetty black or silvery white, and the noble profiles of their race.... It was among such throngs that Christ walked, and from such people that he chose his Disciples and friends.[30]

Howells here, as so often, served as a seismograph for his contemporaries. His swing from distance to appreciation, his mingling of stereotype and sympathy, and his advancing toward and away from the recognition that Christ himself was a Jew, was broadly enacted by late-nineteenth-century ministers, social reformers, and would-be urban ethnographers before and after him. Howells's response is a leading indicator of subsequent cultural responses to Jews: I'll be arguing that, although light-years away in both politics and quality of response, the Christian New Right best sellers of our own moment also evince this same confused response to the relation between the Jew of today and the roots of their own faith, a relation that becomes of increased urgency for them in the context of end-time prophecies that depend on the survival of the Jew to usher in the Kingdom of Christ.

Second, the whitness critics' downplaying of the Jew's Orientalism has also diverted attention from what I see as the crucial importance of the sexual ambiguities that suffuse the construction of the Oriental Jew, especially the Jewish man, and hence the powerful gender and sexual ambivalence that can be found in gentile responses to Jews across the board. To cite one powerful example: in their readings of *The Jazz Singer*, neither Rogin nor Jacobsen nor Melnick, or, for that matter, the much less critical historian Michael Alexander, dwell much on the culturally specific resonances of the sexually polyvalent, sexually ambiguous, just plain *odd* quality of Jolson's screen presence—the rolling eyes, the rictuslike smile, the nervous, jerky, compulsive hand movements. For all these (not to mention what even that period knew as a mother fixation) marked him for his audience as a nonnormative man, a sexual oddball, and this dimension of his character makes the film's portrayal of his love and conquest of a *shikse*, his gentile girlfriend Mary Dale, all the more striking. (Yet more striking, and also underappreciated in the criticism, is Jackie's continued cleaving to the mother even as he wins Mary: in the famous shot of Jack Robin/Jackie Rabinowitz singing to his yiddishe mama at the end of *The Jazz Singer*, the *shikse* is marginalized, left backstage while Jack/Jakie kneels to his true beloved: the Jew, that is to say, is granted public success and defined as a hopeless, Oedipalized neurotic by one and the same gesture (see figures 1 and 2).* Nor do any of them dwell on the association between these qualities and others (hyperemotionalism, for example) that, as we'll see in more detail, the period bundled with the ambiguous sexuality and hysterical mind-set of the (Saidian) Orient in a way that led one contemporary observer to assert, "[Jews] have a nervous make-up that is not easily susceptible to the formation of habits of body and thought, and it would often appear that their mental processes were not of the western order, but, after all, the Hebrew is only a more or less modified Oriental still."[31]

The biggest problems with this lacuna, however, have to do with its effects on contemporary cultural life. For one thing, it effaces a genealogy whose aftereffects resonate in the politics of our own time—the shared

---

* Rogin, interestingly, got the shot wrong in his first pass through the material—the article version of "The Jewish Jazz Singer Finds His Voice" in which he positions Mary Dale in the audience, rather than as marginalized, backstage, looking adoringly to Jackie's performance from behind while his mother beams at him from in front. It's important to Rogin's argument that Jack gets *both* the shikse and the mama at the end of the film—and this moment complicates the argument, since it suggests that his cleaving to one comes at the cost of the other. In the book version of the argument, Rogin deals explicitly with this duality. See "Blackface/White Noise: The Jewish Jazz Singer Finds His Voice," *Critical Inquiry* 18 (1992): 417–453.

1   The oedipal jazz singer: Jack Robin greets his mother after a long absence. *The Jazz Singer*, Warner Brothers, 1927.

2   The sidelined shikse. *The Jazz Singer*, Warner Brothers, 1927.

Orientalization of Jews and East and South Asians. Although, as Rogin puts it, "a common set of racial stereotypes... bound together Jews, Asians and blacks under the orientalist umbrella" in the 1920s, the Orientalizing process also worked (at different times, to be sure) in such a way as to separate Jews and Asians *from* blacks—and also from normative whites—both in terms of their putatively non-normative sexuality (demasculinized men and domineering mothers are stereotypical in representations of both communities) and, more important, under the heading of the "model minority," as embodiments of successful assimilation and hence cynosures of proper ethnic behavior. Reading the struggles of both communities with their Orientalization may at the very least cast a different light on each—allow us, for example, to tell the story of Jewish assimilation differently, as one of the disavowal of Orientalized ascriptions as well as the adoption of whiteness via the appropriation of blackness—as well as to add texture to the accounts, in the culture at large, that would conflate them.

Finally, and for me most consequentially, the lack of attention to the Orientalizing of the American Jew sidelines, or simply eliminates from interpretive view, the new forms of Jewish self-consciousness and cultural production that grow out of this Orientalized matrix and/or seek to return to it. Indeed, as I devote much attention to contemporary Jewish American culture makers—to figures like Tony Kushner and Uri Caine or Gary Shteyngart as well as the Radical Jewish Culture crowd—I want to show that many of their works embrace and further—sometimes under the sign of parody and play, sometimes as "straight"—all the things that their rejection of Orientalizing ascriptions forced Jews to jettison: exoticism, foreignness, alterity, queerness in both the original and the current sense of the word. Without contesting the narrative of Jews' accession to whiteness, in other words, I want not only to account for but to celebrate the work that gets done out of traditions that either accompanied or rejected that assimilating move—and to the critical possibilities with respect to gender and sexuality as well as race and ethnicity that grow out of these alternative histories.

In addition to these field-specific questions (albeit ones with large implications), the second big quarrel this book seeks to pick is with established notions of Jewishness, particularly those espoused in recent critical accounts of the Jewish experience by such diverse figures as liberal par excellence Alan Dershowitz (*The Vanishing American Jew*) and conservative eminence grise—Norman Podhoretz's son-in-law, Iran-contra conspirator, and now, incredibly, the man in charge of our Israel policy—Eliot Abrams (*Faith or Fear*). In these accounts assimilation, intermarriage, intermingling of various sorts are positioned as threats to the maintenance of the Jewish identity in America, and it is only through the return to a program of cultural education (Dershowitz) or an active articulation of traditional faith (Abrams) that Jews can survive, much less prosper. To be sure, these books are different in manner and method: Dershowitz ultimately works his way around to accepting his son's marrying out of the faith—the occasion for the book; Abrams remains in jeremiad mode throughout. Nevertheless, the discomforts each evinces strike familiar chords in any Jew who attends traditional services, reads the bulletins of the official Jewish organizations, tries to marry a member of a different faith. The anxiety they register, it seems to me, is not significant in and of itself—clearly those who identify with traditional Jewish identity politics of either a secular or a religious nature are going to want to stress their embattlement for strategic reasons—but it is an indicator of an impulse in Jewish intellectual and cultural life with which I am in profound disagreement, one that stresses the need for purity, consistency, essence, limits, boundaries in defining what is and is not Jewish. This is of course one impulse in Judaism as a religious practice itself, one in which the delineation of the clean and unclean, the pure and the corrupt, is central, definitional. But it's more powerfully, and more problematically, a repeated impulse in the critical response of American Jews in a multiracial, multicultural America—an impulse to (as it were) circle the wagons, to define Jewishness as well as Judaism (itself a notoriously multiple religious practice and identity) in monolithic, essentializing terms.

This gesture, it seems to me, is motivated largely by a residual anxiety about otherness, both religious and ethnoracial. Having (as Norman Podhoretz, a prime example of the process might have put it) made it, Jews still face the shadowy afterimages of their problematic past. There are many ghosts haunting contemporary assimilated Jewish culture: religious antisemitism in a Christian America (the subject of Abrams's work: his advice to Jews is to get over it and make common cause with born agains), economic antisemitism (as the ugly slurs of Abrams's friends on the Republican right against billionaire George Soros attest),[32] most strongly of all, perhaps, the lingering sense of Jewish alienness in a culture where other forms of difference are proliferating wildly. And the last of these specters leads to particularly loaded, if highly ambivalent responses. The title of Dershowitz's book is enormously suggestive in this regard: its (unwitting?) echo of the familiar topos of "the vanishing Indian" affiliates the Jew with the Native American example, quite paradoxically: after all, if one works out the metaphor, it is the assimilation of the Jew that makes that figure most like the ethnically marked other, the (soon to be exterminated) Indian.* If the Jews have become white, then haven't the other Others become what once was considered "Jewish" in the positive sense: fascinatingly exotic, virtuously marginalized, culturally rich?

It is these anxieties that this book is devoted to engaging. Speaking as a first-generation American Jew who has always felt like both an outsider and an insider in the national frame (as the son, that is, who had to explain the rules of baseball to his German Jewish immigrant father—but, luckily, learned the rules of soccer from him), I want frankly to reclaim the filiation between the career of Jews in America from 1880 to the present day and the experience of immigrants across the board, particularly those we have been calling new immigrants—the economic and political refugees largely from the East and the South who are transforming the American social, cultural, and political landscape as fully as did their predecessors (of whom Jews, as I suggested above, were the symbol even if they were not the majority) in the previous wave of immigration a century ago. And one of the things this means is that, in addition to registering and acknowledging some of the resentments this relation generates for this new influx of immigrants, the present volume wishes to call Jews back

---

*The association between Jews and Native Americans has a long and fascinating history well before Dershowitz's invocation of the vanishing Indian topos. It was commonly believed in the seventeenth century, for example, that American Indians were descendents of the ten lost tribes of Israel. More recently, Alan Trachtenberg has reminded us, Yiddish poets and writers identified themselves with the plight of the Native Americans, positioning themselves ambivalently both as an Asiatic other speaking in sympathy with Indians and as white Americans making poetry out of their plight. See Alan Trachtenberg, *Shades of Hiawatha: Staging Indians, Making Americans, 1880–1930* (New York: Hill and Wang, 2004). All sides of this tradition, perhaps, speak through Tony Kushner's Rabbi Isidore Chemelwitz from *Angels in America*, who eulogizes Lewis Ironson's grandmother, Sophie, as both "the Last of the Mohicans" and a Puritan-like voyager seeking freedom in a distant land. See also here the work of Rachel Rubinstein, especially "Nathaniel West's Indian Commodities," *Shofar* 23 (2005): 98–120.

to their sense of structural isolation and alienation in a society marked, for all its claims of honoring diversity, by a persistent impulse to ethnoracial conformity. In the face of nativist and religious antisemitism and a very hostile world (a context rarely acknowledged in the work of leftist critics of Jewish whitening), American Jews may well have had good reasons to wish to fit into that culture in the 1940s and 1950s in particular. But the relative security of the American Jews—the residual nature of even the antisemitism I noted above—has paradoxically given us the security to affirm our difference, our uniqueness, our alterity. It may be that, as historian Stephen Whitfield has put it, America has not seemed like exile.[33] But the salience of the example of the other Others among whom we find ourselves—sexual others, racial others, ethnic Others—ought to remind us how complicated a relation we have—and ought to maintain—to the idea of home.

One last, and I hope less parochial, word about the salience of this work. The process of thought that led to this book began in 1994, which is to say in a world we can barely remember: before religious fanatics influenced by the antisemitic politics of the Christian identity movement blew up a Federal Building in Oklahoma City; before a gentile president's affair with a Jewish woman led to a constitutional crisis; before adherents of radical Islam, largely Muslims who were educated in the West, attempted to blow up the World Trade Center and then succeeded in piloting planes into that same building and the Pentagon and while an ostentatiously born-again, macho president announced a "war on terror" with no seeming end, with rhetoric striking in its apocalyptic and crusader-like overtones. This is to say, in other words, that the twinned and reinforcing claims of ethnic and religious identity have achieved an ever greater power in the world of contemporary modernity, particularly as they have been placed in the pressure cooker of sexuality and gender—especially as masculinity comes under particular challenge in a world where traditional verities of all sorts have been dissolved. Although worlds apart in their backgrounds and orientation, Timothy McVeigh and Muhammed Atta were both young, disaffected men who turned toward traditional models of maleness to negotiate their disoriented experience in the complex world of nineties America and Europe—not coincidentally, the time when the Berlin Wall and the Soviet Union fell, the stock market exploded, and global capitalism proclaimed its triumph over any other form of political or theological belief.

In the next decades, in other words, an understanding of the world that takes the swirling and uncertain effects of culture, religion, national, or regional identifications into account is clearly crucial, and all the more so as global population flows—of North African and other Muslims into Europe, of Asians and Latinos into the U.S., and so on—challenge traditional national boundaries and cultural patterns. And it's also clear that one powerful dimension of this interface is the way the culture of modernity impacts upon sexual and gendered identity across the board, and masculinity in particular. And here, the precedent of the Jewish experience—of peoples shaped by culture and religion, adapting variously to different nations and experiences, defined as ethnic or racial groups but challenging those definitions, understood in complex and ambivalent gendered terms—provides an important precedent and guide to the social and cultural experience of the future. If I am arguing for a klezmerical reading of that experience—an experience that stresses the Jews' persistent ability, most evident in their experience in the U.S, to engage in a syncretic, hybridizing engagement with a national culture in ways that transform both their own identity and experience and that of the culture at large—it is because I believe that such interchanges and the transformations they bring will mark the modernity that is to come as fully as they have the modernity that has prepared for it.

1. ANGELS, MONSTERS, AND JEWS
From Kushner to Klezmer

> *The foreignness of Jews is a kind of difference unlike others. They are "those people" whom no label fits, whether assigned by the Gaze, the Concept or the State. For Jewishness, the type is the exception and its absence the rule; in fact you can rarely pick out a Jew at first glance. It's an insubstantial difference that resists definition as much as it frustrates the eye: are they a people? a religion? a nation? All these categories apply, but none is adequate in itself.*
> —Alain Finkielkraut

IN THIS PASSAGE from his resonantly entitled book, *The Imaginary Jew*, French critic Alain Finkielkraut neatly encapsulates the conundrum that Jews have long posed to the imagination of the West. Jews are doubtless different—but somehow differently different, in ways that differ markedly over time. To sample just a few of the major Western understandings of the Jew is to see how diverse and contradictory models of Jewish identity have been. Installed since biblical times in a position of national marginality, constructed by medieval theologians as outsiders to revealed truth, persecuted in the early modern period as usurers or pawnbrokers (from whom governments did not hesitate to borrow), defined by eighteenth-century philosophers as members of a debased tribe in need of cultural improvement, and viewed by nineteenth-century ethnologists as an irrevocably inferior race whose members should be deported, sequestered, or ultimately exterminated, Jews have historically been defined as many contradictory things. And as a new generation of critics has powerfully argued, this multiply constructed figure has an additional property. Although essential to the many different categories by which human difference has been constructed, the Jew challenges the coherence of these classifications. If Jews are a race, why do they look so different from one another? If they constitute a religion, how are they to enter the secular nation-state? And if a nation is defined by shared language and culture, how can these people who speak numerous languages and who cleave stubbornly to a culture of their own belong?[1]

Nowhere have both these properties of "the Jew"—giving a shape to otherness and calling such constructions into question—been more evident than in images of sexual transgression, especially in the later nineteenth century, when entirely new classifications of sexual deviance were elaborated: the degenerate, the pervert, the homosexual. For as Sander Gilman has consequentially argued, these powerful but unstable models of deviance were built on that shifting figure of all-purpose alterity, the Jew—often, to add to the irony, by assimilating Jewish intellectuals like Max Nordau, Cesare Lombroso, and of course Freud.[2] The figure of the monstrous Jewish pervert became a staple of antisemitic propaganda first in Europe, then in the United States in the late nineteenth century, but the link between the Jew and the sexual other had been forged in the imaginative literature of Europe and England long before—for instance, in medieval mystery plays, which emphasized the Jew's sexual ravenousness and extrahuman powers. Shakespeare's Shylock is a figure metonymically connected with that other merchant of Venice, Antonio, whose homoeroticism echoes and is echoed by the Jew's supposed appetite for unnatural reproduction in the form of usury. (According to the medieval philosopher Nicholas Oresme, for example, "it is monstrous and unnatural that an unfruitful thing should bear, that a thing specifically sterile, such as money, should bear fruit and multiply of itself.")[3] And Dickens's Fagin is simultaneously a classic Jewish monster with supernatural powers (Fagin does not leave footprints on marshy ground) and one of the first and most fearsome representatives of the child molester, that new figure of sexual pathology in the late nineteenth century. In a more positive vein, Proust's *A la recherche du temps perdu* can be read as a lengthy attempt to play images of the *race maudite* ("the damned race") of Sodomites against an equally othered race, the Jews.[4] The Jewish other and the sexual other were thus frequently placed in vibrant contiguity in the literary traditions of the West well before sexologists or psychologists or race theorists codified that relation.

And yet the overlapping and mutually constitutive discourses on the Jew and the sexually perverse generate questions about each other that disrupt established categories. Shylock's rapacious Jewishness and Antonio's noble homoeroticism measure each other in a way that undermines any simple characterization of Jewish vice or Christian virtue. And in contrast to Dickens's use of anti-Jewish sentiment to enhance the evil of a perverse villain, the dazzling interplay of images of sexual deviance and

Jewish otherness in Proust works to undo any stable code of identity, whether rooted in the Faubourg Saint-Germain or the rue du Temple. Indeed when discourses on queer and Jewish identities in Proust come into contact with each other, each destabilizes the already unstable ground upon which the other sits; and the result of this project is the questioning of imaginative constructions and cultural dispensations on a wide variety of fronts ranging from the personal to the ethnoracial to that of class—especially in that characteristically weird Proustian turn in which the aristocracy is identified both as sodomitic (which is not surprising) and isomorphic to the Jewish (which is).

In what follows I want to extend this analytic frame from the Anglo-European to a different national literature—that of America—a different medium—theater—and a different historical moment—that of Ronald Reagan's America. Specifically, I want to turn to one of the most acclaimed texts in recent American literary and theatrical history, Tony Kushner's "gay fantasia on national themes," *Angels in America*. Along with its many other projects, the play undertakes an extensive mapping of the place where figurations of the Jew meet figurations of the sexual other, the deviant, the queer. Indeed, I think that no other text since Proust's gives such sustained and sympathetic attention to both sides of this complex and long-standing conjuncture. But the disappointment of the play, its flawed conclusion, follows ineluctably from Kushner's need to collapse this parallel in order to affirm a vision neither queer nor Jewish. For Kushner desires to create both a dramatic form and an understanding of transcendence that allow a space for queer citizenship in a culture, obsessed with the mythography of rebirth and the inevitability of miracle, that privileges the ideal of family and reactivates the mythos of national coherence and destiny. Much is imaginatively and politically gained thereby, but it is my doleful task to suggest that much is lost as well and what is lost is almost exclusively on the Jewish side of the equation. The play collapses into a traditional assimilationist answer to the questions of Jewish identity it has bravely raised: the price of achieving political efficacy in a Christian-centered culture turns out to be the abandonment of Jewish difference and all that comes with it.

Angels was not the end of Kushner's mapping of this crossroads, however. He went on to experiment with a theatrical piece on Jewish themes, *A Dybbuk*—a new version of a new translation by Jaochim Neugroschel of S. Ansky's (the nom de plume of Shloyme-Zanvel Rappaport) *The*

Dybbuk (1920). Kushner's *A Dybbuk* takes up the project of conjoining Jewish and queer identities in a radically different way from *Angels*, especially in its quite moving conclusion, in which a Jewish woman, choosing death with the spirit of her beloved over life in a traditional marriage, articulates a vision of self- and art-making that is oddly congruent with those of the two queer men who dominate *Angels*, the very Jewish Roy Cohn and the very gentile Prior Walter. The eruption of this monstrous, antinormative vision in the midst of a so-called traditional culture focused on individual and social reproduction alike suggests Kushner's discovery of what I would call a queer diasporism—a cultural form generated by diaspora-dwelling Jews who accept, and sometimes revel in, the rootless quality of Jewish experience by privileging transgressive identities and non-natural forms of individual and cultural reproduction across the board. That diasporic cultural formation enters into Kushner's art at the moment of *A Dybbuk* and then quickly passes out of it, resolving certain tensions and generating new ones as he moved on to new and different projects that take up entangled questions of race and citizenship. But I want in conclusion to suggest some of the ways in which contemporary American Jewish musicians associated with, but moving beyond, the so-called klezmer revival (including some who composed music for *A Dybbuk*, the Klezmatics) extend this formation so as to open up new possibilities not just for queer culture, or Jewish culture, but for that of a nation struggling to come to terms with its complex and differing itineraries of racial and ethnic variegation—of, in short, of the multiple and multiplying diasporas that construct "America."

Angels, Monsters, and Jews

Angels in America is a loose baggy monster of a play, housing in its capacious representational tent (inter alia) Brechtian alienation devices, American mythologies, Broadway shtick, kabbalistic folktales, sitcom wisecracks, vaudeville blackout sketches. But its series of loosely linked scenes is undergirded by a number of recurrent thematic concerns: the rise of right-wing culture in the United States from McCarthy to Reagan, the dawning of gay male identity politics in the face of the plague of AIDS, the place of abjected aliens—gay men and lesbians, Mormons, Jews—in a culture that insists on a national narrative of communal oneness. And as that last formulation suggests, one of the prime unifying structural devices of the piece is its dramatic enactment of the unstable and shifting equation between the sexually transgressive and the Jewish. That equivalency is established in the very first scene of *Millennium Approaches*, the first part of *Angels in America*, and runs throughout to the last words of the final part of the play, *Perestroika*. *Millennium* begins with Rabbi Isidor Chemelwitz's eulogy for Louis Ironson's grandmother Sarah in front of Louis and his lover, Prior; those scenes later, Prior reveals that he has a Kaposi's sarcoma lesion, "the wine-dark kiss of the angel of death," and proclaims, "I'm going to die."[5] The fate of Sophie Ironson in America, that "melting pot where nothing melted," ironically foreshadows Prior's, and it is a reminder that his death, too, is starkly inevitable (10). And the words that Rabbi Chemelwitz speaks of Sarah resonate directly in Prior's experience: "You can never make that crossing that she made, for such Great Voyages in this world do not any more exist. But every day of your lives the miles that voyage between that place and this one you cross. Every day. You understand me? In you that journey is" (10–11). Although the syntax is stage Yiddish, the language is rich with implication for the two gay men: the archetype for the transformation of identity—the mark of queer experience in the play—is a wandering, rootless, shape-shifting Jew like Sarah who never finds a "home," despite her many years of residence in America. "You do not live in America," claims the rabbi. "Your clay is the clay of some Litvak shtetl, your air the air of the steppes" (10). The fate of the Jew is to be eternally other even in the utopian land that proclaims itself a haven for all aliens.

The same thing turns out to be true of its queer characters, almost all of whom also end the play as wanderers, shape-shifters, metamorphosers. Louis leaves his lover Prior after the latter's diagnosis to wander through the shoals of gay male New York—including a trip to a pickup spot known as the Ramble and a relationship with a Mormon; Joe Pitt leaves his marriage, his religion, and at the end of the play, the stage itself; Roy Cohn, cynosure of the family-values right, shuffles off the mortal coil and reappears as a ghost, and then is last glimpsed in heaven as God's defense attorney; Prior Walter undergoes a series of hallucinatory, fever-induced mental journeys and ends the play (like Proust's Swann) transformed from a witty, ironic man-about-town into something of a prophet. The last of these journeys—can we call them also diasporas?—is perhaps the most significant. For, in so doing, Prior brings the play full circle: the message he preaches echoes the note of alienation on which the play began. At the end of *Perestoika* he proclaims, "We will be citizens," underlining his own Sarah-Ironson-like alienness in announcing his very quest to overcome it."⁶

Although Kushner emphasizes the contiguity between the Jew and the queer, like Proust, he does not insist on positing their common alterity. Instead he uses each as a metonym for the other, creating an interplay of similarity and difference that conspicuously resists reduction into identity. Early in *Millennium Approaches*, for example, Mormon Joe's homoerotic desire is articulated by his dream of Jacob wrestling with a "golden-hair[ed]" angel, an image both of male-male desire and of the struggle between prophetic vocation and queer identity that resonates throughout the play (*Millennium*, 49). The dream vision insists on multiplicity and struggle, even in its articulation of a sexually charged oneness—not only in the homoerotically inflected wrestling match between Jacob (soon to be Israel) and an Aryanized angel but also within Joe, whose identifications are multiple. "I'm . . . It's me. In that struggle," Joe tells his wife, Harper, suggesting that he can be or wants to be both a new Jacob wrestling with the angel for prophetic power and an angel yearning to press his body against a Jewish man's (*Millennium*, 49).

But the same phenomenon—the generation or projection of new identities through the conjunction between Jewishness and sexual deviance—occurs on the Jewish side of the queer-Jew equation, too. Louis Ironson becomes aware of himself as a Jew only after he encounters antisemitism from a Jamaican-born black man in a London gay bar. There, he says, "I feel like Sid the Yid, you know I mean like Woody Allen in *Annie Hall*, with the payess and the gabardine coat" (*Millennium*, 91). For Sophie's grandson, a fully assimilated American Jew who cannot speak Hebrew and who only vestigially remembers the Mourner's Kaddish, Jewishness heaves into view only when it is brought into contact with the politics of otherness in the gay community—and, even then, it is a Jewishness mediated through mass-cultural images, like Woody Allen's famous representation of his character, Alvy Singer, being viewed as a Hasid by the hypernormative Hall family in a visit to their home in Chippewa Falls, Wisconsin. (It comes in response to Annie's line, "You're what Grammy Hall would call a *real* Jew," a line that in the present context takes on new salience in the light of Allen's transformation into a "real" Jewish pervert following his liaison with his teenage adoptive stepdaughter.) Jewish, queer, *whatever*: Kushner does not specify which kind of alterity might be more privileged, preferring instead to ironize all possible forms of difference through his characters' experience of their clashing interplay—and the audience's as well.

The richness of this interplay—and I have only begun to trace it here—is a tribute to Kushner's skill as a dramatist and cultural critic; but the process of bringing together Jewish and queer identities and predications has a darker, richer, and more historically pointed side as well. For at the imaginative center of the play stands its most daring and conflicted representation of the queer-Jew interrelation: Roy Cohn, at once Kushner's most historically specific and his most stylized character. The real Roy Cohn was of course a perennially controversial figure in American politics, from his days as chief aide to Joseph McCarthy to his career as a politically connected power broker with ties to right-wing politicians, the mob, and the Catholic Church.[7] He was also a spectacularly self-denying gay man, simultaneously the object of homophobic innuendo by his political opponents and, as one of the first public victims of the AIDS virus, an object lesson to the gay male community of the perils of internalized self-hatred. Cohn's silence, quite literally, equaled death. An anonymously contributed panel in the Names Project AIDS memorial quilt expresses this conflation of qualities; it reads, "Roy Cohn. Bully. Coward. Victim." Kushner cites this panel as the source of his interest in Cohn: "I was fascinated [by the panel] .... People didn't hate McCarthy so much—they thought he was a scoundrel who didn't believe in anything. But there was a venal little monster by his side, a Jew and a queer, and this was the real object of detestation."[8] And, throughout the play, Kushner not only notices but also exploits the process by which Cohn was constructed in the culturally sedimented image of the monstrous Jewish pervert—a "venal little monster ... a Jew and a queer."

Well before Cohn's opponents invoked the stereotype of the monstrous Jewish pervert, familiar in European discourse, it had assumed a specifically American embodiment. For, between 1880 and 1920—a time of extensive eastern European immigration, economic upheaval, and class warfare—antisemitism both accelerated and changed its character. Up until that time, American antisemitism largely focused on the Jew's religious and economic deviance; negative responses focused on the Jew as Christ killer (a view spread widely through McGuffey's readers) or as purveyor of material values and shoddy goods.[9] But, first in works like Telemechus Timayensis's *The American Jew* (1888) and *The Real Mr. Jacobs*

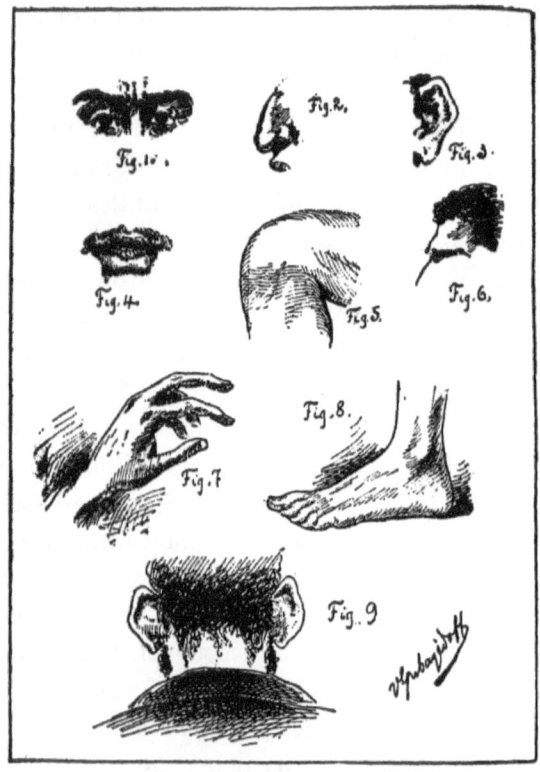

1.1 "How We May Know Him." Courtesy of the University of Michigan Library.

(1890), then in the snippets from the *Protocols of the Elders of Zion* put into public circulation by Henry Ford's *Dearborn Independent* and *The International Jew* (1920–22), the Jew's perverse political power and indulgence in deviant forms of sexuality got foregrounded instead. Thus *The American Jew* follows claims about the Jews' financial power with assertions that Jews imported sexual perversion into an otherwise pristine America: "Those certain hideous and abhorrent forms of vice, which have their origin in countries of the East, and which have in recent years sprung into existence in this country, have been taught to the abandoned creatures who practice them, and fostered, elaborated, and encouraged, by the lecherous

Jew!"¹⁰ This hideous behavior extends into all aspects of the male Jew's being: his bodily *hexis*, which is portrayed in the standard topoi of Western antisemitism (hooked noose, stooped shoulders, cadaverous body, etc., all of which make the Jew look like a droopy walking phallus), his debased culture, even his speech:

> The average Jew is disgustingly bawdy in his talk, and interlards his conversation with filthy expressions and obscene words. On the verandas of summer resorts, in hotel corridors, in the lobbies of theaters, on steamboats, on railway cars, and in public places in general, the Jew indulges in this repulsive peculiarity, to the great annoyance and disgust of respectable Christian women and decency-loving Gentile men. This was one of the habits that made him so objectionable at summer resorts, and has led to his practical exclusion from almost every first-class summer hotel in the land. (Quoted in Selzer 50)

This image of the licentious or lascivious Jew was rapidly inscribed in narratives of female exploitation, either as an instigator of white slavery or as an exploiter of female workers. A 1909 article in *McClure's* claimed that a cadre of mysterious American Jews controlled the prostitution industry in New York—largely by selling their own daughters—and that "one half of all the women ... in the business ... started their career ... in New York" prostitution.¹¹ *The American Jew* extended the concern to gentiles: "In many of the factories operated by Jews throughout the country, the life of an honest girl therein employed is made simply a hell, by reason of the Jews' predominant lechery" (Selzer 53). These fears exploded in 1915 in the Leo Frank case, an event generally considered the worst antisemitic incident in United States history and one that was, as we have seen, made possible by the network of associations that suture the Jew to the sexually deviant. Not only was Frank cast by his chief public antagonist, the populist politician Tom Watson, in the image of the gentile-mad Jewish pervert: "[a] typical young libertine Jew ... dreaded and detested by the city authorities of the North [for] utter contempt of law and a ravenous appetite for ... the girls of the uncircumcised."¹² Throughout the trial suggestions of his sexual deviance ran rampant: not merely an alleged appetite for underage girls, or proclivities for (giving) oral sex, but also out-and-out suggestions of homosexuality were all part of the prosecution's case. Frank's despairing words from prison resonate within and beyond his own experience and shadow the Jewish/queer conjunction in *Angels*: "Is there a man in Atlanta who would deny the charge of perversion was the chief cause of my conviction, or deny that the case, without that charge, would be an entirely different question?"[13]

Hyperphallic but abjuring the proper exercise of the phallus, politically and economically empowered but turning to the seduction of innocent American virgins, the Jewish male thus enters the American populist imaginary as a peculiar amalgam of sexual and political power, perverting gentile bodies and the body politic with a single gesture. This image is imported into *Angels* through Roy Cohn, one conduit for the mainstreaming populist paranoia in the 1950s via the efforts of his first political sponsor, Joe McCarthy. And, in doing so, Kushner is quite attentive to the conjunction of perversion with monstrosity that runs as a subtheme throughout much of this discourse. "He's like the polestar of human evil, he's like the worst human being who ever lived, he isn't *human* even . . . ," Louis cries out when he hears of Cohn's death (*Perestroika*, 95). Kushner's iconography in limning this nonhuman is quite precise. "Playing the phone" with what the stage directions call "sensual abandon," Cohn cries, "I wish I was an octopus, a fucking octopus. Eight loving arms and all those suckers" (*Millennium*, 11). Through the magic of theatrical transformation, he metamorphoses into that very inhuman figure. Fixing cases, buying Broadway seats, cheating clients, placing his protégés in the highest ranks of the justice department, Cohn seems to extend his tentacles everywhere: New York, Washington, the entire country.

Indeed, Kushner's Cohn corresponds with uncanny accuracy to one of the most powerful images of antisemitic propaganda, which I would label, with a nod to Sander Gilman's elegant anatomization of the Jew's body, the Jew's tentacles. In antisemitic discourse of the later nineteenth and early twentieth centuries, the Jew's monstrosity is performed by the transformation of the hand—that emblem of warmth, love, and pleasure—into bat wings, vampire talons, spider legs, or octopus tentacles. For example, a late nineteenth-century illustrated anatomy of the Jew includes not just standard antisemitic attributes—"restless suspicious eyes," "curved nose and nostrils," "ill-shapen ears of great size like those of a bat"—but also "long clammy fingers" that reach out to clutch or caress (see figure 1.1). In much classic antisemitic propaganda, these corpselike fingers extend in a monstrous way that connotes social or sexual power. "The Jew's soft hands and curved fingers grasp only the values that others have produced," claims *The American Jew* (Selzer 99), and, according to *The Original Mr. Jacobs* (1888)—in words appropriated from the French antisemite Éduoard Drumont—"the soft hand, almost melting with the hypocrisy of the traitor" is a sign of "physical degradation," which "closely follows upon moral degradation. This is strongly remarked among Jews, who, of all races of men, are the most depraved" (21). Among visual representations that use this trope is Gustave Doré's famous caricature of Mayer Rothschild, *Dieu Protège Israel*, which represents the banker holding the globe and defiling it with his long, batlike talons. In George Du Maurier's *Trilby* (1894), the hypnotizing musician Svengali is represented as a spider filling Trilby's dreams with images of monstrous pestiferousness (see figure 1.2). Illustrated covers of the *Protocols of the Elders of Zion* depict a brutish Jew pawing a bleeding, violated globe or a spider covering the world with its all-encompassing legs (see figure 1.3).

Kushner's trope of Cohn-as-octopus functions with particular brilliance in this context: it conjoins an image of the Jew as hyperphallic monster with one that stresses the perverse dimensions of that figure.

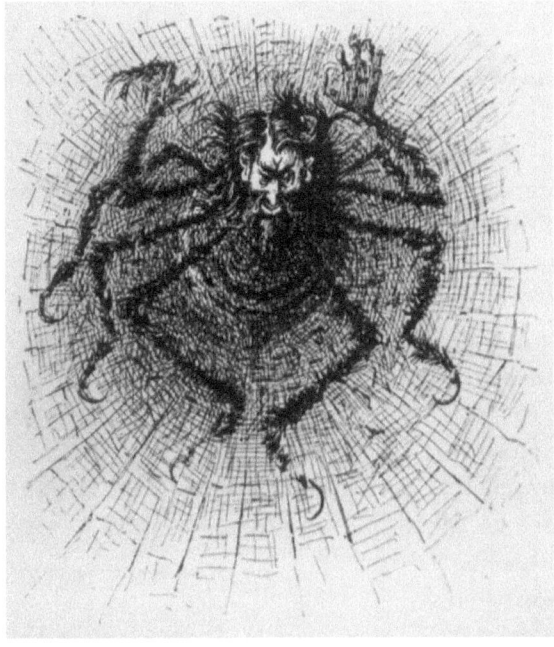

1.2   Svengali as a spider, from George Du Maurier's *Trilby* (New York: Harper, 1894).

1.3 Cover of the French edition of the *Protocols of the Elders of Zion*.
Courtesy of the Wiener Library, London.

Indeed, it is the second image that constitutes Kushner's most original addition to the tradition. An octopus, like a spider, has "eight loving arms," but it also has "all those suckers": the multiplication of phalli suggested by the arms is reoriented by the trope of the suckers, which unites implications of cheating, vampirism, and fellatio in a vivid image of monstrosity that is both recognizably Jewish and demonstrably queer.[14] The figure of Cohn thus represents an audacious attempt to think through to the center of antisemitic imagery, to the cultural queering of the Jew, and finally to the representation of the Jew as at once monstrous, empowered, and perverse—an image Kushner then installs at the center of the play's most malignant icon of queer/Jewish identity.

Kushner invokes this antisemitic iconography throughout the play with amazing accuracy. Cohn is foul mouthed:

Roy: CHRIST!
Joe: *Roy.*

Roy (*Into receiver*): Hold. (*Button; to Joe*) *What*?
Joe: Could you please not take the Lord's name in vain? (*Pause.*) I'm sorry. But please. At least while I'm . . .
Roy (*Laughs, then*): Right. Sorry. Fuck.

(*Millennium*, 14; ellipsis in the original)

Like the stereotypical Jew, Cohn seduces an innocent gentile, Joe Pitt, whom he tempts first into big-city life and then into homosexual practices and a homosexual identity (to Cohn's hypocritical chagrin). Cohn embodies not only stereotypical Jewish lasciviousness but also greed by hogging a cache of AZT—one he procures, as antisemites might imagine, thanks to his possession of secrets about affairs of state, albeit given a distinctively queer twist:

Roy: I have clout. A lot. I can pick up this phone, punch fifteen numbers, and you know who will be on the other end in under five minutes, Henry?
Henry: The President.
Roy: Even better, Henry. His wife.   (*Millennium*, 45)

But the idea of the sexually transgressive is never far from that of the malign Jew, and when antisemitic language explicitly surfaces in the play, it is sutured to the notion of queerness. For example, when Belize confronts Cohn about this selfish appropriation of a drug that can help prolong, if not save, Prior's life, Cohn refuses to share, then launches a shocking series of racist epithets at Belize. Belize responds with a string of his own imprecations: "shit-for-brains filthy-mouthed selfish motherfucking cowardly cocksucking cloven-hoofed pig" (*Perestroika*, 61). It's a strong moment in the play, bringing to the fore the racial tensions between its Jewish and its black character—for all his un-Cohn-like liberalism, Louis's racial sentiments are as susceptible to interrogation as are those of this "polestar of human evil." But the common queerness of all these characters renders both sides of the equation problematic; indeed, at once homophobic and antisemitic, Belize's curse points to self-hatred common to Jews and queers in a society suspicious of its manifold others. For to call Cohn a "cloven-hoofed pig" is to curse him for being both Jewish and nonkosher: cloven-hoofed animals, of course, are kosher;

pigs are not. The curse thus echoes the common antisemitic habit of conflating Jews with that which they abjure, but it also ironically reminds us that Cohn has taken as his totem animal the octopus, a beast as forbidden to observant Jews as the pig. The octopus-loving Cohn proudly casts himself the same way that Belize casts him, as forbidden, taboo, *treyf*, in a self-negation that contravenes both his sexual and his religious identity.

Kushner's representation of Cohn is explicitly political, part of his indictment of the hypocritical—if not worse—cast of an American right full of gay men and women but homophobic in its public embrace of "family values" and murderous in its failure to devote attention and resources to the scourge of AIDS. The construction of Cohn confronts the most regressive element of the right with a reminder that one of its cynosures was also one of its biggest bogeymen, the perverse Jewish power broker. It also outs Cohn in terms that Cohn himself would have doubtless resented. But Kushner evinces a profound fascination with this character, one that lends *Angels* a remarkable inner tension. For, while Kushner keeps killing Cohn off, Cohn keeps rising from the dead, like a zombie or (perhaps more appropriately) a dybbuk. Cohn's death dominates *Perestroika*, all the more so because it seems to occur three or four times. The first instance is the memorable scene in which Cohn fakes his death in front of the ghost of Ethel Rosenberg, convincing her to sing him a lullaby, then triumphantly proclaiming, "I just wanted to see if I could finally, finally, make Ethel Rosenberg sing! I WIN!" (*Perestroika*, (114). By so tricking a ghost, Cohn achieves a Nietzschean triumph over the dead even though he cannot beat death. Cohn dies a few moments later, and the play even manages to have him properly mourned—again, largely through the intervention of Ethel. Discovering Cohn's body while sneaking in to steal his AZT, Belize urges Louis to remember his grade-school Hebrew and say Kaddish, the diasporic-marked, centuries-old Jewish prayer for the dead.*

---

* As a jokey footnote in the the play reminds us, Kaddish is spoken in Aramaic, not biblical Hebrew. Aramaic was the demotic, the language of many peoples of the Mideast, both before and after the period of the Second Temple, and bespeaks Jews' close connection with the other peoples of the Mideast, their exile in Babylonia, where they probably encountered Aramaic most fully, and, after the fall of the temple, the gap between the priestly caste and the popular.

The ghost of Ethel Rosenberg, hovering by the bedside, prompts Louis when he forgets, then comically has him add a curse:

> Louis: Oseh sholom bimromov, hu ya-aseh sholom olenu v'al col Yisroel ...
> Ethel: V'imru omain.
> Louis: V'imru omain.
> Ethel: You sonofabitch.
> Louis: You sonofabitch. (*Perestroika*, 125–6)

Blessed and cursed, mourned and mastered, Cohn may be prepared to depart for whatever afterlife awaits him. But, like a dybbuk—a being cursed in eastern European Jewish folklore to wander the earth to haunt the living (and a creature that Kushner, as we shall see, becomes fascinated with)—he returns again as a ghost that haunts Joe Pitt. Roy's specter, emanation, dybbuk, or whatever he now is, kisses Joe on the mouth in a moment of overt sexuality that pays tribute to Joe's nervously asserted "outness": "Show me a little of what you've learned, baby Joe. Out in the world." Then Cohn announces his departure to the afterlife with a Shakespearean flourish: "I gotta shuffle off this mortal coil. I hope they have something for me to do in the Great Hereafter, I get bored easy" (127). But he is not through yet. Even after this final appearance, Cohn is brought back yet again when Prior, retreating from heaven, sees Cohn agreeing to take on God as his client. And Cohn is in a sense killed again by the excision of this scene from the Broadway and national touring productions of the play.*

This remarkable series of cursings and blessings, ritualized slayings and compulsive revivals make Cohn seem less a monster, more a great vaudevillian in the twilight of his career making one farewell appearance after another before being dragged offstage in mid-shtick. But the persistence of these efforts to kill Cohn, mourn him, revive him, then kill him again, attests to the power he continues to exert over his author.

---

*The scene appeared in the 1988 production at the Mark Taper Theater, which Kushner considers definitive. But its excision in middlebrow venues like Broadway suggests an act of cultural omission that is consistent with Kushner's political project.

It is also a sign of Kushner's need to master Cohn and all that Cohn allegorically embodies: homophobia, the most invidious forms of right-wing populism, and McCarthyism (the regressive witch's stew that fueled the Republican right from the 1950s through the 1980s and continues up to the present day's gay-marriage bashing). Indeed, the symmetry of the two plots of the play suggests that Cohn functions as the objective correlative of the AIDS virus: he infects Mormon Joe with his political vision just as the virus infects Prior. But Cohn's persistence in the face of multiple deaths suggests that he enacts another allegory that attacts and repulses Kushner as well: that of Jewish power. The fantasy culturally inscribed in the supposed monstrosity of the Jew, after all, is that these persistently marginalized members of a Christian-centered culture possess the greatest amount of what Cohn calls "clout" (*Millennium*, 45), a secret power all the more insidious because it is hidden, one that has persisted over the passage of centuries despite all efforts to eradicate it. And it is this image of the Jew with power that I see as key to Kushner's structural, indeed energizing, ambivalence in the play, an ambivalence that expresses itself more on the Jewish side of the equation than that of the queer.

In *Angels* the repository of this ambivalence about Jewishness is Louis, another queer and much more assimilated Jew than the raw, empowered Roy: Swann to his Bloch, we might say. But Louis is also portrayed, at least around questions of Jewishness (in sexual matters, he is more assertive), as something of a neurotic nebbish, a (lovably) talkative, self-dramatizing figure who only sees himself as a Jew when others see him in that guise and can commit neither to affirming nor to critiquing Zionism. (The point here isn't his political positioning, but rather his inability to assert anything other than ambivalence.) Cohn, by contrast, energizes that ambivalent image by refusing the role of nebbish—the ineffectual, hand-wringing Jew—and by arrogantly asserting the voracious, phallic power ascribed to the Jew under the sign of monstrosity. Cohn's willingness to embody this image, to be the Jew with tentacles if not testicles, palpably attracts Kushner. But it also leads to Kushner's equally powerful need to master Cohn dramaturgically—to mourn or to kill him. For, to affirm the play's ideological commitment to the full assimilation of queer citizens into an ideal body politic, Kushner must eliminate Cohn and all the phallic aggression he represents from his idealizing vision. At the end of the play there is room for angels and angelic queers in a utopian America, but there is no place there for monsters.

Cohn's ejection from the play, then, is not to be read as a function of some putative self-hatred but rather as an inevitable aspect of Kushner's social and political program. I am deeply sympathetic to Kushner's politics, but their inscription in *Angels* has disturbing dramatic and ethno-religious consequences. As *Perestroika* lurches toward its climax (like Cohn, it seems to end several times), a Christian thematic surfaces that stresses grace and rebirth. And along with this thematic comes a classic form of emplotment—Shakespearean comedy—that affirms regeneration through the creation of a new, redeemed community. Both these forms have notorious difficulties in reckoning with the figure of the Jew. Like *Twelfth Night*—or, more relevantly, *The Merchant of Venice*—Kushner's play ends with the evocation of a community as a newly formed, extended, inclusive family, albeit a family with a difference. Composed of various forms of otherness, this family is a redeemed version of the community of others that Louis seeks in the gay bar in London: a Mormon with recently discovered lesbian tendencies, a Jew, and a black male drag queen, all presided over by a WASP man living heroically with AIDS. But given the play's preoccupation with the queer-Jew equation, it is all the more disturbing that Louis, the Jewish member of this queer family, should be represented as querulous and ineffectual. The queer Jew enters the postnuclear family, that is to say, not only as a cultural stereotype (albeit one depicted with some affection) but as a particularly disempowered one. More troubling still is the absence of Cohn and anyone associated with him from this community—for Joe Pitt, too, is banished from the final scenes. Shylock, at least, gets to leave the stage under his own power; no such agency, not even negative agency, is granted either to Cohn or his surrogate son. This elision pushes the play into a more explicitly Christian narrative: it emphasizes the near-miraculous rebirth of Prior after his fever-induced dream vision, for he lives on thanks to the AZT stolen from Cohn's deathbed by Belize and Louis. Cohn dies, it seems, so that Prior might live to preside over the new queer postnuclear family, at least for the space of the theatrical enactment.

The turn to Christian thematics suggested by the privileging of the Prior plot is confirmed by the imagery and action of the play's final section. At Central Park's Bethesda Fountain, Prior has Louis begin the story of the biblical pool of Bethesda and directs Hannah and Belize to complete it. As a piece of theater this moment is undeniably moving, but when considered under the sign of Jewishness it remains deeply problematic. Prior asks Louis to perform an act at once typical and typological, to submerge his own Jewish voice in a chorus of Christian ones. The story of Bethesda that Louis tells has distinctly anti-Jewish overtones in the Book of John, where it precedes Christ's healing of a lame man (and, not uncoincidentally, Prior walks with a cane as a result of his disease). The miracle increases the persecutorial furor of the Jews, already aroused by Christ's performing such miracles as bringing back the dead (and again, it is no coincidence that Belize mentions Lazarus earlier in the play). And in response to their contumely, Christ announces that he is the fulfillment of the Old Testament prophecy to the Jews, a prophecy to which they reveal themselves deaf: "Had ye believed Moses, ye would have believed me, for he wrote of me" (John 5:46). These implications were, I suspect, absent from Kushner's consciousness as he wrote; however, they animate the cultural text to which he is clearly referring, and, at this point in the play, that passage is writing him. Louis performs the act that, in the biblical passage Kushner alludes to, Jews exist to accomplish: announce the new Christian dispensation, then get out of the way.*

The Bethesda angel that hovers over the play's conclusion seems to derive more from Marianne Williamson than from Walter Benjamin, and I need here to suggest why. This turn to the Christian grows out of the play's most powerful and moving political aspirations. The particular success of *Angels*, after all, is to speak at once to multiple audiences—gay and straight;

---

*It can be argued that there are enough doctrinal continuities and shared eschatologies in the Christian and Jewish traditions to ameliorate one's sense of the Christian domination of the Jewish predecessor; certainly, that has been the response of many people to the point I made above when I have presented this material to non-Jewish audiences (for Jewish ones, it tends to be a commonplace). But, as Gavin Langmuir observes, typological thinking in the Middle Ages made a primary theological point of the historical insufficiency of the Jews. This view persists in American versions of covenant theology, as Sacvan Bercovitch shows, and in eighteenth- and nineteenth-century Enlightenment philosophy, as Paul Rose argues. More to the point, Kushner alludes to one of the most egregious New Testament passages suggesting the historical supersession of the Jewish people by Christian revelation. According to Ruether, such biblical passages make anti-Judaism (and hence, later in time, fully racialized antisemitism) a vital part of the Christian tradition rather than a blot on an otherwise sympathetic vision.

highbrow and middlebrow; socialist, Democratic, and even Republican—and to argue to those audiences for a mode of civic identity that includes rather than excludes, that creates rather than denies community. To critic David Savran, one of *Angels*'s most incisive readers, this enterprise is problematic, for it recapitulates the liberal pluralist ideology that Kushner has explicitly disavowed. Yet, as Savran grudgingly admits, the play's breadth of appeal and generosity of address are the source of its efficacy in a public sphere dominated for decades by conservative ideologies that articulate the utopian longings historically central to the construction of a distinctive American identity:

> What is perhaps most remarkable about *Angels in America* is that it has managed, against all odds, to amass significant levels of both cultural and economical capital . . . . It does so . . . by its skill both in reactivating a sense (derived from the early nineteenth century) of America as the utopian nation and mobilizing the principle of ambivalence—or, more exactly, dissensus—to produce a vision of a once and future pluralist culture.[15]

The evocation of the queer family at the end of *Angels* is a perfect example of this utopian vision of union by dissensus and of the political ends to which Kushner attempts to turn this vision. He offers the image of redeemed community in the guise of a utopian Americanness where the nation is reconstituted as a postnuclear family made up of quarreling outsiders—in Savran's terms the very embodiment of union by dissensus. That Kushner is echoing a problematic nationalist discourse is ultimately less important than his appropriation of it for a frankly queer political project—and of the family-as-nation metaphor for a nonprocreative notion of both family and nation that includes all forms of family in a new national narrative. When Prior, the reluctant prophet, having wrestled with his own angels, announces his apocalyptic revelation, he intends to include all the members of the audience in this new union, which is more perfect because it is still divided:

> The world only spins forward. We will be citizens. The time has come.
> Bye now.
> You are fabulous creatures, each and every one.

And I bless you: *More Life.*
The Great Work Begins. (*Perestroika*, 148)

Prior predicts that "we"—the members of the queer family—"will be citizens," but to achieve this status, "each and every one" must devise a new form of citizenship and work to construct a redeemed America that can gather gay and straight, black and white, Mormon, Christian, and Jew into a collective identity precisely through the act of quarreling over that identity.

Herein lies the problem with Kushner's achievement, at least when considered from a point of view that stresses the different difference that is Jewish difference. To affirm this project, Kushner must speak in the idiom of mainstream culture while criticizing that culture: he must evoke a utopian ideal of America that exerts political and imaginative power in the social arena but that is substantially less than ideal in practice. As Sacvan Bercovitch has suggested, this American ideal of utopia presents the nation as a perfected version of its flawed predecessors just as in the versions of Protestant theology adopted by American Puritans the Christological narrative serves as a fulfillment of its Jewish antecedents.[16] Ironically, this utopian understanding of America has served for many Jewish intellectuals—including Kushner (and perhaps Bercovitch as well)—as a vector of assimilation into a national drama that had excluded them. "It was impressed upon us," writes Kushner of his childhood, "as we sang 'America the Beautiful' at the Seder's conclusion, that the dream of millennia was due to find its ultimate realization not in Jerusalem but in this country."[17] But, as Bercovitch also reminds us, the deployment of a typological schema in the construction of an American national utopia ultimately swallows up the narrative of Jewish history that serves as its antecedent and gloss. Jewish difference becomes not only one part of an ethnic panoply—of a vision of union by ethnic dissensus—but also the shadowy type whose truth is named America. In such a schema, the narrative of the biblical Hebrews and even that of the Jewish people may be privileged, but, by the very conditions of that privilege, their difference—that which marks them as Jews—is extinguished.

To be sure, Kushner invokes the rhetoric of an American utopia not to elide Jewish difference but to intervene on behalf of a queer politics in a cultural debate over the national destiny: to queer the Puritan, as it were.

However, the narrative schema he deploys situates his endeavor on a firmly Christian terrain in an overtly typological way. This effect becomes clearest in the play's final foray into the typological imaginary, the concluding speech of Prior. Prior the arch-WASP reverses Louis's anticipation of the Christian dispensation and speaks a Jewish blessing, marked as such by Kushner in his commentary on the play, "More Life." But the reversal cannot be complete; although the Protestant imaginary can contain Jewishness under the logic of typology, Jewishness is granted no such power vis-à-vis the Christian. Prior's articulation of a Jewish blessing thus continues and indeed confirms the absorption of Jewish type into Christian fulfillment instead of breaking or reversing that pattern. It is troubling that a play beginning with a rabbi's voice extolling "the melting pot that does not melt" ends with the subordination of the Jew to Christian emplotment. But Kushner is determined to find a place for angels in America—somehow.

Is there a way of conceptualizing the utopia *Angels* evokes that would not amalgamate otherness into a culturally palatable unity? Walter Benjamin, one of Kushner's major sources for the play, thought so, and his writings suggest a different model for the consolations *Angels* offers. As I have suggested, Benjamin is everywhere in Kushner's play, from its imagery of apocalypse to its angelic iconography. But Benjamin's presence is felt most powerfully in the final scene. When Prior cries, "The world only spins forward" (a false claim, since the world, which spins on its axis, could be said in that sense to be moving nowhere), his speech alludes to the moment in the "Theses on the Philosophy of History" when Benjamin defines his own utopian vision through the image of a Klee drawing, the *Angelus Novus*:

> His face is turned towards the past. Where we perceive a chain of events, he sees one single catastrophe which keeps piling wreckage upon wreckage and hurls it in front of his feet. The angel would like to stay, awaken the dead, and make whole what has been smashed. But a storm is blowing from Paradise; it has got caught in his wings with such violence that the angel can no longer close them. This storm irresistibly propels him into the future to which his back is turned, while the pile of debris before him grows skyward. This storm is what we call progress.[18]

Kushner invokes Benjamin but not the full complexity of his argument. With its audacious conflation of the angelic and the monstrous, Klee's image serves as a reminder that the difference between angel and monster is often just a matter of perspective. This is the chastening recognition that Kushner's utopianism conspicuously lacks, especially when compared with Benjamin's muted (in Benjamin's word, "weak" [254]) messianism. That the angel is propelled forward by the wind from paradise is less important than the text's clear distinction between the beholder of the angel and the vision the angel experiences. The same nonidentity exists within the collective subject that is the implicit addressee of Benjamin's text. This storm may be what "we" call progress—but Benjamin leaves thoroughly and disturbingly open-ended the questions of who that "we" is and what the relation is between what "we" see and what "we" want to see.

In the space created by that opening lies a less amalgamative, more open-ended model of collective identity that creates a place for divergent understandings of history, progress, paradise, and utopia—even of America. That space provides an escape from the impulse to amalgamate—we might also say assimilate—the various sorts of otherness that Kushner's utopian project ultimately embodies, despite his juggling of multiple models of alterity until the last act of the play. The beauty and brilliance of *Angels* is that the play points beyond itself—and so imposes hard questions about the nature of identities, Jewish and queer alike, that a less insistent, more troubled vision of utopia would leave in its wake. What that utopianism might look like is the subject of the rest of this chapter.

Toward a Queer Diasporism: *A Dybbuk*

In the afterglow of *Angels*'s remarkable success—its triumphant Los Angeles and London productions, its protracted Broadway run, its multiple Tonys and Pulitzers—Kushner turned to a project that promised further to explore the ramifying conjunctions between Jewishness and queerness: *A Dybbuk*, his adaptation of Ansky's *The Dybbuk*. It proved to be a shrewd choice. That work served, from its very inception, as a discursive crossroads where self-consciously modernist intellectuals encountered, and attempted to come to terms with, so-called traditional eastern

European culture—discovering, along the way, just how complex a life-form that culture was, and just how great a challenge it provided to their own assumptions and understandings. *The Dybbuk* was pasted together from Ansky's collection of the narratives and life experiences of shtetl culture as the lead investigator of the Jewish Ethnographic Expedition (1912–1914), a three-year exploration of the Jewish peoples of Poland and the Pale of Settlement funded by Baron Vladimir Horace Guinzberg.* (Indeed, much of the material for the play was gleaned from responses to a questionnaire consisting of a mind-boggling 2,567 questions that Ansky posed to his native informants, covering virtually every aspect of everyday life.) Originally written in Russian and intended for the Moscow Art Theater, and not entirely untouched by modernist ambitions, the play was refashioned, at the suggestion of Stanislavsky himself, into Yiddish by Ansky before being translated into Hebrew and English and then retranslated into Yiddish: Ansky lost the original Yiddish translation on a train, but retranslated it into Yiddish from the Hebrew version of I. M. Bialyk. And it was multiply translated in a different sense as well, as it was brought to the stage in many of the urban centers that defined Jewish life: Vilnius (the famed Stanislavsky-inspired Vilnius Yiddish Theater), Moscow (the equally famous Habimah Company, which performed it in Hebrew), and New York (first at the also-renowned Yiddish Art Theater, then in an English version by Henry Ahlsberg in a memorable production at the Neighborhood Playhouse—crucible of the twenties avant-garde theater—on Grand Street on the Lower East Side). It was even translated into an entirely different set of media: a magnificently uncanny film, employing not only stars from the Yiddish theater but also townspeople from Kazimierz, Poland, where it was shot on location in 1931.

Ansky's *The Dybbuk* thus served as a contact zone for all the multiple, conflicting, if not warring impulses within Ashkenazic Jewish culture in

---

*I use the term *shtetl* advisedly. Barbara Kirschenblatt-Gimblett reminds us that the connotations that attach to that word in America (a backward rural village à la *Fiddler on the Roof*) don't match the realities of lived experience in which more Jews lived in small and medium-sized towns, often cheek by jowl with gentiles, than out-and-out villages. Indeed, the very term *shtetl* means "little town," and it's this sense that I ask the reader to keep in mind in what follows. See her preface to the second edition of Mark Zbrowski and Elizabeth Herzog, *Life Is with People: The Culture of the Shtetl* (New York: Schocken, 1995).

the last fin de siècle: between *Haskalah*-inspired* intellectuals like Ansky and the putatively indigenous life practices of shtetl culture they sought to excavate; between Yiddish and Hebrew as authentic languages of Jewish self-expression (the so-called Language Wars over whether Hebrew or Yiddish was the proper language of the Jewish people were raging at precisely this moment, touched off by the 1908 Czernowitz Conference that first promulgated the Yiddish revival); between Hebrew or Yiddish and Russian or English or other European languages as proper imaginative and social vehicles of expression; between Jewish-identified and European-identified cultural trajectories for Jewish intellectuals—between, we might say, the conception of a *Jewish* modernism and a Jewish *modernism*. And, as Naomi Seidman has brilliantly argued, the play also created a contact zone where conflicting inscriptions of sexual desire within shtetl culture encountered each other, with equally conflicting results.[19] In the play a dybbuk—a supernatural creature—possesses a young woman, Leah, and deflects her attentions from the man her father wishes her to marry to Chonen, a young kabbalist whose death created that spirit. As the creature is exorcised, we learn that its very origins were erotically overdetermined. Two Hasidic scholars who had fathered Chonen and Leah had, out of their intimacy as young men, promised their children to each other. Chonen's father may have died; Leah's father, eager to marry his daughter to the son of a rich merchant, may have forgotten his pledge; but still the force of

---

* The Hebrew name for the so-called Jewish enlightenment, which flourished throughout the eighteenth and nineteenth century and featured the rise of the so-called *Wissenschaft der Judentums*, the scientific study of Jewishness of which the ethnographic expedition was a poignant part. For it ended with Ansky's realization that not only the traditional culture of eastern Europe, but the actual lives of Jews, were threatened by the war and its aftermath: famine, pestilence, pogrom. In many ways *The Dybbuk* represents Ansky's attempt not only to memorialize this disappearing culture but also to make the lives of Jews palpably alive to his Russian and European countrymen. As David Roskies argues, to Ansky, acquainting a broader audience with popular folktales was "the best way of acquainting non-Jews with the ethical and aesthetic dimensions of Jewish culture" (see *The Jewish Search for a Usable Past* [Bloomington: Indiana University Press, 1999], p. 82). But it has to be conceded that the dybbuk narrative that particularly fascinated Ansky is one of the *least* likely of all the many folktales and customs he collected to teach this lesson, communicating instead the mysticism and superstition of the "ethical and aesthetic dimensions of Jewish culture." Its aesthetics, to be sure, have much in common with those of nativist Russian intellectuals—it's similar to many Russian folktales—but its ethics are, as we shall see in some detail below, far more complex.

their childhood affections drives the wandering Chonen to Leah, and then, after his death from shock at news of her betrothal, creates the dybbuk to possess her. The monstrous dybbuk, therefore, not only enforces the love of the son and daughter but also embodies the forgotten homoerotic passions of their parents. By extension, it also represents the overwhelming eroticism of the all-male world of the *cheder* in which those affections were formed—an eroticism that rises up from the past in a monstrous form that threatens to undo the reproductive, sexual, and gender order of shtetl culture itself, and from within the very normative center of that culture.

Kushner works hard in his version of the play to underscore its transgressive undercurrents. As Alisa Solomon has reminded us, he accentuates the erotic relation of Chonen and his fellow student Sender as well as that of the parents, stages a discussion on the place of women in the synagogue, and expands the version of the Song of Songs that Chonen quotes in the original.[20] But Kushner goes well beyond the exclusive identification of queerness with sexual transgressivity upon which Seidman and Solomon rely and accentuates elements in the play that we might want to think of as queer in the broadest sense of the word: as all that which stands outside of and is subversive to the gendered and sexual norm. Seidman writes that "in Ansky's conflation, the mutual attraction of the young couple emerges simultaneously from the depth of their erotic passion for each other and from the betrothal pledge sworn by their fathers. In a startling move, Ansky suggests that the two derivations—one instinctual and preconscious, the other historical and traditional—are, in fact, one and the same" (233). But in fact, they are not. What makes the play remarkable is that Leah's choice of death with Chonen rather than life without him in a loveless arranged marriage comes *after* she has been freed of the spell of the dybbuk— from the spirit of her father's affection for another man:

> Leah: Come to me, my bridegroom, enter my heart, let me bear you there, my dead man, until in dreams I can deliver you, in dreams at night we can cradle the children we will never have....
> (*A wedding march is heard outside.*)
> Leah: They're bringing the stranger in, they want me to marry him. Come to me, my bridegroom.
> Chonen's voice: I left your body to return to your soul.
> (*Wearing white for the wedding, Chonen appears.*)

Leah: The circle's broken! I am coming to you! I'm so afraid!
Chonen: Please come to me!
Leah: I am!
(*As the wedding march grows stronger, Leah removes her black cloak and approaches the bridegroom. The two become one.*)[21]

To a certain extent, this moment invokes the folk concept of the *zivug* (literally, the twin, the pair—by extension the soul match), the belief that one is fated to marry one person and one person alone, else trouble will follow. The strength of the *zivug* here is even greater than that of the rabbis who have exorcised the dybbuk or, for that matter, of the dybbuk itself, drawing Leah inexorably forward to fulfill its dictates. So much is clear in Ansky's version of the play, *pace* Seidman and Solomon. In Kushner's revised version of the play (and in the Joachim Neugroschel translation upon which he relies) Leah's speech stresses not the inexorability of her *zivug*ian movement toward her soulmate but rather its willedness—not the uncanny power of the love match but that of her own self-assertion. In the Ahlsberg translation, when Chonen calls Leah to join him in death, she responds: "I am coming." [22] In the Neugroschel/Kushner version "coming" is elided, the declarative "I am" left to resonate in the audience's ears. The strong suggestion here is that Leah's desire to merge with Chonen, however linked it may be to the death drive, is ultimately an affirmation of her own agency—that what she truly is can only be fulfilled by embracing her beloved to the exclusion of all else, including family, children, and life itself. Further, in their echo of God's words to Moses when he first appears to him in the guise of a burning bush—"I am what I am"—her words suggests that her act of willed death is also to be seen as an audacious act of self-creation. The allusion suggests that she has taken onto herself this divine power, even if it can only be realized first by linguistic expression and then by death. Erotic transport, gender liberation, and the embrace of the supernatural merge in a vision that questions normativities of all sorts, especially those that restrict mystical experience to men.

This moment of transcendental expression mirrors the end of *Angels* and suggests some of the directions in which Kushner moves from there. As we have seen, Prior's moving speech at the end of *Angels* invokes a progressivist model of history as a means of pushing toward the possibility of queer citizenship; it ends, as Emerson might say, in the optative mood. Leah's is the exact opposite; it invokes a new life that is a form of death, an uncanny and unnatural species of reproduction that perverts—turns from—the biological in favor of a form of being that embraces dream, death, art. As she does so, Leah eschews or even defies communal norms and national identities. Leah's is not the vision of the people of her shtetl or even of the eastern European Jewry for whom Ansky, after World War I, became an impassioned spokesman or the Zionism that was emerging as one solution for their persecution in the European nation-states. To the contrary, hers is a plea for futurelessness, for a turn away from the biological and social reproduction that is at the center of national predications and future-oriented aspirations of all sorts. As such it achieves an uncanny negative power, one that stands powerfully against the version articulated at the end of *Angels*—shall we call it the Prior version? This negative vision of creation is "Jewish" in some sense that the *Angels* epiphany is not; it is kabbalistic in its insistence on the powers of negation as a form of making (a potential borne out in one of Kushner's additions to the play—a beautiful stage direction in which the two dead forms of Chonen and Leah become balls of light, dancing off into infinity). But it is also "queer" in a sense that *Angels*, for all its ostentatious self-positioning as a piece of queer dramaturgy, is not; that is, it does not posit as an emblem of value not a new, reborn family as an image of collective identity, as *Angels* does, but rather insists on a stringent embrace of the negation of family itself and, with it, all that family metonymically betokens: community, religion, nation. In the valorizing of an imaginative power that comes through this embrace of the negative, and in the positing of an individual achieving that self-making through an act of asserted will, Kushner in fact places Leah in the exact same position as Roy Cohn, a figure who achieves, almost despite himself, a dramatic power that transcends even as it embraces death. (Both Roy and Leah end up, in fact, as spirit beings, although in their last appearances Leah is all light, Roy all sass.) To put it simply, at the end of *A Dybbuk* or *Angels* it is the bracing figures who embrace death that live with us as much or perhaps even more than the normative figures who call for "more Life."

Interlude: Metamorphoses of a Dybbuk

What Kushner went looking for in turning to the dybbuk narrative is a genealogy for his own queer project *within* the culture of central and eastern European Jewry. What he finds, like Ansky before him, is just how complex that culture turns out to be, how delving into it involves reconsideration of questions of gendered, national, and religious identity as fully as it does those of sexuality. It is complex in a different way as well. His queer genealogizing is grounded in a work that can be said with some justice to have been written in three different languages and instantly translated into a fourth; a work, moreover, that, disseminated broadly as a portrait of authentic shtetl life, was by the very fact of its proliferation through languages, media, and nations a tribute to the relentless remaking of the authentic throughout Jewish and gentile culture. It is thus unsurprising—it is in fact seemingly inevitable that the odd, reproductionless love celebrated in the play is itself repeated in the play's seemingly parthenogenic dissemination.

Moreover, the diasporic churning of the dybbuk narrative through media and languages continued apace in America, and these avatars might be just as important to understanding the implications of Kushner's project as the eastern European origins of Ansky's "original" text. "I think there is a kind of *klezmer*/east European influence in American popular song that came in through the Jewish community," Kushner told klezmer performer and scholar Yale Strom, and this shared heritage of "sexiness, transgressiveness, and [ecstasy]" that passed from klezmer into American popular culture, a heritage so important to Kushner's own genealogy, can be traced through the fate of *The Dybbuk* in the U.S. as well.[23] The play, as I have suggested above, crossed over from a Yiddish-speaking audience to a more cosmopolitan one in the English version performed at the Neighborhood Playhouse. That production featured, in the role of Leah, a young actress named Mary Ellis who was a close friend of George Gershwin. Gershwin attended the performance and was enormously impressed; so much so that five years later, he took up the subject himself by signing a contract with the Metropolitan Opera—eager for new material on an ethnic theme—for an opera to be based on the dybbuk story, with a libretto by Ahlsberg. After learning that rights had been sold to another composer, Gershwin turned to different interests, ultimately realizing his grand ambitions for an opera on a folk theme on the plane of race, not ethnicity, with *Porgy and Bess* (1935).[24]

For Kushner to turn to this play is thus for him to seek to embed—or perhaps discern—his queer diasporic vision in the tradition of Jewish American theater and music as well as the folk culture of eastern European Jewry. In so doing, he reminds us that the Jewish-queer conjunction of *Angels* has a resonance not only in the world from which comes Sophie Ironson, Louis's shtetl-born grandmother, but in that of the rich cultural mother lode running from the Lower East Side to Broadway and the Metropolitan Opera—that particularly American place where high, low, and middlebrow culture meet and to which *Angels* itself aspires. And these resonances proliferate further, which suggests both the scope of Kushner's project of embedding the queer in the Jewish via the dybbuk narrative and some of the problems that seem to crop up in this project of self-genealogizing—almost, it often seems, impelled by the uncanny force of the dybbuk itself.

In 1974 Jerome Robbins and Leonard Bernstein collaborated on a ballet version of the dybbuk story for the New York City Ballet. The ballet, like the opera Gershwin had planned, represents a bid to use Jewish folk material for esteem at the highest of high-cultural institutions on the part of two cultural outsiders-become-insiders—Bernstein, of course, being the brilliant son of a businessman who had become the first Jew to conduct the New York Philharmonic and Robbins née Rabinowitz (he had, as he himself put it in describing another dancer, "done a fine nose-job on his own name") being the brilliant second-generation New York–born, New Jersey–bred son of a successful entrepreneur who had become the clear successor to George Balanchine at the hyperprestigious New York City Ballet company.[25] Both Bernstein and Robbins, moreover, were adept at moving back and forth between such high-culture venues and the commercial world of the Broadway theater, sometimes separately (Bernstein with the witty *Candide* [1956], Robbins with *Fiddler on the Roof* [1964]), sometimes, powerfully, together: they had previously collaborated on such enormous successes as *Fancy Free* (1944) and *West Side Story* (1957). *Dybbuk*, however, represented a deeply personal collaboration: an effort, it seems, to bring their outsider origins and their insider status together in one grand gesture of ethnoracial uplift and cultural consolidation. The collaboration was an unusually rocky one and as such indicates some of the problems as well as the possibilities inherent in this project. Robbins brought to his friend and collaborator Bernstein the idea for a ballet on the subject of the dybbuk as early as 1944; the two decided to put it into concrete form in 1973 (along, it turns out, with a number of other culture makers: that year also saw a wonderfully innovative version of *The Dybbuk* put on by the National Theater of the Deaf as well as another ballet version by Jewish choreograopher Pearl Lang). But they quickly found

1.4　Jerome Robbins and Leonard Bernstein, *Dybbuk*: "The Chorus." Courtesy of the New York Public Library, Performing Arts Division, and Martha Swope.

what had previously been an easy collaboration turned into a messy, difficult one. Bernstein and Robbins seemed to have different agendas in mind for the ballet, agendas that had much to do with their differing relations to their Jewishness. Robbins—who had done extensive research into the world of eastern European Jewry for *Fiddler*, including attending and watching Hasidic dances in Brooklyn—was unusually conflicted about his own origins, and working on the dybbuk material, reports Amanda Vaill in the recent definitive biography, seems to have brought this ambivalence to a fever pitch. It returned Robbins to the trauma of his own bar mitzvah, where he broke down in tears during what he thought was faulty chanting and cried out for help from his grandfather; it raised his prickly relations with his domineering father, who seems never to have understood his son's choice of careers or his multivariate sexual partners—and it hardly helped matters that, as he prepared the ballet, his father lay ill in a Florida hospital, unable or unwilling to respond to Robbins's attempts to

1.5 *Dybbuk*: Helgi Thomasson and Patricia McBride as Chonen and Leah. Courtesy of the New York Public Library, Performing Arts Division, and Martha Swope.

reach out to him. This ambivalence—about family and hence his own free-floating queer sexuality, about the Jewish past he had rejected when he changed his name, about patrimony in its most extensive sense—was reflected in Robbins's plan for the ballet, which (in his words) attempted to make the story "cleaner"—to conform to a sleek Balanchinean aesthetic of high modernism, not the messier modernism of Ansky, with its distinctive synthesis of European symbolism and Russo-Jewish folk art.[26]

Bernstein had, if anything, the opposite problem: he enthusiastically threw himself into the project of high-culturing eastern European Jewish otherness, of bringing together (in the words of his biographer) "his Ukranian-Jewish heritage" with the world of "abstract music."[27] To that end Bernstein expanded what was going to be a simple project for a small chamber orchestra into a score for a full symphony and voices; as he did so, he worked fiendishly to write the most "Jewish" scenes of the ballet in a modified version of twelve-tone method by deploying for major portions of the score a scale involving twenty-two notes assigned to the twenty-two letters of the Hebrew alphabet. "Every note in the ballet was arrived at by cabalistic or mystical manipulation of numbers" Bernstein proudly told the *New York Times*, adding that, even more ingeniously, his melodies and harmonies in the twenty-two-tone row laid particular stress on intervals of eighteen and thirty-six, the former being the numeric equivalent of the Hebrew letters for *chai* (life) and the latter (the letters *lamed-vav*) designating the thirty-six righteous men who, according to Jewish mystical thought, must exist to justify God's continuing to sustain this manifestly unrighteous world.[28] He even drew a kabbalistic diagram—a tree graphically describing the ten emanations of the godhead—to guide him in his composition. But all this was put in the service of the most advanced high-art practices, the twelve-tone system of Schoenberg, Webern, and Berg that is almost coterminous with Viennese modernism of the most dauntingly abstruse level. In so doing, of course, the self-assuredly Jewish Bernstein was working through his artistic patrimony no less insistently (if more happily) than Robbins was confronting the lineage of his own family. By adopting the twelve-tone technique of another Jewish high-cultural composer, Schoenberg (in his youth a Catholic convert but whose late work, like *Moses und Aron*, turns to Jewish-identified themes), Bernstein sought to bring together high-art European modernism, especially as created by high-culture Viennese Jews, and the "traditional" culture of Ashkenaz that this high culture insistently rejected, stressing implicitly the continuity, rather than the rupture, between the two modalities.[29] At the New York City Ballet, Bernstein's score seemed to suggest, the opposed worlds of Vienna and the shtetl could be as remade as one.

Given these differing agendas, no wonder the two collaborators began to clash over the ballet. "Lenny is depressed," reported Bernstein's friend and producer Helen Coates, "because Jerry can't make up his mind about how the ballet should go. . . . Jerry is the most difficult person with whom to work."[30] Indeed, the two disagreed so violently that at one point Robbins had Bernstein ejected from the theater during a run-through.[31] The ballet, understandably, was a relative failure, a speed bump in the otherwise enormously successful careers of both men. Although a critical success, *Dybbuk* was not popular with the high-toned audience and was unaccountably dropped from the repertory one year after its premiere. The subsequent fate of the material, however, suggests that the problem of its reception, like that of its inception, may not have been with the audience. Bernstein recycled the material into a suite, and it joined other material that defines him as a self-consciously Jewish composer, like his "Jeremiah" and "Kaddish" symphonies. (Tellingly, when Bernstein chose to record *The Dybbuk* suite, he did so twice, once with the New York City Ballet Orchestra, once with the Israel Philharmonic.) Robbins, however, took a different tack. Dissatisfied with the ballet, he took Bernstein's music and refashioned it into a new work called *The Dybbuk Variations* (a reference to his magnificent *Goldberg Variations* of 1971, a work in which Robbins turns as closely as he ever did to nonrepresentational, non-narrative choreographic modalities of high Balanchinean modernism), then in 1980 to a work for an all-male ensemble, *A Suite of Dances*, utterly devoid of any explicit Jewish content. All the various subtexts—the queer and the Jewish, a European-identified modernism versus a stripped-down, self-consciously "American" one, and of course the question of Jewish modernism versus *Jewish* modernism—that course through Ansky's play and the Robbins/Bernstein ballet diverge just as fully and just as fatally as they do at the end of *Angels*—in this case having the additional consequence of breaking up a collaboration sustained for over thirty years. *The Dybbuk*, we might say, was as cursed as its subjects but reversed its effect: instead of uncannily expressing the union of two queer Jewish men over time, it served as the means of their division.*

It's perhaps no coincidence, then, that like Robbins and Bernstein, Kushner quickly moved on to other material. For even as he was finishing *A Dybbuk* (and making noises about following it up with another play on

---

* The ballet has been rarely staged since. It was revived in 2005 by the San Francisco Ballet, and in 2007 by the New York City Ballet, each time earning respectful, but not rapturous, reviews. These manifestations of the dybbuk story are hardly the last or, perhaps, even the most important; rather, what strikes me as significant is that the dybbuk material has been consistently fascinating to artists working in a number of different media. Thus, to add to the ones I have inventoried above, Gershwin's opera was pre-empted by the endeavor of Italian composer Ludovico Rocca, whose *Dybbuk* premiered in 1934. In 1931, American composer David Tamkin began writing a dybbuk opera which premiered in in 1951. More recently, Pulitzer Prize-winning composer Shulamit Ran's *Between Two Worlds (The Dybbuk)* was performed at the Chicago Lyric Opera in 1997. In addition, a Noh-theater version, *Between Two Worlds*, directed by Zvika Serper, was performed at Tel Aviv University in 1999 and a puppet version, by Mark Levinson, toured the U.S. in 2002. Doubtless more—in yet more media—are to come.

1.6   Bernstein and Robbins during rehearsals for *Dybbuk*. Courtesy of the New York Public Library, Performing Arts Division, and Martha Swope.

Jewish themes, *The Golem*), Kushner began *Henry Box Brown*, a play on the subject of a slave who sent himself to freedom in a cargo container, then moved with lightning speed to a splendidly prescient play on the theme of imperialism (*Homebody/Kabul*) before turning back to interrogate his own middle-class Jewishness and its relation to race in his 2005 musical *Caroline, or Change*. More recently Kushner turned to the Mideast conflict with the screenplay for the film *Munich*, one that attempts to balance sympathy for the Palestinians and the Israelis and that, in the eyes of many observers, myself included, falls into Louis-like incoherence as a result. Kushner's themes have broadened, it might be said, from exploring and interrogating an alterity based on sexual otherness first, and ethnic, national, and racial difference second, to an increased attention to the latter categories; although these are clearly on his mind, as we have seen, in

Angels, the latter ones have recently become the sum and substance of his work.

This turn toward race and ethnicity is one that this book will make as well, although, like Kushner, I'll keep coming back to sexuality—normative and otherwise—as an integral component of these alterities. Before doing so, however, I want to pause briefly over the moment of *A Dybbuk*, or, more to the point, the incidental music to that play, as a way of suggesting how all these diverse formations—the queer, the diasporic, the Jewish—can continue to be successfully intertwined. For that music was provided by the downtown New York klezmer band I mentioned briefly in the introduction, the Klezmatics, and, indeed, like Bernstein's score for the ballet, it has been gathered into something resembling a suite and included in their 2001 CD, *Possession*. The progress of their music through and beyond the queer/Jew conjunction can provide not just an interesting gloss on Kushner's uneasy wrestling with these issues, but a warrant for thinking about a resolution of the conundrums that he poses under the heading of what I'll be calling a queer diasporism.

From Kushner to Klezmer

> *I think there is something that is profoundly useful and morally elevating about the position of recognizing oneself as not being an inheritor on sight. By this I mean in some degree eternally disinherited and struggling for something rather than working to defend what you already have. I think that position, that terrible yearning for what was lost, the desire for the future that is expressed in the* Toyre *and in the holy scriptures, is what has given Judaism and the Jewish people its moral genius. It is what has produced Marx, Abraham Joshua Hescheles, Freud, and various other great Jewish thinkers. I think what I love of the culture of* klezmer *and the culture of Yiddish is its disloyalty to an idea of Jewish power as expressed in the State of Israel. I feel* klezmer *positions this. And as far as I know there aren't very many conservative* klezmorim.
> —Tony Kushner, quoted in Yale Strom, *The Book of Klezmer* (249)

Not only the music of the Klezmatics—and the turns it has taken in recent years—but, more important, the musical traditions that lead up to their remarkable oeuvre itself can help us point through and beyond the questions that Kushner and the queer critics who were working in his wake pose to the larger implications of their vision. To see this, we need to spend a bit more time thinking about klezmer. Although, like so much of eastern European culture, klezmer musicians have been bathed in a wave of nostalgia—particularly during the 1950s and 1960s, as American Jews seemingly suburbanized en masse—the music we now call klezmer* originally bore a thoroughly marginal, almost subversive, relation to the "traditional" world of eastern European Jewry in which it originated. From the first, the *klezmorim*—the musicians who were hired to grace weddings and other joyous ritual celebrations—were liminal characters, or, more properly, quintessential insider/outsiders: central to the life of the community, but existing in every possible way on its fringes. Music making itself had a theologically problematic status in the Diaspora; commentators of the rabbinic period (c. 70 CE to roughly 1000 CE, had proscribed instrumental music in mourning for the loss of the Second Temple; music was permitted, however, at special events like weddings or the festival of Purim, an escape hatch that led to the development of a caste of music makers for those occasions. The klezmorim became, by the middle of the eighteenth century, an integral part of the wedding festival; their admixture of sad and gleeful music accompanied every ritual act, from the bride's dressing to the procession to the joyous dancing afterward (and sometimes even the consummation of the marriage itself, from outside the bedroom window). In addition, parodic commentary was offered by the ceremonial figure of the *badchen*, or master of ceremonies *cum* wedding jester, who worked alongside the klezmorim and in some cases was one of them. Although he often lampooned the rabbi's discourse and language, the *badchen*'s Bakhtinian role was frequently (and increasingly) also to bring the obscene, the scatological, the gender-bending into this communal celebration—to invoke, mimic, or apotropaically summon the disasters that are to beset the married couple as they move into their new life together. Sholem Aleichem gives a good, if perhaps hyperbolized, description of this aspect of the group endeavor—one that, as we shall see, was kept alive in the American klezmer tradition—early on in his 1891 novella *Stempenyu*:

---

*The Yiddish word *klezmer* itself is derived from the Hebrew for "musical instrument"—*klay zemer*—and came to denote in Yiddish the musicians who played them. Indeed, to a Yiddish sensibility the term *klezmer music* (the origins of which Slobin traces to the 1980s) would be nonsensical: "musician music." In this it shares the fate of many foreign words in the macaronic mishmash that is American English: for example, *shrimp scampi*.

a fine rhymester, a crafty prankster, [Beryl the Bassist] disguised himself as a beggar at all weddings, twisted his eyes, danced like a bear, mimicked a woman in labor yelling "Oh God, oh God, I swear on a stack of Bibles it'll never happen again! . . . ." Or else he let out a stream of water in the middle of a room so that all the men rolled up their coattails and the women lifted their skirts. Or else he hung some sort of rubbish on the mother-in-law's apron, and he played further tricks and hoaxes galore.[32]

Integral to the wedding ceremony, in other words, the klezmorim were also marginal, or rather, brought the marginal, the forbidden, the taboo, into this community-affirming ceremony in a (somewhat) safely packaged guise. This dual function extended to their place in the community itself, in which they existed as a semi-autonomous guild, a licensed band of somewhat disreputable insider/outsiders who passed on musical training, trade secrets, and shtick from one generation to the next, even speaking in their own argot, *klezmerloshen*. More to the point, they extended the boundaries of that community. Wandering Jews par excellence, the klezmorim were part of multiple or overlapping social worlds: their own, those of the other (usually Christian or Rom) musicians with whom the played, the larger communities of gentiles at whose wedding celebrations or parties they also performed or whom they also met on the road, in taverns or inns or houses of ill repute. And the signs of these larger social transactions are inscribed in the music itself, which perforce mingled traditional Jewish melodies and harmonies with those of the Balkans, Greece, Ukraine, Russia, the Rom peoples, and even those of the Arab and Muslim world, all finding their way into the musical experience of klezmorim in Romania and the Balkans. The klezmorim didn't just imbibe these musical influences, they playedgentile musics, too, as they worked the dining halls and parties of their neighbors. Greater social forces and transformations leave their traces in klezmer as well: the military music from the Russian army in which many found themselves conscripted, for example, or the tonalities of American jazz klezmorim heard on the records that began to circulate, even in the Pale, by the early years of the twentieth century.

Although a part of the traditional life practices of eastern Europe, klezmer was, in short, both a sign of the multiple diasporism of this culture—its many contact points with the shifting peoples among whom eastern European Jews lived—and a part of the burgeoning culture of modernity that impacted these communities, all the more so as the klezmorim moved, along with so many Jews, to cities like Odessa or to Paris, London, and, of course, New York in the later years of the nineteenth century and the first decades of the twentieth. Indeed, as I suggested in the introduction, in its relentless hybridity, its negotiation between the soundscapes of a traditional religious culture and those of the larger, circumambient world, klezmer doesn't just reflect the enormous changes undergone by eastern and southern European Jewry at the moment of modernity; it is itself a leading indicator of those changes.

And it is a leading indicator of something else as well, of the sexual and gender complexities of traditional—and modernizing—eastern European culture. While the klezmorim may have accompanied and facilitated the wedding ritual, they were themselves frequently understood to be sexually threatening outsiders to the mores and gender identities of the community. We can get some sense of this from the classic—indeed, perhaps definitional—fictional account of the klezmorim I quoted earlier, Sholem Aleichem's *Stempenyu: A Yiddish Romance*. This influential fiction was no doubt an exaggerated version of the on-the-ground realities of the klezmer musicians' lives and their place in the community, but it offers a splendid reflection of the kinds of associations that not only affected the eastern European response to klezmer musicians, but that traveled with them to the United States.

The protagonist of Sholem Aleichem's novel is a wandering klezmer musician who woos and beds a different girl in every town and whose musical powers are as great as his powers of seduction—and vice versa. One of these women, Freydl, manages to marry Stempenyu, and she proceeds to create a kind of living hell for the free-spirited musician—relentlessly interrogating him about his contacts with other women, monitoring his free-spending ways, imprisoning him in her world of marketplace transactions. Stempenyu's escapes from Freydl are two: his life with the band and his adoration of a beautiful woman named Rachel who is married to an unpleasant vulgarian, Haim-Hynkel. Stempenyu sends Rachel a near illiterate love letter asking her to meet him; frustrated at her intended's crude behavior (he and his mother are in the midst of a particularly pointless fight about the cost of a coral necklace, purchased from Freydl, that he has given to Rachel), she decides to meet Stempenyu in a late-night assignation, allegedly to give him a piece of her mind for writing him, but also of course because she is as attracted to his freedom as he is to her beauty. But when she does rendezvous with Stempenyu, a vision of her dead best friend Haiah-Etel, who had entered unhappily into an arranged marriage before dying, appears before her eyes and she flees the scene of potential transgression. At the story's end, she and her husband have moved to a different town, where he makes a great success for himself as a small businessman. Stempenyu remains a henpecked husband, albeit an ever greater musician.

What's interesting in the current context is the series of parallels the story draws between Stempenyu and Rachel. Trapped in marriages with materialistic, insensitive spouses, each is, nevertheless, a figure of boundless romantic desire found in the popular European romantic fiction that Sholem Aleichem sets out to critique and parody in his self-proclaimed "Yiddish romance."* In both cases the figure for their aspirations for something more than that marital fate is music: not only is that "fine scoundrel" Stempenyu the most expressive and moving klezmer violinist the shtetl world has ever seen (109), but Rachel possesses an extravagantly beautiful voice, singing of freedom to escape, imaginatively, her loveless marriage: "Flying, flying, / The golden birds, / Over all the seas, / Say hello, / You golden birds, / To my mother dear!" (132).[33] Music provides a further ground of similarity between them: Stempenyu's musical genius is itself gendered anomalously. Although he speaks "for the Yiddish [or Jewish] soul," his great success as a musician is grounded not only in his giving voice to the sentiments and aspirations of the community but also in his ability to speak to the sadness and disappointment faced by women in marriages:

> Ah, how hard it is for my pen to describe what Stempenyu did [as he played]! This was no scraping, no mere playing. It was like a religious service, a divine labor, with a lofty feeling, a noble spirit!

---

* And in so doing, of course, he places himself and his art in the main line of European realism, which itself depends crucially on the parody and deconstruction of romance plots and their underlying ideologies, especially romantic love. From *Madame Bovary* through William Dean Howells's *The Rise of Silas Lapham*, literary romance and especially romance novels are shown to be inadequate, often dangerous guides to the realities of love and the institutions of marriage.

> Stempenyu stood opposite the bride and played a sermon on his violin, a long, lovely sermon, a poignant sermon about the bride's free and happy life until now, about her maidenhood, and about the dark, bitter life in store for her, later, later. Gone was her girlhood! Her head was covered, her long, beautiful hair was out of sight, forever and ever.... No more joy! Farewell youth. Now you're a married woman!... How bleak and cheerless—may God forgive me!...
>
> That was what came from Stempenyu's fiddle. All the wives understood the wordless sermon, all the wives felt it. They felt it and wept for it with bitter tears. (107)

Indeed, Stempenyu ultimately proves to be more than the articulator of these unspoken thoughts of married women; he becomes, as it were, one of them. In his barren marriage to the unpleasant Freydl (herself the daughter of a klezmer musician), Stempenyu feels as constricted as any of the women to whom he plays. Indeed, to emphasize the point his fate and Rachel's continue to mirror each other at the end of the story. Both of their partners, Freydl and Haim-Hynkel, become successful shopowners. Rachel, to be sure, seems to have made some peace with her marriage, largely, one suspects, because she is happy as a mother. Stempenyu, on the other hand, grieves for the loss of Rachel—and makes of his grief yet more beautiful music:

> Stempenyu played as he had never played before. One can say that in his playing he reached the highest possible level...
>
> That's the kind of joy we feel when a bird sings in its cage. The bird is dreaming of green leaves, gorgeous blossoms, open air, a free world, an open world, a great wide world, and it feels like singing to pour out its bitter heart—and it sings, it weeps, it pours out everything it feels! And we feel joy and delight, we have true pleasure. (179)

Homesick, Rachel sings of the freedom of birds; lovesick, Stempenyu has become an encaged one. It is not clear who has made the worse bargain.

Stempenyu the archetypal klezmer musician is thus positioned by Sholem Aleichem's story as an exemplary insider/outsider: he is essential to the

1.7 A Real-Life Stempenyu? (*Jewish Daily Forward* caption in Yiddish): "A small-town 'klezmer' [folk musician]." (In English:) "The village fiddler . . . posing barefoot in playing position outside a log house." *Jewish Daily Forward*, March 2, 1924; photographer, Irving Berkey. With the assistance of Chana Pollock at the *Jewish Daily Forward*. From the archives of the YIVO Institute for Jewish Research, New York.

maintenance of the community's norms of sexuality and reproduction, but he also represents that which questions, subverts, or stands outside its dictates. To be sure, the story firmly embeds this dualism in a community-affirming response: it is his sadness that gives "us"—the readers of the tale and, by extension, members of the extended community of Yiddish-speakers it addresses—"*true* pleasure"(emphasis mine). In this sense Stempenyu is (as Anita Norich has stressed) a very slightly exaggerated figure for Sholem Aleichem himself, the writer who positions himself as both articulator of communal norms and maker of delicately subversive narratives about them.[34] But in Stempenyu's subversive doubleness, his wanderings (put to an end by Freydl), his relations with his fellow musicians (his dialogue with them was rendered in a version of *klezmerloshen* so alien to the Yiddish audience that Sholem Aleichem included a glossary for them), his gender ambiguity—at once horny man, encaged woman—Stempenyu also articulates values that can be thought of as at once diasporic and queer, in a manner far more subversive than Sholem Aleichem can allow himself to be.

He, it might be said, is Sholom Aleichem's Leah or Roy, a character who dramatizes the culturally and sexually transgressive that is embedded, via the klezmer tradition, in the very heart of the norms and values of so-called traditional culture, but whose full power is deferred, denied, or pushed out of awareness by that tradition.*

As I suggested above, this dimension of the klezmer maintains itself in a more or less unbroken fashion even as the klezmer musicians themselves diasporize, largely to the U.S.; as I shall suggest below, this dimension helps fuel the klezmer revival and the radical Jewish culture phenomenon that follows it. A fine example of this continuous tradition of klezmer-borne (and born) diasporic queerness *within* the unfolding of Jewish culture in America—and its consequences for the alignment of Jewish diasporic experience with that of other others in the U.S.—is provided by the experience of a virtuoso whose persona and performance style alike remarkably resemble those of Stepenyu: Naftule Brandwein. Born into a Hasidic family in the Pale around 1885, Brandwein was one of fourteen children of a klezmer musician, many of whose children were also initiated into the craft. True to the klezmer ethos, however, Brandwein ranged widely, both as a musician and as a Gypsy-loving roustabout: "He played for everyone and everyone thought he was one of them," his daughter Sadie told Henry Sapoznik, "Poles, Gypsies, Jews." "Pictures of him from

---

* The term *queer diasporism* is analogous to the "Queer Yiddishkeit" celebrated by Alisa Solomon and contextualized by Jeffrey Shandler. According to Solomon and Shandler, the affinity between Yiddishkeit and queerness called into being by contemporary queer/Jewish culture makers (Shandler cites klezmer band Isle of Klezbos, performance artist Sara Felder, and Solomon herself); it is grounded in the discovery of a common "diasporism; rootless cosmopolitanism; a penchant for transgression; border-crossing; and being proudly, defiantly different" in Yiddish and queer cultures alike. See Shandler, *Adventures in Yiddishland: Postvernacular Language and Culture* (Berkeley: University of California Press, 2005), pp. 187–188; he quotes Solomon on p. 187. As the example of *Stempenyu* suggests, such a possibility is built into Yiddish culture to begin with via the wandering transgressors we call the *klezmorim*, which we might well add to the examples Shandler gives of the phenomenon in eastern European culture before moving to the present "postvernacular" moment. I will be interested below in a cognate phenomenon, one I wouldn't restrict to Yiddishkeit, however broadly construed, but to the development of Jewish culture in the U.S. beyond the reanimation of Yiddish: the move to the avant-garde, for example, which may begin with the klezmer revival but quickly speeds beyond it to a space of avant-garde praxis.

1.8 Naftule Brandwein (center). From Henry Sapoznik, *Klemzer! Jewish Music From Old World to Our World* (New York: Schirmer, 1999).

this time," Sapoznik adds, "showing a dark-skinned young man with broad, high cheekbones, make it easy to understand how he could pass for one or the other of these ethnic identities."[35]

Brandwein emigrated the United States in 1908, where his absolutely prodigious technique and imaginative soloing quickly marked him as a master of the klezmer clarinet. So too did his antics, which (as every commentator on his career cannot forbear from mentioning) included dressing in an Uncle Sam suit festooned with Christmas tree lights, turning his back on the audience (some think that he did so in order to keep rivals from learning his fingering), and, when in a particularly gnarly mood, mooning the audience. Brandwein was famous, as well, for his unruly personal life. A notorious drunk and womanizer, he was adopted by those Jewish gangsters who had transferred their operations from Odessa to Brooklyn and came to be known in their new home as Murder, Incorporated. Brandwein played at their all-night parties and presumably drank in their speakeasies and partook of their houses of prostitution. Meanwhile, Brandwein found a home in two of the most prominent klezmer orchestras of the 1920s and 1930s, Abe Ellstein's Klezmer Orchestra and Joseph Cherniavsky's Chassidic-American (or, alternately Yiddish-American) Jazz Band, making a number of recordings with them and on his own in the 1920s. His virtuosity and his antics soon wearied his fellow band members, and he was replaced by a much more tractable but no less skilled clarinetist, Dave Tarras. Brandwein set out on his own, but his career started a downward spiral, partly personal, partly a reflection of the decreasing interest in klezmer among second- and third-generation Jews. He ended his career on the Borscht Belt, playing for the parents while the children presumably bolted the room, eager to boogie to the siren strains of rock and roll. Tellingly, he pushed his son to a career as a classical musician rather than a klezmer—that life, Brandwein feared, being impossible to sustain in 1950s America.

Brandwein's example is crucial in a number of ways, particularly to the further development of the klezmer tradition in America, which can, in some sense, be divided into those who have followed in his footsteps and those who have pursued the paths blazed by his great contemporary and rival, Dave Tarras. Unlike the profoundly orderly Tarras, Brandwein served as a kind of a bridge to the more disreputable side of klezmer—the klezmer as antic parodist of social norms, articulator and deflater of communal ambivalences—and he so served for both his moment and our own.[36] As far as the first is concerned, I am particularly struck by the anecdote of Brandwein performing in an Uncle Sam suit made of Christmas tree lights (the anecdote goes on to claim that he almost electrocuted himself when his sweat short-circuited them), suggesting that he served as a kind of an expression of ambivalence about the project of assimilating to American middle-class norms and identities that his audience was undertaking. Festooning himself with emblems both of Americanness and of its secularized but still normative Christianity, the dark-skinned, high-cheekboned klezmer was mocking both the emblems and the audience that would metaphorically dress in that garb.

As for my second concern, Brandwein served as a bridge in another sense as well. His musical example achieved near legendary status among those few enthusiasts who were devoted to klezmer music and helped fuel the more experimental, less reverent, dimensions of the klezmer boom of the 1980s and 1990s. Transcriptions of his amazing solos and the few recordings he made, in the late twenties and early forties, continued to circulate among aficionados, and klezmer revivalists in the 1990s frequently adopted them. Brandwein's compositions were given prominent place on the Klezmatics' first recording, which includes no fewer than four of them, and have also been repeated by a number of other klezmer revivalist and soloists (e.g., Dave Douglas and Alicia Svigals, both of whom have recorded a number of Brandwein compositions). Perhaps more significantly, his work has inspired larger projects: a brilliant and wild klezmer band with ambitions to crossover with ska and jazz has entitled itself Naftule's Dream, and clarinet virtuoso David Krakauer recorded an equally eclectic album, entitled *Klezmer, New York*, in which he imagines and stages an encounter that might well have taken place in the late 1920s between Brandwein and the equally virtuosic jazz clarinetist Sidney Bechet.

Not only do Brandwein's brilliant solos, in other words, serve as an example and a goad to these musicians, so too do the hybridity and experimentality of his music. As opposed to Tarras, who, as Walter Zev Feldman has observed, normalizes the manifold and warring melodies and harmonies of klezmer into a single mold (Besserabian) and form (the so-called bulgar), Brandwein's work remained militantly eclectic, mixing, far more than did other klezmer musicians, tunes and influences from the full range of musics that shaped the distinctive sound of klezmer.[37] Specifically, many of Brandwein's tunes look to the Middle East modally, melodically, and in terms of subject matter. He recorded such compositions as "Araber Tanz," "Ein Terk in New York," "Ein Yid in Jerusalem" (A Jew in Jerusalem); even Brandwein's bulgars—tunes from the Bessarabian matrix that were a defining component of Tarras's work—are entitled "Turkish-Bulgar Freilachs." This persistent self-identification with Arab and Turkish (Ottoman) cultures and musical traditions has proved to be appealing to contemporary klezmer revivalists—"Araber Tanz," for example, has been recorded by many of them—and for cultural and political reasons. Culturally, his music identifies klezmer music as grounded in a world of multiple cultures rather than the eastern European or the Yiddish American with which it is associated. (Brandwein's identification of the klezmer as "Ein Terk in New York," for example, reminds us that Constantinople was as powerful a site of origins for Jews in the early twentieth century and that klezmer musicians lived, recorded, and emigrated from there as fully as they did in and from Odessa or Vilna.) Indeed, for the more politically advanced among them it relocates Jewish-identified music, and hence Jewish identity itself, away from the sphere of eastern Europe and the cultural politics of nostalgia and places both music and identity in the midst of the cultures of the Levant, with obvious implications for the current relations of the State of Israel and the Zionist project to the cultures that surrounded and interpenetrate it.

But Brandwein's importance for the klezmer revivalists did not stop there. Rather, he served as a bridge in a third way as well, linking the klezmer tradition flourishing in eastern Europe to the great popular art being produced in America in the early years of the twentieth century, jazz. Virtually every commentator on Brandwein compares him not only with his great rival Tarras but also with jazz contemporaries like Sidney Bechet and Louis Armstrong. And, I would suggest, with good reason: his work mirrors developments in jazz—developments that, to complete the circle were to be of consequence in the extended sphere of klezmer. The 1920s, jazz historians tell us, was the moment of the arrival of the great jazz virtuosos, especially Bechet and Armstrong: when the nature of jazz performance changed from a collectively improvising group playing repeated choruses of a tune, with brief solos by differing instruments, to one in which an instrumentalist repeats a solo that lasts several choruses, dominating the piece and, though in dialogue with his fellow players (now interlocutors), turning all the attention to himself.[38] The same shift is evident in a comparison of Brandwein's to contemporary klezmer recordings, like those of Abe Schwartz's orchestra in which Brandwein briefly played before striking out on his own. Consider, for example, his *Turkishe Yalle Vey Uve* recorded in 1924, just as Louis Armstrong was stepping out from the shadow of King Oliver's band with his virtuosic recordings with the Hot Fives and Sevens, released in 1925–1929. The structure of the recording is simple: a violin, piano, and drums repeat what musicologists call a stop-time figure while Brandwein reiterates the melody with different trills, *krechts*, ornaments, until the fadeout. But the effect is complex, foregrounding (as it is intended to do) Brandwein's supple virtuosity, the enormous complexity of the ornaments, and the subtle differences in each iteration of the chorus. Given the persistent comparisons critics have made between Brandwein and Armstrong, one might profitably juxtapose this cut to the Hot Fives recording of "Yes I'm in the Barrel," released in 1925. The band (consisting of banjo, clarinet, and piano in addition to Armstrong's trumpet) launches into the same repeated stop-time figure as Brandwein's; after three or four iterations, however, the band breaks into a freer, syncopated double-time theme led by Armstrong's strenuous trumpet, after which the clarinetist Johnny Dodds takes a solo that lasts two choruses. The band then returns to the more stately stop-time figure and a final recapitulation of the theme.*

To compare the two is to see how complicated is the intertwining of the development of Brandwein's klezmer and Armstrong's jazz. Stop-time—when the rhythm section stops playing, or plays a repeated figure, to foreground the virtuosity of a soloist—itself is a jazz device, deployed by musicians like Jelly Roll Morton even before jazz was named as such; that Brandwein's band adopted it suggests how great an influence American jazz began to have on klezmer music in the 1920s, just as second-generation Jewish composers like Gershwin were rejecting (and being rejected by) Jewish identification in favor of jazz. More important still, the coalescence between Brandwein's transformation of klezmer from a group endeavor into a vehicle for virtuoso performance suggests that klezmer and jazz were, in the 1920s, paralleling each other—moving away from the ensemble, toward the foregrounding of individual instrumental performances. Indeed, it could be argued that, from his own tradition, Brandwein is getting there earlier than Armstrong—or even the jazz tradition itself, which moved in what one might fancifully call a Brandweinian direction several decades later. For on *Turkishe Yalle Vey Uve* he takes not one or two choruses, but six (particularly impressive when technology limited recording length to two minutes and forty-five seconds maximum), so dominating the record that there's time for little else on it—indeed, he is still soloing as the music fades out. This is remarkable both in the klezmer recordings and in the contemporary recordings of "jazz" or "race" music, like Armstrong's or that of another figure frequently compared to Brandwein, Sidney Bechet's, who also takes six choruses on *Blue Horizon* in 1944. Indeed, for something that explosive—something challenging so strenuously the constraints of the form itself—we might best compare Brandwein with Paul Gonsalves's famous 1956 solo on the Duke Ellington *Live at Newport* or John Coltrane's *Chasing the 'Trane* (1961), where, as Gary Giddins argues, Coltrane blows up utterly the structure that had dominated jazz by

---

* Stop-time is extensively used in other recordings of Armstrong's during this period; for an equally sophisticated version, consider *King of the Zulus* (1925), which begins with an extensive stop-time figure played by banjo and piano following its opening theme with an Armstrong solo; this is followed by a brief bit of dialogue then continues with the solo, which is then followed by the banjo breaking into a melodic solo before concluding with another statement of the theme.

taking twenty-five separate iterations of the chorus.[39] Add to this the extensive use of modal scales, glissandos, ornaments, and *krechts* by Brandwein in the 1920s and the deployment (via entirely different traditions) of similar techniques by John Coltrane and Miles Davis in the 1960s, and Davis's adoption (without, of course knowing it) of many of the same performance tics as Brandwein's, especially turning his back on his audience, and one can see why artists who attempt to fuse klezmer and jazz modalities should be so drawn to the example of Brandwein. Precisely because he remained true to the complex stew of musical, national, regional, ethnic, and religious traditions that produced klezmer—performative, virtuosic, Stempenyu-like—he anticipated the directions in which not only klezmer but also jazz was going.

Radical Jewish Culture

When David Krakauer stages in *Klezmer, New York* a fictitious meeting between Brandwein and Sidney Bechet, he is actually fabulating a musical conjunction that had occurred long before—a conjunction in which these two traditions, separated from each other by oceans, race, religion, cultures, have always already been in the process of dialoguing with each other, even ex post facto. (For more on interweavings in the middle of the twentieth century, especially as superintended by the figure of Artie Shaw, see chapter 3.) This conjunction, to think more expansively, is one that is central to the development of klezmer in America, especially as it morphs from a revival led by enthusiasts into a full-scale phenomenon into new avatars I associate not so much with the klezmer revival per se—that revival has, as I suggested in the introduction, more or less run its course—but rather with the radical Jewish culture movement into which it has developed: a fusion of Jewish and jazz traditions that, we shall see, brings into the cultural mix other musical traditions as well. Sometimes these figures play explicit tribute to the conjunction of jazz and klezmer; anticipating Krakauer's *Klezmer, New York*, for example, an early klezmer revival band, Brave Old World, performed Bechet as an encore after regaling the audience with hours of klezmer. In a more contemporary vein, John Zorn's band Masada freely mixes the free-jazz tradition of Ornette Coleman with Jewish-inflected modes, subjects, and instrumentations. On the other side of the jazz/klezmer coin is of course Don Byron, who moved freely back and forth between both idioms in his *Don Byron Plays Mickey Katz!* project and continued to do so in his *Bug Music*, which brought together great tunes from Ellington and the cartoon scores of Raymond Scott (née Harry Warnow, from Brooklyn). Contemporary jazz musicians Uri Caine and Matt Darriau also migrate back and forth between Jewish-themed and identified music and jazz: Darriau, to cite just one case of many, supplements his work with the Klezmatics with a group called Ballin' the Jack, which specializes in jazz of the 1920s and 1930s, especially that associated with Ellington's "Jungle Band" period. And, to broaden the canvas, a number of contemporary musicians are exploring the conjunction between the musics of the African and the Jewish diaspora—most notably the Klezmatics, whose most recent CD, *Brother Smote the Waters*, adds to the group a gospel singer, Joshua Nelson; and one can list such excellent endeavors those of Steve Bernstein (*Diaspora Blues, Diaspora Soul*) and David Chevan and Donald Byrd's Afro-Semitic Experience. Some of these musical endeavors are better than others—one can hear just so many versions of *Eliahu Hanavi* set to a jazz or soul or even a New Orleans beat before wearying of the attempts, however resonant or ingenious (and in some cases inadvertently comic: the version offered by the otherwise estimable David Chevan, Donald Byrd, and their band makes this piece of sacramental music sound something like Frank Loesser's *Hernando's Hideaway* from *The Pajama Game*). But, taken as a whole, this work represents a consistent and sustained attempt to suture these two always already intertwined musical traditions.

That sustained endeavor, of course, bears many readings; the Jewish/African American relation is, as we have seen, one deeply fraught on both sides, and the kind of rhetoric that these artists deploy in meditating on their endeavor can remind us of just how loaded it might remain. We are reminded, yet again, that while American Jews have accessed, to a large degree, the promised land of religious tolerance and material prosperity, many African Americans justifiably feel themselves still wandering in the desert, awaiting a deliverance that Jews can celebrate. That having been said, it also needs to be said that the klezmer movement has a number of features that correct or complicate (or both) the black-and-white politics that one might assume lie behind the conjunction between jazz and klezmer and the agonizing narratives of comparative victimology that have fueled the long-standing tensions between the two communities. Indeed, the insistence of many of the klezmer revivalists and/or new Jewish music makers on expanding the diasporic Jewish musical lexicon has interesting resonances for expanding our understanding of the construction of Jewishness.

For one thing, many of these music makers move back and forth freely not only between the world of klezmer and African American jazz but also between klezmer and the musics of Central and Latin America that also inflected American jazz—musics that were shaped by the *other* great diaspora of Jews, the one that followed their expulsion from Spain in 1492. There are a number of exemplary cases here. One of the most renowned examples is Larry Harlow (born in Brooklyn in 1939 as Lawrence Ira Cahn), also known as *el Judio Maravilloso*: one of the pioneers in the making and dissemination of the Cuban/jazz/rock blend known as Salsa. Or one thinks of Anthony Coleman, a fiendishly versatile pianist in John Zorn's Masada band, whose own endeavors include a project called *Sephardic Tinge* (a play on Jelly Roll Morton's description of the Latin element in jazz as "Latin Tinge").* Here's Coleman's description of the processes that led him in this direction:

> I started thinking about the music which had accompanied most of my life in some way or another. I thought about the fact that the Mambo and Cha-Cha had both been dance crazes in the Borscht Belt during the '40s and '50s. I thought about Sephardic (Spanish) Jews and how strange and mysterious I had always found the idea of their language, Ladino. I added to this the uses that Jazz composers have made of what Jelly Roll Morton called the "Spanish Tinge," Habañerea and Mambo patterns, montunos.[40]

Another excellent example is provided by the work of Roberto Juan Rodriguez, a Cuban-born percussionist (and a Sephardic Jew on his father's

---

* That there's substantial interest in this crossover between Jewish and Latin music can be attested to by the fact that another Jewish musician, Mark Levine, fronts a band called Latin Tinge. Such interest extends beyond jazz: a rap group named the Hip-Hop Hoodios has issued two impressive CDs, produced by Happy Sanchez of the Latino band Los Moscicos and including guest artist appearances by figures like Loren Sklamberg of the Klezmatics, mixing (inner city) Latino and Jewish idioms and agendas. Most germane to our concerns here is their "1492," which attempts to remind both U.S. Latinos and Jewish Americans of their common origins in pre-Expulsion Spain.

side). Rodriguez emigrated to the U.S. at age nine from a family of musicians. Growing up in Miami, he played bar mitzvahs and weddings and frequently went with his grandfather to Wolfie's Delicatessen and the beach "to see old Jews dance the mambo and the cha-cha."[41] (One of his most plangent pieces is entitled "Wolfie's Corner.") After stints with the Miami Sound Machine he moved to New York where, in addition to serving as an excellent studio musician (he played, for example, with Paul Simon), he found himself working with many of the artists in the radical Jewish culture movement, including David Krakauer and Frank London of the Klezmatics and Marc Ribot. What's interesting about Rodriguez's music in the present context is the role that the always already hybridized Jewish music plays in it—creating what we might want to call hybridity to the nth degree. "A hallmark of [his] sound is the *guajeo*; an ostinato-like pattern played by violin and cello that bridges rhythm with melody and allows players to solo and improvise," writes jazz critic Elliot Simon, which is to say that, in creating a "Cuban sub-genre interwoven with Jewish harmonic overtones," Rodriguez has also returned to a differently inflected version of the structure of Naftule Brandwein's stop-time recordings. It's no coincidence, then, that Rodriguez testifies to the importance of Brandwein's example to his own ensemble. "To have David perform with my band a Naftule Brandwein piece—it's awesome."[42]

That piece is "Turkish-Bulgarish," which Brandwein recorded in 1924 and Rodriguez covers on his second CD, *Baila! Gitano Baila! (Dance, Gypsy, Dance!)* in a powerful revision to which he adds the subtitle *Vedado Street Mix*. (Vedado is a fashionable commercial and entertainment district in downtown Havana.) And what a mix it is: the version of the song begins with the sound of Matt Darriau playing the *guida*, a Macedonian bagpipe, which is then backed up by Rodriguez's strikingly Middle Eastern percussion (timbales, cymbals) that gives, as Rodriguez writes of his music, the distinctive air of the marketplace, the *souk*. Then Brandwein's theme is announced in a more familiar klezmer orchestration: clarinet, trombone, and violin, which, however, are arranged contrapuntally against each other, to further the effect of fracturing, segmentation, dialectic that energizes the piece. The Balkan Middle Eastern and the eastern European continue to play off against each other throughout, brought together only by the relentlessly energetic Cuban-inflected percussion. The effect is as striking culturally as it is musically. Rodriguez is taking Brandwein's synthesis of the "Oriental" and the eastern European seriously, reuniting these two closely affiliated branches of the Jewish Diaspora, however, by a third term that seems different from them but is intimately a part of each: the Sephardic. To draw attention to this modality of Jewish cultural production is to disrupt the normative narratives of Jewish American identity as traced through the eastern European Diaspora, ratified by and enhanced in the first iterations of the klezmer revival; it is to direct our attention to the other waves of Jewish wandering and homemaking, whether southern European, where the Sephardim gathered under the indulgent eye of the Ottoman Empire, in Arab-dominated lands (those of the so-called Mizrachic or Oriental Jews), or in Latin America. The streets of Havana's Vedado become the place where these various streams of the Jewish Diaspora "mix," before wandering from Havana along with Rodriguez not only to Miami and New York but out into the larger world.

It's at this point we need to return to Kushner's *Angels* and to the problematics from which we have ourselves been wandering. What the klezmer revival and its successors, the postklezmer radical Jewish culture scene, have done is to create a new language for framing Kushner's project in *Angels* of bringing together Jewish and queer identities in a different, more expansive way. Under the sign of the musically scattered, the orally and culturally diffuse, they create what I've been calling a queer diasporism, a vision of identity that rejects origin, nationhood, cultural reproduction in favor of a vision that embraces cultural syncretism, wandering, exile without any sense of the moral imperative of returning to origins. As guitarist Marc Ribot put it in a brilliant and as yet unpublished manifesto collected by a latter-day Ansky, musicologist Tamar Barzel, "The biggest problem with believing in the authenticity of an inherited past, and especially of speaking of it in organic metaphors such as 'roots' and 'blood,' is that it's a very short step to mistaking the metaphor for reality, and believing that like the relation of branch to root, we are genetically connected to the culture of the past."[43] * What Ribot is suggesting here is a critique of the very notions of "authenticity" that governed the first iterations of the klezmer

---

* Ribot's work itself exemplifies his persistent sense of both the extensiveness and the factitiousness of cultural and national identities. Not only has he played with many of the epigones of the radical Jewish culture movement, he's also been leading a band called Los Cubanos Postizos—the fake or made-up Cubans—with which he sings in what can charitably be called a Spanish that is calculated to draw attention to its own inauthenticity. Ricardo Rodrigues, discussed below, plays on this CD.

movement. But what he is also, perhaps inadvertently, reminding us of is how completely hybrid that culture was in the first place and, by extension, how radically hybrid—assimilative rather than assimilating or assimilated, transformative rather than transformed—Jewish cultures have always been and continue to be. It's not for nothing that Ribot for many years fronted a band called Rootless Cosmopolitans—Stalin's term for intellectuals, Trotskyite deviationists, and Jews.

To bring matters back to the sense of queer cultural reproduction with which I began, it's also important to note that his critique is one of a genetic, organic connection to the past unified by metaphors of roots and blood. In the countervision that lies at the heart of the radical Jewish culture project stands a vision of culture as a nongenetic, non-normative form of genesis, making itself by shaping prior and contemporary cultural forms into new patterns of mixing and matching—a recombinant form of reproduction mysteriously undertaken without any DNA. But as I have been arguing implicitly throughout this chapter and now want to state explicitly, this countervision is part of "radical" Jewish culture in the paradoxical sense in which the word "radical" etymologically—that is to say in its root sense—invokes the very notion of roots. The critique of the metaphor of roots gestures toward a different sense of rootedness, one that nourishes such strange, beautiful, if sterile second growths as Sholem Aleichem's Stempenyu, Brandwein, Ansky and Neugroschel/Kushner's Leah, Kushner's Cohn, self-created, transgressive wanderers all, in theory and practice. And it is one that generates new forms of cultural cross-fertilization—hybridization in the horticultural sense of the term, but with a Bakhtinian or Bhabhian twist as well—in places real (the *shtetl*), semireal (Rodriguez's reimagined Vedado as *souk*), or utterly imaginary, like the space of Kushner's theatrical reenactments. Such a movement brings us from klezmer beyond klezmer, into a space where even so-called radical Jewish culture looks very much like the (transatlantic) avant-garde. To cite a different culture maker (one who has also worked with Ribot), Anthony Coleman:

> I started from an idea of born-again Jewish pride: "Playing klezmer brings me in touch with my roots" and all that—creating a relationship to East European music out of a wish, a hope, an idealized relationship to their personal histories. I asked myself, "What about de-ethnicized Ethnic Pride?" Pride in having been nowhere, with nothing.... Suburbs, TV, Christmas trees, station wagons, Passover

and "Never Again" . . . What is can be more important to thematize than what we wish would be. . . .

Then, take a look at the instrumentation. Standard klezmer: clarinet, trombone, keyboard, drums—and look at the roles, look at the scales and the phrases—consider all of that in relation to Webern's "expressing a novel in a single sigh," Beckett's theatre, DeKooning's women: abstractions where the ghostly traces of figuration remain as hints to a past, hints to a narrative, hints to a culture which no longer exists; read the quotes from Bellow and Beckett which I used (in the notes to the first CD).[44]

This move from klezmer beyond klezmer, through Jewishness beyond Jewishness to an avant-garde modernity that is shaped by Jewishness but transcends any specific ethnic identification, has significance for the rethinking of what Jewish culture can be and can do in the United States, and I don't want to underemphasize these possibilities: indeed, I'll be exploring them in the pages to follow. But it has a greater salience still. As may also be suggested by my invocation of terms like *hybridity* (derived from postcolonial criticism, especially the work of Homi Bhabha) and *cosmopolitanism* (an equally powerful predication in current cultural theory, given recent and powerful articulation in the postcolonial context by Anthony Appiah's theorizing of a "rooted cosmopolitanism"), the possibilities I have been sketching here—rootless cosmoplitanism, queer diasporism—have implications for cultural criticism across the board.[45] They represent a significant alternative to the ways in which cultural production and/as social reproduction are being retheorized in the context of a globalizing public sphere at large. These possibilities represent, we might say, moments of hybridity to the second power—a hybridity that has intimate knowledge of the conditions of alienation that call it into being and comments on those conditions even as it embraces them—and a cosmopolitanism that denies the aspirations for universality that lie at the center of cosmopolitan ideologies despite their own best instincts. Indeed, bringing the Jewish example explicitly to bear on these discursive arrangements, I hope I have shown in this chapter, and I shall attempt to show in the chapters that follow, suggests virtues of precisely (*pace* Appiah) a rootless, not a rooted, cosmopolitanism: one that bears the marks of historicity (the term, after all, testifies to the twentieth century's long succession of pogroms, massacres, and genocides) but nevertheless seeks to trope or refashion it through a variety of adaptive mechanisms, including appropriation, transformation, mimicry, parody, play. The art of the queer diasporite, of the rootless cosmopolitan, is the art of *Angels*, of *The Dybbuk*, of the klezmer virtuosos in America, as of their successors in the klezmer revival and the radical Jewish culture movement alike: an art that, by its relentless and systematic syncretism, challenges simple, reductive predications of national, ethnic, racial, or religious identity across the board (including but not limited to Jewish identity) even as or especially because it composes itself out of their raw material. It's for the generative creative work that can get done through this antinormative, antigenetic model of cultural reproduction that this book argues—and to further instantiations of that project, and of responses to it, that I turn in what follows.

2. ARTHUR MILLER, MARILYN MONROE, AND THE MAKING OF ETHNIC MASCULINITY

WHAT DOES IT MEAN to be a man—a father, a son, a husband, a lover? These questions were, until recently, central to the delineation of Jewish identity in America: as countless critics have reminded us, Irving Howe didn't exactly entitle his groundbreaking book *World of Our Mothers* (a book with that inevitable title wasn't published until 1988).[1] To be sure, generations of excellent feminist-inspired scholarship have challenged this masculinist tradition, altering both the canon and the very discursive frame in which the Jewish American experience has been construed. But the questions raised in and around the constitution of Jewish masculinity have not gone away. Indeed, a new generation of scholars, informed by feminist, queer, and other such skeptical dispensations, have started asking them again, but from a different, more theoretically vigilant, angle. The time may thus well be propitious to go back to the classic texts of Jewish American male tradition and look at them again, in light of the critical constructions that cast a cold eye on the established ways of thinking about Jewish masculinity, both in and of itself and in the context of U.S. culture at large.[2]

There's no better place to start this process than with the work and—of equal importance—the life of Arthur Miller, who over the course of his career explored the contradictory penumbras of meaning surrounding maleness with a persistence and an intensity that often quite literally reduced audiences to tears. One such access of sentiment was particularly significant. As Miller recalls in his autobiography, *Timebends*, when *All My Sons*—the title is significant in this context, as is the play's Abraham-like narrative of sons sacrificed to the greed of the father—opened in Boston,

> I was surprised to see [his salesman uncle] Manny among the last of the matinee audience to leave. He had a nice gray overcoat on his arm and his pearl gray hat on his head, and his little shoes were brightly

shined, and he had been weeping. It was almost a decade since I had last laid eyes on him. Despite my name on the marquee he clearly had not expected to see me here.

"Manny! How are you? It's great seeing you here."

I could see his grim hotel room behind him, the long trip up from New York in his little car, the hopeless hope of the day's business. Without so much as acknowledging my greeting, he said, "Buddy [Miller's older, sexually rambunctious cousin] is doing very well."[3]

Manny's gratuitous mention of his son sparked a reflux of Miller's resentment of his lower-class, uninhibited relatives—"my boyhood need of his recognition, my resentment at his disparagements, my envy of his and his sons' freed sexuality, and my contempt for it too" (131). But it also sparked, he claims, his most famous achievement. This was precisely the crystal of experience, Miller later claimed, in which the method and, it would seem, much of the matter of *Death of a Salesman* was formed. The image of the appropriately named Manny's "hopeless hope of the day's business" combined with his empathic vision of Manny's life, Miller claims, to give the impetus to the play with which Miller was to be associated for the rest of his career.

If this is a crucial moment in the history of American theater, it is also, I would suggest a crucial moment in another, equally theatrical, history: that of the making of ethnic masculinity in general, and Jewish masculinity in particular. The relation between Manny's family and Arthur's experience represents a divergence between an ideal of maleness that conjoins business success with sexual potency and one associated with more refined sentiments—with cultural attainments and cosmopolitan amplitudes. The anecdote I have begun with suggests the triumph of this form of masculinity over Manny's, for (not to be *too* Nietzschean about the matter) to empathize with someone who once frightened or appalled us is also to stage a victory over them—a victory that confirms the very values Miller opposes to those of his uncle, those of art and imagination itself. The anecdote traces a second triumph as well. The quite worldly success of that play brought with it fame, fortune, and the love of a movie star—an undeniable achievement in Manny's world as well as in Arthur's.

Miller's double triumph has cultural as well as personal ramifications, for they accompany, and perhaps even accomplish, the creation of an entirely new ideal type of Jewish masculinity: the persona of the pipe-smoking

Jewish intellectual as star-marrying stud muffin—a persona that over the decades Woody Allen and Philip Roth also came to represent in the publicity-mad public sphere, to the delight and chagrin of all three. It is the construction and ramifications of this new social type that I will be stressing here. In this chapter I want to argue that the Miller/Monroe conjunction represents an important and neglected stage in the Americanizing process. In its many manifestations it emblematized both the desires of assimilating Jewish men to break out of the spaces in which they had been contained and the ways in which organs of entertainment and publicity constructed new boxes in which to contain them. In this sense the creation of "Arthur Miller"—the name to which I will give the public face of the man in what follows*—is either a sign of the cultural transformations that bring to an end the centuries-long process of constructing Jewish masculinity in problematically double terms or a sign that that process has shifted into a new, and not necessarily more expansive, key. Moreover, the Miller/Monroe conjunction suggests how problematically that process registers when it is brought into contact with the idiom of so-called whiteness. For Monroe's indisputable whiteness—she is one of those "pure products" of America who William Carlos Williams reminds us, went "crazy"—raises interesting questions that whiteness discourse doesn't address. That idiom has been very strong on asserting the kinds of desires that led Jews—and largely Jewish men—to wish to assimilate to the normative patterns of American identity defined in racialized terms. But it is less interested in the

---

*I should stress in doing so, especially after his death, that despite my deep respect for Arthur Miller the man and playwright, he is subsidiary to my interest in "Arthur Miller" the cultural phenomenon. (His marriage to Marilyn, Miller told an interviewer in 1983, "is not part of my life now . . . except when some stupid jerk says something about it"; it is my hope in what follows to be as little a jerk as possible; see Arthur Gottfried, *Arthur Miller: His Life and Work* [New York: Da Capo, 2003], p. 442.) To be sure, there are points of overlap between the two, particularly as Arthur Miller repeatedly commented on or attempted to come to terms with "Arthur Miller" the public figure. Works like *Timebends* or *After the Fall* meditate, paradoxically, on the ways in which a private man's private life becomes the subject of public knowledge, obsession, scandal. So does his last play, *Finishing the Picture* (2005). Although in that work the Marilyn-figure, a recalcitrant actress refusing to shoot a scene, remains offstage for the entire play while her motives, history, and actions are discussed by husband, lover, producer, and director, the fact that Miller found himself in his eighties writing about the lover and wife of his forties suggests that, at the least, the subject that he sought to escape continued to preoccupy him until practically the moment of his death.

ways in which that white culture identified as saliently attractive to Jews in particular and ethnic otherness in general—for Marilyn, of course, was famously attached not only to a Jewish American in Miller but also an Italian American in Joe DiMaggio and one or perhaps two Irish Americans in John and Robert Kennedy. Their varied engagements with Monroe, it seems to me, help us fill out the picture of the whitening, suggesting that the process is far more complicated than our paradigms have hitherto allowed us to see. Caught up in the dialectics of white nonethnic desire for a putative ethnic authenticity, this process was impelled, I want to show, by a powerful libidinal charge that flowed forward and backward between Jew and white gentile, remodeling both in their erotic encounters with each other.

Miller, Monroe, and the Remaking of Jewish Masculinity

To understand this process, we need to understand something about the changing shape of Jewish masculinity, first in Europe, then in America. For, as a number of critics have recently reminded us—and as I've been implying in the previous chapter—from at least the eighteenth century forward, the Jewish man has been persistently defined in double terms. On the one hand—like his companions, the working-class man, the swarthy southern European, or the colonial subject—the Jewish man was seen as primitive, more fully sexual, impulsive, and hyperphallic. On the other, the Jewish man (unlike these other figures) was also seen as unmanly, weak, effeminate, or otherwise outside the norm of properly assertive masculinity. Thus in the antisemitic literature that flooded to the surface in late nineteenth-century Europe—much of which had its origins far earlier, in the anti-Jewish polemics of the medieval period—Jewish men were seen either as debased lechers yearning for Christian girls (or boys) or as men-women: this is the famous allegation of Otto Weininger's *Sex and Character* (1903), with which artists as various as Marcel Proust and James Joyce were to play in the early decades of the twentieth century. As these works begin to suggest, the cultural contradiction was ameliorated when the two got merged into a new character type, the Jewish pervert: a figure who conjoined the will-to-power of the hyperaggressive Jewish male with the sexual non-normativity of the feminized Jewish man.[4]

At once more and less of a man than gentile men: this was the odd position in which Jews were placed in early twentieth-century America and to which they were forced to respond as they sought to assimilate into that culture. But to tell this story only this one way—as being about gentile constructions—is to miss its full complexity, for it is also a narrative about changing models of masculinity within an assimilating Jewish community. Within traditional Jewish culture, critics have recently reminded us, conventional ideals of Western manhood were contravened by an ideal that stresses study, passivity, physical inactivity, which places ideal men in the *beit midrash,* the place of study, rather than the battlefield or the marketplace, loci of, respectively, the residual chivalric and the emergent bourgeois ideals of masculinity. The result is a strikingly different notion of what constitutes ideal maleness than is the norm in Euro-American culture. As Daniel Boyarin writes,

> In direct contrast to the firm handshake approved (for men and businessmen) in our culture, a *Yeshiva-Bokhur* [traditional scholar of the Talmud in Orthodox Jewish culture], until this day, extends the right hand with limp wrist for a mere touch of the other's hand. If the handshake is, as frequently said, originally a knightly custom, the counter-handshake of the ideal Jewish male elegantly bears out my thesis of the *Yeshiva-Bokhur* (and his secular grandson, the *mentsh*) as antithesis to the knight of romance. . . . The very handshake of the ideal male Jew encoded him as femminized in the eyes of European heterosexual culture, but that handshake constituted as well a mode of resistance to the models of manliness of the dominant fiction.[5]

To a certain degree, in other words, what gentile culture read as Jewish male effeminacy was a different order of masculine value, one that, when brought into contact with the gentile world, merits Boyarin's term *resistance.* But from the Jewish side of the equation, *resistance* was even more complicated: assimilating Jewish men had to differentiate themselves from traditional Jewish models of masculinity even as they were distancing themselves from antisemitic ones. Whether in the trade union movement, or in Zionist youth groups, or in the Bund, young Jewish men sought to define themselves against the traditional mode of maleness, positioning themselves instead as fully muscularly embodied. No wonder that Zionist critic (and foe of racial degeneration in gentile culture) Max Nordau vociferously argued for what he called "the muscle Jew"—a Jew capable of overcoming internal and external constraints and affirming a new, assertive form of masculinity appropriate to the project of draining swamps and irrigating deserts in barren and far-off lands.[6]

Boyarin's narrative of fraught Jewish masculinity restricts itself to Europe. But the dynamics that he traces got even more sharply complicated when eastern European Jews emigrated, in enormous numbers, into the United States. For what they found here was an entirely different social order—one in which the traditional models of Jewish masculinity, already under attack from within and without, were found not to be subjects for contempt, as they so frequently were in a European context, but at best irrelevant, at worst dysfunctional. In adapting to American life, argued University of Chicago sociologists Robert Park and Herbert Miller, the very model of study so highly prized in the Old World proved to be useless.[7] And in his ethnography of the Lower East Side, *The Spirit of the Ghetto*, Hutchins Hapgood eloquently summarized some of the reasons: "In spite, therefore, of his American environment, the old Jew of the Ghetto remains patriarchal, highly trained and educated in a narrow sectarian direction, but entirely ignorant of modern culture; medieval, in effect, submerged in old tradition and outworn forms."[8] Establishing a dynamic that was to play itself out for the rest of the century, Jewish boys rebelled against their foreign parents by vigorously adopting the most aggressively American of guises:

> The boys not only talk together of picnics, of the crimes of which they read in the English newspapers, of prize-fights, of budding business propositions, but they gradually quit going to synagogue, give up "chaider" promptly when they are thirteen years old, avoid the Yiddish theatres, seek the up-town places of amusement, dress in the latest American fashion, and have a keen eye for the right thing in neckties.... Then, indeed, the sway of the old people is broken. (27)

What's important here is not only that the second generation secularized and assimilated in self-conscious revolt against their parents—this is a familiar enough dynamic in American Jewish life—but that they did so through their participation in American mass culture: in the world of amusements, prize fights, and advertisements spread in large measure, through the later years of the nineteenth century and early years of the twentieth, by the proliferation of new media, like penny newspapers, mass-market magazines, nickelodeons, and the motion picture industry. But, as they came into increasing contact with American constructions of masculinity, they faced a persistent question: namely, which of the various models of American masculinity were they to assimilate to? Middle-class norms of self-abnegating achievement—as does the "cadaverous" but upwardly mobile Bernstein in Abraham Cahan's 1896 novella, *Yekl*? Working-class models of physical self-assertion, like those embodied by his romantic rival, the dance-hall-frequenting would-be-boxer Jake? Urban models of aristocratic flânerie, like the Lower East Side poets who frequented coffeehouses and published Yiddish verse in art magazines? Or organized expressions of muscular Judaism—like the efforts of the Jewish Agricultural Society to create a return-to-the-land movement for American Jews in the 1910s and 1920s, leading to agricultural settlements in New Jersey, the Catskills, and Petaluma, California?

Amidst this welter of possibilities, two distinct models emerged in the 1920s—and were to find their reflection in Arthur Miller's family. On the one hand stood ideals of bourgeois but disembodied respectability (if you can't beat 'em, join 'em), on the other, a more rambunctious but embodied assertiveness (if you can't join 'em, beat 'em up). To be sure, the first of these patterns predominated, as Jews marched into small businesses or the professions starting in the 1910s and continuing well into the 1920s and beyond—indeed, so much into the latter that law schools and medical schools as well as Ivy League universities started closing their doors to Jews. Although, as we shall see in more detail below, the power of this ideal type was to be challenged by the Depression, its greatest salience to Miller's own life was doubtless one of its offshoots, the high-culture intellectual. Indeed, the very notion of the intellectual entered American parlance at the same moment as eastern European Jews flooded into New York, and often in discursive tandem with them. The term, originating in the Dreyfus affair in France in the 1880s, in which it was a term of abuse adopted by the right for Zola and other Dreyfusards, was first deployed in an American context by William James in 1906; it was subsequently applied to describe the vigorous cultural life on the Lower East Side by a number of critics, including William's brother Henry and sociologists

Robert Park and Herbert Miller, who cited the presence of "intellectuals" as one of the most distinctive factors in New York Jewish life. Indeed, one conspicuous pattern of Jewish assimilation for much of the 1920s and 1930s was via the traditionally antisemitic mechanisms of high culture, which Jews transformed as they entered, even as they sloughed off the more visible signs of their Jewishness. As literary men, publishers, even professors, Jews entered the cultural mainstream that had marginalized them, claiming for themselves a power not equal but superior to those of the genteel WASP authorities who excluded them from their universities and reviled them in print: the power of modernity itself.[9]

But even as the yeshiva *bokher* metamorphosed into the high-culture intellectual, another, more bodily model of Jewish masculinity started to appear alongside it. Valorizations of assertive, embodied Jewish masculinity were always present alongside the middle-class and intellectual ones I have mentioned above, but became all the more important as the second generation of Jewish youth rebelled against the seemingly uptight strictures of their parents, particularly as the Depression made their parents' faith in success through bourgeois restraint seem risible and raised the specter of ineffectuality or even emasculation as their businesses failed, their professional careers withered or were blocked. Their model of Jewish masculinity met antisemitic constructions of feminized Jews and Jewish constructions of yeshiva *bokhers* head-on, affirming the Jew's toughness, worldliness, power. Its cultural embodiments took the form of boxers, athletes, and proletarianized workers; but by the late twenties its main cynosures were the gangsters, pimps, hangers-on who defined the Jewish mob in large cities like New York, Philadelphia, Detroit. I am thinking here of men like Arnold Rothstein, who essentially created the modern mob by unifying the Jewish and Italian gangsters and who was immortalized by Scott Fitzgerald as Meyer Wolfsheim, "the man who fixed the World Series," Sammy "Red" Levine, the Orthodox hit man who wore a skullcap to work and took the Sabbath off, Bugsy Siegel, the man who used the mob's money to build Las Vegas. Some of these were family men, like Rothstein, who was known wide and far to be a criminal mastermind but who was indistinguishable in appearance and habits from a banker or a lawyer; others were flamboyant womanizers, like Siegel. Some were part of the underworld alone—Murder Incorporated was a Jewish-dominated enterprise; others had links to labor unions or politics or the legal profession—one thinks here of a figure like Roy Cohn who (as we have seen) was the tough Jew par excellence, one who placed his considerable talents for threatening, manipulating, and extorting in the service of such varied clients as Senator Joseph McCarthy, the mob, and the Catholic Church. The entertainment industries, then and now, were particularly shaped by the image (if not the actuality) of the tough-guy Jew—it was a significant element in the persona of studio heads like Harry Cohn, not to mention in the those of such actors as Emanuel Goldenberg (aka Edward G. Robinson), Meshelim Weisenfreund (aka Paul Muni, Howard Hawks's Scarface), Jacob Julius Garfinkle (aka John Garfield), and, in a later decade, Issur Danielovich (aka Isadore Demsky, aka Kirk Douglas) or Bernard Schwartz (aka Tony Curtis)—all of whom may have "passed" as normative white Christians but were known and treasured by Jews as people of their tribe who had made it big in gentile America.[10]

It is against this background, with its welter of sharply contrasting, if not contradictory, models for Jewish manhood being offered from within and without the Jewish community, that we are to understand Arthur Miller and, more to the point, "Arthur Miller." As far as the former—the "real" Arthur Miller—is concerned, the relation between Arthur and Isidore Miller on the one hand and Arthur and his cousins on the other suggests (as it did for so many of his generation of Jewish men) the inadequacy of both the businessman and the tough-guy models—and indeed of the Jewish ones entirely. The business failure of Miller père—one enhanced and ratified, according to Miller, not only by his relentless nag of a wife but also by his own mother, who refused him a loan when his business failed—played off against the relative success and rambunctious sexuality of his uncle and cousins in ways that are virtual paradigms of each model of manliness. And both were plainly unviable for Arthur, who needed to find—as did generations of Jewish sons from at least the turn of the century—a different form of manliness in order to negotiate the social hurly-burly in which he was enmeshed.

At least for the Arthur Miller of the 1940s and early 1950s, that model followed out of the tradition I have sketched above of finding in the mechanisms of high culture a form of superiority to both his own family origins and a decreasingly but still palpably antisemitic culture. Like many of his peers, Miller rejected available models in his neighborhood and followed the assimilation-by-high-culture trail, asserting an identity for himself as the ethnicity-transcending Artist, writing plays despite the opposition of his father, who urged upon him a more conventional career. And, as it did for many of his fellow travelers on the assimilation-by-high-culture path, such a choice also meant rejecting the Jewish family itself, rejecting his parents' wishes by marrying a woman of Irish Catholic background, albeit one who, like Miller himself, was self-alienated from her own ethnicity, seeking to identify with "mankind rather than one small tribal fraction of it" (70). Indeed, his first wife Mary's sense of the "tribal," the particular, afflicting her Irish American culture of origin and blocking her aspirations for the universal, persistently suffuses Miller's writings about—or wrestlings with—his own Jewishness. When he considers Jews as Jews, that is to say, he often emphasizes their exoticism, their otherness, as in the vivid (and beautiful) description of his grandfather's Hasidic dancing in *Timebends* or his association of the New England Puritans with Jews—as fanatics, driven "crazy" by the same "fierce idealism, devotion to God, tendency to legalistic reductiveness, the same longings for the pure and intellectually elegant argument" (42). But when he thinks about his own Jewishness in positive terms, it is usually as a species of universal belief—a bulwark against "nihilism," as he says in an interview as late as the 1980s—or a vital but indistinct principle of life itself.[11] As Miller charmingly put it in the 1995 preface to a reissue of his autobiography—this after the performance of his most Jewish-obsessed play, *Broken Glass*: "I may have forgotten the little Hebrew I knew as a child, I never go to synagogue, and even find it troublesome to accurately remember which high holiday is which and what they signify, but something in me insists that there must continue to be Jews in the world or it will somehow end" (xiv).

But, despite his efforts to escape or evade the "tribal" aspects of his Jewish origins, Miller's personal commitments and, perhaps more important, the representations of him in the public sphere were powerfully linked to the double constructions of Jewish masculinity I have been outlining above. Or, to be more precise, Miller's rise to fame was in large measure a response to the more invidious of those constructions, as American society in general started to overcome its aversion to Jews. Miller came to public attention in the period after World War II at a moment when opposition to Hitler, knowledge of the death camps, and a general opening up of an insular America to the world at large forced underground the antisemitism that had flourished in the early years of the twentieth century and had been given new impetus during the Depression by figures like Henry Ford and Father Coughlin. (Miller himself contributed to this process with his 1945 novella *Focus*, in which—characteristic of his mixed strategies of Jewish self-identification and disaffiliation—he limns antisemitism through the experience of a gentile antisemite who, when fitted with glasses, discovers himself treated as a Jew by those around him.) At this moment Jewish artists and writers were entering the cultural mainstream, not as marginalized figures, but as full participants in middlebrow production; the 1950s were not only the time of writers like Miller attracting a new audience to Broadway—"an audience impatient with long speeches, ignorant of any literary allusions whatever, as merciless to losers as the prizefight crowd and as craven to winners, an audience that heard the word *culture* and reached for its hat" (244)—but one when writers like Herman Wouk and Leon Uris, following in the footsteps of Fannie Hurst, were extending both the subject matter and the reach of mass fiction. As Jewish writers moved into the previously WASP-dominated cultural and literary spheres like Broadway or the bestseller lists, however, new inscriptions of Jewish identity needed to be crafted. And the representation of Miller, who emerged in this welter of new talent as its most towering figure, was an integral part of this process. For the popular press constructed Miller in terms that united the dualities of Jewish male identity, positioning him as someone who straddled the lines between mental and manual labor, body and intellect, high and mass culture, art and business—and, ultimately, between normativity and perversion.

Consider, as a prime example of this process, the following, a *Saturday Evening Post* profile of Miller just after *Death of a Salesman* opened on Broadway:

> "A man who can't handle tools is not a man" says Willy Loman in the title role of *Death of a Salesman*. Willie speaks for his creator. Before *Salesman* was written, Miller built a house in which to write it. He owns some country property in Roxbury, Connecticut, and a year ago he dug a cellar, poured a concrete foundation, built a one-room shack with windows and door, installed workable plumbing and finally got the roof up. The roof gave him some trouble, working alone, but he devised a way to fit the rafters on the ground, get them on top of the house upside down, climb up on the beams and flip the rafter joists over and into place.
>
> Then Miller sat down in front of a thirteen-year-old secondhand portable typewriter . . . and started to write *Death of a Salesman*. Six

weeks later, the play was completed. Produced with only the most minute changes, it may become the most profitable six weeks' work ever undertaken in the history of show business.[12]

Note here how this figure—the first glimmerings of what I am calling "Arthur Miller"—unites the antitheses between which Jewish male identity had been divided in such a way as to modify or normalize their more troubling aspects. The negative side of the gentile construction of Jewish masculinity—Jews as ineffectual, intellectual sissies, if not queers—and the negative side of the Jewish counterresponse—Jews as working-class, manly, tough guys—both get ameliorated as they are mainstreamed. Indeed, the mainstreaming of this "Brooklyn Boy" who "Makes Good" (as the title of the profile has it) casts that "goodness" in the most traditional of American terms, terms in which his identity as a Brooklyn Jew or even an intellectual are effaced in favor of values more finely homespun, if resolutely un-Jewish:

> The man responsible for this solid milestone in theatrical history . . . until recently insisted that there was no truth to his friends' belief that he resembled a beardless Abraham Lincoln. Not long ago, his wife showed Jane Ellen Miller, age four and a half, a shiny new Lincoln penny. "Daddy on money," she said knowingly. Daddy sighed and accepted the inevitable.

This is, not to put too fine a point on it, what we mean by assimilation: Miller is admitted into the ranks of the normatively American, but the price of that admission is an extinction of his own ethnic difference, the collapse of it into a sanitized version of one of America's most canonical heroes and then the placement of that image on the most thoroughly American of objects, a piece of money. Thus far, though, there seems nothing unexceptional about Miller's metamorphosis, at least as that metamorphosis is treated by the American publicity machine. But, less than a decade later, "Daddy on Money" was to launch first an affair, then a marriage, with the most sought-after woman in America, the actresss-cum-sex-bomb Marilyn Monroe—and it was in this guise, I am suggesting, that his transformation from Arthur Miller into "Arthur Miller," or at least the "Arthur Miller" that was to do such powerful cultural work, was wrought.

To be sure, such a process would seem to involve some of the more insidious stereotypes of Jewish masculinity, that of the showbiz variant of the tough-guy Jew. For this is the precedent set by the numerous liaisons between Jewish men and gentile women throughout the 1930s and 1940s, perhaps the most salient being that between Miller's precursor Clifford Odets (to whom some of the most powerfully ambivalent pages in *Timebends* are devoted) and Frances Farmer, a beautiful free spirit who was to go mad and be, infamously, lobotomized. As no less an authority than Philip Roth's Alexander Portnoy observes, such conjunctions were common throughout the 1950s: Eddie Fisher and Debbie Reynolds, Phil Harris and Alice Faye, even Elizabeth Taylor and Mike Todd—and "you know what Mike Todd was—a cheap fascimile of my Uncle Hymie upstairs!"[13]

The liaison between Monroe and Miller makes Portnoy's list, too. But it is important to note that, especially in comparison with these other liaisons, matters between this last couple were far more complicated. For one thing, it was not as a tough Jew like Harry Cohn (who more or less used Monroe as a concubine early in her career, then dropped her from his studio after he tired of her services) or a business Jew like Mike Todd but rather as an intellectual Jew—and hence an exception to the Hollywood norm—that Miller and Monroe wrought their relationship. Indeed, part of Miller's appeal to Monroe was his gentlemanliness: when the two first encountered each other in 1950, they spent a long time talking at a party during which Miller, coyly but chastely, sat holding her toe. As such, Miller was at distinct odds not only with the wolves with whom Marilyn had been afflicted in her early career as Hollywood party girl but also with his own friend Elia Kazan, who was conducting a torrid affair with Marilyn at the time, for which Arthur served as something like a beard during his first trip to Hollywood. As a man of sensitivity and tact, as a New York playwright, as an intellectual, Miller was at distinct odds with the prevailing ethos of the male-dominated Hollywood entertainment industry, an industry that served as both the lure for and a validation of Jewish men of Miller's generation.

But, interestingly, the actress's response to the playwright was very much like his daughter's, and the *Post*'s—and Arthur, infatuated, was not above using it to his own advantage. For, after their first meeting, "Miller wrote Marilyn within days," according to one biographer, "with a reading proposal":

"If you want someone to admire, why not Abraham Lincoln?" Marilyn, as the world could hardly fail to know, admired Lincoln already. Her idolatry had started, she said, in junior high school, when her essay on Lincoln was judged the best in the class. By happy coincidence, Arthur Miller had attended Abraham Lincoln High School. Five years later, before her marriage to Miller, Monroe would enthuse to Joshua Logan, director of *Bus Stop*, "Doesn't Arthur look wonderfully like Abraham Lincoln? I'm mad for him."[14]

The two did not consummate their relationship, it seems, until many years later, after Monroe's ill-starred marriage with the Yankee Clipper, Joe DiMaggio, failed, although things between them clearly simmered through the intervening years. But the anecdote also suggests how fraught and charged were the issues involved in the transformation of Miller's persona. On the one hand, there is an undoubted transferential dimension here: Monroe is reported to have told Maurice Zolotow, "My father is Abraham Lincoln—I mean I think of Lincoln as my father. He was wise and kind and good. He is my ideal, Lincoln. I love him," which makes her relationship with Miller, and its failure, perhaps too easily explained.[15] (Two further nuggets: when Monroe began sleeping with Miller, she put a portrait of Lincoln above her bed; in public, she called him Arturo, but in private—as with all her lovers—her pet name for him was Daddy.)

But there was a powerful political dimension to this conjunction, too. Especially in Monroe and Miller's circles (and as opposed to those of the *Saturday Evening Post*), to be identified with Lincoln was not an innocent conjunction. The Great Emancipator was a favorite icon of the Popular Front—it was not for nothing that the antifascist, integrated Abraham Lincoln Brigades identified themselves with *that* particular president— and he was even more frequently evoked by less radical leftists like Carl Sandburg, whose hagiographic biography of Lincoln was completed in 1939, or Aaron Copland, whose *Fanfare for the Common Man* was first sounded in 1944, with Sandburg as narrator. And Marilyn was a passionate Hollywood liberal, particularly with respect to civil rights: although, unlike Miller, she seems to have had no involvement at all in the Communist Party, she nevertheless attracted the attention of J. Edgar Hoover long before her dalliances with the Kennedys filled his file. Miller and

Monroe, dancing with the possibility of a relationship that was not to be consummated for six years, thus concocted together first a private, then a public image of Miller that was distinct from the normative one of his family or the popular press. But that image, it is crucial to stress, was made out of many of the same materials—the Lincoln-like artist, here reinterpreted as the man of political integrity and leftist sentiments. When Miller and Monroe were married, the then quite liberal (how times have changed!) *New York Post* reported on their nuptials with the following banner headline: *Our Man Kissed the Bride!*—referring not only to Miller's New York origins but also to the legitimacy of the Jewish liberal-left that Miller, like that newspaper, represented to the culture at large. (The *Post*'s rival, then as now, the *New York Daily News* was, predictably, dyspeptic.)

To remind ourselves of the leftist spin that Miller and Monroe gave their union is also to observe the difficulties it faced—difficulties, I would suggest, that helped cement the transformation of Arthur Miller into "Arthur Miller," with considerable aid from Arthur Miller and Marilyn Monroe themselves. For there is no doubt but that Miller's dalliance with Marilyn brought him to his greatest test, the one that remade his persona a third time: his appearance before the House Un-American Activities Committee in 1956. It does not seem to be the case, as Miller later claimed, that his long-simmering affair with Monroe was the sole reason he was called as witness. Nevertheless, the committee did indeed make as much of the publicity that attended from Miller's engagement to Monroe and his desire to leave the country with his new wife during her filming of *The Prince and the Showgirl* in London. (Indeed, the chair of the committee reportedly offered to let Miller out of his obligation to testify if he could pose for photographs with Monroe.) But Miller himself was not above using his marriage to help him ease his political difficulties; he mentioned her as frequently as he possibly could (as, to be sure, did the press, for whom the word *Miller* was conjoined as frequently to *Monroe* as it was to *testimony*). Monroe, for her part, stood by her man, demurely standing behind Arthur when he spoke to the press even as she participated in his private war councils urging a resolute stand. Because of her celebrity she served an invaluable purpose. One of Monroe's most sympathetic biographers, Barbara Leaming, describes the scene outside the HUAC hearings, after an uninspired performance by Miller, as follows:

2.1 June 22, 1956: Marilyn Monroe Whispering to Arthur Miller. Their first joint appearance before the press after their plans to wed had been announced. Photographer: Sam Schulman. Courtesy of Corbis.

Finally, Marilyn Monroe and Arthur Miller emerged hand-in-hand from the apartment-house lobby. She looked adorable, yet properly subdued for the occasion . . .

"I've never been happier in my life," said Marilyn, nuzzling Miller for the cameras. He looked sweaty in a dark suit and tie.

As the couple stepped out onto the sidewalk, Marilyn leaned very hard on Arthur as if to emphasize that she depended on his protection, though in fact it was very much she who was going to protect him today. It wasn't enough to give a brilliant performance; she had to be a director, too. . . . She had to show people an Arthur Miller they had never seen before.

"You better stop that," Miller whispered to Marilyn. "If you lean too hard, I'm going to fall over."

Marilyn, all smiles and giggles, responded by closing her eyes and kissing Arthur's weathered cheek.

"Do that again, Marilyn!" the photographers cheered.

She did—numerous times.

"It's a good thing that we'll only be getting married once," Miller remarked to reporters. "That's all I can tell you."

Marilyn whispered something in Arthur's ear that caused him to hold her very tightly, burrowing his nose in her forehead. He was the image of a man deeply in love, a man who certainly deserved to be permitted to go on his honeymoon.[16]

Leaming's account of the scene seems partial, in every sense of the word. Miller was thirty-nine when he married Monroe, and she was ten years younger, which is to say that he was no more the *senex amans* that Leaming sketches than Monroe was the blushing young bride. But her sketch does capture something important about the Miller/Monroe dynamic, at least as it was represented in the public sphere. For, as in their initial dalliance with each other, it seems as if these two are collaborating to create a collective fiction. But here the fiction is meant to be public rather than personal, an improvised performance for the cameras, rather than an erotic pas de deux for each other. Indeed, the drama they created is essentially a transformation story—an American Pygmalion or, perhaps more appositely, a real-life version of the smash hit musical and film *Born Yesterday*.[17] Like Judy Holliday—star of both the stage and screen versions—Monroe plays the innocent but sexy guttersnipe redeemed by the love of a decent, if awkward man, the naïf sex bomb tamed—and elevated—by the power of culture. For his part, Miller is cast—or casts himself—as the other role in the drama: the ugly duckling redeemed by the love of a beautiful woman, the powerful, severe intellectual whose austerity is overcome by his swinging, sexy beloved—but one whose chief role remains that of savior.

It is *this* mutual transformation story—which only partially catches the complexity of the relation between these two—that initiates, I think, the most significant act of metamorphosis in the Miller saga. For what is crucial about it is not just that Miller is the man who succeeded with the woman who dumped Joe DiMaggio and whom countless other American men wished to win, but he succeeded *because* of his status as an awkward, nervous, press-shy, artistic, sensitive, man: all the things that had defined the Jewish man as effeminate or at least nonmasculine in the American popular imaginary. And more: Miller was transformed into a figure of such potency in the media—the entertainment industry—to which Jewish men turned for their models of American masculinity on the non-Jewish plan. Just as Marilyn was (literally) converted to Judaism through her encounter with Miller, so Miller was transformed, not so much into a gentile or a goy—this was the point of his previous incarnations—but into a celebrity in his own right. Whatever else one can say about it, none of the subsequent events of the marriage—its inevitable breakdown in mutual mistrust and the inability to conceive a child, the strain of two quite incompatible career paths, Marilyn's death, Arthur's grief and guilt—would or could change the cultural salience and importance of this development.

I want to be clear here: I am not writing about this moment in a spirit of cynicism, nor am I suggesting (as does Leaming or, in a different form, David Savran) that Arthur was deploying his wife in a merely tactical manner.[18] Miller and Monroe at this moment were under enormous pressures, pressures that no reader of this volume (much less Leaming or Savran or myself) will ever endure: pressures from the press, the HUAC, their lawyers, their own internal needs and desires. Nevertheless, considered in cultural terms, the moment is absolutely crucial. For the construction of "Arthur Miller" and the cultural work that circulated in his wake initiated a new style of Jewish masculinity among the subsequent generation of Jewish writers and intellectuals, one in which the kind of notoriety that Miller found, the kind of celebrity he achieved, became an explicit goal rather than (as I think it was with Miller) the byproduct of a series of life events and choices. Not only do a number of Jewish intellectuals who came to maturity during the fifties and early sixties play out the Miller pattern—I have mentioned already the two most prominent, Woody Allen and Philip Roth, but one needs to include Norman Mailer in this list as well—but many make explicit reference to the Monroe/Miller conjunction as they do so. Such references suggest that Miller (or rather "Miller") served as something of a rival and a blocking figure for these writers: a figure, that is, who had to be overcome for them to claim masculine literary or cultural authority for themselves—an authority that could best be accessed through an appropriation of Marilyn's image, memory, or even body.

One prime example of this was set by Norman Rosten—a friend of Miller's from college and himself a prolific poet, playwright, and fiction writer officially crowned the "Bard of Brooklyn." Rosten and his wife befriended Monroe as she and Miller began their affair, often serving as a cover or beard for the two of them as well as providing a place in New York for the two of them to tryst. He was so close to the two during this phase that he announced the wedding to the press and was to have been the best man, only supplanted at the end by Arthur's brother. As the marriage cooled and failed, Rosten stayed close to Marilyn, often ducking out to museums with her while Miller kept busy elsewhere. After her death he cleaved to her memory in ways that Miller felt—not unjustifiably—crossed the line from inappropriate to the ghoulishly appropriating: Rosten wrote two books about Marilyn (*Marilyn Monroe: An Untold Story* [1973] and *Marilyn Monroe—Among Friends* [1988]; cooperated with Norman Mailer in the writing of the latter's scabrous *Marilyn* (about which more below), and even penned a folksong with Pete Seeger called *Who Killed Norma Jean?* (to the tune of *Who Killed Cock Robin?*) that included a direct jab at Miller in its fourth verse:

> Who'll make her shroud?
> I, said the Lover, my guilt to cover,
> I'll make her shroud.

No wonder Arthur cut off all contact with Rosten and barely mentioned his oldest friend in *Timebends*: Rosten had succeed in doing in death what he could not fully do in life, make Marilyn his own, publicly humiliating his old and more successful friend and garnering a considerable degree of literary success (or at least notoriety) in the process.[19]

A similar pattern, with a more overtly political spin, is evident in the career of Alvah Bessie, a screenwriter and member of the Hollywood Ten who presumably moved alongside Miller and Monroe in the circles for which they were called to account by the HUAC. In 1966, after he had been able to write again in his own name, Bessie published a potboiler of a novel called *The Symbol*—one that told the Marilyn story very much from her perspective (much of it is made up of fictionalized versions of the tapes Miller's psychiatrist allegedly kept of her sessions, tapes that have recently, allegedly, "surfaced"). Bessie, in other words, appropriates not only Monroe's story but her very voice—makes her *his* literary creation, not Miller's. The competitive/appropriative dimension of this response is enhanced in the sections of the book written from the perspective of the book's surrogate

Arthur Miller, a name-changing Jewish painter named Calvin Bernard. Bernard is cold, directive, self-centered. His relations with the Monroe figure, Wanda, are circumscribed by his creative block ("Since I met my sexpot wife I have not done a tap of work," he thinks), on the one hand, and, on the other, her failure to achieve orgasm with him (or any man—a female fan does so by performing oral sex on her, a thrilling inversion of her own sexual servicing of studio execs early in her career).[20] Indeed, although she adores him as a mentor and an intellectual, their initially thrilling (to him) sex soon leaves him feeling less than fully satisfied or even potent:

> [in] their private life . . . he sat like a potentate upon a throne and she crouched literally at his feet, waiting to catch any pearl of wisdom that dropped from his lips. She sat with her mouth open, staring up at him, adoring, asking for advice and counsel, believing anything he said about anything under the sun, because she was a poor, ignorant orphan child and he was a Man of the World—wise, educated, cultured, accomplished, traveled.
>
> She snuggled up to him day and night, and when this—as it almost inevitably did—aroused him physically, she submitted but she did not really participate. He could sense it. Although he had admonished her *never* to accept him unless she also wanted him and never to fake a response she did not feel, he became aware that somehow she had learned to do this and she could not control her "need" to pretend she was in ecstasy. (180)

His politics, however are more resolute, less caught up in the mechanisms of authorial ambivalence. Like Miller, Bernard's relationship with a Hollywood star brings him to the attention of the HUAC and, even more than Miller, he stages a principled confrontation with that body. Boldly walking in (Wanda is off on the other side of the country—although she does receive horrific hate mail), he not only refuses to name names, but denounces the committee for its affront to the "dignity of an artist, a man, and an American" and, when asked by the chairman what he means by the word *dignity* gets off a truly heroic riposte: "'I would not expect you to know the name, sir,' Calvin replied coolly, to almost universal applause" (198). Cited for contempt by the committee, and held in contempt by the full House of Representatives, Bernard is indicted by a grand jury only to be saved from imprisonment by a reversal from the court of appeals—much of which present direct echoes to Miller's story.

Bessie's response to Miller is a nuanced and complicated one, a representation of a principled man caught up in desires and needs (his own as well as Wanda's) that defeat his best intentions and compromise his idealized vision of himself. The paradoxical formulation "admonished her *never* to accept him unless she also wanted him" suggests how self-defeating his enterprise is: the very terms on which their relation is constructed prevent its mutual fulfillment. Self-defeating, too, is his mixture of guilt and excitement at his dominant role in their relation: admonisher, potentate, unproductive—sterile—genius. However compromised or hypocritical he might be on an affectional level, though, he remains true to his best instincts in his political convictions. Indeed, given the complexities of Miller's performance adverted to above, Bernard's steadfast cleaving to principle without the benefit of Wanda/Monroe's company makes him even more admirable and forthright than Miller—and allows him to have received the instant gratification of an applause Miller only received later. In short, Bernard is a composite of Miller and a wish-fulfillment version of Alvah Bessie himself—imprisoned for ten months as a result of his refusal to cooperate with HUAC, condemned to odd jobs for many years before slowly making a comeback with projects like *The Symbol*.

The richest example of this phenomenon of male competition with Miller staged over the memory, example, and even the body of Monroe is provided by Norman Mailer's spectacularly bitchy *Marilyn: A Life* (1972), in which the rivalry over Monroe's body and the desire to appropriate that body are explicitly thematized. The book is, as is well known, a commentary on a series of photographs, especially new and hitherto unpublished ones from late in her life taken by Bert Stern (although it's also woven together from a number of contemporary revisionist takes on Monroe, including Norman Rosten's), and Mailer understands that his enterprise is the complex one of using his powers of writing to make love to a dead woman—or, more appropriately, Orphically to call that woman into being from beyond the grave so that he can make her body, and its history, his own. (And quite successfully, too: it's in Mailer's narrative that the story of Marilyn's death being an assassination by some mysterious person or persons eager to cover up her putative affairs with one or two Kennedys got its start.) To do so, of course, he has to wrest Marilyn's ghost away from Miller, whose literary and cultural paths he had been crossing for thirty years, and with whom he had been expressing his rivalry since the moment they first met, after which Mailer announced that he could easily write as good a play as Miller's *All My Sons* (Gottfried, 112). Indeed, one suspects that, as is the case with Bessie, the enterprise of summoning up the voice and the very being of Marilyn is as much about the author's urge to do in Miller as about his desire to do Marilyn. Thus Mailer writes on one of the earliest pages of *Marilyn*:

> Once in Brooklyn, long before anyone had heard of Marilyn Monroe—she had been alive for twenty years but not yet named!—he [i.e., Mailer, who refers to himself throughout in the third person] had lived in the same brownstone house in which Arthur Miller was working on *Death of a Salesman* and this at just the time he was himself doing *The Naked and the Dead*. The authors, meeting occasionally on the stairs, or at the mail box in the hall, would chat with diffidence as they looked for a bit of politics or literary business to mouth upon—each certainly convinced on parting that the other's modest personality would never amount to much. In later years, when Miller was married to Monroe, the playwright and the movie star lived in a farmhouse in Connecticut not five miles away from the younger author, who, not yet aware of what his final relation to Marilyn Monroe would be [i.e., none], waited for the call to visit, which of course never came. . . . The novelist [couldn't] . . . condemn the playwright for such avoidance of drama. The secret ambition, after all, had been to steal Marilyn . . . a conceit which fifty million other men may also have held. . . . It was only a few marriages (which is to say a few failures) later that he could recognize how he would have done no better than Miller and probably have been damaged further in the process. In retrospect, it might be conceded that Miller had been made of the toughest middle-class stuff—which, existentially speaking, is tough as hard synthetic material.[21]

This passage, like many of the passages devoted to Miller, is a masterpiece of carefully controlled character assassination, in which Mailer both stages his rivalry with Miller and seeks to downplay it. His implication here is that Mailer has always already transcended his older rival—that, as he goes on to amplify with some mean but not entirely inaccurate comments later, Miller's career never again reached the heights he achieved in

Death of a Salesman and was in a particularly bad slump at the moment he met Monroe, while Mailer's star was, from the moment of *The Naked and the Dead* forward, to be in the ascendancy. Their meeting on the stairs, Mailer implies (but wickedly never states) is one after which he is to head up, and Miller down, down, down. The wickedness doesn't stop here. In a maneuver worthy of the late stories of Henry James, Mailer defines Miller as the less worthy artist by installing him in the position of the person more successful in the art of living than in the life of art (this is the point of a host of James stories from his "middle years," including most conspicuously *The Lesson of the Master*). Miller, unlike Mailer, is made of "the toughest middle-class stuff," and the "hard synthetic" Naugahyde of which he is composed stands in direct opposition to the more pliable, perhaps even organic material that constructs the true Artist. The condescending dialectics here, however, take on an even more specifically intraethnic cast, as Mailer keeps insisting on putting Miller down not just as a man, but as a *Jewish* man. For Mailer obsessively returns to two features of Miller's identity, features he implicitly links to one another: Miller's Jewishness and his (putative) sexual lack. After the success of *Salesman*, Mailer tells us, Miller became

> sufficiently pontifical to become the first Jewish Pope, he puffed upon his pipe as if it were the bowl of the Beyond, and regaled sophisticated New York dinner parties with tedious accounts of his gardening and his well-digging.... The stinginess for which he was famous—find the witness to testify that Miller had ever picked up a check—now seemed to have become a species of creative thrift. He was tight, he was tied up, he was abstemious—an artist in a time of such orderliness and depression can feel he has nothing to write about. Experience repeats itself with the breath of a turnip. (143)

If comparing Miller to a celibate and dwelling on his clenched, anal, uptight nature (Mailer is soon to write that Miller is "as guarded in his synapses as a banker") doesn't make the point obvious enough—that an uptight, conventional Jewish man couldn't sexually satisfy a woman like Monroe—Mailer more or less says just that: "If she has known the best sexual athletes of Hollywood (that capital of sex)," writes Mailer, ventriloquizing Marilyn, "and Miller at his worst has to be an inhibited householder from Brooklyn, nonetheless she loves him" (167) and then proceeds to dilate for a long paragraph on the metaphysics of sexual self-delusion that enmeshes these two lovebirds until its inevitable decline, in the wake of Marilyn's miscarriages, depression, pill taking, and Miller's assumption of various paternal roles: caretaker, business manager, *noodge*.

Monroe's body, in Mailer's perfervid imagination, is the prize that Miller has won as a result of his workmanlike writing and Mailer explicitly writes his book to "steal" away from him, yet he pushes beyond even that relatively primitive scenario. In the first passage I have quoted, the as yet unnamed Marilyn (she was to take that name definitively a few years later) and the anonymous Mailer (who refers to himself throughout the book in the third person) seem oddly conflated with each other: two then-unknowns brought together by the unlikely figure of Arthur Miller. Although, he told *Time* magazine in a cover story celebrating the publication of *Marilyn*, "I come from Brooklyn . . . and she had the basic stuff out of which Brooklyn dream girls are made," nevertheless "I felt some sort of existential similarities with Marilyn Monroe."[22] And indeed, in the next paragraphs, Mailer is to rewrite her name as an anagram in such a way as to conflate it with an anagram of his own: "the letters in Marilyn Monroe (if the 'a' were used twice and the 'o' but once) would spell out his own name, leaving only 'y' for excess" (20). Mailer, it would seem, doesn't just yearn to sleep with Monroe, like fifty million other American males; he writes this book in order to *become* Marilyn—a glittering celebrity *cum* sex symbol. Seeking to ventriloquize Monroe, he ends up being possessed by her spirit—leaving, of course, only the "y" (chromosome) for excess.*

To put the matter this way, of course, is also to imply that his rivalrous relationship with the older Miller is not untouched with homoerotic desire—to seek to be Marilyn is perforce to become his rival's lover; and to say this is also to reiterate the obvious truth of literary rivalry, that one loves the thing one wants to transcend, transume, or destroy. But it's also to suggest that what's at stake for Mailer, writing in the wake of the sexual

---

* And that fixation continues through the rest of Mailer's career no less than it did Miller's. Mailer wrote another long meditation on her photographic image in *Of Women and Their Elegance* (1980) and—perhaps in response to Miller's *After the Fall*—a play, *Strawhead* (1986) on the subject of Marilyn that starred his daughter Kate during its brief run at the Actors Studio (!).

2.2 Monroe Meets Mailer—Time Magazine. July 16, 1973. TIME Magazine ©1973 Time Inc. Reprinted by permission.

revolution and very much its exponent and avatar, is precisely the issue of Jewish masculinity I have been foregrounding throughout this chapter. Mailer clearly wants to escape—indeed thinks he has escaped—the traps of Jewish masculinity into which Miller has fallen. Positioning his rival Miller as a version of Cahan's Bernstein—as the studious yeshiva *bokher* turned guardian of middle-class mores and morality—he projects himself as a kind of Jake—a muscle Jew, bursting with heterosexual energy and potency. But, even as he does so, he ironically inscribes himself in a different position: that of the haunted androgynous, queer Jew—a version of Otto Weininger's Jewish man/woman made fit and hip for the era of sexual liberation and self-expression.

This weird admixture of misogyny and queerness, Mailer's *Marilyn*, helps to clarify what was at stake for Jewish men in the Miller/Monroe encounter and suggests one way out of the double binds that such an encounter articulated, toward the construction of what can only be described as a sexually transgressive identity formed in alliance with—rather than in distinction from—the female object of male rivalry and desire. A clearer—perhaps the clearest—example of this move to the non-normative as a response to the constrictions of assimilated Jewish masculinity—and the salience of Miller's example to Jewish American male intellectuals—is that of Philip Roth, who not only followed the great-American-writer-marries-a-Hollywood-star-and-lives-to-regret-it pattern but has also written about Miller and Monroe in at least two crucial contexts. One of them is his novel, *I Married a Communist*, which turns back to the days of the Hollywood blacklist and imagines a marriage between a movie star and a Jewish radical radio personality in which she betrays her husband and ruins his career by penning a novel with the same name as the book's title. (That the novel was published just after Roth's former wife, the actress Claire Bloom, published a tell-all memoir with long sections detailing her relationship with Roth is part of the story, too.) There is indeed a Hollywood backstory to this novel, but it seems to me to be more germane to a figure we will consider in the context of another Roth novel—the jazz clarinetist Artie Shaw, who, after retiring from music, moved to Hollywood and married a succession of gentile women, one of whom, romance novelist Kathleen Winsor (author of, *inter alia*, *Forever Amber*) denounced him to the House Un-American Activities Committee for sponsoring a concert series of Soviet composers. I want briefly instead to focus on the engagement with Miller in Roth's most famous (or is it infamous?) novel, *Portnoy's Complaint*, because this novel suggests just how enduring the cultural forces called into being in and around the Miller/Monroe conflation turned out to be—and just how enduring are the patterns of Jewish masculine definition that Arthur Miller's career seemed to transcend.

At least two important points of contact between "Arthur Miller" and Alexander Portnoy are woven into the text of the novel. The first, and to my mind most systematically underappreciated, is the way that the novel stages an important aspect of its revision of modes of Jewish masculinity on the back of Miller and Miller's most famous play, *Death of a Salesman*.

For the character who is most systematically forgotten in critical accounts of the novel, but who dominates its second section (the memorably titled "Whacking Off"), is Alexander Portnoy's father, by profession an insurance salesman. And, like Willy Loman, he is a figure who has bought into the American Dream with ironic results, although, of course, Roth plays these for comedy, not tragedy. Although like Isidore Miller, Arthur's father, Jack Portnoy is eclipsed by "the potent man in the family—successful in business, tyrannical at home," (51) his older brother Hymie, he is most notably a driven Lomanesque salesman, one who "work[s] the longest day of any insurance agent in history," in his case, vending insurance policies to poor, vulnerable African Americans in the poorer sections of Newark and pouncing on them to collect their small payments on Sundays and weekends (117). This occupation is doubtless galling to his rebellious son, a civil rights liberal from his youth and the New York Assistant Commissioner of Human Opportunity in his middle age; but even he understands that, although Jack is clearly an exploiter, he is treated by his employer with the same indifference that Willy Loman discovers from his. Alex apostrophizes "this father! this kindly, anxious, uncomprehending, constipated father! Doomed to be obstructed by this Holy Protestant Empire" (39) of the insurance company upon whose behalf he toils, in which his progress is blocked, and from which he retires with just a gold watch. More important, perhaps, he is like Willy, Alexander thinks, in cheating on his wife from the front office. In this case, the woman in question is not known as "the Woman" but rather a *shikse* named Anne McCaffery—a new cashier, Jack Portnoy tells Sophie, who wants to come home for a real Jewish meal. Her arrival in the home precipitates a most un-Loman-like battle royale between Jack and Sophie Portnoy; but it also provides the psychogenesis of Alexander Portnoy's own form of sexual expression. Whether or not Jack is (as Alex puts it) *shtupping* Anne McCafferey, Sophie seems to think he is, and, as she confronts her husband, turns and hugs Alex's sister Hannah to her breast, consigning the two Jewish men in the family to what Alex perceives, years later, to be a commonality of guilt that becomes "the most prevalent form of degradation in erotic life"—Alex's need for exogamous relationships with gentile women, as if to do openly what his father could only do covertly.

I want to suggest, then, two things: that the impress of Arthur Miller's literary example is felt on the character of Jack Portnoy, who is an ethnic version of Willy Loman, a Willy Loman who is definitively a Jew and whose treatment by his insurance company is tinged with systemic antisemitism—but also a Willy Loman without any tragic or transcendent dimension. (Could one imagine the life of Jack Portnoy being celebrated with a requiem—the title Miller gives to the last scene of *Salesman*?) I am also suggesting that the force of Miller's personal example is felt here as well, that Jack Portnoy brings into the novel the thematics of Jewish/gentile sexual attractions that get played out in the experience of Alexander Portnoy with direct allusion to the Miller/Monroe relationship. As with Roth's rewriting of Willy as Jack, his reinscription of Miller and Monroe takes what seems to be a comic form, although it turns out to be quite powerful indeed: he rewrites it as Alex's affair with the character he knows as "the Monkey"—a model and actress whose name literally echoes that of Norma Jeane Baker: Mary Jane Reed. Like Norma Jeane/Marilyn Monroe, Mary Jane/"the Monkey" is born into a dirt poor white trash family, in her case Appalachian rather than the descendents of Appalachians who emigrated to California, as was the case with Monroe. Like Norma Jeane/Marilyn, Mary Jane/"the Monkey" enters the entertainment industry (in her case, the fashion industry) via her spectacular beauty, but is also taken up by a string of rich men who use her sexually and then discard her—Harry Cohn's abuse of Monroe, for example, is mirrored in "the Monkey's" marriage to a kinky millionaire who remakes her image (he pays for a new set of teeth) but who forces her to participate in degrading sexual shenanigans. Like Norma Jeane/Marilyn, Mary Jane/"the Monkey" enters into a protracted analysis with an orthodox Freudian shrink, one of the results of which being her attraction to a seemingly stable Jewish man—in this case, Alexander Portnoy, at exactly the same age, and with many of the same motives, that Marilyn seems to have entered her relation to Miller: "Now she's thirty, wants to be married and a mother, wants to be respectable and live in a house with a husband (particularly as the high-paying years of her glamorous career appear to be just about over)" (135). Alex's role in this drama is to be exactly that Miller portrayed in the public (and, I want to insist again, *not* the private) relation with Marilyn: to be the stable family man who grants her her wishes, the intellectual who helps elevate her tastes (on one of their most idyllic weekends, he reads her "Leda and the Swan," for which she rewards him with a particularly inspired bit of oral sex). And, finally, Mary Jane has, at the end of the novel, attempted (in the best Marilyn fashion), to force Alex's hand by attempting suicide—and caused Alex to retreat into a state of guilt-induced impotence. No wonder Alex concludes his first description of Alex's relation with Mary Jane/the Monkey with an explicit invocation of the Arthur Miller/Marilyn Monroe relation:

> What was I supposed to be but *her* Jewish savior? The Knight on the Big White Steed . . . [who] turns out to be none other than a brainy, balding, beaky Jew, with a strong social conscience and black hair on his balls, who neither drinks nor gambles nor keeps show girls on the side; a man guaranteed to give them kiddies to rear and Kafka to read—a regular domestic Messiah! . . . What we have before us, ladies and gentlemen, direct from a long record-breaking engagement with his own family, is a Jewish boy just dying in his every cell to be Good, Responsible, & Dutiful, to a family of his own. The same people who brought you Harry Golden's *For 2¢ Plain* bring you now—the Alexander Portnoy Show! If you liked Arthur Miller as a savior of *shikses*, you'll just love Alex! (153–154)

To be sure, in the context I have been discussing in this essay, this is a deeply insightful passage; but it is also a troubling one. It is insightful in its recognition that the Miller/Monroe relation sets the stage for subsequent Jewish-gentile relations and, more particularly, that such a relation is quite literally a "show"—a spectacle, a TV sitcom or variety special in which Jewish men are granted their full masculinity (indeed a proliferatively powerful one; they have so much "black hair" on their bodies that some of it even appears on their testicles), yet are made to play a domesticated role as family men, educators, "saviors of *shikses*." Indeed, as that last word implies, as Jews, they are asked to assimilate into a thoroughly Christian pattern, one in which their mission is not only to sleep with gentiles but also to redeem them. And, even more problematically, Alex-as-Miller fits himself into the gentile imaginary in other ways as well. Here he stands in the midst of the not-enough-too-much-of-a-man pattern we have seen afflicting Jewish men in America: either he is a kind of a ravening beast filled with transgressive desires (the larger context of this passage, as of much of his relation with "the Monkey," is her reproaches to him for initiating a sexual threesome with a prostitute from Rome) or he is to be the very model of the good Jewish boy that Jewish boys like Portnoy, from at least the beginning of the century, found to be confining at best, emasculating at worst. Indeed, at the very end of the novel, Portnoy is quite literally caught in this double bind: he finds himself afflicted with guilt at Mary Jane Reed's suicide attempt and thoroughly impotent even—or especially—when he attempts to force himself on a sabra soldier he has picked up in Israel. It is this double bind that not only defines "Portnoy's complaint," but that leads him to the long, heartfelt cry of anguish that concludes the novel—and to Dr. Spielvogel's comic punchline: "Now ve may perhaps to begin. Yes?" (274)

Roth's hope here is clearly for a new beginning not only to Alex Portnoy's story but to narratives of Jewish masculinity. But this is not what he finds—to the contrary. As Alex both explores his own sexuality over the course of the novel and revolts against it in the novel's comic conclusion, he clearly reinscribes himself as an all too familiar character type: the Jewish pervert, with the added intensity that this vision of himself comes not only from gentile and Jewish culture, but from his own guilt-inducing superego, which continually reproaches him for his deeply felt transgressive desires. And this is the fate of the new beginning of Jewish masculinity represented by the construction of "Arthur Miller" as well. Although Miller's transformation into "Miller" in many ways registered the amelioration of the most invidious double binds of Jewish masculinity, it also suggested that such an amelioration came at a price. Not only could Jewish men not be Jews, but they weren't allowed to be human, fallible, governed by the same desires and demonstrating the same fallibility as their gentile peers. Rather, they had to display exquisite ethical sensitivity, perform acts of earnest self-sacrifice, display strenuous intellectualism. If they failed in that task, Jewish men of the 1950s and 1960s had to see themselves as degenerates, perverts— as the very figures this ethical imperative was intended to relieve them from embodying.

The response to that dilemma is one I see as one that shapes Mailer and Roth's distinctive versions of masculinism—to revel in the role of the Jewish pervert, to play it to the hilt, and to subject the mechanisms of amelioration to comic scrutiny and hence critique. But as I have been implying with respect to *Portnoy*, this solution for them is no solution at all, merely a different version of the familiar situation in which Jewish men found themselves in the first place. But, as my readings have also tried to suggest, they contained within them the seeds of a new dispensation, one in which the familiar figure of the Jewish pervert is tweaked to yield a different outcome, to become the cynosure of sixties libidinal radicalism not outside but rather within the defiles of masculinity at its most aggressively phallic. Were I a different sort of critic, one more psychoanalytically inclined, I'd start using the language of reaction formation here, as if Marilyn's desire to become Marilyn or Roth's embrace of an impotence that defines him as an assimilated Jew couldn't be read as the core of perverse desire that leads to their hypermasculine poses. (Indeed, by the time of *The Human Stain*, Roth's stand-in, Nathan Zuckerman, is wholly impotent—a condition that clearly makes him a better narrator—more empathic, less insistent on his own prerogatives and needs—as well as a better man. A negative sexuality, in other words, generates a negative capability.) Or were I yet more a different sort of critic, I'd push toward a queer reading of these figures, of the homosexual desire that seeps into Mailer's rivalrous engagement with Miller, of the polymorphous perversity that defines not only Portnoy, but the Rothean protagonist tout court. But, as someone most interested in an ethnoracially inflected historical criticism, I want to stress the transitional role between their positions and those of their successors, the queer Jewish critics and artists whom I have discussed in the previous chapter. Roth and Mailer transform notions of Jewish masculinity in ways that look back to the model of the Jewish pervert, but that also look forward to the appropriation of that figure by Arthur Miller's grandchildren, the Jewish men of our era. To be sure, the muscle Jew is making a comeback—the current champion of the World Wrestling Federation, a former pro football player, goes by the name "Goldberg" and neoconservative policy wonks like William Kristol posed alongside generals like Colin Powell as part of the "new Warrior elite" on the pages of *Vanity Fair* before their dreams came crashing down in the Iraqi desert. But, as we've seen in the previous chapter, Kushner, and with him a generation of Jewish men, proudly, if complexly, step into the guise of the sexually transgressive Jew. The open question that remains is whether they do or do not move beyond the double binds implicit in the Miller model. On the one hand, one way of reading Louis in *Angels in America* may be as a kind of Portnoy, infatuated with gentiles—Republicans, even!—and yet at the same time repulsed by the consequences of that desire. On the other, it may well be that within the defiles of radical Jewish culture, and especially the enthusiastic adoption of the model not only of the Jew as queer but the Jew-as-queer-as-outsider, exists the potential for a masculinity that escapes the double binds that have beset Jewish men in America from Miller's time—or for that matter Cahan's—to our own. If so, then it is either a historical oddity and a dialectical inevitability—or, more likely, both—that they will owe much indeed to two heterosexual writers generally considered to be arch-misogynists, and to their career-long fixations with the tantalizing and frustrating figure of Marilyn Monroe.

Marilyn Monroe and the White Desire for Ethnicity

But rather than ending on this affirmative note, I need to observe that I've done here exactly what I've critiqued Miller, Bessie, Allen, and Roth for doing: that is, appropriating Monroe for the purposes of delineating Jewish masculinity. I don't mean to make this self-critique in a cheap or obvious way; in the absence of any real authoritative evidence, it's difficult to know as much about the nature of Marilyn's desire for Miller as we so abundantly do about Miller's desire for Marilyn. And even if we had other evidence—perhaps those long-rumored tapes of her psychiatric sessions; something more than a sketch of her autobiography—it would be difficult to know what to do with it. If psychoanalytic theory has anything to teach us, it is that desire is a fickle and mutable thing, capable of shifting permutations at the best of times; and Marilyn, the most intensely desired woman of her time, was also notoriously alienated from her own appetencies and needs. And, even if we could know the shape of her own inclinations in any determinate way, Marilyn was also an intensely public person who (doubtless the source of much of her appeal) nevertheless represented herself slyly, elusively, self-parodically, so it is all the more difficult to move from what records we do have, public or private, into any determinative judgment.

That being said, it seems important to take her affectional life seriously, and for two linked reasons. The first is the pattern of her object choice. For—getting beyond the Miller conjunction or, perhaps it would be better to say, putting it in context—Marilyn's desires can be best read through the prism of her actions, which is perhaps the best way to read anyone's desires. And here the pattern is clear: while she slept with countless men, and had affairs with fewer but still a large number, her prime, long-lasting emotional attachments were to men of a certain background or variety: to men of white ethnic descent. Joe DiMaggio, Arthur Miller, John and (probably) Robert Kennedy. And these men were all the children of immigrant families (second-, second-, and third-generation) who made their way into the center of American cultural and civic life through means common to—indeed stereotypical of—white ethnics in the 1940s, 1950s, and 1960s: sports, culture, politics, or, to put it differently, through the exercise of the body, mind, and will. This pattern is of particular moment because one of the most common constructions given to Monroe in current criticism is not only as an embodiment of an overwhelming if self-alienated sexuality but also as the very cynosure of whiteness itself. As film critic Richard Dyer put it, in 1987, in a formulation that has proven to be enormously influential for both film studies and the critical interrogation of whiteness across the board:

> Monroe conforms to, and is a part of the construction of, what constitutes desirability in women [in the 1950s]. This is a set of implied character traits, but before it is that it is also a social position, for the desirable woman is a white woman.... Monroe could have been some sort of star had she been dark, but not the ultimate embodiment of the desirable woman.
>
> To be the ideal Monroe had to be white, and not just white but blonde, the most unambiguously white you can get. (She was not a natural blonde; she started dyeing her hair in 1947).... [And] blondeness, especially platinum (peroxide) blondness, is the ultimate sign of whiteness.... Blonde hair is frequently associated with wealth, either in the choice of the term 'platinum' or in pin-ups where the hair color is visually rhymed with a silver or gold dress... and with jewelry. (We might remember too the title of Monroe's nude calendar pose, *Golden Dreams*.) And blondeness is racially unambiguous. It keeps the white woman distinct from the black, brown or yellow, and at the same time, it assures the viewer that the woman is the genuine article.[23]

The ironies here are of course multiple; Monroe—who was about as white as they come in origins (the daughter of an Okie family in Los Angeles whose mother was a devotee of Aimee Semple McPherson and who was first discovered while working in an aircraft plant)—still had to dye her hair blonde in order to achieve her status as "the most unambiguously white you can get," "the genuine article": whiteness itself, in other words, is always already simulacral, factitious. But the ironies are greater still. Just as Marilyn's identity has taken on a greater symbolic significance as archetypal of white identity across the board, so her desires may be taken as having a larger implication. For the period of Marilyn's accession to fame, the 1950s, was also the period of the white ethnic's accession to cultural respectability, if not centrality. Baseball, the movies, politics—all places where ethnics had either been unrepresented or "passed"—joined the theater (where Jews and other ethnics had long been ensconced) and popular music (ditto) as loci in which ethnics could thrive *as* ethnics without apologizing for that status, celebrating it even as their contemporaries suburbanized, assimilated. That celebrated move, as I've been stressing throughout this book, is one that contemporary critics tend to read in racializing terms, as being about the ethnics' assimilation via their accession to the magic status of whiteness itself, an accession masked or occluded by the idiom of ethnicity. But Monroe's desire for white ethnic men puts front and center the unasked question in this criticism: what cultural desires on the part of white, Protestant mainstream culture made the ethnic's assimilation to "whiteness" possible? What qualities did this culture identify or valorize in the not-yet-always-already-white Jewish or Catholic ethnic—and, more to the point, why? And what is the relation of this larger pattern of white response to ethnicity to our subject here, the shifting and volatile dynamics of Jewishness?

To view the three chief relationships of Monroe's life as a single structure, as I propose to do briefly, is to see them as a set of Venn diagrams in which the points of intersection spell *Jew*. To be sure, each of these diagrams might be best conceptualized as a slightly shaded circle, each tinted by the faint aura or tinge of the others. I've already suggested that what the conjunction of Miller and Monroe represented in the public eye was the mainstreaming of qualities associated with the intellectual—brainpower, sensitivity, creativity, and so on—as they get validated by the desire of a culturally desirable sex bomb. To this we might want to add an association I haven't yet stressed above, namely, the virtues of family—Marilyn, for example, remained so close to Isidore Miller, Arthur's father, that, even after the separation, he accompanied her as her "date" to the birthday party at which she sang "Happy Birthday, Mr. President" to her lover, John Kennedy, much to the chagrin of Arthur himself, whose relations to his own father were strained. The notoriously close-knit ties of the ethnic family contrasted, in other words, with Monroe's own scattered upbringing to define the former as a locus not only of cohesiveness in an increasingly mobile, chaotic world but also as a conflictual haven of emotional authenticity: of warmth on the one hand, sturm und drang on the other. (One can't help but thinking here of such later texts that defined the Jewish family in this loaded guise: not only Portnoy, in which Alex is astonished when he visits the Iowa home of the shikse girlfriend he names the Pilgrim to discover that, in some families, people don't shout at each other, but of the split screen in Woody Allen's *Annie Hall*, in which the emotional repression of the Hall clan is vividly contrasted with the outrageous volubility of Alvy Singer's Jewish family.) But such was also her connection to other ethnicities across the board: during her relationship with DiMaggio, she also bonded quite powerfully with DiMaggio's sister and mother, a relation lasting well after her marriage ended. And, if the rumors of her relations with Robert as well as John Kennedy are true, she took the complex and intense dynamics of family (as well as the classic account of ethnic families as incestuous, inbred) to new heights.

But it's with respect to the assimilation narrative that I see the conjunction of Monroe and whitening ethnics at its most powerful and socially contumacious: for the qualities she validated for the larger culture helped conduce to the mainstreaming of the ethnic, the accommodation of the previously Other to larger, emergent patterns of social value. The narrative I associate with DiMaggio, for example, focuses on the body and, more generally, athletics as modes of accommodation to dominant norms (think of the role that boxing and baseball as objects of immigrant self-definition serve in Cahan's *Yekl*: the upwardly mobile characters identify with the Yankees, the working-class ones like Jake with the rough-and-tumble sport of boxing). Baseball is a fine case in point; dominated by rural whites in its first instantiations, major league baseball teams were largely located in big cities with large immigrant populations: New York, Boston, Detroit, Cleveland. German-originated ethnics became stars in the 1920s—Babe Ruth and Lou Gehrig are classic examples; Jews entered into prominence in the 1930s (Hank Greenberg, who starred for the Detroit Tigers, famously hesitated to play on Yom Kippur in the 1934 World Series) as, even more powerfully, did Italian Americans, particularly on the New York Yankees: Phil Rizzuto, Tony Lazzerrii, as well as Joe Di Maggio were the great stars of the greatest teams of the post-Gehrig era, and, as if miming the parade of white ethnic succession in the U.S., with DiMaggio taking over the mantle of starhood from the aging, sick Gehrig. And, of course, as such the career of baseball powerfully enhances the salience of the whiteness argument, since these figures, however ethnically marked, hazed, and even discriminated against, were at least allowed to play in the Big Leagues, while baseball players of equal or greater ability who happened to be black were consigned to the lesser-paid, but in many ways higher-quality, Negro Leagues until the 1950s.

Of all these, DiMaggio bore a special cachet, one betokened by his nickname, the Yankee Clipper: his athleticism, his long and elegant strides, his putative patriotism (DiMaggio, of course, devoted some of the best years of his career to military service, although not so enthusiastically as his PR would suggest): all these affiliated him with an ideal of athletic ease associated with the WASP rather than with the bodily *hexis* of the sweaty, exerting, or even dissolute ethnic. Spectacularly successful, he never tried too hard—or never seemed to; rather, his game on the field and at the plate was predicated on his grace, his patience, his calm and ease. Although he did have other, less favorable nicknames—Dago was the monicker by which he was known by his teammates—the Yankee Clipper appellation bestowed upon him by the Yankee broadcaster sutured these abilities onto a mythic, WASP-centered narrative of American identity. That this fisherman's son from San Francisco could embody both the bodily ideal and the putative adventuring spirit of the New England Yankee ratified (as he enacted physically) the narrative of assimilation that was being performed throughout American culture in the 1940s and 1950s—and was being theorized by Jewish social scientists on the model of the Jewish American experience. Likewise, the circle we might associate with the Kennedys betokens the classic assimilation story, but one centering on politics (not untouched with a previous generation's criminality)— on power, accumulated and exercised—rather than sports. The story of the Kennedy family is almost as well known as that of DiMaggio (or for that matter Monroe) and I won't go into it here, except to note that the rise of the Kennedy family was itself a manifestation of the move into respectability of a once stigmatized ethnicity. With respect to this issue, to be sure, scholarship tends to fall into two camps: one emphasizing Kennedy's assimilation to Americanness as part of the melting-pot ideology and his family's continued and continuing sense of their Irishness—their conditions of outsiderhood in America that no amount of success at Choate or Harvard, not even the presidency, would ever ameliorate. Of course, this doesn't need to pose itself as an either/or; these may, in fact, prove to be two different ways of looking at the same thing: what better triumph than claiming for oneself the status as representative of the melting pot itself? And Kennedy chic, to call it by its proper name, involved, as did the cult of the Yankee Clipper, the stapling of a narrative of white ethnicity onto a WASP model of cultural authority: what is Camelot but a mythic tale of the origins of the British, and therefore most definitively *not* the Irish, nation? To remind ourselves that Kennedy did much to craft this image for himself (he was, from childhood, a life-long admirer of the Knights of the Round Table as well as, in his adulthood, of the uber-Brit James Bond) is, of course, simply to reassert the terms of the problem.

But however one construes it, the ascension of John Fitzgerald Kennedy represented a moment in American life that is of profound importance: the mainstreaming not just of a man but of a cultural ideal, that of white ethnicity itself, of peoples who, as recently as a previous generation, were seen as lesser, primitive, drunkards, lesser than or off-white. As Matthew Jacobson has recently reminded us, Kennedy himself did much to craft this myth: penning a book entitled *A Nation of Immigrants*, visiting his ancestral home in Ireland, and so on.[24] And while it may not have been fully perceived as such at the time by the U.S. publicity machine—those responsible for promulgating the WASPy Camelot mythos—it was as an ethnic hero that Kennedy was viewed by his fellow ethnics, especially white ethnic intellectuals. In beautifully crafted paragraphs from *Beyond the Melting Pot*, for example, Daniel Patrick Moynihan celebrates, very soon after Kennedy's death, Kennedy as representing as much the much reviled Irish political machine of the past rather than the advent of modern celebrity politics of the future. Had Kennedy lived, he might have represented a "new American style, combining . . . the tribal vigor of ward politics with the deft perceptions of the chancellor. But he is gone," Moynihan laments, "and there is none like him.

> The era of the Irish politician culminated in Kennedy. He was born to the work and at every stage in his life a "pro." He rose on the willing backs of three generations of district leaders and county chairmen who, like the Good Thief, may in the end have been saved for their one

moment of recognition that something special had appeared among them. That moment was in 1960 when the Irish party chieftans of the great Eastern and Midwestern cities, for reasons they could probably even now not fully explain, came together to nominate for President the grandson of Honey Fitz.

It was the last hurrah. He, the youngest and newest, served in a final moment of ascendancy. On the day he died, the President of the United States, the Speaker of the House of Representatives, the Majority Leader of the United States Senate, the Chairman of the National Committee were all Irish, all Catholic, all Democrats. It will not come again.[25]

Conflating a wide variety of texts and myths—Kennedy is at once compared to Frank Skeffingon, the defeated Irish machine boss mayor of Frank O'Connor's magnificent 1956 novel, *The Last Hurrah*, and Christ himself—Moynihan situates Kennedy's apotheosis in an ethnically specific drama of Christian triumph and sacrifice, one bundled simultaneously with the Irish immigrant experience in America, machine politics, and Catholic dogma. His is, in other words, a narrative that connects Kennedy not just to Irishness, but to a whole panoply of histories, belief systems, and collective experiences—to ethnicity in the broadest sense of the word: in some sense, he dies to redeem the Barabbas-like corrupt pols who were so intimate a part of the Irish American experience.

Although he is more poetic than most, Moynihan is not alone in the associations of Kennedy with a larger collective drama that conflated ethnicity and religion. Consider, for example, a classic political science study from the era, *John F. Kennedy and American Catholicism*, written in 1967 by Lawrence Fuchs of Brandeis (later in his career the author of *The American Kaleidoscope*, a summa of 1980s thinking about race and ethnicity). Although the book is deeply shaped by some of the now superannuated assumptions of American studies and history of the period (Perry Miller is a particularly strong influence, for example), it remains undeniably powerful in its understanding of the ways in which Irishness and Catholicism alike function in terms of the dominant "Arminian-Pelagianism of America's culture-religion": a "culture-religion" that doesn't admit, as the Catholic and Irish do, of the tragic and the collective in their predications of human identity and destiny and that moreover has lost its original ordering religious frame, leaving American subjects foundering in a morass of individualist self-definition and self-doubt.* Writing very much as a "Jew by birth and conviction who has long been interested in politics and religion in America," Fuchs binds Kennedy's legacy in America to the messy project of accommodating others from around the world in the process of becoming American, which Fuchs understands in terms unusually complicated for his own time: "no metaphor yet invented describes the process: neither a melting pot, pressure cooker, nor rainbow" (244). But the heart of that process remains a fundamental dialectic between identity categories that know themselves as such (Jew, Catholic, Irish) and a postreligious culture that maintains, in and through its individualist ethos, the Protestant drama of doubt, election, in the theater of isolated, individual self-definition.

What Fuchs and Moynihan identified on a ethnoreligious-political level—Kennedy's connection to a larger collective drama (Fuchs almost goes so far as to call it *tribal,* the very term that Miller used to describe his Jewishness at roughly the same time)—is what Monroe sought on the level of intimate life, and not just with Kennedy but with all the ethnic men with whom she was emotionally and/or sexually involved. (The list, it should be said here, was longer than just the three I have been foregrounding in this chapter: it includes Joe Schneck, her first Hollywood agent and lover; Elia Kazan, whom as we have seen was passionately involved with her when she met Miller; Frank Sinatra, with whom she was friends for many years and an on-again, off-again lover; or even—or especially—her controlling psychiatrist Dr. Ralph Greenson, née Romeo Samuel Greenschpoon.) We can read the ethnoracial dimension of Monroe's desiring life, in other words, in sociological terms; view her not as a pathological case, a fascinating and sexy aberration from the psychic norm, but rather as an archetypal subject in an America whose "culture-religion"—a radical individualism growing out of Protestantism and enhanced as it spins into the turbodrive of a capitalist economy—hypostatizes the conditions an assimilating European Jew, Emile Durkheim, described

---

* Roughly put, Pelagianism is the fifth-century doctrine, deemed heretical, that all people did *not* fall with Adam; that each individual is given the choice as to whether to withstand sin or succumb to it. Arminianism is the belief that God gives each of us the choice as to whether to accept or reject Him. Both, Fuchs is arguing, replace the Calvinist core of American Puritanism with emphasis on the individual's freedom of choice, as opposed to the dismal drama of election. Fuchs, *John F. Kennedy and American Catholicism* (New York: Meredith, 1967).

as "anomie": a society in which individuals are cut off from communal or for that matter any sense of interconnection and, with it, the sense of limitation on the boundless, but unfulfillable, desires imposed by belonging to a group larger than oneself. And to do this is to understand more fully the historical and cultural implications of Monroe's desiring life: that if Marilyn is a metonymy for whiteness, her desires are a synecdoche of white desires for ethnicity across the board.

As for the first of these: floating in radical suspension in a social world bereft of regulation—external or internal—the anomic subject is, Durkheim argues, prone to precisely the kinds of behavior that Monroe both exemplified and died from: that excess of choices, that minimum of constraints, that "erethic" enhancement of desires of all sorts without any hint of satisfaction, led to what Durkheim called "anomic suicide."*

> Nothing gives satisfaction and all this agitation is uninterruptedly maintained without appeasement.... All classes contend among themselves because no established classification any longer exists. Effort grows, just when it becomes less productive. How could the desire to live not be weakened under such conditions?[26]

I cite Durkheim here but I could also of course have cited another assimilated Jew, Freud, whose understanding of constraints internal and external is interestingly cognate with the former's (what Durkheim calls *regulation* Freud calls the *superego*). I do so not so much to define Monroe's drama in "Jewish" or "ethnic" terms (although shortly I'll do just that) but to see in its full dialectical force the drive or quest that I would argue is at the core of her desire for these ethnic men or, to be more precise—because "desire" implies an individual libidinal cathexis that I'm

---

*Implicit in my argument is my belief that Marilyn either committed suicide or, more likely, got into such a stuporous condition that she overdosed on barbiturates. Mailer was the first to suggest that there are a number of inconsistencies in the testimony about the night of her death; the implication that Monroe was murdered by some unknown assassin, presumably to conceal her relationship with the president and/or attorney general has flourished in the years after *Marilyn*. I can't rule out this understanding of her death—but my argument here doesn't depend on cleaving to the suicide option, since the last years of her life were marked by a downward spiral (drug addiction, thanks to her unusually inept analyst; unusually self-destructive sexual liaisons, etc.) consistent with suicidal impulses, if not actually eventuating in them.

trying to complicate here—the structures of social experience that she tried to access through her encounter with them. It's too easy, in other words, merely to read her desire for these ethnic men as being motivated by the thrill of exogamy, although I think that thrill runs through not only her experience but also that of a good deal of the work on ethnic whiteness. It's perhaps a little harder, but nevertheless well within the bounds of the familiar discourse on Monroe, to read her as a poor little orphan girl searching among these ethnic men for the family she never knew. Again, there's more than a little truth to this reading; but the Marilyn-just-wanted-a-family explanation for her marriages is not incompatible with the Durkheimian reading that I'm offering here, since Durkheim sees the breaking down of family bonds as one of the factors most resoundingly conducive to "anomic suicide." But neither of these quite plausible etiologies encompasses, I think, the common denominator in all these cases, a denominator that extends beyond desire altogether or rather expands it from the libido or the unconscious into the social and binds them together: the urge to connect oneself with history, community, connection itself. For all these were understood in the 1940s and 1950s through the conceptual vehicle of ethnicity, which was constructed by Jewish and Irish American intellectuals in particular as a turning to an alternative to the anomic "Pelagian-Arminian" culture of radical individualism.

What I am suggesting (with full knowledge of its discursive oddness) is that what Monroe was in search of in her relations with these ethnic men was a social hermeneutic as much as family, or respectability, or even the additional kick of systematic exogamy. Tossed into the anomic hurly-burly of postwar America, she sought to make her life mean something—anything—first in the context of a culture, Hollywood, that provided one such heavily ethnicized structure and another, the Broadway of the Actor's Studio, of which very much the same can be said, and then in that free-floating world of the bicoastal celebrity. In doing so, not uncoincidentally, she turned as well to another meaning system, psychoanalysis, that was read in her time, and mutatis mutandis in our own, as a "Jewish science."*

---

*The phrase was also used to insult Durkheim and his circle, and at roughly the same time that it was applied to Freud; see Ivan Strenski, *Durkheim and the Jews of France* (Chicago: University of Chicago Press, 1997), p. 6. Strenski's point here, it should be said, is to disar-

(Her analyst's analyst, with whom he consulted considerably about her case, was none other than Anna Freud.) Along the way, she was drawn, most important of all, to men who would provide some kind of metanarrative of experience and identity in the everything's-up-for-grabs world of postwar America—access to history, to transindividual structures of identity, to community itself. With all of them, for example, she bound herself into the ethnic assimilation narrative, if only as the prize who legitimated that project; with Miller she bound herself into the agenda (also apparent in her self-refashioning via the Actors Studio) of self-remaking through the acquisition of cultural capital; with the Kennedys in the project of gaining political power as a means of self-legitimation; with DiMaggio, with the mythos of the physically superior immigrant supplanting the attenuated modalities of WASP manhood. In all of this endeavor, more saliently for our argument, she persistently bound herself to group identity, to collective structures, whether political, social, or religious, ideological, or therapeutic. It was a moment of great cultural as well as individual significance in America when a girl raised by a mother who was a devotee of Christian Science and Aimee Semple McPherson converted to Judaism: it can be taken, among all the other things it might mean, as a paradigm of the collapse of an ultraindividualist, free-floating post-Calvinist religiosity, what Harold Bloom calls "the American religion"—the near gnostic belief in the individual's confrontation with the Godhead—and a collective, communally based ethnoreligious identity. One could also read her avid participation in liberal politics with the Kennedy brothers in the same light, as a quest to join a party and a political project that was associated with ethnic politics, big-city machines, the assertion of communal—of tribal—values. Similarly, one can even read her long engagement with a pan-ethnic (even pan-racial) group, the Rat Pack of Sinatra, Dean Martin, Sammy Davis, and Peter Lawford that facilitated her original access to John Kennedy, in these lights. In all these cases Monroe turned away from the anomic individualism of her own chaotic upbringing toward structures that emphasize community, collectivity, historical embeddedness,

---

ticulate Durkheim from the connection with Jews or Jewishness, although he was part of a circle of intellectuals of Jewish descent, including Marcel Mauss. Strenski argues that Durkheim's thought is to be considered outside the vague sociologism that would impute religious characteristics to his musings on sacrifice or community.

and rootedness—all the things that ethnics were going to discover about themselves years later.

And, to give the screw one last turn, in this project the role of Jewishness is, as I have been stressing throughout this book, key. For the legitimating narratives by which ethnicity itself rose to the fore in the 1950s and 1960s, of which Monroe's quest was both a part and an example, were largely by Jewish commentators who have joined gentile societies, as did Durkheim, Freud, and Fuchs by Seymour Martin Lipset, Milton Gordon, Daniel Bell, Nathan Glazer, Will Herberg. To be sure, not all of these were Jews: Daniel Patrick Moynihan, to cite one towering counterexample, is perhaps the most important, and culturally as well as politically significant writer on ethnicity from this period. But, taken at large, what's striking about the writing of this period was that it analyzed ethnicity in its confrontation with American society in terms that referred back to, and hypostatized, the quite anomalous experience of Jews: that put family, education, assimilation at the center of the cultural narratives associated with the drama of success or failure of ethnic or racial groups. And, not coincidentally, this critical work grew out of a culture created, nurtured, and sustained by assimilated Jews. Consider the (still quite influential in policy circles, if universally derided in academic ones) example of Moynihan and Glazer's *Beyond the Melting Pot*, written the same year as Monroe's and Kennedy's death, 1963. Glazer—already the author of two studies that emphasized Jewish cultural experience in the making of a distinct, postimmigrant ethnic identity—was asked to coordinate a study of New York's ethnic communities by James Weschler, then editor of the liberal-left *New York Post*, whose ethnocultural resonance we have already had occasion to discuss above. He expanded the articles into a book, supported not only by the New York Post Foundation but also with aid provided by Martin Meyerson, head of the Joint Center for Urban Studies at Harvard and MIT. Glazer undertook to write the sections on the Jewish community; he asked Daniel Bell to suggest an Irish American to write on New York's Irish, and Bell recommended Moynihan. (The sections on Italian American, African American, and Puerto Rican communities, the controversial emphasis on family as a marker of social success or failure, and the even more controversial prophecy that African Americans and Puerto Ricans would follow in the white ethnic path, were joint products.)

In other words, while ethnicity itself was being probed, analyzed, and privileged across the social board, liberal-left Jewish culture was at the epicenter of this privileging of white ethnicity—precisely the culture, I am arguing, to which Monroe turned either directly, via Miller, or indirectly, as she did through her ventures into psychoanalysis or the Actors Studio. As Jacobson has shown quite convincingly, the road thereby gets paved for the so-called ethnic revival of the 1970s to eventuate in the rise of neoconservatism, of the privileging of this model of "ethnic bootstrapping" and upward mobility via educational achievement, with consequences for the attack on affirmative action, the enrollment of the model minority model, and the withering of the welfare state whose consequences we are living with today. What he doesn't say—perhaps out of politeness—is that, throughout this latter work, Jews are frequently instanced as the first among equals, the most model of ethnic minorities, the group whose continuing ethnic cohesion, attachment to family, bootstrapping, and entrepreneurial spirit can and should provide a paradigm for other ethnic communities. (We'll trace the consequences of this identification with respect to Asian Americans more fully in chapter 6.)

But this is still to beg the central question I am posing here—how did this model come to be persuasive not to the white ethnics themselves, but to the white Protestant majority? Jacobson ends his account of this process not with Michael Dukakis's disastrous 1988 campaign, but with George Bush's successful appropriation of the neoconservative privileging of family, ethnic community, and even the model of gemeinschaft observable in the white ghettos of the first half of the twentieth century. He doesn't linger (long) on the oddity of a patrician WASP claiming for his own narrative the very antithesis of his own experience, which tended to the country clubs and Old Boy institutions that systematically excluded Jews and other white ethnics—Andover, Yale, the CIA, the Republican Party—turning instead to demonstrate how the Bush campaign used the angle of race and nativism to disarticulate the bootstrapping ethos from the experience of the majority of white Americans. But perhaps looking at the process through the lens of Marilyn Monroe rather than George Bush Sr., and at the beginning of the process of the privileging of ethnicity rather than its end, can help us see it more richly—can help us see the mixture of ideology and desire, belief system and appetency, that impelled the privileging of the ethnic by the nonethnic. At the very least, reminding us of her headline-grabbing liaisons with ethnic men would rewrite the reprivileging of white ethnicity as a collaboratively constructed fiction, shaped not only by those ethnics themselves—although they undeniably did that—but by nonethnic white people who came to those ethnics for specific things they came to feel were missing in their own increasingly anomic postwar experience. As what existed of traditional communities splintered via suburbanization, the rise of the freeway system pushing people into farther and farther-flung suburbs, as capitalism reached its Fordist apotheosis and traditional, defining antagonisms (labor versus capital) broke down into ambiguous new class structures, as mass postwar education helped to create what some theorists have called a new professional-managerial class, as the rise of white-collar employment in heavily bureaucratized corporations created a host of (or at least a discourse about a host of) alienated organization men, as the Arminian-Pelagian dramas of American Protestantism seemed increasingly inadequate to a post-Holocaust world—at the moment, in other words, that has been evoked for us by the likes of William Whyte, Sloan Wilson, and C. Wright Mills—white nonethnic Americans started to turn via figures like DiMaggio, Miller, and Kennedy (not to mention Sinatra) to cultural narratives and social projects not their own.[27] Or, at the very least, they began to enthrall themselves with the spectacle of Monroe, perhaps the first and certainly the greatest cynosure of the enlarged celebrity culture emerging after the war, not only coupling with but linking herself to the social projects of white ethnics, thereby helping to position them as objects of esteem, value, and, most important, desire. Indeed, it is perhaps the last of these that is the most enduringly significant. Via Monroe, the Italian athlete, the Irish politician, the Jewish intellectual, and all the values and cultural possibilities associated with them, didn't just become legitimated: they became fashionable, cool, even sexy.

Plugging Monroe, and with Monroe the swirling currents of desire, into the discourse on whiteness then, allows us to identify the libidinal impetus behind the reconstruction of American ethnicity. It shows us that the so-called "ethnic revival" is not only a bid to weave new ideological justifications for the ideological state apparatus that produces "America"—now remade on the multiethnic plan as a "nation of immigrants." For, before America could be reconstructed as a "nation of immigrants," before the ethnic could become fully white, before the national drama could be identified with that of assimilation, before Irish pols could become

Christ figures and Jews a routine part of the national conversation, normative Americans had to fall in love with white ethnics in general, and Jews in particular, as passionately and as problematically as did their archetypal representative—the most "unambiguously white you could get"—Marilyn Monroe.

3. ANTISEMITISM WITHOUT JEWS
Left Behind in the American Heartland

EVERY NOW AND THEN, I teach a course entitled "Jewish and Other Others," and, to remind my largely assimilated, predominantly Jewish students that Jews were once something other than comfortable suburbanites like themselves, I begin with a conceptual tour upon which I now invite the reader of this chapter. I am writing these words from my office at the University of Michigan in Ann Arbor—a leftist enclave in a liberal town in a moderately conservative "battleground" state. Forty miles or so east of here is the city of Dearborn, Michigan, in which Henry Ford published the *Dearborn Independent* in the 1920s—a notorious venue for the publication of a number of antisemitic articles and editorials, many of them adapting to the U.S. context the notorious slurs of *The Protocols of the Elders of Zion*. Although Ford publicly recanted his antisemitism (the sincerity of that recantation is much debated by historians), its effects linger on. A compendium of slanders issued by his press, *The International Jew* (1920–22), is still available for sale through numerous extreme right-wing organizations (e. g., the Liberty Lobby) and can be easily downloaded online from such venues as possecomitatus.com or jewwatch.com ("Keeping a Close Watch on Jewish Communities and Organizations Worldwide").

Ten miles farther northeast stands the town of Royal Oak, now a trendy suburb but once a working-class enclave whose Shrine of the Little Flower Church was the site from which Father Charles Coughlin made his radio addresses in the 1930s—addresses that began with a brand of Christian socialism directed at his Depression-scarred audience but that turned to outright antisemitic slurs, including the continuing propagation of the *Protocols* libel along with perfervid denunciations of Roosevelt, the New Deal, and those who would bring America to war against Germany. And his endeavors even extended to what we today would call terrorism. In addition to (perhaps) being involved in a plot to overthrow the government of Mexico, (probably) taking money from the Nazi regime, and (undoubtedly) building close ties to the Nazi-supported German-American Bund,

Coughlin's organization horded a cache of armaments—or so claimed the FBI when they raided his headquarters in 1941, although for what end the guns were intended remains murky.

Shortly thereafter, Coughlin rapidly became too much of an embarrassment even for his indulgent superiors and was reined in, falling into obscurity. So too did another radio minister, the Protestant Gerald L. K. Smith, whose fulminations against Jews and in favor of a Protestant-dominated America were nationally broadcast on Detroit's powerful WJR and who won thirty-six thousand Michigan votes in the presidential election of 1936. But the connection between right-wing politics, antisemitism, and terrorism lives on a few miles farther away from my comfortable office. About a hundred miles to the northeast of Royal Oak is the so-called Thumb of Michigan, a peninsula sticking out into Lake Huron consisting largely of farmland. Relatively impoverished since the rural depression of the 1970s and 1980s, the Thumb is one home of the so-called Michigan Militia, a group devoted to the proposition that America is governed by a cabal of Jews they call the Zionist Occupational Government. It is also the home of Terry Nichols, Militia-inspired coperpetrator of the second most heinous terrorist act committed to date on American soil, the Oklahoma City bombing. And just to conclude this litany of heartland antisemitism, indeed to bring it, as it were, back home, the janitor in the building in which I write these words was (until he was imprisoned) Mark from Michigan, one of the chief spokesmen for the Militia: an extreme right-wing ideologue broadcasting his survivalist, antigovernment, and anti-ZOG views on short-wave radio when not emptying my wastebasket.

To be sure, this area is somewhat exceptional; it would be hard to find such a rich archive of antisemitic hatred in other parts of the country. Hard, but not impossible: for, as I will be suggesting here, the map of Southeast Michigan I have sketched can provide a template for some of the varieties of antisemitism that have flourished in America and a suggestion as well of why the people reading this volume might not recognize it any more than I did Mark from Michigan before he rose to notoriety in the wake of Oklahoma City bombing. This is not to say that the area is still visibly full of these sentiments. Terry Nichols faces execution for his role in Oklahoma City; Mark from Michigan is safely tucked away in the state prison on a spectacular driving violation (fearing that a routine traffic violation was a ZOG-inspired arrest, he sped away from police, crossed the median, and attempted to escape by driving the wrong way on Interstate 94 at the height of rush hour); the militia movement is in a decade-long decline, presumably because of revulsion against its spasm of violence. Father Couglin's Shrine of the Little Flower Church has been replaced by megachurches in farther-flung suburbs, where a form of philosemitic—or at least pro-Israel—commitment is established fare on the theological menu. But this is not to say that antisemitism has disappeared—to the contrary. The set of narratives and images, predications and associations that construct and define classic American antisemitism is undergoing renovation and is moving from the fringe—from the likes of Terry Nichols and Mark from Michigan—back into the center in ways not seen since the days of Ford and Coughlin. And, in this new guise, it is all the more powerful, in that it is being actively refitted for use against a variety of Semites, real and imagined.

An excellent case in point is the flourishing of the most popular series of books in contemporary America by far, the so-called Left Behind series. Coauthored by Christian Right theologian and activist Timothy LaHaye and prolific free-lancer Jerry Jenkins, the books combine apocalyptic theology with science fiction and motifs; they have sold quite literally tens of millions of copies (their publicity copy trumpets an astonishing sixty-five million). Vended by their canny publisher, Tyndale House, in Wal-Marts and Costcos, they are advertised not in the trade press, or even the mainstream press at all, but through such innovative means as the sponsorship of a NASCAR vehicle and aggressive and innovative use of the Web. (On the Left Behind Web site, for example, one can not only participate in chat rooms devoted to theological questions raised by the series or discussions of one's favorite character; one can also sign up to receive a daily e-mail from Timothy LaHaye himself giving a prophetic gloss of the day's news.) They exist, that is to say, outside the organs of official cultural dissemination and thus have, until recently, remained unseen in the venues that define the cultural sphere for most upper-middle-class Americans and certainly for most academics (although, as Rachel Donadio has reported in the *New York Observer*, Random House has signed a blockbuster multimillion dollar deal with the pair for a new series of Christian fantasy-novels).[1] The novels are intensely interested (as is the religious right at large) in Jews generally and in the State of Israel specifically as intimate, if not essential, parts of the story of Christianity itself. They are, to a certain extent, signs of the increasingly palpable philosemitism on the Christian right, although, given their emphasis on the conversion of the Jews as a necessary precondition of the Apocalypse, this is a philosemitism of which Jews might wish to be wary. But the classic antisemitism that also circulates in the American populist imaginary, that has left its traces all over Southeast Michigan and in extremist groups whom LaHaye and Jenkins disavow, doesn't disappear in these books. Despite, or perhaps even because of, their ostensible philosemitism, the basic narrative structures and figurative associations that have marked antisemitic discourse—that, in fact, define it *as* a discourse in the Foucauldian sense of the word—remain strikingly in place. Indeed, they are effectively reanimated, retrofitted for a seemingly tolerant, multicultural age, for tactical reasons that I will be discussing more extensively at the end of this chapter. And, I would further assert, as a result, these antisemitic topoi are thereby rendered all the more dangerous and potentially effective.

For those who have not had the pleasure of reading the novels that make up the Left Behind series, let me offer a brief synopsis of their narrative arc. In the first (and best, although that's not saying much) of the novels, *Left Behind* (1995), pilot Rayford Steele, alienated from his wife by her increasing interest in Christianity and flirting with a beautiful stewardess, Hattie Durham, finds that his passengers—and millions of other people, including his wife and beloved son—have disappeared from the face of the earth. Later he discovers that they have been carried to heaven in the Rapture, the first stage in the seven-year process in which Christ returns to earth to smite his enemies and found a thousand-year kingdom on earth. Meanwhile, star journalist Cameron "Buck" Williams witnesses an amazing event. In a newly secure, demilitarized Israel—after its deserts have turned to arable land, thanks to the invention of superscientist, Nobel-prize-winning biologist Chaim Rosenzweig, it has made peace with its neighbors, whom it supplies with food and technical know-how—he witnesses a sneak attack by a suddenly (if inexplicably) desperate Soviet Union. But, before their planes could drop their bombs, they are all vaporized by a mysterious source that can only be supernatural in origin. Soon thereafter, Rosenzweig—the archetypal secular liberal—schemes with British financier Jonathan Stonagal to name as secretary general of the United Nations an ambitious Romanian politician named Nicholae Carpathia. Once elected—indeed, he is ushered into office by a starstruck United States president—Carpathia promulgates worldwide disarmament, a universal currency, and, ultimately, a universal religion that just happens to apotheosize him as its leader. Carpathia, of course, turns out to be none other than the Antichrist, a fact that Steele, Williams, and a small band of other believers organized around an evangelical congregation in suburban Chicago are among the few to recognize. Indeed, his powers are founded on a form of mind control to which only committed Christians are immune. As a somewhat gratuitous demonstration of his power, he kills Jonathan Stonagal in front of the United Nations and the assembled press, then hypnotizes all but Williams into believing that they have witnessed a murder-suicide.

Steele, Williams, their friends, relatives, and fellow congregationalists form a small band of guerrilla fighters, known as the Tribulation Force, to resist Carpathia's new world order, a band later joined by a former student of Rosenzweig's named Tsion Ben-Judah, a brilliant rabbinical scholar who proves that Christ has returned as Messiah, after which he promptly and publicly converts to Christianity on Global CNN. Ben-Judah becomes the spiritual leader of the resistance, issuing interpretations of the swirling world events that form the background of the battle between Carpathia's Global Community and the Tribulation Force—earthquakes, plagues, wars, and so on, which succeed in wiping out half the world's population in no time. (Indeed, through his television appearances and Internet-disseminated commentaries, he becomes such an important spiritual adviser to the world at large that all those who come to accept Christ are known as Judah-ites.) The books of the series trace the battle in ways that make it resemble a sci-fi epic—think of a Christian version of Robert Heinlein's *The Past through Tomorrow* series crossed with earlier installments of the *Star Wars* movies. But they also play out a version of the seven years of Tribulation allegedly foretold in Revelation, as interpreted for the growing band of Christian converts in the Tribulation-suffering world— and for the readers of the series itself—by Ben-Judah. Thus when, midway through the series, Carpathia is killed in a public square—initially, it is thought that Williams has committed the crime, but it is actually accomplished by the wily Rosenzweig, who has faked a stroke in order to approach Carpathia with a sword concealed in his wheelchair—Ben-Judah prepares the faithful for Carpathia's resurrection and fervent attempts at revenge, both of which happen like clockwork. And he continues to guide the Tribulation Force and the entire world through the increasingly frenzied events that presage the final battle between a newly returned Christ and Carpathia and his minions, a battle in which the dialogue and narrative teetering, for this reader at least, on the edge of self-parody, pass over the edge into outright raving loony tunes. It's one thing to tolerate long pages of exegeses of biblical prophecy from the increasingly loquacious Ben-Judah (who is killed defending Jerusalem in the penultimate book in the series) or his exegetical successors—a black minister in Detroit and the newly converted Rosenzweig, who assumes the role of a Jewish prophet/leader named Micah. It's another actually to witness a deadpan account in Tom Clancyesque prose of the Apocalypse and the Last Judgment in which Christ appears to smite all his enemies, separate the sheep and the goats, and consign the latter (the millions who have somehow managed to survive the Tribulation) into the pit of Hell, where they remain for a thousand years before a *final* Last Judgment. Indeed, in a teaser conclusion, we learn of Satan's possible escape from the fetters to which he has been consigned, setting up the possibility of a renewal of the whole cycle of temptation and Fall—and the possibilities of a new set of sequels, conveniently supplied by the team of LaHaye and Jenkins in their recently-released *Kingdom Come: The Final Victory* (2007).

Techno-thriller and theology, in other words, vie with each other as representational modes, with the latter increasingly taking over the lead as the series continues, although the former continues to have a strong role to play: for example, the Tribulation Force hacks into the Global CNN feed to broadcast news of Christ's arrival or, on a more mundane note, the Redeemed consult their still-working wristwatches to marvel at how long it takes Christ to parade the saints of heaven before them. And there is a third modality in the series, one that, I think, is equally important to its success, its exploration of what we might want to call Christian depth psychology. The genius of the series is in focusing on the responses to the Rapture and the subsequent Final Days of those "left behind"—that is, of those who are not yet fully believing Christians and are not called up to heaven in the Rapture. Their complex responses to the loss of their loved ones—their mixture of grief, anger, incomprehension, and a dawning sense of respect for the commitment that has taken their wives, their children, their husbands from them—clearly strikes a chord in the millions who have read the books, people who are similarly struggling to reconcile their faith with their practical lives, ambitions, fears. So does the continuing focus (familiar from the Protestant tradition of narratives of self-examination) on the internal lives of those Left Behind. In her reader-response study of the series, *Rapture Culture*, Amy Johnson

Frykholm focuses us on the Hawthornesque example of Minister Bruce Barnes, who realizes at the moment of the Rapture that, for all of his faith and erudition, he has too much pride in his own accomplishments to be worthy of being unfolded onto Christ.[2] But internal struggle is evident in many of the book's central characters. Williams spends much of the series in increasing self-doubt about his capacities as a newly found Christian as well as a leader of men; he agonizes about not only his soul, but his capacities as a self-assigned assassin of Carpathia, an act that he must finally leave to Rosenzweig to accomplish. Or we witness the internal conflict of Chang, the teenage computer genius who serves as the Tribulation Force's technological mole in the center of the Global Community's media network. Through various plot turns, he wears both the Mark of the Beast and the Mark of the Saved, and he spends much time agonizing about whether he will be among those who are saved (as of course, he turns out to be). This emphasis on internal conflict is so marked that, when Christ returns, He not only scourges the wicked, but speaks in personal terms to each of the characters about the feelings that have been troubling them. Appropriate to our thoroughly therapeutic culture, this Christ heals their traumatized psyches as well as their physical wounds.

Given this canny attunement to the reading and life experiences of a contemporary American lower middle to middle class (the people who regularly shop at Costco and Wal-Mart or watch NASCAR races), the persistence in the series of the *structures* of antisemitic expression, the topoi and plot structures of antisemitic discourse, is all the more striking. But before we turn to this phenomenon, it's important to note that the novels are quite explicitly, even audaciously, philosemitic in a number of important ways. Some, of course, have to do with the privileging of the State of Israel, which has long served as a signal to Apocalypse-minded Christians of the arrival of the Final Days. Israel is spared a nuclear attack by divine intervention early in the first book; Carpathia's signing of a peace treaty with Israel on behalf of his one-world government (which is only a prelude to his invasion of it) signals the onset of the seven-year period of Tribulation; the rebuilding of the Temple is an important step in the unfolding of the End Times; the final battle between the forces of Good and Evil begins to unfold in the Old City of Jerusalem and climaxes as a million converted Jews hold out against the forces of the Antichrist in Petra, and so on. Indeed, the novel can not only be read as a form of "Christian Zionism," in the words of critic Melani McAlister;[3] it can even more explicitly be read as a kind of a synthesis of U.S. and Israeli right-wing paranoias and attendant political programs.[4] Israel may be protected by God, but it is betrayed by peace-loving liberals like Rosenzweig into unilaterally disarming itself.

And even more explicitly philosemitic is the crucial role played by Jews in the unfolding events of the Tribulation period. Although as nonbelievers they can't be carried up in the Rapture (unlike the pope, who must have been a secret Protestant), 144,000 Jews promptly convert and testify to the Messiah's return. The remaining Jews, however, continue to be crucial as witnesses of the first signs of Christ. The last few books are taken up with the enormous logistics of transporting the entire Israeli population to Petra, in the Jordanian desert, where, led by Rosenzweig/Micah they prepare to do final battle with the forces of the Antichrist. And, as the Antichrist's reign crumbles (the battle is totally anticlimactic, since all Jesus has to do is to show up and the forces massed against him drop dead), Chang sits "at his computer, staring at the reports coming in from all over the world about people, especially Jews, putting their faith in Jesus Christ as their Messiah" All the while, a hacked GCNN

> transmit[s]images of a tiny band of anti-Carpathia Jews kneeling amidst the lightning flashes [signs of the Second Coming] beneath an ancient Israeli flag, a Star of David, and a rough-hewn cross . . . thumbing their nose at the god of this world, boldly showing that they had never received the mark of loyalty to the supreme potentate, but had now staked their claim with Messiah.[5]

With its striking conjunction of the Israeli flag and the cross, this moment seems the very quintessence of what McAlister calls Christian Zionism. But it more powerfully testifies to the belief system that animates it, the centuries-long Protestant/eschatological belief that the conversion of the Jews is not only a desirable outcome in and of itself but also a necessary precondition for the unfolding of the Apocalypse. The two, to be sure, are linked: the ground of contemporary fundamentalist dispensationalist premillennialism—the American adaptation of the eschatological belief system first articulated by English itinerant preacher Joseph Derby in the 1820s—is the belief that the End Times were to be ushered in by the return of Jews to the Holy Land. As Bernard McGinn puts it, in the 1920s for the premillennialists the most significant event connected with World War I was not the epic struggle that cost millions of lives or the collapse of the Russian Empire and the Bolshevik Revolution, but rather the 1917 [Balfour Declaration].... In the words of one of the most important premillennialist spokesmen [John Valvoord, writing in 1990]: "The most significant prophetic event in the twentieth century has been the restoration of the people of Israel to their land." Not even the advent of the atomic bomb... had quite the same impact.[6]

But here matters with respect to Jews become murky. Some dispensationalist premillenarians cleave to the belief that the proper role of Jews is to prepare for the Apocalypse by founding the State of Israel—then either convert or get out of the way of the Second Coming. LaHaye and Jenkins, however, don't stop at this theologically familiar place, but extend the engagement with Jews into what looks like a definitively philosemitic polemic. In the didactic final pages of the last installment in the series lies the suggestion that some—indeed, many—Jews will not be confined to the pit of fire by the Last Judgment but rather admitted into the redeemed world *as* Jews. (They are, to be sure, exclusively Orthodox practicing Jews: as we shall see later, the secularity of the secular Jew remains fundamentally problematic for LaHaye and Jenkins.) And further, they even suggest that, on Judgment Day, gentiles will be sorted out on the basis of their treatment of the Jews. There is much to judge. In the later days of his reign, Carpathia and his chief henchman, Fortunato, launch a pogrom: "I will sanction, condone, support and reward the death of any Jew anywhere in the world," cries Fortunato: "Imprison them. Torture them. Humiliate them. Shame them. Blaspheme their god. Plunder anything they own."[7] And, as if the reference to antisemitic thuggery doesn't suffice to identify their specific form of evil, Carpathia explicitly invokes the Nazis when he calls the encampment of Jews in Petra "a concentration camp" (*Remnant*, 225). LaHaye and Jennings are clear that this racial and religious persecution is itself grounds for eternal punishment. "Some call this a Semitic judgment," says Eleazar, a wise Jew who speaks with the same authority as Ben-Judah at the end of the last novel in the series. "Jesus will judge you Gentiles on how you have treated His chosen people. Those who honored the Jews are the sheep, and those who did not are the goats" (*Glorious Appearing*, 388).

As if this weren't enough to make clear that they themselves would pass "the Semitic judgment," the authors also part company with one of the most egregious slurs in the evangelical roster: the claim that the Antichrist is himself a Jew. This association is virtually as old as the concept of the Antichrist itself—Bernard McGinn, in his authoritative survey of the Antichrist legend, dates this ascription to St. Jerome (c. AD 400), and, as Joshua Trachtenberg has reminded us, popular culture throughout the Middle Ages confidently identified the Antichrist as Jew.[8] With the Reformation, Catholic figures were slotted for the role, most importantly the Pope, Luther's candidate for the job. And it would be safe to say that the exact origins of the Antichrist remained hotly contested for much of the eighteenth and nineteenth centuries. But, as Robert Fuller observes in his fascinating study of the life of the Antichrist in Protestant America, U.S. evangelicals have startlingly little doubt about his lineage. "Although scholars had often vacillated between the Jewish or the Roman heritage of the end-times 'beast,'" he writes, "the matter was much less murky for mid-twentieth-century fundamentalists.... Arno Gaebelein, a much-respected premillennial writer, weighed the evidence and also concluded that Bible prophecy offers unmistakable proof that the antichrist will be a Jew."[9] Armed by the authoritative counsel of Gaebelein as well as a host of lesser figures, leading fundamentalists continue to cleave to this belief. Jerry Falwell, for example, caused a minor storm when he asserted in 1999 that the Antichrist was alive and that he was Jewish. (Falwell, needless to say, insisted that his claim was merely a matter of historical fact and not intended to cast aspersions on the Jewish people at large).

I cite this history to give a sense of just how audaciously LaHaye and Jenkins revise the fundamentalist tradition. Carpathia is not only represented as being un-Jewish, he is portrayed as the antithesis of the Jewish Antichrist. With blond hair and the features of a "young Robert Redford," Carpathia is visually coded a white Caucasian, despite his Middle European origins.[10] Indeed, the text goes to some lengths to suggest that he is an Italian-descended Romanian, which (also given the origins of the name Romania itself) I take to be a subtle invocation of a Luther-like identification of the Antichrist with the prelate of the Church of Rome as well as with the home of Dracula.[11]

To that extent, the text can be read not only as philosemitic in the traditional Protestant sense, in which the conversion of the Jews is needed to facilitate the Second Coming, but also in a more extravagant manner, one that contests some of the central tropes and topoi of the antisemitism of the evangelical fundamentalist Protestant tradition. But this is not to say that the text is free of antisemitic topoi; indeed, to the contrary. Jewish stereotypes of an almost startling crudeness recur throughout the text, sometimes attached to Jews, but more often, and more interestingly, floating free of them. As far as the former is concerned, consider the case of Rosenzweig. A brilliant scientist and a much revered figure—he complains that he can't walk the streets of his hometown, Jerusalem, without being besieged by well-wishers—Rosenzweig is also that familiar figure from antisemitic discourses: the political fixer, the would-be power behind the scenes. To confine ourselves to the U.S context, this accusation was a commonplace on the antisemitic right for the first fifty years of the last century; entering these shores with the republication of *The Protocols of the Elders of Zion* in the twenties, it was lodged against the likes of Bernard Baruch, the Jew in Roosevelt's kitchen cabinet; in the 1960s the same aspersions were made against Lyndon Johnson's right-hand man, Abe Fortas, in the Republican campaign to deny him a position as Chief Justice on the Supreme Court. Kindly and benign as he may be, Rosenzweig fills precisely this sinister role of Jewish power broker. He helps discover Carpathia while the latter is an obscure member of the Romanian parliament (apparently, one of Rosenzweig's hobbies is following even the most obscure political entities), becomes his conduit to the media elites—through his friendship with Smith, for example, he brokers an exclusive interview with Carpathia that is to benefit both men's careers—then serves as Carpathia's political adviser, naively seeking to advance the careers of Williams and Ben-Judah in his new world order, until he discovers the full extent of Carpathia's evil plans. The point is clear and not inconsistent with an explicitly antisemitic aspersion. It is through the efforts of the power-mongering Jew, no matter how well-meaning or naive he may be, that the Antichrist enters the political world.

This is not to say that Rosenzweig is an antisemitic caricature; to the contrary. But it is to suggest the strategy, conscious or unconscious, that LaHaye and Jenkins deploy throughout their books, to allude to, without endorsing, an identification that possesses a resonant and powerful antisemitic history. In so doing, they drain those associations of their worst antisemitic tonalities—it's impossible to read Rosenzweig as anything but a sympathetic figure—while deploying the energies they invoke. And through that process, powerful cultural, and ultimately political, work gets done.

In the case of Rosenzweig, for example, this work has less to do with invoking the historical association of the Jew as fixer than with the more labile and powerful identification of the Jew as intellectual. As with the topos of the power-broking Jew, this identification has a long history on the American right, or at least what one might want to call its populist wing, and it's one that the novels frequently invoke. As a cultured secular intellectual (one who takes an interest in such things as the Romanian houses of parliament), as an inventor of a revolutionary scientific process, as an all-around and revered genius, Rosenzweig embodies the stereotype Sander Gilman has described as the "smart Jew."[12] Indeed, the text, never subtle in its ethnoracial characterizations, represents him as the quintessence of the type: physically unprepossessing, schlumpy in dress, and European, not Sephardic, in appearance and origin: "wiry, clean shaven, slight, in his late sixties, pale for an Israeli, and with hazel eyes and wisps of wild white hair reminiscent of pictures of Albert Einstein. Normally, the decorated statesman and Nobel Prize winner wore wire-rimmed glasses, bulky sweaters, baggy trousers, and comfortable shoes."[13] Irritating as they are, such stereotypes are not necessarily antisemitic; they are, it might be said, one place where philo- and antisemitic inscriptions of the Jew meet and turn each other inside out. But that despite his intelligence Rosenzweig should turn out to be a dupe of the Antichrist suggests that, from LaHaye and Jenkins's point of view, he is a *too* smart Jew, a Jew who is the bearer of poisoned intellectual fruits.

What is at stake for the authors in this dual response to the Jew's putative intellectual superiority is made clear in an inadvertently hilarious interview that LaHaye gave in 1999 to a Jewish reporter, Jeffrey Goldberg:

"Some of the greatest evil in the history of the world was concocted in the Jewish mind," LaHaye told me, for reasons that aren't entirely clear—he knew what the name "Goldberg" generally signifies. "Sigmund Freud, Marx, these were Jewish minds that were infected with atheism." I asked LaHaye to tell me more about the Jewish mind. "The Jewish brain also has the capacity for great good," he explained. "God gave the Jews great intelligence. He didn't give them great size or physical power—you don't see too many Jews in the NFL—but he gave them great minds."[14]

Rosenzweig is the perfect example of the powers, for good and ill, of the atheism-infected Jew, and his journey from secular humanist to biblical prophet (a journey in which he more than occasionally looks ridiculous—as, for example, when huge locusts descend upon the earth to plague nonbelievers, he dons beekeeper's garb and cowers in a back room) suggests what LaHaye sees as the ordained fate of that particular species. Indeed, one crucial turning point in the series may be the moment when Rosenzweig, rejecting the call that he might be a "modern-day Moses" (*Desecration* 8; repeated in *Glorious Appearing* 134), transforms himself into the prophet Micah. As he dons his prophetic robes, he is full of trepidation and rendered as a classic Jewish weakling: "his was still the plaintive, weak voice with the thick Hebrew accent that reminded Buck of Jewish comedians or storytellers or timid scholars" (*Desecration* 87). But, when he accepts his prophetic destiny, his voice becomes clear and strong, even though, or precisely because, his words are pure theologese, and his actions become equally courageous and resolute. He sheds his stereotypical skin as Diaspora Jew and becomes the biblical type of his people at the moment he converts to Christianity.

The implications for Jews across the board are clear. Insofar as they represent the forces of secularism—the forces associated with the likes of Freud and Marx, much less comedians—they are pawns of the devil; only when they are called back to their messianic destiny can their "native" intelligence help enfold them in the ranks of the redeemed, where that racially encoded quality becomes essential. Ben-Judah's brilliance as a Talmudic scholar allows him to become the worldwide expert in interpreting the unfolding signs of the Final Days (although when the earth's oceans turn to blood, his interpretive expertise is perhaps less necessary than in earlier stages of the process); Rosenzweig's genius allows him easily to accept the mantle of prophet; and, whenever there is high-tech work to be done for the Tribulation Force, hundreds of Israeli scientists appear out of nowhere to get it accomplished. The "God-given" intelligence of the Jew can be part of God's plan indeed, but only when it is put to the use of the Christian.

To be sure, in this instance, LaHaye and Jenkins's use of a familiar antisemitic topos demonstrates a considerable amount of ambivalence. Theirs is not the simple anti-intellectualism that Richard Hofstadter diagnosed as a consistent impulse in American cultural life, but rather one that seeks to define a place for the intellectual and the fruits of his labors in the midst of a dispensation that puts faith and feeling ahead of the matters of the mind.¹⁵ What is at stake for LaHaye and Jenkins finally, it would seem, is nothing less than modernity itself: a modernity that is feared and despised for its tendency to atheism and doubt, but whose technological fruits are essential tools for the Tribulation Force—for those who, like Rayford Steele, "cast their lot with God and the miracle of technology" (*Desecration* 1). As such, it's not only appropriate, I suppose, but also inevitable that the books' "smart Jews" become objects of esteem as much as they are of critique. The dual representation of the "smart Jews" becomes the expression for the dual attitude toward the modern taken by these technology-loving Christians. Through their mixed representation of the secular, intellectual Jew, LaHaye and Jenkins can simultaneously accept, celebrate, deploy, and even innovate with respect to the tools that modernity produced and condemn the epistemology and the ontology that made those tools possible.

As, inter alia, Bryan Cheyette and I have both argued in a different context, the representation of the Jew in the discourses of the West often partakes of precisely this gentile ambivalence, the figure of the Jew (in all senses of the term *figure*) becoming both the expression and the resolution of the conundrums thereby faced.¹⁶ What's striking in this text, however, is the coexistence of this structure (not in and of itself unproblematic, since it reproduces the tendency of the cultures of the West to subordinate the Jews in their number to their own needs, desires, and sign systems), with a cluster of classically antisemitic aspersions—aspersions, however, that are projected not onto the novels' Jews, but rather onto some of their gentiles. These focus, not surprisingly, on the character, actions, and tactics of the most resolutely gentile Antichrist. Consider, for example, Carpathia's charisma. As we have seen, he possesses the power to charm, command, emotionally affect the political figures he moves among—except committed Christians, who are mysteriously immune to his powers, especially after they have been fortified by prayer and sanctification. As such, he takes on the role of the mysterious, satanic Jew right out of the Middle Ages—that cursed, well-and-crop-poisoning, devil-identified figure with magical powers, including the evil eye. This stock stereotype is enhanced by the specific associations that later accrued to that figure, especially in George Du Maurier's immensely best-selling novel, *Trilby*, in which a pestiferous Jew, Svengali, hypnotically controls the beautiful Trilby until—and even beyond—her death. Not only does Carpathia have this "Jewish" power in general, he plays out the Svengali scenario in particular when he directs his mind-controlling powers toward the beautiful stewardess, Hattie Durham, who has been attempting to seduce Steele: she becomes Carpathia's mistress and perhaps the bearer of his offspring, until she is abandoned by him and poisoned by his people. (She subsequently spontaneously aborts his hideous offspring and becomes an agent for the Tribulation Force before confronting Carpathia on his way to coronation in the rebuilt Temple, where she is slain by his security forces.)

Even more problematic is the way the novels call upon a penumbra of associations that link the terms *jew* and *mind control* throughout contemporary antisemitic discourse. The latter is a favorite staple of the more paranoid fantasies of both right- and left-wing fringe groups; referencing CIA experiments and suspicious research at universities, crossing them with fin de siècle fantasies like *Trilby* and science fiction movies and books of the present day, the notion of a nefarious state or state agency actively brainwashing its citizens is a powerful topos of extremist groups across the political map. It's no surprise, then, that such fears and fantasies have a particular purchase in the racist, antisemitic cosmos, although the notion rapidly morphs into a critique of civil society as such. The antisemitic Web site jewatch.com I mentioned earlier, for example, has as one of its major subdivisions "jewish mind control," in which they include some of the following subheadings: "judaism," "communism," "socialism," "liberalism," "civil rights," "atheism," "Freudianism," "psychology," "psychiatry," "secular humanism," "press monopoly," "film monopoly." In short, anything on the political left is part of a worldwide Jewish conspiracy analogous to or indistinguishable from mind control, and it is through the Jew's control of the opinion-shaping organs of civil society that the masses, as well as the elite, are hypnotized. And not only is Carpathia as Antichrist associated with precisely these forms of belief—he espouses left-wing beliefs (universal disarmament, world government, ecumenicalism, religious tolerance, "a utopian society based on peace and brotherhood," he attempts to achieve these ends through control of the media (*Nicolae*, 128). It's no coincidence that much of the novel is told from the viewpoint of Steele, crackerjack correspondent for a major newsweekly not unlike *Time* or *Newsweek* and Carpathia's "media guy" (*Desecration* 259) until he publicly defects to the "Judah-ites." His role allows us to see Carpathia's plan for world domination explicitly involves the press, either by playing to their all-too-palpable one world, peace-loving bias, as he does early in the series, or by co-opting its members into his propaganda apparatus—and so Steele's superiors are hired as journalistic or public relations flunkies for Carpathia—or by simply purchasing all the news outlets, worldwide, as Carpathia's Global Community ultimately does to avoid pesky negative editorials. And it also allows the authors to establish their vision of a Christian-centered alternative public sphere in which computer genius Chang, Israeli scientists, and Steele all combine to produce a newsweekly for Christians chronicling the end times, circulated on the 'net beyond the efforts of the Global Community to censor it.

Again, the point here isn't that LaHaye and Jenkins are adopting the idiom of the Jewish-controlled media as a species of mind control from the antisemitic imaginary. Indeed, to the contrary: it is that they drain explicitly antisemitic content from this discourse while leaving intact a demonstrably antisemitic trail of associations, the path that leads from magic to hypnotism to mind control to press control to mass brainwashing. And it is this dual effect that makes the Left Behind series so ideologically powerful, and so problematic, particularly in the dispensation of our own particular moment. It not only sanitizes these associations of the antisemitic taint that has historically attached to them; more powerfully and consequentially, it reprocesses them, enlisting them for use against a whole host of other enemies—humanists, liberals, ecumenically spirited folk, etc.—who are by the very same operation Jewified, their suspicious Otherness limned in terms drawn from antisemitic discourses.

This effect is enhanced—and connected to yet another antisemitic obsession—in another aspect of Carpathia's power play and a curious object of interest that courses through the entire Left Behind series: economic concentration. "The same control we now have over all media," Carpathia announces to the world leaders whom he has enthralled in every sense of the term, "we need over industry and commerce,"[17] and much of the middle of the sequence is devoted to demonstrating how he establishes that control and what he does with it: after Carpathia imposes a universal currency, the entire world industrial production becomes devoted to standardizing human behavior (including, ultimately, constructing grim factories where the Mark of the Beast can be placed on the heads of all members of the Global Community) and building his pleasure palace in New Babylon. Much of the attention of these books is paid to the efforts of the Tribulation Force to build an alternative economic entity, an international Commodity Co-op, by means of which Christians can barter goods and services with each other over encrypted Internet connections, established by Steele's brilliant daughter Chloe until she is captured and beheaded by Global Community goons.

This particular economic turn suggests the complexity of LaHaye and Jenkins's engagement with the topoi of antisemitism and the equally complex use they make of it. The idea of Jewish power brokers controlling the banks and factories, and ultimately the capitalist market system itself, is, of course, a classic feature of antisemitic propaganda—it goes without saying that it is a staple of *The Protocols*, *The International Jew*, the rabble-rousing of Coughlin and Gerald L. K. Smith, and so on—but it is important to note that it has deep resonance as well in the heartland antisemitism I inventoried at the beginning of this essay. Although, as we shall see in more detail, this aspersion suffused the populist movement of the 1890s, it is not a relic of the distant past in rural America: one of keynotes of the rural depression of the 1980s and early 1990s—the milieu that fostered the extremism of American terrorist Terry Nichols, whose radicalization began when he lost his farm to foreclosure—was the rise of the militia movement, which often articulated these kinds of antisemitic sentiments and had a loose informal alliance with (or, more properly, has largely morphed into) the more explicitly antisemitic Christian identity movement. And it flourishes on the contemporary fringe, the ever morphing netherworld of the neo-Nazi, Christian identity right. Here's a sample from one such, *Light for Nations*, a publication of a militia-promoting, Nazi-sympathizing outfit, the Vanguard News Network:

> Capitalism may be "all-American," but the type of colossal capitalism that bankrupts family-owned retail stores is not. Big capitalism drives corner grocers out of business and outsources jobs to third-world countries. It encourages materialism. And it leads to the importing of inexpensive goods in massive quantities, which also causes American jobs to vanish.
>
> Even though Jews are known for their leftist behavior, they nonetheless pioneered giant capitalism and corporatism. Jews especially pioneered conglomerates, in which one large company owns a dozen smaller companies.[18]

LaHaye and Jenkins are clearly alluding to these kinds of fears, invoking these kinds of energies, and even affiliating themselves quite explicitly with these political programs. Thus the U.S. rebels who belatedly take up the anti-Carpathia fight call themselves a militia rather than, say, an army or even a battalion. Or, in a slightly more benign way, Chloe Steele's Commodity Co-op alludes to a long history of U.S. agrarian reform, from the Grange movement to the Farmers' Alliance (the prototype and indeed origin of the populist movement) to the contemporary farmers' market, in which rural producers attempt to step outside of a market system they feel (not without reason) exploits them.[19] But, as they do so, they are careful to stay away from the antisemitic tinge that these movements, or the sociopolitical critique that animated them, frequently took on. Here, even more clearly than in the representation of Carpathia and Rosenzweig, LaHaye and Jenkins invoke an explicitly populist discourse with an antisemitic cast while stripping it of its explicitly antisemitic associations. But this is not to say that they disavow the basic structures of thought that underlie these associations. They gesture in their direction allude to them, invoke their energies, and, in so doing, enlist them for use in battle against other enemies.

We can perhaps see this strategy most clearly in my final example, the books' seemingly inexplicable obsession with currency. When Carpathia makes his appearance on the world scene, it is not only as an advocate of universal peace and disarmament, but in tandem with an effort to support a worldwide currency led by British bankers Jonathan Stonagal and Joshua Todd-Cothran,[20] an effort he implements himself after he murders his former allies. Indeed, not only are they backing this charismatic Romanian, but it is hinted that they are part of a secret worldwide conspiracy that meets in France and possesses the unlimited capacities to influence governments, control markets, murder their foes. The exact relation between this group and currency reform is a bit dubious—surely financial whizzes would want to continue to make money from currency arbitrage, as did the radical right's current bête noir, George Soros—but, like the invocation of the militia movement, this plot turn is a bow to fringe politics that originates in, and continues to have a strong resonance with, a movement from the American heartland. For Left Behind's odd fascination with the potential rationalization of worldwide currencies is an echo of the politics of more than a century ago, the populist movement's obsession with the gold standard, an obsession in which both Christian imagery and antisemitism played a considerable role.

Like "universal currency," the criticism of the gold standard focused on the fact that it imposed a universal, internationally commensurable benchmark on a currency that had previously been backed by more than one metal—silver as well as gold. By backing the currency with relatively expensive and relatively rare gold rather than the more abundant silver, or with both, money itself became relatively expensive—tight—to the benefit of the big Eastern banks and to the detriment of farmers. Populist critiques of the gold standard therefore invoked the specter of warfare between financial interests and "the people," in which the former were identified heavily with not only American bankers like J. P. Morgan or Augustus Belmont, but foreign financial interests that had invested heavily in American railroads during this period. And, given both historical associations and the role of the British wing of the Rothschild family in the railroad-investment frenzy (a precursor to our own dotcom boom-and-bust cycle of the 1990s), a certain degree of antisemitism entered into these critiques. Although the real financial damage was done to the U.S. economy by the failure of a gentile British house—the bitter enemies of the Rothschilds, Barings' Bank—the culturally loaded ensemble of East Coast bankers, British financial interests, and Jews were frequently confused with one another and were given an explicitly antisemitic—even apocalyptic—significance. Often this antisemitic linkage was explicit. In his wonderful study of Coxey's Army—a populist group that marched on Washington in 1894 demanding redress from the mass unemployment that followed from the panic of 1893—religious studies scholar Michael Barkun quotes the lyrics of their "Commonweal Rallying Song":

> See our stars and stripes are streaming
>   See our banner glow;
> In Christ's Second Coming Triumph,
>   O'er our usury foe.
> ...
> 'Tis the glorious non-interest legions
> Foes of Sheene [sic] gold.[21]

The play on *shiny* and *Sheeney* links the Jew, and the "Jewish" practice of usury, decisively to the gold standard—and the antigold force of the populist army is with equal decisiveness enfolded into the body of a returning Christ fighting his enemy, "the usury foe": a Jewified manifestation of

Satan or his chief deputy, the Antichrist. Indeed, for the chief theoretician of the movement, Carl Browne, the march itself was construed as a vital step on the way to the millennium, a manifestation in earthly terms of the body of Christ itself returned to fight his earthly foe: "the March brought together a critical mass of the 'soul matter' of Christ; . . . [this] Second Coming would be a collective phenomenon, in which the gathered people would be, as it were, the body of Christ" (34). The same associations resonated throughout the populist movement. Sometimes, the association was more implicit, in the widespread use of the rhetoric of Christian suffering that suffused the movement, climaxing of course in William Jennings Bryan's famous "cross of gold" speech at the 1896 Democratic National Convention. (Later, Bryan responded to the defeat of a pro-silver piece of legislation in the Senate by quoting extensively from Shylock's more bloodthirsty speeches; and references to Shylock, and by extension to the idea of the Jew as cannibal or desecrator of the Christian body, were commonplace in populist rhetoric.) But, even in these relatively benign versions, the antisemitic overtones of the Christological rhetoric are clear—who, after all, crucified Christ?—and are made explicit elsewhere in the movement. *Coxey's Sound Money*—the official newspaper of the marchers and, by extension, the pro-silver wing of American populism—printed a cartoon by Watson Heston in 1896 entitled *History Repeats Itself* in which Uncle Sam is posed on a cross, with the words "This is the U.S. in the hands of the Jews" posted above his head. As Democrats and Republicans alike drain his pockets, and a stereotypical Jew joins a figure labeled "Wall Street" to poke his side with a spear, Uncle Sam cries: "My god, my God, why hast thou forsaken me?"[22] The national body itself here is imaged, as was the corporate body summoned up by Coxey's Army, not just as a symbol or a type but as an actual collective image of Christ's body, and the foe inextricably tied to the Antichrist-like, usurious Jew.

I have gone into this coalescence in such depth because it seems to me to be a key to the political strategy of the Left Behind books and hence to their coy but unmistakable use of antisemitic topoi—its remarkable creation of an American antisemitism without Jews. For the authors shrewdly understand currents in American culture and history whose power those of us who live in the leftist-liberal world of the academic sphere don't usually grasp. The most important among these is that bundle of contradictory impulses that go under the heading of *populism,* and that outlasted the actual populist movement, which had run its course by the 1920s—a

3.1 "Crucified Between Two Thieves," *Coxey's Sound Money* April 7, 1896. Courtesy of the Ohio State University Library.

suspicion of elites, an often justified sense of economic victimization, a nativist paranoia often tinged, as we have seen, with an explicit antisemitism, a powerful recourse to conspiracy theories, all coexisting with a powerful impulse toward democratization, social and economic justice, even multiracial or multiethnic coalition building. The shrewd political program of the Left Behind series, and hence by extension of the current crop of Christian right ideologues it represents, is to tap into this deep well of populist ressentiment without appearing to do so, while neglecting, or even contraverting, the impulses in American populism toward radical social and economic justice. The Christian right understands the power of populist sentiments and narratives, particularly in the American South and Midwest where the movement flourished, and understands as well the fundamentally Christian-apocalyptic nature of the tropes and narrative structures that underlay it. Thus, again to turn to Coxey's Army as a paradigmatic instance, we can see many of the same elements that are to emerge in the Left Behind sequence. As Barkun suggests, premillennialism—the belief in the impending arrival of the Apocalypse—had collapsed in 1840, when William Miller's prophecy of the impending end of the earth on October 12 of that year turned out to be erroneous; but Browne imported much of that discourse into the mishmash of beliefs that he pulled together for the marchers, whose songs, slogans, broadsides, etc. all conjoined apocalyptic rhetoric and imagery—indeed, an apocalyptic conception of their own endeavor—with a populist political program, as if the latter were a direct manifestation of the former. Barkun convincingly suggests that Browne's collocation of various creeds and impulses created a precedent for or even a matrix out of which has grown the Christian identity movement of our own time:

> Like Browne's homegrown "theosophy," in which each individual inherited a quantum of Christ's soul, the [Christian identity] myth that the "Ten Lost Tribes" are the ancestors of contemporary Europeans and Americans is a gratifying and unfalsifiable fantasy for believers. Like Browne's belief system it too melds together a traditional millenarian scenario with . . . beliefs that lie outside both major denominations and fundamentalist sects. The deviant beliefs serve the catalytic function of demonstrating to believers that the final, millenarian times are near; that the movement's political aims are God's aims, too; and that in a world polarized between Good and Evil, a Jewish conspiracy is the ultimate adversary. (38–39)

With the exception of the word *Jewish*, that last sentence could read as a summary of the theology of the Left Behind series; and this fact suggests, I think, the nature and dimensions of LaHaye and Jenkins's endeavor and that of the political force they represent. The contemporary New Right with which LaHaye and Jenkins are explicitly involved is seeking to appropriate populist rhetorics for ends quite different from the Christian identity movement but with equally problematic goals: tapping populist energies, reenergizing populist narrative structures, reinforcing populist resentments, not in the service of social reform but rather, as it were, in reverse: to use populism in order to remake America as a functioning Christian theocracy.* To

---

* That they should choose to do so by making their bed with the corporate elites who do not have the best interest of lower-middle-class and impoverished Americans at heart is one of the great political mysteries of our times (it's the subject of Thomas Frank's excellent best

this end, the explicit antisemitism that has always been present within American populism, that rose again in the 1930s with figures like Coughlin and Smith and that has been injected, wholesale, into the Christian identity movement remains a persistent problem. As Leonard Dinnerstein has argued, and as experience suggests, in contemporary American civil society *explicit* antisemitism is just not acceptable anymore, even though it continues to flourish on the fringes, and, after the Oklahoma City bombing, it became even more disreputable.[23] Moreover, the tactical alliance between the Christian and the Jewish right, consummated in a shared support of the most regressive policies with respect to Israel, means that the taint of antisemitism that attaches to populist activism becomes that much more of an embarrassment to the movement.

While the preceding generation of Christian right leaders has mimicked some of the most embarrassingly antisemitic sentiments of their predecessors—Falwell offers a particularly egregious example; so, persistently, does Pat Robertson (whose comments that the stroke suffered by Ariel Sharon as a punishment sent from God were offensive enough to cause the Israeli government to cancel his plans to build a Christian theme park in the Holy Land)—LaHaye and Jenkins quite ostentatiously do not: indeed, as we have seen, to the contrary (LaHaye seems to have learned his lesson when he was removed as a campaign coordinator for Jack Kemp in 1996 when his anti-Catholic and anti-Jewish sentiments were made public). What they do instead, however, is to reference populist obsessions in such a way as to keep their antisemitic dimensions alive, independent of the aspersions they cast on Jews. In so doing, they cleanse as they Christianize those energies and resentments, draw upon them without leaving themselves open to the charges of open intolerance that have dogged the American right for the past thirty years, and in so doing reanimate them—dusting them off for use in other, newer battles.

As such, these books represent not a "New Antisemitism" that can be distinguished from its previous avatars, but rather a new, more dangerous deployment of the same old antisemitic tropes, topoi, and metonymies of

---

seller, *What's the Matter With Kansas* [New York: Metropolitan, 2004]), and whether it can be sustained in the midst of a serious economic downturn like the ones that motivated populism in the first place remains to be seen. But as I write—in the aftermath of George Bush's reelection, with support from evangelicals in the American heartland—their strategy for gaining political power seems stunningly effective.

what I've been calling heartland or populist antisemitism. It is more dangerous not despite but because of its ostensible philosemitism, its invocation not only of Christian Zionism but of such theological innovations as the "Semitic judgment" and the clear condemnation of Nazi-style antisemitism. For, as such, it represents the renovation rather than the rejection of antisemitic topoi for a seemingly more tolerant age. The theology of the Left Behind series, Melani McAlister tells us, is "not your father's fundamentalism" (782), by which she means that it accepts—embraces—racial and ethnic difference: fighters for redemption include African Americans, Asians, and Jordanians as well as Jews and white Christians. Although, as we have seen, each of these remains thoroughly stereotypical, their appearance in books is clearly aimed at nudging fundamentalist/New Right sensibilities closer to the multicultural realities of the current America. Complex relations to Jews, however, reveals the limitations of Left Behind's strategy, not so much on the theological side, which is more or less inevitable, but on the racial/ethnic side, in the use of slurring associations and narrative devices that float free of any one racial or ethnic group and instead become associated with the career of the Antichrist at large and, through that identification, with a host of programs (peace movements, ecumenicalism, reproductive choice, feminism) and institutions (the media, business, industry) that are seen not as wrong or misguided or even horrific, but as satanic. This inability to let antisemitic discourses go, the need instead to use them to turn populist ressentiment into a Christianizing program, suggest some of the darker passions to which not only the series, but the Christian New Right at large appeals. Even though the results of the most recent election suggest that the New Right's power may be on the wane, these passions are worth keeping in mind. One must never forget that, for all its kindly rhetoric about Jews, for all its worrying about the "Semitic judgment," for all its philosemitic gesticulation, Left Behind proposes in both its form and content that, unless we accept the most narrow definition of Christian faith and unless we subscribe to the political program of the Christian right, we are all—Jews and gentiles alike—placed in the position of Jews at their most insidious and stereotypical. And we are all damned.[24]

4. THE HUMAN STAIN OF RACE
Roth, Sirk, and Shaw in Black, White, and Jewish

NO AUTHOR HAS WORKED as hard as Philip Roth to keep the novel alive as a socially significant form, all the more remarkably since he has done so at an age when many of his contemporaries have slid into self-parody or grumpy retrenchment. Defying the distractions of the body and energized by those of the body politic, he has addressed with uncompromising ferocity the central concerns of our moment—terrorism (*American Pastoral*), McCarthyism (*I Married a Communist*), soi-disant political correctness (*The Human Stain*)—while adding charged subjects like race (*The Human Stain*) and mortality (*The Dying Animal*) to his signature concerns with Jewishness and the farthest shores of human sexuality. And in this later-life renaissance Roth has even been placing new arrows in his representational quiver. As suggested by the best recent account of Roth's best recent novel, *The Human Stain*, that of Ross Posnock, Roth has been taking on more exalted company to match his more exalted themes: Hawthorne, Melville, Emerson, Whitman. As Posnock observes, "Roth's creative reimagining of classic American literature deserves to be taken seriously" both in its own right and as "an act of affiliation that reverberates [throughout] *The Human Stain*."[1]

To be sure, measuring himself by the highest of high-cultural standards is nothing new for Roth: his engagements with Kafka and with contemporary eastern European writers were, for example, crucially formative to the fiction of his "middle years"—*The Prague Orgy*, for example, or his rewriting of *The Metamorphosis*, *The Breast*. Nor is his engagement with canonical American writing all that surprising: we may tend, mercifully, to forget *The Great American Novel* (1973), but, as I've argued elsewhere, and as Posnock is currently suggesting, the spirit of Henry James is not far from his experiments in literary form.[2] There is, however, another side to Roth as well, one that has been engaged fully with the popular and mass culture of the last century, particularly the culture in which Roth himself grew up in the 1940s and 1950s. Played in the early fiction for bracingly comic effect—one thinks of Alexander Portnoy's diatribe at the end of the novel, in which he casts himself in the image of Jimmy Cagney in *White Heat*, hurling defiance at the coppers who would arrest him for tearing a label off his mattress—this engagement is no less evident in his more recent deepening of thematic concerns. What, after all, is *I Married a Communist* but a novel that pays homage, with its very title, to the form as well as the matter of pulp fictions?

I want to suggest here that engaging with this side of Roth, or, more properly, juxtaposing it with the mass cultural texts he weaves into his novels, might give us a greater appreciation for the successes and failures of his current work, especially those of *The Human Stain*. And such a juxtaposition might also allow us to put into perspective a form of current academic criticism in which Roth's text participates—the study of racialization as a process and of Jewish assimilation to whiteness as one of racialization's crucial instances. Reading Roth reading mass culture reading race—which is one of the things I think *The Human Stain* sets out to do—can help us understand what is and what is not valuable in the critical reorientation of racial understandings this scholarship implies, a reorientation to which both Roth's text, and the contexts it invokes, have much to contribute.

In what follows I focus on two such contexts in particular: sentimental melodramas of the 1950s like *Lost Boundaries*, *Pinky*, and (especially) *Imitation of Life* and the big band music of the 1940s, especially that of the Artie Shaw Orchestra featuring Roy Eldridge. In all these cases, I'll be arguing, the thematics of passing, the interrelation of black and white cultural formations, and the capital (economic and artistic) made out of them enters Roth's novel in such a way as to open up larger questions about the efficacy (or lack thereof) of even the most supple critical and creative orientations that envision race in terms of black and white. Adding Jewishness to the mix—as Roth, somewhat despite himself, manages to do—destablizes this critical orientation even as it is destabilized by it, a process that points to and beyond current racial dispensations to newer ones still in the process of forming. I conclude with an example of an artist I think is engaged in this work, jazz pianist Uri Caine, whose audacious attempts to overwrite the classical canon with jazz and klezmer intonations, suggests what cultural production in this somewhat utopian mode might well look like.

Roth, Sirk, and the Sentiment of Race

What's interesting about *The Human Stain*, for longtime readers of Roth, is how it does and does not comport to the example of his previous fiction. Nathan Zuckerman, the novel's narrator, is of course a fixture of Roth's fiction of the middle and later period. Readers have followed Zuckerman's growth and development from the eager young apprentice of *The Ghost Writer* to his full priapic maturity in *The Counterlife* and now witness, with heightened appreciation of its ironies, his post–prostate operation old age, complete with colostomy bag. Roth's witheringly accurate portrayal of the politics of college life is familiar from *Letting Go*. The concern with the abusive deployment of political correctness on campus (which he links to American puritanism by interweaving his narrative with that of the Clinton impeachment imbroglio) is an extension of Roth's fascination with tactics of political repression evident in novels as disparate as *Our Gang* and *I Married a Communist*. Indeed, the nub of Roth's critique would seem to be that the old right has become the new (not the New) multicultural left, that the same lack of concern for the idiosyncrasies of individual thought, the same spirit of mindless conformism, animates both.

Whether such a critique is substantial or not—at the moment of Fox News it seems to have been overtaken by events—what is new in this novel seems as germane as it has ever been: Roth's heightened concern with race. This is not to say that matters of black/white conflict and contact have been absent from his work—one thinks, for example, of the awkward case of the black boy in *Goodbye, Columbus* or of Swede Levov's encounter, in *American Pastoral*, with racial conflict in Newark during and after the 1968 riots. But nowhere else in Roth's fiction, I think, have the complex matters of racial identity been so close to the subject matter of his book, in form as well as content. Indeed, it is the embeddedness of race in the novel's narrative method that composes *The Human Stain*'s most striking attribute. To be sure, there is a kernel of fact behind the novel's scenario, the posthumous "outing" of New York litterateur and seeming Jewish intellectual Anatole Broyard—the revelation of his black identity having been made first by Henry Louis Gates Jr. in the pages of the *New Yorker*, then amplified by the publication of Broyard's memoirs. The Broyard connection provides Roth with a good deal of material in the novel, including its central trope. Eric Sundquist has reminded us that Broyard's own remarkable passing performance included an essay in *Commentary*, "A Portrait of the Inauthentic Negro," in which Broyard repeatedly uses the figurative term *stain* to describe the presumably inexpugnable physiognomic basis of black identity that Broyard's own appearance, like that of Roth's protagonist, Coleman Silk, contraverted.[3]

But Gates's narrative of Broyard's experience, like that experience itself, has a specific generic cast: it is the latest in a long line of narratives about ambiguous-appearing black people passing as white. Including such illustrious African American examples as Frances Harper's *Iola Leroy* (1892), James Weldon Johnson's *Autobiography of an Ex-Coloured Man* (1912), and Nella Larsen's *Passing* (1929), the passing narrative also found its way into highbrow white culture—a version of the passing plot is central, after all, to the denouement of Faulkner's *Absalom, Absalom!* (1936)—and into white middlebrow culture as well. The passing plot is crucially referenced in Fannie Hurst's 1923 novel *Imitation of Life* and in the two enormously popular film versions of the text, one directed by John Stahl in 1929 and the other by Douglas Sirk in 1959. And it was centrally instantiated by two films directly referenced in Roth's novel, Otto Preminger's *Pinky* (directed by Elia Kazan), which swept the Academy Awards in 1949, and the much less popular *Lost Boundaries* (1949). All three of these have some relevance to *The Human Stain*. *Lost Boundaries*, with its contrast between a New England setting as a site of racial passing and an experience in the navy as the site of racial self-discovery, comes nearest to being a "source" for Roth's plot. *Pinky* was the subject of a major Supreme Court decision in favor of free expression trumping censorship on the grounds of the 1950s own version of political correctness—miscegenation taboos. But, as I shall argue in greater detail below, the text that seems closest in spirit and substance to his novel is Sirk's 1959 masterpiece, whose astringency is indeed even greater on the subject of race than that of the notoriously unsaccharine Roth.

Placing Roth's narrative in this generic context suggests the dimensions of its ambitions: by this "act of affiliation," no less than by his invocations of Hawthorne and Melville, Roth is clearly seeking to write the Great—or at least quintessentially—"American" novel and, in doing so, he identifies race as the defining obsession of that enterprise. But it also suggests the distinctiveness of Roth's enterprise. Like that of many passing narratives, Coleman Silk's story is ultimately a tragic one, but for different reasons than those which predominate in the texts I've named. In Johnson's novel, and in the genre as a whole, passing is often presented both as an opportunity and as a betrayal—one remembers the famous last lines of the *Autobiography*, in which, in an uncharacteristic rush of affect, the nameless ex-colored man laments that, even though he has successfully passed to the point of raising three white children, he feels "a coward, a deserter" and cries out that he has "sold his birthright for a mess of pottage."[4] This striking turn gets at a central ambivalence in the passing genre. The ex-colored man's conclusion affirms the racialist notion of identity the genre at large is devoted to complicating. Although they may end otherwise, passing narratives flirt with the possibility that there is no necessary link between racial appearance and human identity. They suggest that the infinite vicissitudes of the former—the wide variation in skin color and other facial markings created by the intermingling, whether by force or consent, of the races—forestalls the racialist leap from phenotype or physiology to predications about essential qualities of intelligence or character. Indeed, in one powerful if perverse reading of *Ex-Coloured Man*, Samira Kawash has argued that there is no actual evidence in the book that the ex-colored man isn't "really" white; while her claims are somewhat debatable, they speak to the central point of the novel, which is that race thinking can, by overemphasizing variable factors like skin color and facial appearance as markers of identity, create epistemological eddies that spin into ontological whirlpools.[5] Yet at its powerful conclusion Johnson's narrative ends up reinstalling racial identity as a crucial category, albeit—and powerfully—in a different register, that of affect. When the ex-colored man first rejects the idea of "passing" as a white man, his white benefactor tells him: "This idea you have of making a Negro out of yourself is nothing more than a sentiment" (145), and, at the end of the novel, the now ex-colored man confirms the truth of his words when he hymns his "birthright" in language that testifies, in form of expression as well as denotative meaning, to the power of feeling: "I feel that I have been a coward, a deserter, and I am possessed by a strange longing for my mother's people" (210). Whatever complicating work that *Autobiography* may wish to do with respect to deconstructing race as an ontological or even cognitive category, in its last paragraphs race rushes back as a powerful category of value, reinscribed in the language of sentiment: as feeling, possession, longing.*

Although he fully participates in the passing genre, Roth seemingly will have none of its return to the racial under the sign of sentiment. Instead, his character Coleman cleaves to the bitter and unsentimental end to the passing project, one that comes, therefore, to have the force of principle as well as that of convenience. Coleman could dispel charges of racism—that he referred to two absent students as "spooks," intending to mean spectral presences, but taken by those students vulgarly to refer to their race—by simply outing himself as a black man, due to a simplistic belief among his accusers that prejudice against African Americans could only be deployed (or even felt) by someone white or, more accurately perhaps, that a speech act performed by a black man would have a different meaning than one with the very same content performed by a white one. His refusal to do so thus indicates his commitment not only to his masquerade but more importantly to the principles upon which he has staked his intellectual life or, again to be more precise, his life as an intellectual: that language and thought, like identity itself, are independent of racial classification, that the words we use and the predications we assert through them can be willed by an act of self-assertion that transcends socially determined categories like race. (The irony here of course is that Coleman's speech acts and silences alike also give testimony to a different capacity of language: its capacity to veil, obscure, and lie.) If he is punished for this faith—and he is, multiply—it is finally not by the university that treats him abominably or the town that turns its back on him; ultimately, he

---

* Significantly, the exact same scenario is played out at the end of Cahan's *The Rise of David Levinsky*. There the assimilated, successful millionaire (who also loses his mother at an early age) confronts the sense of deracination that comes from his Americanization and describes it in a language startlingly similar to Johnson's. He, like the ex-colored man, is called back to a sense of his true identity by musical performance: "I love music to madness. I yearn for the world of great singers, violinists, pianists. Several of them are of my race and country, and I have met them, but all my acquaintance with them has brought me is a sense of being looked down upon as a money-bag." And he, like the ex-colored man, discovers that "I cannot escape from my old self... David, the poor lad swinging over a Talmud volume at the Preacher's Synagogue [in Russia], seems to have more in common with my inner identity than David Levinsky, the well-known cloak-manufacturer." A maker of cloaks—of garments designed to cover or hide the body—he may be; but he cannot cloak what he truly is—a racially encoded Russian Jew. Cahan, *The Rise of David Levinsky* (New York: Harper, 1917), pp. 529–530.

transcends these fallible communities, creating, with the help of Viagra, a lover's paradise that effectively transcends his surroundings. Rather, he and his lover Faunia are killed by "a guy with a subconscious mind full of PTSD," Faunia's Vietnam vet ex-husband Les, who acts out of white-militia-inflected antisemitic rage at Silk and anger at Faunia for her culpability in the deaths of their children, but remains as ignorant of Coleman's true identity as the rest of the community.[6] Coleman is "buried as a Jew," the narrator Nathan Zuckerman thinks, "and, if I was speculating correctly, killed as a Jew. Another of the problems," he adds wryly, "of impersonation" (325). But also, one might add, one of its ironic blessings as well. Having lived his adult life as a white man, and having been murdered for being a certain kind of white man, he becomes fully in death that which he has pretended since his twenties to be. The only bearers of his secret are either dead—Faunia—or silent keepers of his secret—like his sister Ernestine.

Roth's intervention in the passing narrative, then, is an audacious one. He rejects the genre's inherent if contested racialism by affirming, however grimly, what we would call an Emersonian vision of identity asserted as an act of will. Or, to be more precise, Roth generates an Emersonian dialectic between freedom and fate, contingency and necessity, the self-created self and the forces of historical circumstance, whose oscillating motion generates both Coleman's tragedy and his triumph (which, in Nathan's account, and I think in Roth's as well, are indistinguishable).* Coleman is "the man who decides to forge a distinct historical destiny,

---

*It's this note in the novel, I think, that Amy Hungerford captures in the best academic treatment next to Posnock's I have yet encountered. To Hungerford the question of race is finally something of what Hitchcock would call a MacGuffin, a plot contrivance that motivates the action of the text but is finally irrelevant to its real concerns, which for Hungerford are the attempt to claim via secrecy a "valued human identity" for oneself (146)—a process as fully embodied by the white Faunia, who is "passing" as an illiterate, as by Coleman, and hence one independent of race. By contrast, I see the matter of secrecy as being ubiquitous in the novel and as liable to perversion as to the achievement of authenticity (Delphine, as her name ironically indicates, is a keeper of secrets too); hence racial and ethnic passing occupy a different, if analogous, space, to the keeping of secrets tout court. To be sure, histories of race and ethnicity don't determine identity in the novel, but they do *overdetermine* it (even Delphine's secret history contains a narrative of multiple attractions to black men) and overdetermine as well the possibilities of escaping such determinations via the maintenance of secret identities. See Amy Hungerford, *The Holocaust of Texts* (Chicago: University of Chicago Press, 2003), pp. 141–146.

who sets out to spring the historical lock, and who does so ... only to be ensnared by the history he hadn't quite counted on: the history that isn't yet history, the history that the clock is now ticking off" (335). "All he'd ever wanted ... was to be free: not black, not even white," writes Nathan, but it's clear that the inevitabilities of racial history prevent the fulfillment of the agenda of Emersonian self-reliance (120).

There's another sense of history at work in *The Human Stain*, however, one that ends up working differently, ultimately undercutting Roth's own attempts to move through and beyond the passing narrative. I refer here to the history that is simultaneously embodied and apotheosized by Coleman's sister Ernestine, light-skinned like her brother ("her complexion was no darker than a Greek's or a Morroccan's" [316]), encountered by Zuckerman at Coleman's funeral late in the novel, but who, in the recursive narrative structure of the text, also supplies him there with much of the information about Coleman's early life that shapes his earlier narrative exposition. (In this respect, and not a few others, the novel echoes the narrative structure of another sort of American passing novel, the sentimentalized story of Jay Gatsby né Jacob Gatz.) At the funeral Ernestine provides the novel both narrative information and its didactic payoff. In a long speech she gives Nathan—and the reader—a history lesson. Repeating the role of her own mother, she tells the family about the history of African Americans at large as well as their own family, informs Nathan—and us—about Coleman's past, about that of his family, about the black experience in New Jersey, dilates into a defense of the traditional canon ("in East Orange High they stopped long ago reading the old classics. They haven't even heard of *Moby-Dick*, much less read it" [329]), then concludes with a reminder of the kind of multiple work that such historical consciousness can do, recalling to Nathan Zuckerman the story of Dr. Charles Drew, the black discoverer of the clotting factor in blood who died for want of a blood transfusion from a hospital that wouldn't treat him because of his race. Crucially, it is in Ernestine's insistently grammatical phrasing (she, like Coleman, like all the children of their father, is a believer in precision of language) that Roth launches his most scathing attack on academic p.c.: "I don't believe I've ever heard anything more foolish being perpetrated by an institution of higher learning. ... Sounds like the people there forgot what it is to teach. Sounds like what they do is something closer to buffoonery. Every time has its reactionary authorities, and here at Athena they are apparently riding high" (328–329).

Ernestine clearly steps into the role of Roth's surrogate with far more authority that the self-confessed unreliable narrator Nathan. But, in so doing, she also seems to have been rendered into a stick figure rather than a character, a mouthpiece for her author's opinions rather than a representation of a complex human being who holds a bundle of contradictory ideas that exist in taut and complex relation to the rest of her life, like her brother Coleman or the narrator Nathan. One sign of this is how fully Roth's characteristic fluency with dialogue deserts him here—try speaking the last sentence I quoted above out loud and see if it would be uttered by any living human being, even (or especially) a dignified middle-aged African American woman with concern for precision of language. Another, more troubling index of Roth's move into the one-dimensional is the utter absence of any of his characteristic perversity. Ernestine is simply *too* earnest, to make the inevitable pun. Indeed, she embodies the hectoring didacticism one finds elsewhere in Roth, frequently ameliorated or qualified by its expression by unreliable narrators like Nathan. Here instead Roth's tendency toward didacticism is heightened, rather than qualified, by his placement of these sentiments in the mouth of a thoroughly admirable, self-possessed black woman.

More to the point, Ernestine's appearance in the book can best be described as "sentimental" in the technical, generic sense of the word: the sense associated with a form of writing immensely popular in nineteenth-century England and America and one that, as I have suggested above, bears a complicated relation to the passing narrative. Although scholars agree that sentimentalism as a representational mode originated in the eighteenth century in dialogue with new understandings of affect, subjectivity, and gendered identity—I am thinking here of such classic formulations as Goethe's *Sorrows of Young Werther* or Sterne's *Sentimental Journey* or Richardson's *Pamela* and *Clarissa*—they have also taught us that the development of the genre in Victorian England and nineteenth-century America was coupled with the testing of the virtues of that emergent social form, the bourgeois nuclear family.[7] In the admittedly different (though mutually reinforcing) projects of Dickens or Susan Warner or Mrs. E. D. E. N. Southworth, the white middle-class family itself is constructed as a fallible but essential unit, struggling against manifold threats from a hostile world: sexuality, drink, the vagaries of the urban metropolis. Critics have been pushing this insight further by arguing that sentimental fiction became a key locus in which the claims of biology and culture fought it out on the terrain of the idealized family—frequently with unexpected results. Cindy Weinstein has recently shown, for example, how the recurrent plot device of adoption in the American sentimental novels of the 1850s allowed them to participate in a larger dialogue about whether the family is to be seen as an affective or a reproductive unit, a voluntary and malleable form organized by the logic of "love" or a fixed form organized by a logic of blood. In these texts, Weinstein convincingly argues, the force of sentiment itself is so great that it overwhelms, complicates, or otherwise contradicts the biological agenda the bourgeois nuclear family is designed to encourage or enhance; she further shows how contradictory are the results when the expansive power of sentiment comes face-to-face with the consanguineous logic of race.[8]

The use of the sentimental as a way of negotiating the boundaries of the familial continues well after the sentimental novel per se declines in popularity or, perhaps it would be more accurate to say, transfers its energies into other venues, including narratives of passing. Indeed, in these narratives precisely the scenario Weinstein locates with respect to the nineteenth-century sentimental novel gets played out, albeit with a series of ironic twists. Thus the cultural work Weinstein identifies in the 1840s gets done in reverse in the most popular sentimental melodramas of a century later: in the so-called women's pictures of the 1930s and 1940s where mothers are repeatedly asked to give up their daughters in the interest of the child's social advancement. For here the sentimental story is told, as it were, from the other side of the mirror. I am thinking here of a prototype of the form, *Stella Dallas* (1925, 1937), in which a lower-class woman gives over her daughter to her upper-class ex-husband so that the girl may enjoy the privileges of his class: in the tear-soaked final scene of the film, Stella stands in the rain outside her daughter's college graduation, watching from afar as her daughter, her ex-husband, the girl's stepmother, and the daughter's fiancé celebrate her glorious future. Or, more apposite to Roth's novel, one thinks of *Imitation of Life* (1934, 1959), in which a self-sacrificing black woman first resists, then plays along with her daughter's passing masquerade before dying of a broken heart at the loss she has sustained.*

---

*There's much more to be said about the novel on which the film was based, Fannie Hurst's *Imitation of Life* (1933). Hurst was one of the first mass-market middlebrow

Precisely this version of the sentimental drama is also at the core of Ernestine's history lesson. For, as she narrates Coleman's story, she foregrounds the rejection of his mother necessary to make it work and emphasizes the mother's premature death of a broken heart at the loss of her son. And when Nathan narrates/describes/imagines the discussion between Coleman and his mother as he tells her of his intention to pass and walks entirely out of her life, he puts words in her mouth that script a scenario right out of sentimental passing films, most relevantly, perhaps, *Imitation of Life*:

> "I'm never going to know my grandchildren," she said.... "You're never going to let them know who I am. 'Mom,' you'll tell me, 'Ma, you come to the railroad station in New York, and you sit on the bench in the waiting room, and at eleven twenty-five A.M., I'll walk by with my kids in their Sunday best.' . . . And you know very well that I will be there. . . . You tell me the only way I can ever touch my grandchildren is for you to hire me to come over as Mrs. Brown to baby-sit and put them to bed, I'll do it. Tell me to come over as Mrs. Brown to clean your house, I'll do *that*." (137–138)

There's a precisely correlative scene in Sirk's great version of the melodrama. when the black mother Annie follows her passing-for-white daughter Sara Jane (who, just to complicate things further, is played by a white Jewish American actress, Susan Kohner) to Las Vegas and visits her in a motel room as the girl prepares for a date. Sarah Jane, like Coleman (or for that matter the ex-colored man), understands that the price of her passing is a rejection of the mother and tells her so directly. "Please, mama," she tells Annie in a much discussed shot-counter-shot (Sarah Jane is at the left of the screen, facing the camera; Annie on the right, her back to the camera, paralleling but also negating her daughter in image as she does in diegetic life; the shots then reverse positions, suggesting the linkage but also

---

novelists—writing for a group which Roth has spent most of his career seeking to offend; and, as Daniel Itzkovitz observes in his fine introduction to the 2004 reissue of the novel, Hurst's own treatment of the race narrative is handled with a considerable degree of projection and ambivalence, such that, among other things, Hurst explored her own sense of Jewish outsiderdom and alienation through her black characters (there are no Jews to speak of in the novel). See *Imitation of Life*, ed., with introduction, Daniel Itzkovitz (Durham: Duke University Press, 2004).

the divergence between these two), "will you go? And never do this to me again. And if—by accident—we should ever pass on the street, please don't recognize me." Annie agrees, renouncing her efforts to track the girl, telling her only that she wishes to hold "my baby, my beautiful baby" one last time before she returns home, to die of a symbolically resonant failing heart. And this is not the end of these sentimental theatrics: as Sarah Jane's white roommate enters, the roommate assumes that Annie is the maid; to protect her daughter from yet another humiliation, Annie quickly adopts a different role, telling the roommate that she has just been by to visit her former charge "Miss Linda." As she leaves, Sarah Jane/Linda bids her farewell, then mouths the word that she dare not speak: "Mama." And the pathos heightens when the roommate tells Sarah Jane, "I didn't know you had a Mammy"; Sarah Jane sobs in reply, "yes—all my life."[9]

This scenario—of maternal loss accepted as an inevitable concomitant of the passing scenario—provided Roth, according to the author in a recent interview, with what another one of his role models, Henry James, might call the "germ" for his novel.[10] And Roth isn't the only one to focus on the connection. Commenting on the novel in the wake of its release as a (not very successful) film, Brent Staples remarked on the frequency of the kinds of contortions that the families of those passing for white would undergo: "The most heartbreaking moment in 'The Human Stain' comes when the near-white Coleman Silk informs his darker-skinned mother that he is engaged to a white woman and has told her that his parents are dead. White moviegoers will see this as tragic. Black moviegoers who lived through American apartheid—the prime period of passing—will find it not just tragic but familiar."[11] Staples's use of the language of feeling reminds us of how close the novel comes at this most powerful moment to Sirk's film. But it also reminds us of how Sirk and Roth extend the scenario in order to defamiliarize the expected, almost routinized, tragedy of race: in both cases it is not merely the death of the mother, but the fantasy of her own self-abnegation in order to make the passing performance work that gives the event its affective kick. To be sure, this act is not without its perversities; Coleman is well aware that in a very real way he was "murdering [his mother] on behalf of his exhilarating notion of freedom" (138). But to fantasize the death of your mother is one thing; in some sense this is what individuation may demand of us, at least if Julia Kristeva is right. To tell your mother to her face that she is dead to you—and to hear her willingly embrace that death sentence in order to allow your passing performance to work: this is truly, one might even say existentially, egregious. To underline that egregiousness, both Sirk and Roth call forth all the theatrics of the sentimental tradition: its scenario of boundlessly sacrificial mother love, its eliciting of sighs, tears, outrage, affective distress.

This frankly sentimental use of the maternal is a fairly radical turn for Roth, whose fictional representations of motherhood have, to this point, ranged from the vague to the monstrous (he is, after all, the creator of Sophie Portnoy). A similar phenomenon is evident at the end of the novel, when Roth plots through Ernestine a closure by which—as I am claiming sentimental fictions also often do—to keep alive the coimplicated ideals of race and family that the would-be passer has rejected. Well after the funeral and Nathan's investigation of Coleman's death, Ernestine invites Nathan to visit: "I thought you might like to see the house . . . there's Coleman's room, where Coleman and Walter slept. The twin beds are still there" (342). She goes on to promise Nathan photographs from the family album, tells his brother Walt about Coleman's death despite Walt's wish never to hear about Coleman again, and justifies all of these actions with the simple, resonant phrase: "We're a family" (343). Nathan is on his way to visit her and see this family for himself at the end of the novel; it is, in short, "the Family Silk plenty that Coleman jettisoned" that endures, not Coleman's desire to "[jettison] . . . the whole ramified Negro thing," "to become a new being. To bifurcate" (342).

Like *The Autobiography of an Ex-Coloured Man*, *The Human Stain* is not "simply" sentimental (then again, neither is sentimentality). But, in its final turn toward the affective, it undercuts the rigorous Emersonian irony that it displayed elsewhere on the subjects of race and identity. Such gestures seem to me to be out of keeping with the main tendency of the novel, which turns much more discordantly (and valuably) ironic when it invokes other ways of going at the race problem. More to the point, the turn toward the affective and the echoing of the language of family at the end of the novel read as sentimental in the admittedly reductive sense of "mawkish," "manipulative" in comparison with Sirk's film, which manages to make its raid on sentiment without giving up—while in fact enhancing—a critical sense of the difficulties involved in that activity. The scene of Annie's death is followed by one of equal, if not greater, emotional intensity in which Sarah Jane, learning of her mother's death, comes home for the funeral and flings herself on the coffin, begging her forgiveness. (It is not the only way in which Sarah Jane, a performer in life as well as in her career, mirrors her mother's histrionic employer, Lora, as opposed to her own mother, whose racial performances are far subtler.) There Sarah Jane accepts, under precisely the sign of the sentimental, her family and her history, affirming publicly the identity as a black woman she has been trying to deny. And, just to augment the sentimental theatrics, the film ends with Sarah Jane joining Lora, her husband Steve, and her daughter in the funeral car: the family that has been fractured throughout the film is reconstituted, with Steve firmly at its head. This family is a multiracial anomaly; it is neatly cordoned off from the African American community that has turned out, in moving and abundant numbers, to mourn Annie's death. But, in this very gesture, the film enacts the dual work I have been trying to locate in the passing narrative. Sarah Jane is at once fully black and newly white, at once her mother's daughter and Steve and Lora's assimilated stepchild: all the contradictions of racial identity with which the film has been playing are, if not resolved, at least held in taut and successful suspension, by means of an invocation of family right out of the closural gestures of the sentimental tradition—along with, as Weinstein's analysis would predict, a privileging of the new, adoptive family unit as a suitable replacement for the old, biologically based "consanguineous" one.

Sirk being Sirk, however, things are not so easily resolved. As the funeral car bearing the newly reconstituted family proceeds past a revering, largely black, crowd, the film cuts to a shot from inside an antique shop looking out onto the procession: the objects in the window hiding the car from us, the partially frosted glass of the window refracting our view, the segmented window pane fracturing our view yet again. Whatever else one can say about it, this moment formally complicates the message its narrative intends to display thematically. As Lauren Berlant observes in her hypnotically eloquent reading of the film, lettering on the antique store window spells out "Costume Shop"—an ironic reference to the film's recognition, via Lora's passing story, that race is a masquerade, a performance, a travesty in both the current and the root sense of the word.[12] But I'd also draw attention to the gesture toward historicity made by this distancing, alienating (in the Brechtian sense) shot. That we peer through the antique shop window suggests the film is gesturing its own anachronism. Sirk wants to suggest to us that in 1960, six years after *Brown v. Board of Education* and five years before the passage of the Civil Rights Act, the brand of black identity that Annie represent has passed away, its place to be taken by the new postracial family represented by Sarah Jane's admission to Lora's clan. But, at the same time, the very form of the shot suggests that difficulties of perception will continue to trouble this new era. That there is a barrier of thick glass between the spectator and the funeral cortege emphasizes the difficulty of perception that dogs the very articulation of "race"; we see the funeral procession, quite literally, through a glass darkly. And that the glass is segmented by the lines of the windowpane is to say that it presents an image of continued and continuing division—division of consciousness on the part of the (normatively white) spectator, racial division in a world where race is defined, as W. E. B. DuBois famously put it, in the spatial imagery of a line dividing or, as Roth puts it, bifurcating the social field. And, finally, that the window itself is shaped to mimic the aspect ratio of the screen image itself links these complexities to Sirk's own mimesis. *This* imitation of life, the image is telling us, reproduces the troubled and troubling perceptual process that generates the articulation of race itself.

For all the overt sentimentalism of his conclusion, in other words, Sirk complicates that move, shows how the desire for sentimental closure in its familial and racial context is caught up in a drama of false perceptions that renders it (like the glass through which the scene is shot) only semi-

4.1   Through a glass darkly: the view from the antique shop. Douglas Sirk,
Imitation of Life (Universal, 1959).

transparent, if also at the same time not fully opaque. Intuiting and exploiting the sentimental reaffirmation with which the passing text so frequently finds itself complicit, Sirk turns such a reaffirmation inside out, questioning his audience's stake in the very affective turn he has so brilliantly made. Race, Sirk reminds us, is at its core a matter of perception first and affect second; in the admixture of sentimental mode and of Brechtian alienation effects designed to disrupt that very mode he forces his audience to confront their own investments on the level at which they are truly lived: the level of sentiment itself.

It's perhaps unfair to compare Sirk and Roth, although it's a comparison Roth's text unwittingly invites. But the comparison also suggests what I see as the chief deficiency of *The Human Stain*: its failure to follow through its own logic vis-à-vis race to that logic's ultimate conclusion. In this respect, as I already suggested, the novel mimes the gestures of the genre in which it participates, in which ambivalence on precisely this score (the impulse to affirm the possibility of passing; the desire to affirm, or at least not to expunge, the experience of race) is resolved on the terrain of sentiment. But generic logic alone cannot account for Roth's failure of nerve, for the prominence he gives to Ernestine and to the family narrative she articulates. Rather, it seems to me that for all of his vaunted obstreperousness, race considered under the heading of black and white makes Roth if not nervous then at least timid. And this timidity, brought to the fore in comparison with Sirk's greater rigor and irony, becomes all the more pronounced when we turn to a different set of contexts—ethnoracial and mass-cultural alike—that do allow Roth to commit fully to his own most audacious impulses.

For, elsewhere, the novel achieves the ironic sublimity I have associated with Sirk. That achievement, it will not surprise the reader to learn, is conducted not through Roth's concern with matters of black and white—although those matters are implicated in it—but rather his invocation of the complicated and complicating example of Jewishness. This concern is of course explicit throughout his career; it seems—and, I will be arguing, only *seems*—to be tangential to the passing narrative of this novel, but indeed turns out to be central to it. And here again, it is a set of mass-cultural associations that do this work for Roth. As we shall see in more detail, it is accomplished through a recurring—if oddly occulted—comparison of Coleman's passing-as-a-Jew masquerade to the life and career of a Jewish jazz musician who passed for a gentile: Artie Shaw.

"That Big White Thing": Roth, Shaw, and the Musical Mysteries of Ethnicity

If *The Human Stain* contains a range of references to sentimental passing melodramas, particularly those of the 1950s, it is also shot through with references to music of all varieties and eras; indeed, it is perhaps the most musically attuned of Roth's novels, many of which feature (as Mark Schechner has noted) a substantial and ongoing engagement with the music of Roth's adolescence.[13] Nathan hears big band music of all varieties coming from his neighbor Coleman's house well before he even meets him—Coleman listens to an FM big band program that includes the likes of Dick Haymes and Tommy Dorsey and ends with "a ritual weekly half hour of Benny Goodman" (14). And, in the memorable scene of their first real encounter with each other, the two men dance cheek to cheek to the music of Frank Sinatra. Late in the novel, bookending this moment, the triumphant (if endless) last movement of Mahler's Third Symphony is played at Coleman's funeral. In between, music shadows the affair between Faunia and Coleman in a number of ways. At Tanglewood he takes her to hear a concert by Israeli émigré pianist Yefim Bronfman—one of their few public outings together, but the one that, in Nathan's best words, represents Coleman's attempt at "bringing recalcitrant, transgressive Faunia to life as a tastefully civilized Galatea . . . educating her . . . influencing her— . . . saving her from the tragedy of her strangeness" (208). More saliently, that affair is conducted to the tune of Artie Shaw's version of George Gershwin's song "The Man I Love," which figures three times. Coleman's first white girlfriend, eighteen-year-old Steena, does a long, langorous, sensual striptease to Shaw's rendition of that song. Later, at Coleman's request, his middle-aged white lover Faunia also strips to the tune, bringing a lifetime of knowledge, erotic and otherwise, to her performance. At the end of the novel the tune is referenced again, movingly and plangently, when Nathan tells the reader that he wished he had heard Steena singing to a piece of big band music at Coleman's funeral rather than, or in addition to, the Mahler reverently played there.

While it's the various iterations of "The Man I Love" that will be taking up the majority of my attention, I want to point to a common thread that runs throughout these musical examples: the thread of racial crisscrossing subtended by Jewishness. Whether represented by the Jewish-born Catholic convert Mahler, the Tashkent-born multiple émigré Bronfman, or the American-born Goodman or Gershwin's engagement with the distinctively African American form of expressive musical culture we call jazz, the crossing of expected lines and norms of national and ethnoracial identity are implicated in the seemingly value-neutral aesthetic sphere of music. Roth has said in an interview that the drama of the novel "has nothing to do with the ethical, spiritual, theological or historical aspects of Judaism"—which is quite true, since the only sign of Judaism I can see in the novel is the moment, at Coleman's funeral, when his rebellious son Mark stands to say Kaddish for his father, believing him, like everyone else, to be the Jew he has played for most of his life.[14] But Jewishness permeates the musical references that run through the novel as a kind of undersong—or soundtrack. And more: these references connect Jewishness to the thematics of passing and the dynamics of race in ways that ramify well beyond Roth's invocation of the passing narrative.

Such work is performed most vividly—and linked to the intensities that grip the novel most fully—in the novel's flashback to the late 1940s, when an eighteen-year-old Steena Olfsson, new to New York and newly in love with Coleman, does her striptease to "The Man I Love." Here is Roth's description of that moment:

> She astonished him—astonished *herself*—with the dance she did one Saturday night, standing at the foot of his foldout sofa bed in her half slip and nothing else. She was getting undressed, and the radio was on—Symphony Sid—and first, to get her moving and in the mood, there was Count Basie and a bunch of jazz musicians jamming on "Lady be Good," a wild live recording, and, following that, more Gershwin, the Artie Shaw rendition of "The Man I Love" that featured Roy Eldridge steaming everything up. Coleman was lying semi-upright on the bed, doing what he most loved to . . . watch her take her clothes off. All at once, with no prompting from him—seemingly prompted only by Eldridge's trumpet—she began what Coleman liked to describe as the single most slithery dance ever performed by a Fergus Falls girl after little more than a year in New York City. She could have raised Gershwin himself from the grave with that dance, and with the way she sang the song. Prompted by a colored trumpet player

playing it like a black torch song, there to see, plain as day, was all the
power of her whiteness. That big white thing. (115–116)

In the present context this passage suggests two things. First, it tells us how Roth brings into his novel the concern with whiteness circulating in academe at the moment he was writing the novel (and that, as we shall see, he had something to do with creating) and, second, it suggests that he does so in order to complicate, irrevocably, that discursive matrix. Steena is singing and dancing to a black man's version of a Jewish man's version of a black-inspired musical idiom, and each element in this chain deserves separate attention. George Gershwin, Jeffrey Melnick has reminded us, famously took the elements of jazz and spirituals and recast them into his own Tin Pan Alley–inflected idiom and essentially (if memorably) made his bid for high-culture status, *Rhapsody in Blue*, by unifying the Western art music tradition and the African American vernacular form to which he owed so much.[15] Jazz musicians returned the favor by riffing on, and transforming, Gershwin's melodies, sometimes explicitly so, sometimes without acknowledgment. Indeed, Richard Crawford has shown, the chord structure of "I Got Rhythm" became the basis for a number of jazz standards—so much so that, to this day, they're referred to as Rhythm changes. Most notable among these were the endeavors of Charlie Parker who, as Crawford elegantly observes, frequently "employed the 'I Got Rhythm' chord changes to create a kind of obstacle course that only the best players could negotiate"—witness, for example, his elegant and intricate "Cherokee."[16] Parker thus implicitly riffed on the title of the tune as well as its chords; to be able to follow along with the chord changes was to demonstrate that one possesses the magical quality that the song praises, "rhythm" and, indeed its correlative in the lyrics of the song, "music." Implicitly, he also riffed on Gershwin's act of racial appropriation in claiming that quality for himself. Parker seems to be saying to Gershwin: you may say you have rhythm of the sort that is conventionally (and even racistly) associated with African American cultural production, but we *really* have rhythm—not the sort you ascribe to us, but a kind even more virtuosic and complex than yours; and we show it by rendering your admittedly adventuresome chord changes truly dazzling.

So too Roy Eldridge, in Roth's account, transforms Gershwin's standard into a "black torch song," an act both of racial transformation and of racial reappropriation à la Charlie Parker. The words of the song ("Some day he'll come along / The man I love; / And he'll be big and strong / The man I love") take on an ironic double meaning that tends toward the undecidable—is Eldridge's virtuosic and steamy solo paying mock tribute to Gershwin the racial appropriator or to his white bandleader, Artie Shaw?—all the while running rings around both.* But Steena's song and "slithery" dance to the black man's magical music performs yet another reversal of these power dynamics. Her performance (in every sense of the word) is what Roth, like Michael Rogin in his famous account of the Jewish accession to whiteness via blackface minstrelsy, would identify as "racial cross-dressing": a moment, that is, where a white person enacts a black role in order to access for her or himself the libidinal freedom stereotypically associated with "blackness."[17] Indeed, Steena's performance is quite directly reminiscent of the most egregious form of "racial cross-dressing," blackface: for she is recreating the role of Billie Holiday, who sang "The Man I Love" to the trumpet of Roy Eldridge briefly and unhappily with the Artie Shaw Orchestra (one of the few integrated swing bands of the era, but one in which black performers like Holiday and Roy Eldridge still found themselves in uncomfortable enough positions—facing separate accommodations, for example—to make their time in the band relatively brief). But the ramifications of the scene do not stop there. For Steena's cross-dressing comes to be mimicked by Coleman's. He turns very soon thereafter to adopting the masquerade of a white man playing the role of a Jewish intellectual. Indeed, I would go further: her blithe performance seems to inspire his. Witnessing Steena display of the "power of ... whiteness" by dancing to and then imitating the music of a black man teaches Coleman not only how to lie about his own racial identity but also (how) to imitate and then master the high-white culture that he, as a graduate student, is encompassing and of which he becomes an exponent, first as professor, then as dean. Coleman may be the man she loves; but through her performance he learns not just to love but also to become the Man.

---

*Roth's syntax is ambiguous. The phrase "the Artie Shaw rendition of 'The Man I Love' that featured Roy Eldridge steaming everything up" could refer to the steaming effect of the entire orchestra or to that of Eldridge alone. Whatever reading one gives to this particular phrase, the emphasis throughout the passage is on Steena's dancing to Eldridge's trumpet, not to Shaw's clarinet—to "a colored trumpet player playing [Gershwin] like a black torch song," not, as I am suggesting, a Jew-passing-for-gentile playing it like a klezmer clarinetist.

Roth's scene thus participates in and comments on the critical tradition that seeks to revise the hallowed process of Jewish assimilation by reframing it in racialized terms—as an accession to the privileges of whiteness.* Whether it be Al Jolson triumphantly singing "Mammy" in blackface to his appreciative *yiddishe* mama or George Gershwin adopting the spiritual "Sometimes I Feel Like a Motherless Child" to shape the tonalities of "Summertime," whether it be rapacious Jewish entrepreneurs sewing up the music publishing industry or the Warner Brothers rescuing their studio from financial catastrophe and remaking the movies through the magical appeal of blackface in *The Jazz Singer*, critics like Rogin, Matthew Frye Jacobson, and Melnick remind us that Jews moved from a fraught category of off- or nonwhite into ambivalent admission to the hallowed and respectable halls of whiteness through their donning of—and exploitation of—the mask of blackness. Coleman simply—one might even say neatly—reverses the process: he becomes white by playing at being a Jew. But, Roth suggests, this reversal is actually part of a long chain of imitations, appropriations, revision that serve as an act of racial requital. Coleman's Jewface performance may imitate Steena's imitation of Gershwin's appropriation of the African American tradition of jazz, but, whatever its distance from the original, his appropriation of the guise of Jewishness poses itself as a counterappropriation no less intensely satisfying in its implications than Parker's reworkings of "I Got Rhythm" into "Cherokee." Passing as—for all intents and purposes becoming—a Jewish intellectual is a "colossal sui generis score-settling joke" on the world, one that requites a long series of racial slights, the very first one of which—the one that Nathan chooses to begin the chapter that describes his past as a black man—is the offer by the Jewish parents of one of his classmates, the

---

*I want to be careful here about what I am and am not claiming. I'm not asserting that Roth read Rogin, Jacobson, Melnick, etc.; it's not outside the realm of possibility, given his attunement to the academic zeitgeist, but I tend to doubt it. On the other hand, as I suggest more fully below, his position vis-à-vis Jews and whiteness anticipated their critique as early as *The Counterlife* (1986), which is, no doubt, why Jacobson uses it so powerfully in his own argument. And there are reasons for this, having to do with the general position of alienation Roth takes toward the generation of Irving Howe, and the American Jewish establishment in general, which puts him in an oddly isomorphic position with a figure like Michael Rogin, only a few years younger than Roth at the time of his death and equally irreverent with respect to the pieties of the Jewish American liberal-left establishment. Generational politics makes strange bedfellows.

Fenstermans, of a thousand dollars for Coleman's agreeing to louse up his high school final exams and hence make their son the senior class valedictorian (131). Coleman not only outdoes the hapless Fensterman by becoming a member of the tribe—"what a great all-encompassing idea the world had had to turn him into... his father's Fensterman son" (131); he triumphs further on their chosen terrain of academic achievement, becoming that most successful of upwardly mobile Jews, a college professor—even, indeed especially, a dean who delights in pruning his New England college of its manifold encrustations of WASP deadwood.

But the ironies don't stop there; they ramify throughout the scene and well beyond. Indeed, as with the musical subtext of the novel itself, Jewishness is present everywhere, yet mentioned nowhere, in the scene; it works in ways that are multiply ironizing, destabilizing. That effect is created by the version referenced in the text, that of Artie Shaw's band featuring the black trumpeter Roy Eldridge. As we have seen, according to Roth, Eldridge's performance is most remarkable for its revision of the Gershwin standard, for its "steam[y]" transformation of his original into "a black torch song." Regrettably, the technology does not yet exist for me to reproduce this song here, but what's most notable about it to my admittedly uneducated ear is the *lack* of what Roth calls "steam" in Eldridge's solo.[18] There are none of the characteristic touches of Eldridgean virtuosity—none of the upper-register blasts or inspired whoops and hollers that I associate with Eldridge at his most unbuttoned; nor does the solo boast the suave sinuosity that Eldridge's playing also frequently achieves. Rather, he offers a very elegant, very taut, and very brief restatement of Gershwin's tune, with little or no embellishment. Whatever this solo might be, it is no "torch song." Its restraint and lack of embellishment contrast strikingly with Shaw's playing, which dominates the recording both temporally (fully a minute and ten seconds of its three minutes and eight seconds of recording time) and stylistically. Indeed, Shaw's solo here is a particularly virtuoso performance, nothing but arabesques and ornament, chromatic runs and modal swoops. And this solo, too, bears an ethnoracial reading, for it further complicates the game of racial appropriation and reappropriation to which Roth's passage alludes. The dominating sound of Shaw's clarinet here has the distinct intonations of the music with which Artie Shaw grew up. The solo alludes to the stylistic devices—the use of augmented seconds (the so-called Phrygian mode) and fourths in a minor key, the "smears" between notes, the longish trills and mordents—that define the eastern European Jewish popular music or "Jewish jazz," as it has been sometimes dubbed, which has come to be known as klezmer.

In the big band recording around which Roth builds his scene, in other words, we don't so much hear a black musician reappropriating the musical appropriation of black expressive culture by the Jewish composer Gershwin, but rather the music of a white clarinetist playing insouciantly with the music to emphasize Gershwin's Jewish origins and musical roots. (Klezmer, after all, was as germane to Gershwin's musical development as jazz—a fact noted by the gentile clarinetist who, at a rehearsal, mockingly improvised a klezmerlike glissando at the beginning of *Rhapsody in Blue*, which Gershwin promptly added to the score.)* And more: in that performance Shaw slyly, allusively proclaims himself to be a Jew. Such a gesture is not so simple, in Shaw's case, as one might think. Named in his youth Arthur Arshawsky, named at his birth Abraham Isaac Arshawsky (!), Artie, or, as he preferred to be known, Art Shaw spent much of his earlier career engaged in the same enterprise as Coleman: that is to say, passing—in his case, as a gentile. His pointing to his own Jewishness here was not for him, in other words, a simple or routine matter. To be sure, many Jews were openly such as they entered the jazz scene of the late 1930s and 1940s, especially the big band/swing world: the famous bandleader Benny Goodman and the sideman Ziggy Elman (née Harry Finkelman) come to mind—it was Elman, Seth Rogovoy suggests, who brought the klezmer tune "Der Shtiler Bulgar" to Goodman's band, where it got transformed into a 1939 tune called "When the Angels Sing," with lyrics by Johnny Mercer.[19] Some of these sought to pass for black in that world. Such was the case with Mezz Mezzrow, the original "white negro": hipster, appall-

---

*And, to keep the chain of allusion going, klezmer virtuoso Dave Tarras parodied this glissando (à la Charlie Parker with *I Got Rhythm* and, with some of the same reappropriating wit, putting Gershwin back in the ghetto where he belonged) in his "Nicolaev Bulgar" (1940). See Seth Rogovoy, *The Essential Klezmer: A Music Lover's Guide to Jewish Roots and Soul Music, from the Old World to the Jazz Age to the Downtown Avant-Garde* (Chapel Hill: Algonquin, 2000), p. 71.

Recordings of *Rhapsody in Blue* vary tremendously in their rendering of this glissando and other klezmer effects. The one that to my ears is most insistent on these is, interestingly, Maurice Peress's attempt to recreate as "authentically" as possible the original 1924 concert, *The Birth of Rhapsody in Blue* (CD 60113-4, Musicmaster, 1987), based on the advice of jazz scholars and in consultation with the Whiteman archives at Williams College.

ingly bad clarinetist, and Louis Armnstrong's drug connection, who genuinely considered himself to be black. (As Melnick reminds us, Shaw went through a brief period of white negroism in Harlem, under the tutelage of the Yiddish-speaking jazzman Willie "the Lion" Smith, but this seems to have been a brief phase in his long career.)[20] Still others foregrounded their Jewishness by alluding to, or even participating in, the klezmer tradition in which they grew up. Manny Klein, with whom Shaw played during his unhappy years of work in the CBS orchestra, began his career in the Paul Whiteman band and, before becoming an accomplished studio musician in Hollywood, moved easily into Mickey Katz's raucous klezmer/comedy band. Or, to adduce a later example too delicious not to mention, one thinks of eminent vibraphonist Terry Gibbs née Julius Gubenko, who got his start playing klezmer in his father Abe Gubenko's Radio Novelty Orchestra, then starting his own band, which cut a disk, *Terry Gibbs Plays Jewish Melodies in Jazztime* (recently reissued on CD) that intermixes bop passages with straight klezmer (and, just to complicate the matter, featured a young pianist named Alice McCord, later and better known as the deeply Afrocentric Alice Coltrane).

But Shaw was not one of these. In both his life and his music, traces of his Jewish origins were veiled, muted, or simply ignored. To be sure, as was the case with many of the above named, there was often a "Jewish" note—however ill-defined that may be—in Shaw's style, a "Jewish flavor, an emotional predisposition, something cantorial: the catch in the voice, the certain keening, grieving, quality that distinguishes the *Kaddish* and *Kol Nidre* of Jewish liturgy," according to jazz critic Richard Sudhalter.[21] But it's important to note there was just as often—indeed there was more frequently—*not* such a note in his playing. Shaw's tone throughout most of his career was light, almost airy; his playing simple, compact, if virtuosic. It was not until the mid-1940s—relatively late in his career—that Shaw began to indulge in the crossover game played by many of his Jewish contemporaries, to "out" himself musically as a Jew, although in ways that read as edgy, ironic, self-deprecating. Consider the prime case: a recording of "Dr. Livingstone I Presume?" from 1940 ends with a solo that is pure klezmer, based, according to scholar Henry Sapoznik, on the Russian theme *Kamarinskaya*.[22] But here the act of ethnoracial affiliation is complex. Playing the white Stanley to the equally white Livingstone, Shaw's klezmer allusion sutures eastern European culture to that of the Congo, positions it as the primitive but entertaining other to the great white explorer—himself. Or consider the 1947 a version of "My Heart Belongs to Daddy," which Shaw himself described as containing a direct allusion to the Jewish. The song begins with a violin solo that uses klezmer melodies and harmonies, then moves into a version of Shaw's signature tune, "Nightmare" (!), then segues into a vocal of the song. All these elements wittily allude to even as they deconstruct the "Jewish science" of psychoanalysis, in which Shaw was himself at the time deeply involved.

Thus, even as he introduced Jewish elements into his music via klezmer, Shaw was insistent on the necessity of his veiling them, distancing himself from the Jewishnessness that he was in the process of affirming. So too in version of "The Man I Love" that Roth foregrounded—as opposed to the more unbuttoned playing in the weirdly primitivistic setting of "Dr. Livingstone"—the klezmer influence is muted, there but not there, a matter of allusion, of hinting, of veiling and revealing: a kind of Coleman-like passing, perhaps, or even a Steena-like striptease, rather than an out-and-out form of self-revelation. [7]* And this is exactly how Shaw spoke of the relation between his Jewishness and his music. "Certainly I can't deny the influence of my Russian-Jewish-Austrian ancestry," Shaw commented. "But how it comes out, how it makes itself felt—that's a mystery" (quoted in Sudhalter 583: no source given). As in art, so in life: for much of his adulthood, Shaw mystified his own origins. Born on New York's Lower East Side and raised on the rough streets of New Haven, Connecticut, Shaw describes in vivid detail his day-to-day encounter with the antisemitism it is quite easy, from our own historical moment, to forget but with which Shaw's second-generation Americans were quite familiar: the humiliations by schoolmates, the beatings by street toughs, the general sense of being a cultural outsider in a gentile world. In his autobiography, *The Trouble with Cinderella*, he tells us that it is this sense of alienation that caused him to change his name from Arshawsky to Shaw. While playing an early gig with a group called the Kentuckians, he simply renamed himself because, as he puts it, he realized that being Arshawsky would "not

---

*The peekaboo klezmer game was not only one played by Jews. African American clarinetist Barney Bigard opens a 1942 version of "Are You Sticking?" with the Duke Ellington Orchestra with a solo that is pure klezmer; the rest of his quite brilliant playing on that cut references all sorts of musics, including most prominently the big band stylings of Goodman and Shaw. It reads to this listener at least as a kind of musical "outing"—a knowing reference to the Jewishness of big band–leading clarinetists of the time.

bring him any real benefits." He describes the process by which he became "Artie Shaw" in remarkably Coleman-like terms:

> As for this new kid we'll be dealing with from here on—let's see now... Art Shaw. Doesn't *sound* very "foreign." Certainly doesn't sound much like a Jewish kid either, does it?
> Well, what's he look like, maybe we can tell something that way? Dark hair, dark brown eyes, fairly regular features—could be almost anything, almost any nationality, Spanish, Italian, French, Russian, Greek, Armenian, damn near anything at all. Could be he's a mixture of a bit of every one of those. In short, an American kid—may as well let it go at that. Although Shaw *sounds* Irish, wouldn't you say? Or maybe English? Anyway, what difference does it make? At least he's not a Jew or a "foreigner," so that's all right.
> Or is it?[23]

Throughout the passage, Shaw enacts the Coleman-like pattern of self-reinvention through ethnoracial masquerade, a term that Shaw uses quite explicitly when he refers to the new self who forms around this name change as "this Art Shaw kid who was now beginning to masquerade as me" (93). And the passing game worked, particularly in the still antisemitic worlds in which Shaw was moving in the late 1930s and 1940s (as Sudhalter puts it, accurately if a bit uncomfortably conveying the spirit of the times, "his new name didn't even *sound* Jewish; handsome and assured, he didn't *look* Jewish in any stereotypical way" [606]). But, as distinct from Coleman's, Shaw's passing always seemed to be accompanied by a lingering sense of guilt or, perhaps, shame. ("That's right," Shaw says in *The Trouble with Cinderella*, "I was ashamed of my name. I was ashamed of being a Jew.... And it's only because I am no longer ashamed, no longer ashamed of being Jewish, *and no longer ashamed of having been ashamed*, that I can speak about it now" [91].)

Indeed, *The Trouble with Cinderella* narrates this act of passing as a primal fall into the sense of inauthenticity that plagued him for the rest of his life—an inauthenticity that he connects, via his psychoanalysis with noted Hollywood shrink May Romm (who also treated both David Selznick and his wife) to his shame at his Yiddish-speaking father ("my fear and shame of my father made me feel guilty, which made me fearful and hateful of myself... I was so ashamed of his guttural accent that I didn't want other kids to hear him talk to me, to have further reason to despise me for 'being Jewish'" [138]). Combine this with his overinvestment in his Americanizing mother, his trouble with the bitch goddess success (aka Cinderella), a goddess who keeps finding him despite his best efforts to hide from her, and we can read the book as tracing an impossible set of dilemmas in which Jewish self-hatred, passing, and cultural achievement are all complexly interrelated—in which Shaw's fame as a jazz musician and his shame at the act of passing that seems to have made it possible get conflated, at least in his own mind. It's not till the end of the experience the volume records, in fact, that he is able to resolve this conundrum. There he simultaneously proclaims himself a Jew and turns his back on the popular success that has so tormented him and prepares to turn to what he now identifies as his true love—the pursuit of culture. And, indeed, soon after writing his autobiography in 1952 Shaw abandoned the clarinet altogether and spent the rest of his life studying philosophy, composition, and the arts. In this new identity as a high-culture intellectual, he seems to be saying, he has found his authentic self, and it is a *Jewish* self, although it is one that is no longer named Arshawsky. The Lower East Side–born Arshawsky becomes more and more of a Jew the more he assimilates to *high*, not popular, culture—the more he becomes, as it were, Art as well as Artie Shaw.

As he did so, powerfully if problematically, Shaw seemed to become more and more a Roth character—a model for Coleman Silk, to be sure, but also a model for a character type that populates Roth's fiction from Portnoy forward: the sex-and-culture obsessed Jewish man who is both made and unmade by his gentile women. For Shaw soon entered Hollywood, where he embarked on a Roth-like march through the many gentile starlets who, Steena-like, threw themselves at his feet. He married five of them, including Ava Gardner, to whom (very much like Coleman with Faunia at Tanglewood or Roth's Portnoy in his relation with "the Monkey") he devoted considerable efforts at cultural improvement even as he basked in the glory of Hollywood's sexiest star sharing his bed. Even more memorable, perhaps, was the denouement of his disastrous marriage to the romance novelist Kathleen Winsor. In their bitter divorce battle she denounced him to the House Un-American Activities Committee (while they were still married) for the crime of championing Russian and folk classical music—a gesture that, given his interest in the Slavic-tinged klezmer of his roots, had ethnoracial as well as political overtones. (He

THE HUMAN STAIN OF RACE

was, in other words, denounced for being both a Jew and a Red.) Following the denunciation, Shaw withdrew entirely from public life, spending most of the next two decades in seclusion. And these plot points only confirm our sense of Shaw as a kind of Rothian figure, for such—the denunciation by a Hollywood wife, the conflation of Jewishnesss and Communism in the hysterical right-wing response, the withdrawal into seclusion—mark exactly the fate of Ira Ringgold, the protagonist of Roth's novel about the blacklist, *I Married a Communist*.

So why does Roth, to return to the passage with which we began, focus on Roy Eldridge rather than Artie Shaw, especially when the latter provides so perfect a model for Coleman Silk—aspirer to high culture, self-remaker, sex maniac? And what can this tell us about the whiteness argument with which he seems to be struggling via this set of allusions? The answer to the former is the same as it is to the latter: because Jewishness complicates everything—including Jewishness (a lesson Roth elsewhere knows well and teaches us throughout his work, when he's not

4.2   May 4, 1953. Artie Shaw Wiping his Eyes During Testimony (before the House Un-American Activities Committee). "He shed a few tears while recounting his rise to fame from a poor beginning." Courtesy of Corbis.

intent on making a Big Statement About Race). Passing, desire, sexuality, levels of cultural aspiration and achievement: all these things look complicated enough when they're a matter of the "big white thing," as Steena's cultural and social performance suggests, or when they're a matter of appropriations and appreciations colored in black and white, as Coleman's revisionary version of her performance would also imply. And, indeed, Roth wants to tell this story as just that, of culture and passing as a matter of the cultural interchange between Gershwin and Eldridge, between Steena and Coleman; and he wants to make the passage very much about the satisfactions and possibilities of racial reappropriation: of what Eric Lott might have called "love and countertheft." But, when he turns to the idiom of Jewishness to do this, each of these already volatile and unstable terms becomes set in yet more fluid motion. The unacknowledged but palpable presence of klezmer in Shaw's (repressed, unmentioned) solo in "The Man I Love," of both Shaw and klezmer in Steena's dance of white appropriation and appreciation, of all of the above in Coleman's ultimately successful masquerade as a white Jewish intellectual: all these bring elements of a deep undecidability into the novel's ethnoracial cultural mix. Roth's layering of impersonations raises this question: who is masquerading as whom, if the person one is masquerading as is himself masquerading as something else? Like the mocking speech of Faunia's pet crow Prince, who, we learn in a pivotal passage in the book, "imitates the schoolkids that come here and imitate him," the layers of appropriative imitation know no bounds, possess no origin and no end; all we know is that new forms of expression proliferate, generating new, uncanny, unexpected forms of cultural expression as they do so. For this intricate set of imitations does not represent echoings or mimetic performances alone; each also represents a new, revisionary creation. "'When the kids on the school trips imitate a crow?' Faunia explains. 'That's his impression of the kids. The kids do that. He's invented his own language. From kids.'" "In a strange voice of her own," Roth's novel continues, "Faunia said, 'I love that strange voice he invented'" (243).[24]

Inconclusion

In her contribution to the *Slate* exchange with Brent Staples on the subject of *The Human Stain* from which I've quoted above, Judith Shulevitz channels Michael Rogin: "No matter how true *The Human Stain* is to the affective experience of African Americans, Roth is using Coleman for his own ends," she writes. "Call it using the black collective experience to talk about Roth's encounter with the Jewish one."[25] In some ways I have been arguing the same thing, with this qualification: that talking about the Jewish experience is not only the *only* thing that Roth can do, as Shulevitz implies, but that talking about race through the Jewish experience is the best thing that *Roth* can do: the questions he is able to raise through and around Jewishness resonate more deeply with respect to race than do the questions he raises by approaching race through a lens of black and white.[26]

Vis-à-vis Roth, this should be no surprise, but vis-à-vis cultural and social criticism across the board that recognition might lead us in surprising and productive directions. To a certain extent, seeing this allows us to place with more precision the valences of the influential Jewish-assimilation-by-blackface argument with which, I have been claiming, Roth's text has been engaged. For one thing, putting Roth and the whiteness critics together suggests that the Jewish multicultural left and the increasingly neoconservative Roth display a surprising affinity to each other: they are all, to put it one way, people who have problems with Irving Howe. Thus it is no coincidence that Jacobson's *Whiteness of a Different Color* begins with the explication of a long passage on the subject of whether the Jew is a Caucasian drawn from another novel featuring Nathan Zuckerman, *The Counterlife*, a passage Jacobson uses to set the tone for the rest of the analysis of the processes by which ethnics became white and to which he returns later as a clinching example.[27] For both Roth and the whiteness critics, working from different ends of the political spectrum, the putative intimacy of the Jew and the African American manifested by turn-of-the-century Socialists, Depression-era adherents of the Popular Front, white liberal participation in the civil rights movement, et by now all-too-familiar alia, do not betoken the ostensible ethical sensitivity of the American Jew but rather testify to the troubling gap between the idealized Jewish self-image and the realities of Jewish practices in matters of race.

But the use to which Jacobson puts Roth might also serve as a key to the ways in which Jewishness as a cultural example performs a more complex function than the whiteness critics seem to allow. For these critics, Jewishness finally is of importance for the manner in which it signals the transformation of ambiguously raced European-born ethnics into white people, with the property and privileges attending thereunto. As such, they continue a long tradition of using the example of Jewish experience as a synecdoche for European immigrants across the board, a practice at best misleading. This is not to say that Jewishness can't provide one model among many of the various paths by which immigrants enter into the American "mosaic," "melting pot," or "salad bowl"; nor, as I've been insisting throughout this book, that Jews haven't "become" white in some significant way. But, as I've also been suggesting throughout, there are other lessons one could derive from the Jewish experience in the U.S., patterns of significance that don't necessarily end in a reified whiteness but rather eventuate in more destabilizing possibilities—in this case, in a model of identity that is mobile, multidimensional, transactional. To be Jewish, as I've been arguing throughout this book, is to be constructed simultaneously in racial, ethnic, cultural, religious terms, and this very multiplicity seems to be germane to the discussion about identity that underlines whiteness criticism, at least at its most provocative. So, too, is a long chain of discourse from the 1910s through the 1940s that emphasized the ability of the Jew to escape simple identity cateogories. For example, as Zygmunt Bauman has also powerfully suggested, even before their transformation from off-white to white was undertaken, Jews historically functioned as shifters, metamorphosers: likewise, in Daniel Itzkovitz's powerful reading of racialized discourses of the 1920s, they are identified as chameleons—as color-shifting entities that, transforming and retransforming, veiling and reveiling, have imitated many conceptual, ethnic, and racial entities without being fully encompassed by any one among them.[28] What would it mean, one wonders, to use either of these two models (the Jew as multiply constructed identity, the Jew as shape-shifter) to think about racial identity itself in a new—or at least newly self-conscious—multiethnic America, one in which the black/white binary has been fatally disrupted but no new model of racialization has fully emerged to take its place? Could it be possible, to extend this chain of speculation further, to think about racial equivocality or racial metamorphosis on the Jewish plan as a genuinely redemptive option—as Coleman Silk and Artie Shaw variously do, only to be punished for their presumption, the one by external, the other by internal Furies?

What I'm suggesting is that the example of Jewishness powerfully and uniquely raises these questions *as* questions, disrupting the certitudes and rigidities that mark not only American race thinking, but race thinking across the board. It's significant, at the very least, that even (or especially) within the black/white dichotomy, Jewishness often functions in just this way, not only as a signifier of whiteness but also as a sign of multiple affiliation and fluid identity construction. Contemporary novelist Walter Mosley, son of a black man and a white Jewish woman, proudly defines himself as a Coleman-like race crosser without the necessary secrecy; in his interviews and his writing he identifies himself as both Jewish and black, but (*pace* whiteness critics) with a significant qualification: "Mosley does not consider [his Jewish mother] or any other Jew as being white. . . . By his reasoning, Jews, in the eyes of Europe's Aryan supremacists, were an extinguishable race. He is Jewish in a cultural sense, but a black man in a racial sense, he said, because his father was a black man. Because the world sees him as a black man."[29]* In this complex self-identification, he's at one with a number of children of multiracial families, including writers Rebecca Walker Gordon and James McBride, who have written identity-blowing autobiographies that meditate on the dual allegiances of Jewish and African American histories and their intricate imbrication with each other. (McBride's is particularly relevant to the inquiry of this chapter, in that the narrative of his mother's trek from an oppressive traditional Jewish background to the matriarch of a black church is rich with echoes, some ironic, others direct, of sentimental and passing narratives alike as well as a salutary reminder of how powerfully Christian is the rhetoric that underlies both these genres.)

Or to cite a different example of the deployment of Jewishness in the discourse of race, consider the recent book by anthropologist John Jackson, *Real Black: Adventures in Racial Sincerity*. Not only does Jackson take his organizing trope from Lionel Trilling, a Jew who had some issues, to put it mildly, with racial sincerity *and* authenticity.[†] The center of the

---

* But here is how the British newspaper, the *Observer*, sees him: "Walter Mosley is a bear of a man, with soft features, olive skin and a face that, even in repose, has a quizzical look"—which is to say that, with the exception of the girth, he is perceived as a racial double for Coleman. Sean O'Hagan, "Time for a New Black Power Movement," *Observer*, August 18, 2002.

† Indeed, Trilling's antithesis can be read in fairly autobiographical terms: as the first tenured Jew in the Columbia English department, yet one who maintained a studied distance from his own Jewishness and adopted a mandarin, Anglophilic persona, he is a

book is occupied by two chapters on black Jews—on African Americans who consider themselves "authentic" Jews and American (or for that matter any other) Jews to be false claimants to their own history, Esaus to their Jacob. Jackson's argument here is rich with compelling ethnological detail about the competing forms of black Judaism and the ways in which black Jews court what one might call paranoia, if there weren't generations of experience to support that paranoia. What's important about his argument are the purposes for which Jackson invokes these "Real Jews": he cites them as "tangible example of how racial authenticities fold in on top of one another, and on top of our proffered sincerities, to rewrite our overly monolithic iterations of racial identity."[30] While there are numerous other possible examples he might cite of the same phenomenon (the Nation of Islam or Rastafarianism, for example, or the multiple national identities of many Caribbean-originated African Americans, including, by his account, Jackson himself), it would seem that only the overdetermined discourse of Jewishness—a discourse so powerful and labile that it can be invoked to de-Jewify Jews themselves—is strong enough to do the work of disarticulation in the service of which Jackson invokes it.

This disarticulation becomes yet more important as we approach a new millennium in which black and white are both soon to be superseded by Latino and other minority groups in the racial and ethnic composition of the U.S. Here, too, Jewishness is frequently a labile identity marker—and a marker of the essential lability of identity. I'm thinking of a response that the film version of *The Human Stain* garnered in, of all places, *People* magazine. *People* illustrated the passing story of Coleman not only by finding African Americans who would or could have passed as Jews but also by highlighting the experience of a Puerto-Rican who converted to Judaism because, as she put it "I don't like to be stereotyped," passed as the descendent of a Sephardic family, dated and almost married an Orthodox man but now self-identifies as a Latina, since that is how she is identified in the culture at large.[31] Her experience has broader implications—as we'll see in

---

prime representative of the stance of "sincerity"—of the adoption of a subject position that may or may not be factitious, but that can be played to the hilt and opposed to notions of "authenticity," or subject positions grounded in something imagined to be genuine, nonsocially crafted. Trilling's whole career can be said to have played out between these two possibilities.

chapter 5, the Sephardic diaspora functions in many recent Latino/Latina narratives as a figure for repressed historical memory itself—but it also reminds us of the power with which Jewishness functions in public discourse to disrupt the reflex demarcations of racial and ethnic identity that our culture insists on crafting.

The point of invoking these examples is not to suggest that the Jew-as-white-person model is invalid. Rather it is to insist that it is inadequate, increasingly so in this time of vast transition in the very makeup of U.S. racial and ethnic identities. In this sense, both *The Human Stain* and the whiteness discourse in which it is entangled are both reflections of—and climaxes to—a racial dispensation that is passing, but whose basic logic lingers on well after its time: one in which the tangled and complicated relation of Jewish and African Americans is not only read but *comes to symbolize* a racial regime constructed in terms of black and white. In its place we might profitably turn to that which such a logic represses, more complex narratives of racial and ethnic mutability that underlie the Jewish experience across the board, in order to weave new narratives fit for the multicultural future that *The Human Stain* and whiteness discourse have only begun to explore. We stand in the first decade of the twenty-first century, in other words, at an analogous juncture to the one that Sirk's film records: a moment when the old terms for thinking about race and ethnicity are inadequate, but no new lexicon has emerged to replace them—who uses the term *multiculturalism* any more, even as the dominant culture becomes, well, multicultural? At such a moment, Parker's revision of Gershwin, Roth's revision of the passing narrative, and Shaw's syncretic allusions to both the jazz and the klezmer traditions in the course of a move (back?) to Western art music remind us of the ways in which culture makers, in creating these revisionary representations, began long ago the process of guiding us into a new millennium rich with ethnic and racial recombinations.

As Rogin, Melnick et al. properly remind us, the process of such cultural recreation has involved unequal distributions of power, never more shockingly (but not, it should also be added, uniquely) with Jewish culture entrepreneurs. But—despite their political vigilance to the power dynamics involved in this transaction—it's important to note what gets left out of these accounts. The works I have been advertising to expose a logic—and an economics—of appropriation involved in the chain of revisionary remaking. But they also trace a counterlogic of theft and countertheft in which the "original" gets remade but is never fully effaced. Parker and Roth and Shaw's often on-the-fly improvisatory remaking of the cultural materials they were given don't merely repeat the appropriation of African American cultural expression upon which cultural criticism has focused so intensely: they also seek to imagine appropriation itself in newer guises, ones that have a racial salience but also transcend it, ultimately challenging established and stable notions of *any* racialized identity. To be sure, we look at such interventions, as Sirk asks us to look at the sentimentalized closure of racial passing narratives, through a glass darkly, our vision still irrevocably organized by the bifurcations of the color line. But, like Sirk as well, these writers and musicians ask us to come to terms with our own investment in race even as they challenge us to think through and beyond it. The human stain of race may smudge our vision; but Roth and the welter of contexts that his text evokes all ask us, sometimes despite themselves, to imagine a world where we can see differently. Or, to switch registers, these texts ask us to appreciate the strangeness, as well as the impossibility, of such a postracial vision and to speak it in a strange voice of our own.

Coda: Uri Caine, the Artie Shaw de Nos Jours

I want to conclude on a musical note. For, as I've been suggesting in other chapters, this working toward more complex articulations of the racial-ethnic dynamic is well underway among musicians, especially jazz musicians, and the destabilizing example of Jewishness is often at the center of this revisionary work, particularly in the downtown klezmer/radical Jewish culture scene to which I have been drawing attention. And it long has been so: I would point, for example, to the original constitution of the Klezmer Conservatory Band, organized by a then instructor at the New England Conservatory of Music, Hankus Netsky, that included in its number Don Byron and now-eminent musicologist Ingrid Monson, neither of whom is Jewish and both of whom are master klezmer performers.[32] The klezmer scene that has emerged in the last ten years is, as I argued in chapter 1, as multiracial as it is multicultural: jazz and klezmer music makers collaborate on a frequent and regular basis; racially, ethnically, and religiously diverse musicians jam, play in bands with, reshape the musical traditions of, one another. More generally, the black/white/Jewish collaborations that flourish in the avant-garde downtown scene have begun to spin out of even that context into a larger world of contemporary jazz, and I want in closing to focus on one of the more prominent of these, contemporary jazz pianist Uri Caine. Impressive in his own right, Caine is of particular importance in the current context because he systematically crosses over the divides that structure the cultural norms of contemporary American music making and of the culture at large that they reflect—and the ones that Artie Shaw so clearly chafed at: not only those between black and white, but also between Jewish and gentile, classical and jazz, U.S. and world musical tradition.

Caine grew up the son of a Law and an English professor at the University of Pennsylvania, speaking Hebrew as well as English, and studied both jazz theory and classical composition in high school. While attending Penn, his musical ambidexterity continued; he studied composition by day while playing with, inter alia, Philly Joe Jones, Grover Washington, and Hank Mobley at local clubs by night. Since leaving school, he has played in bands led by Rashid Ali, Sam Rivers, as well as the Woody Herman Orchestra; he is a regular sideman for Don Byron, having in fact played on all of Byron's recordings, as Byron has on many of his. His first CDs paid tribute to his pianistic precursors Thelonius Monk and Herbie Hancock; but he also joined Christian McBride and rap rhythmicist Ahmir "?uestlove" Thompson in a 1991 recording in which they assayed music ranging from Sun Ra to Marvin Gaye to Grover Washington. And he has himself played with many of the musicians who have refracted the klezmer revival in avant-garde directions—for example, not only on Don Byron's Mickey Katz album but also his klezmer-goes-Hollywood-inflected *Bug Music* and on David Krakauer's *Klezmer Madness!*—as well as on their nonklezmer works. But, although he performs classic jazz with his own trio, Caine's efforts have been increasingly moving in the direction of a number of fractured versions of classical music, including revisionary treatments of Mahler, Wagner, Beethoven (*The Diabelli Variations*) and Bach (*The Goldberg Variations*).

What's important about Caine in the context of this inquiry is the Shaw-like way he challenges the assumptions that structure so much of our thinking about the musical expression we put under the heading of jazz: those of race, of course, but also those of cultural hierarchy (jazz or other popular music versus European art music) or those of the "jazz canon," of what counts as "real" jazz (for example, music in the Armstrong/Ellington tradition, à la Wynton Marsalis, versus that in the avant-garde or experimental vein). To be sure, there have been a number of other figures who have posed challenges to these recurrent oppositions—Charles Mingus, who studied Varèse while he was thinking through Ellington, for example—but none, since Shaw, has done so in the way that Caine does: by systematically, wittily, invoking Jewishness. Such efforts pervade his work but are most evident in his systematic engagement with—and transgressions against—the classical tradition. His early effort in complicating that tradition, the wonderful *Wagner e Venezia*, for example, pricks the pretentious Wagner balloon by rearranging his thunderous symphonic scores for a string quartet augmented by piano and accordion playing in a square in Venice, complete with applause from a smallish crowd. Moreover, in this cheekily parodic, pastichy revision, Caine also contests Wagner's antisemitic discourse on musical expression. Wagner, of course, argued vociferously in *Das Judenthum in der Musik* (*The Jewish Spirit in Music*) that, because they lacked a national culture of their own, Jews were not capable of true musical originality, the highest expression of *Kultur*. Mendelssohn, the great German Jewish composer of Wagner's time, was incapable of creating original art, since he lacked any organic connection to German culture; Meyerbeer, the most prominent Jewish opera composer of Wagner's time, was capable only of creating tinkling, showy melodies since he lacked the true depth of feeling that underlay genuine cultural expression.[33] For Caine and his mini-band to take Wagner's own melodies and transform them into something precisely tinkling and parodic is not only to poke fun at his stereotypical vision of the Jews as insubstantial parodists but to play the antisemitic card against the antisemite. It is also to suggest that there is a ground of similarity between Wagner's own melodic expression and the kind Wagner identified with the Jew.

Similar effects pervade Caine's other efforts at "variation"—a classical form that, in an interview, Caine suggests is isomorphic to jazz: "If you're talking about variation form, it's also reminiscent of the way jazz players take a theme and then improvise on the same harmonic structure.... The game is to make each piece wildly different from the others and to still emphasize that they're all unified by a central adherence to the harmony. Bach himself does that."[34] As is suggested by that last statement—which essentially turns Bach into a jazz musician rather than, like the Swingle Singers or the Modern Jazz Quartet, the other way around—these variations are not just sophisticated efforts at difference within similarity; they're also powerful ideological statements aimed at the undoing of cultural hierarchy.[35] This effect is particularly pronounced in Caine's version of the most famous of all the theme-and-variations work that virtually defines this alternative tradition within the canon of Western art music, Bach's *Goldberg Variations*. His two-CD-long set of variations on Bach's variations persistently introduce klezmer and especially African American motifs to the work of the man who vividly illustrated the most famous Passion texts pre–Mel Gibson. Tellingly, Caine's own opening version of the canon upon which Bach signifies inflects that familiar tune with intonations of jazz, blues, and especially gospel. Of equal importance, Caine's persistent musical partner-in-crime Don Byron riffs on the Goldberg theme in a piece called "Don's Variation" by beginning with a klezmer lick followed by a glissando reminiscent of the opening of Gershwin's *Rhapsody in Blue* before moving into squeaks and squeals reminiscent of Albert Ayler and avant-garde jazz. The effect is not only to render indistinct the lines between classical, jazz, and klezmer traditions. It is also to recapitulate in a few bars the history of Jewish and African American musical exchange and thereby to redraw the lines that the classical tradition and jazz traditionalists like Marsalis alike enforce between "art" and "popular" music, "canonical" and "avant-garde" jazz, and imaginative expression coded black and white and Jewish.

It is Caine's sustained engagement with the work of Mahler, I think, that brings together the klezmer, the jazz, and the classical in ways that do powerful cultural and political as well as aesthetic work. Mahler was of course an utterly deracinated Jew—born to a Jewish family in Bohemia, he moved to Vienna early in his life and was raised in complete isolation from his origins (although he was widely and controversially perceived to be Jewish). Famously, he converted to Catholicism, more or less de rigeur for a state-sponsored career that climaxed with his position as chief conductor of the explicitly antisemitic Vienna Opera (whose charter forbade Jews to serve as conductor) and a tumultuous four-year stint at the equally antisemitic Vienna Philharmonic. The question of the Jewishness of Mahler's music is notoriously vexed. As Theodor Adorno—not always so attuned to these issues in his own life as he might have been—famously

4.3 Uri Caine on Broadway. Photographer: Jan Caine. Courtesy of Uri Caine.

put it: "One can no more put one's finger on [Mahler's Jewish element] than in any other work of art: it shrinks from identification yet to the whole remains indispensable."[36] On the one hand, in Wagner's terms, Mahler's music was *Jewish*—full of parody, pastiche, and paraphrase, it eschews or deconstructs the ideal of musical originality itself and hence severs the connection between national culture and musical expression that Wagner and other ideologues of German *Kultur* articulated. ("Just as words and constructions are hurled together in [their] Jargon with wondrous inexpressiveness," writes Wagner, "so does the Jew musician hurl together the diverse forms and styles of every age and every master" [92].) On the other, Mahler only infrequently brought Jewish motifs or melodies into his seamless web of musical allusion and often identified himself with the traditions of high German Romanticism and of Christian music making that were, to say the least, hostile to Jews. Nevertheless, or therefore, Caine's repeated deployment of Jewish motifs in his two jazz albums devoted to the music of Mahler, *Dark Flame* and *Gustav Mahler in Toblach* creates a striking and not un-Shaw-like effect: it brings to the fore the Jewish dimension that is always already there in Mahler's life and work. And, in so doing, Caine transvalues our understanding not only of the classical canon but also of the nature and possibilities of the music we call jazz.

Thus he brings into his band both the essential Don Byron (replacing him on the live recording, *Gustav Mahler in Toblach*, with David Timlin) and a whole band of multicultural, multiracial performers, including DJ Olive* and Aaron Bensoussan, a Moroccan-born cantor *cum* professional musician whose specialties include bridging the gaps between Ashkenazic and Sephardic cantorial styles *and* between cantorial singing and the vocal styles of grand opera. Bensoussan plays the *oud* on a number of pieces, chants on his powerful version of the *Abschied* (the last, longest, and most beautiful of Mahler's *Lied von der Erde*), recites the opening of the *selichot* prayers from the Yom Kippur service and improvises freely on them in Caine's version of the song "The Little Drummer Boy." All of these conflations are significant, but the last is of particular significance. "The Little Drummer Boy" anticipates what Mahler, living in the most antisemitic city in all of Europe, must have felt but could not know: the impending pressure of historic catastrophe. Not only does the drumroll that opens the song resonate with the pressure of the two world wars to come, but its Kafkaesque narrative—it is the story of an imprisoned drummer boy who envisages his march to the gallows the next day—trembles with anticipation of the impending genocide whose force was to burst out of its Viennese cocoon less than thirty years later:

> O gallows, you tall house,
> You look so frightening.
> I don't look at you any more,
> Because I know that's where I belong.

Words that Adorno wrote about Mahler's Tenth Symphony are apposite here: "The ground trembles under the feet of the assimilated Jew ... [and]

---

*DJ Olive is a turntable-and-mix artist who emerged from the Williamsburg avant-garde club scene in the 1990s, perhaps second only to DJ Spooky Tooth in fame. Olive's real name is Gregor Asch; he claims to have lived in America, Trinidad, and Australia before making his name in the all-night parties in Brooklyn lofts. His name testifies to his racial-ethnic self-identification.

by the euphemism of foreignness, the outsider seeks to appease the shadow of terror" (150). Or perhaps it would be better to say: even by seeking to adopt the euphemism of the German folk song for his ends, the insider/outsider Mahler cannot appease the shadow of terror; instead, he is prescient to its shape and gives it musical form.* But Caine goes Mahler, and for that matter Adorno, one step better. By adding to his version of "The Little Drummer Boy" prayers from the Yom Kippur service that denote collective self-affirmation by the Jewish congregation—the moment when the congregation asserts its own communal guilt and in so doing expiates it for a year—Caine presents us with a dense and productive conundrums. Is the drummer boy's internalization of his criminality a weird version of the *Viddui*, the repeated moment in the Yom Kippur service when each member of the community beats his or her breast and accepts the sins committed by all? Or is the latter to be distinguished from the individualized guilt of the drummer boy?—*Viddui*, after all, expiates as well as enumerates. Or, to add to these, is Mahler to be seen as standing inside or outside the Jewish community into which he was born? On the one hand, the conjunction of a (revised version of a) Jewish prayer and a (revised version of an) ur-German folk song suggests the distance between Mahler and the extended Jewish community at large. On the other, the prayer could be read as including Mahler's own transgressions—his willed disavowal of his Jewish origins—in the list of those that are being communally expiated, enfolding Mahler back into the Jewishness he disavowed

---

*There's another important intertextual link to be suggested here; Leonard Bernstein (who of course brought Mahler back into popular esteem, largely through some amazing performances with the highly antisemitic Vienna Philharmonic) produced for PBS a special devoted to the question of Mahler's Jewishness entitled *The Little Drummer Boy*. (Caine clearly worked through Bernstein's Mahler as he worked up to *Dark Flame* and *Gustav Mahler in Toblach* and references his encounters with the Vienna Philharmonic in an interview.) It's an extremely interesting performance in which he wonderfully demonstrates the formal deployment of Jewish harmonies (the use of the flatted second) as an index of Jewish identities in the music and shows how Mahler constructs a dialectic between them and Christian, liturgical quotations. Bernstein, however, is less secure on the question of the cultural hermeneutics of Jewishness. Jewishness variously betokens, for Bernstein, Judaism; Yiddish-speaking, ghetto-dwelling, being an object of persecution, being impoverished, being assimilated, being middle class, being riddled with guilt, being suffused with sentiments of communal joy. In other words, all the various contradictory inscriptions of Jewishness in the West are bundled together in Bernstein's account of Mahler's Jewishness.

through the interlacing of this liturgical moment with his music. Whichever of these options one adopts, Caine would seem to be interrogating the notion of Jewishness itself: questioning who is and is not a Jew, who does and does not count as part of the community that is performatively constituted by the Yom Kippur rituals. He uncovers, that is to say, the layered and contradictory constructions of Jewishness within European discourse and makes them legible in terms of our own equally confused, if not quite so contested, cultural moment.*

But, at least in the present context, the most powerful effect is created by Caine's version of the third movement of Mahler's First Symphony. That movement (one of Mahler's many funeral marches) is constructed in the form of a rondo, with a version of the folk song "Frère Jacques" repeating ominously, in a minor key, then followed by other melodic material, after which Mahler returns to the original "Frère Jacques" theme, then back to another, and so on until its tumultuous end. In the first of the interpolated passages, the violins and clarinets lurch into a folk wedding dance whose melody and harmony are demonstrably eastern European. (Indeed, according to one critic, the melody is found among the fifteen hundred known klezmer melodies, presumably those collected by the Ansky ethnographic expedition.)[37] Or they seem to be: certainly they were identified as such by Leonard Bernstein (who cites them in his PBS special on Mahler's Jewishness) or by Norman Lebrecht, the critic I quoted above, or, as we shall see, by Uri Caine. The klezmer context of the song was not so clear, however, to Adorno, who does not mention the First Symphony at all in his enumeration of Mahler's musical Jewish moments, or to an earlier critic in the *Musical Times*, who, writing in 1960, ascribed the wedding dance to gypsy origins.[38] And perhaps not to Mahler himself, in the sense that the klezmer wedding march tune is just one of many European folk elements that are assimilated into this, as into all of, his symphonies (and of course is being put on a par with, even as it is being contrasted with, a

---

* By having Bensoussan improvise on the sacred melodies of the Yom Kippur service, Caine may also be referencing one of the most famous anecdotes about Mahler's Jewishness. In 1899, two years after his conversion to Catholicism, Mahler employed a young singer named Magnus Dawison (née Davidsohn) to sing in a performance of Wagner's *Lohengrin*. After one rehearsal, Mahler invited Davidsohn out for a beer and, learning that his first hope was to be a cantor, replied, "But then you would have been lost to the world of art." Mahler then suddenly asked Davidsohn to sing for him:

popular folk tune such as "Frère Jacques"). The effect, in other words, may well be to assimilate Jewish material in every sense of the word, to make its themes and harmonies part of the swirl of symphonic sound—an effect heightened by the increased chromaticism of Mahler's treatment of the klezmer theme, which, like "Frère Jacques," is transposed from the Phrygian into the minor mode, making it sound both like itself and different at one and the same time.

But Caine's version of the movement undoes Mahler's act of radical assimilation by musical incorporation. Instead of a troped, Mahlerized klezmer wedding dance—klezmer with quotation marks around itself—he gives us an out-and-out *frailach*, or klezmer dance, complete with wailing violins and stertorous trumpets. This passage, interestingly, is followed by a period of jazzlike improvisation by the violin, then a return to the *frailach*, then further, yet more jazzlike improvisation by trumpeter Ralph Alessi. Caine thus turns Mahler's musical structure inside out, giving us a rondo within a rondo—an oscillation between klezmer and jazz in the section that alternates with the "straight" classical theme (which is itself, to multiply inauthenticities, a parody of a folk song). Again, as with Caine's version of "The Little Drummer Boy," the effect is multiple. First, it's of course to accentuate the Jewish element in Mahler's own work—to, as it were, remove the quotation marks Mahler placed around it: to recite or even remember the original that Mahler himself sought to chop up in the course of his First Symphony into a stew of local references and regional

---

> I asked him if I might improvise on the basis of the words of prayer. . . . I sang with all my heart and soul, I put in all the Jewish *Weltschmertz*, but also the all the meaning of the words. The master listened. And as I came to an end, the old Day of Reconciliation prayer: "Do not forsake us when our strength falters," he whispered in a dry voice, "Yes, that is religious! That's how I heard it as a child, sung by the old prayer-leader in the village synagogue." He sat silent for a while, lost in thought. Suddenly he sat down at the piano and began to play. To improvise. I heard phrase for phrase the melody I have used and which I could not have repeated since I had only improvised it. It had become something quite different. He clothed the heavy minor mode in other, wonderfully blossoming harmonies. And I sat spellbound, thinking only how much our religious worship would have gained if only he, the great man, had not turned away from it and from all that he regarded as a frustrating burden.

Quoted in Henry-Louis de La Grange, *Gustav Mahler. Vienna: The Years of Challenge (1897–1904)* (New York: Oxford University Press, 1995), p. 173.

folklorisms. The effect may be to recompose Mahler himself, to reintegrate the Jewish element Mahler repressed but kept compulsively resurrecting into a new, more inclusive vision of his work. At the very least, in the current context, Caine's revision of Mahler can help us understand that that musical choice at Coleman's funeral—between Mahler's Bach-haunted Third Symphony and Shaw's "The Man I Love"—is no choice at all: considered ethnoracially, they are, Caine helps us to see, versions of the same thing.

But, more than that, it is also to confirm Faunia Farley's imperative of creative remaking through transformative mimicry—here in a reverse of what critics have called, in another context, appropriation. In Uri Caine's version of Mahler's version of the klezmer *frailach*, Caine doesn't just quote a klezmer tune, but actively makes it mean something quite different, first by playing it in a setting in which it is truly estranging (as part of a Mahler symphony, performed live by a jazz band in front of a group of Mahler enthusiasts); then as something itself reshaped again and again and again as it becomes the basis for jazzlike riffing and improvisation. Indeed, in the klezmer/jazz rondo alternation within the movement, he suggests a basic affinity—not an identity, but an affinity—between these two demotic idioms, and an affinity as well between both of them and the European folk tune that forms the basis of Mahler's own riffing. And to put the matter this way is to suggest that, just as he outs Mahler as a Jew, so he also transforms Mahler into something of a jazz musician: Caine works to suggest a continuity between Mahler's methods and those we associate with jazz. Or, more precisely, he works to unify the various traditions he's triangulating by seeing them all working by analogous principles of spirited syncretism. The jazz musician, the klezmer, Mahler: all for Caine are masters of pastiche, appropriation, and inauthenticity who make sumptuous music out of their diasporic condition.

Caine's achievement here is an extraordinary one, and I want to celebrate it in and of itself, just as much as Caine's work celebrates Mahler's. But I also want to instance it as an example of the process that I have been foregrounding throughout this chapter, and indeed throughout this book—the creative revisionism involved in the acts of appropriation and reappropriation embedded in and evident throughout Jewish responses to gentile cultural forms. Whatever we want to call it—I have called it over the course of this book queer diasporism, transgressive reinscription, hybridization to the second power, reappropriation, and I'm sure other, better names might emerge to describe the phenomenon—this response challenges the simple logic that undergirds the cultural articulations of race (black versus white), taste (high versus low), and canon (traditional versus avant-garde) that jazz and cultural critics of the last thirty years have persistently invoked even as they have interrogated them. Of course, I'm not suggesting that avant-garde Jewish musicians are the only people to exemplify these practices; nor that they annul the hard realities of racism (as embedded in the Jewish/black interchange in the U.S.) or antisemitism (as evidenced by Mahler's conversion in Vienna or, for that matter, Artie Shaw's passing in the U.S.). But merely to remain with these hard realities is to miss the new examples such art and artists suggest for us, the new aesthetic as well as ethnoracial trails their cultural experiments blaze.

5. CONVERSOS, MARRANOS, AND CRYPTO-LATINOS
Jewish-Hispanic Crossings and the Uses of Ethnicity

A FEW YEARS AGO I found myself with a seat at the table where most of the real work gets done at the contemporary university: on a hiring committee. This committee faced a more interesting challenge than most; we were charged with hiring a junior person, in any department, who specialized in any aspect of Jewish cultural or social life in America. Needless to say, the jockeying among representatives of the various fields was intense (I am happy to say that we literature folks prevailed). But the meta-jockeying was equally intense, or so I discovered to my doubtless naive shock when I proposed that we consider hiring someone whose specialization was Jews in the Americas of Sephardic descent, that is, peoples who traced their descent to the Diaspora from Spain in the wake of the political and social persecution spearheaded by the Inquisition and consummated by the Expulsion of 1492. Such an appointment, it seemed to me, might profitably widen the field of Jewish American studies itself or supplement the study of Yiddish with that of Ladino, the Hebrew-Spanish amalgam that has been the lingua franca of many Sephardic Jews. It also promised to open up the kind of dialogue that this book is dedicated to furthering: between Jewish studies and those done under the heading of "ethnic" or "Latino" or even "Atlantic" studies. But my suggestion, I found, was not met with universal applause; indeed, I was the only person who supported it. As an older, very distinguished colleague informed me, "the Sephardim are of no importance, in the U.S. None. At best—they're a footnote."

Despite his salty language, my colleague may have had a point: although the first Jews in the U.S. were Sephardic—the first Jewish house of worship in the U.S., the Touro Synagogue in Newport, for example, was built by Jews of Sephardic descent from either Holland or Curaçao on the model of the Grand Synagogue of Amsterdam—they were rapidly supplanted in numbers and influence by Ashkenazic Jews from Germany in the mid-nineteenth century and then by a second, larger influx of

Ashkenazim from the collapsing Russian Empire in the later years of that century. But nevertheless, I persisted in thinking that the experience of the Sephardim might give us an opportunity to ask a new set of questions about some very familiar issues. For one thing, integrating the Sephardic experience into our accounts of Jewishness would complicate a number of the metanarratives I have been contesting throughout this book: rapid assimilation to Americanness, upward mobility, even the accession to whiteness. Well after their expulsion from Spain, the Sephardim were considered—and considered themselves—aristocrats of the Diaspora: founders of some of the great trading and banking houses, progenitors of prime ministers (Disraeli), philosophers (Spinoza), economists (David Ricardo), and poets (Emma Lazarus). But in the 1880–1925 period, those Sephardim who emigrated to the U.S. (largely from Greece, Turkey, Rhodes, and the Balkans) were by and large neglected, marginalized, frequently more impoverished and less mobile than their Ashkenazic peers. Moreover, since they came from areas other than northern or eastern Europe, cleaved to their own distinctive religious practices, and located their sense of loss and dislocation differently than did Ashkenazim—with respect to a mythical and often hyperinvested Spain as well as, or even in the place of, the ubiquitous Jerusalem—their tension with the dominant Ashkenazic culture often took on a racially or ethnically tinged spin. "'They used to call us black Jews,'" recalled Morris Calderon, an eighty-two-year-old volunteer at the Sephardic Home for the Aged in Brooklyn who used to live on the Lower East Side. "'We called them *Zigazuk*, which is how Yiddish sounded to us.'"[1]

A focus on such a multiply marginalized group, in other words, might extend the geographic frame of Jewish identity formation to include not just Iberia and all that it represents to the places to which the Sephardim fled—the Balkans, the Maghreb, the Mediterranean.[2] More piquantly, and more relevantly to American studies broadly construed, it would extend the frame to the Caribbean and Latin America, to which many of the Sephardim found their way, and in a fascinating array of guises. Some emigrated as out-and-out Jews (largely via Holland, in which many Sephardim had found refuge, to the Caribbean); others came as conversos or "New Christians," Iberian converts to Christianity (under considerable pressure and duress) who nevertheless found themselves persecuted in post-1492 Spain; still others were so-called Marranos or crypto-Jews, those who practiced what they retained of their Jewish faith in secret.* And bringing into the picture this particular influx might enable a wider discussion of two hot-button topics. First, it would bring into view the implication of Jews in the slave trade in which they played, it would seem, a not insubstantial but not central role, especially as they composed what Jonathan Israel has called a powerful "transatlantic trading network," largely moving the goods made possible by slave labor (sugar, cocoa, etc.) rather than slaves themselves.³ And focusing on the Sephardic experience raises the question of Jewish implication in the colonial enterprise itself. After all—to cite but one spectacular case—Columbus (who some think may well have been a Marrano himself, although recent scholarship tends in the other direction)⁴ led a crew full of Marranos and conversos on his first expedition and had his second financed by wealthy Spanish conversos. Conversos played an important part in the colonizing of Peru and Mexico, among not only the administrative elite but also the rank and file who fought for them, and sometimes both. Here's a fairly typical scenario, the story of the first known converso to emigrate from Old to New Spain:

> Hernando [Alonso], a blacksmith by trade . . . embarked in the year 1518 for Cuba [and then] worked under the orders of the famous carpenter, Martín López, in building the brigantines which played so important a role in the conquest of Tenochtitlán. Later, he took part in the pacification of Pánuco. For all these services, he was granted the signory of

---

*Matters of definition here are complex, because members of these groups frequently shifted affiliations of and identities over time, moving so frequently among them that one critic employs the term *cultural commuters* to describe many. Merely for the sake of lucidity, I adopt here Yosef Yerushalmi's distinction between so-called New Christians or conversos, on the one hand (the Hebrew *anusim*, or "forcibly lost," is also a relevant marker here), and Marranos, or crypto-Jews, on the other, understanding that this is a rough-and-ready distinction at best; these categories frequently overlapped and need to be supplemented with more subtle ones suggested in recent scholarship, which has written of *cultural commuters* and *fuzzy Jews* to emphasize the continuing traffic between religious identities and affiliations among Jews of the Sephardic Diaspora. But as provisional as this distinction must be, as we'll see below, it's not an unimportant one. See Yosef Hayim Yerushalmi, *From Spanish Court to Italian Ghetto: Isaac Cardoso: A Study in Seventeenth-Century Marranism and Jewish Apologetics* (Seattle: University of Washington Press, 1981), p. 6; for the other definitions, see, inter alia, Renee Melammed, *A Question of Identity: Iberian Conversos in Historical Perspective* (New York: Oxford University Press, 2004).

Actopan as an *encomienda* [that is, a grant of land plus the right to compel labor from the people inhabiting it]. From then on, he devoted himself to cattle-raising and mining, and between the years 1524–1528 he managed to be the principal meat supplier for Mexico City.[5]

Invoking the converso/Marrano experience in the context of Jewish participation in the colonial project, however, also serves to place these matters in a remarkably complex light. Jews were, in Israel's felicitous phrasing, "simultaneously agents and victims of empire."[6] After all, the Marranos who manned Columbus's ships were fleeing an institution known to torture, flail, and burn alive its objects of inquiry; and the wealthy conversos who financed his second expedition did so to avert the confiscations that helped finance his first. And as for Alonso . . .

> In early autumn of 1528, he was accused of having celebrated Passover in the company of some Crypto-Jews in Cuba, having rebaptized or washed out the holy water poured on the head of a mestizo . . . son and, finally, for forbidding his wife to go to church during her period. . . . Weeks later, he was burned in the first public Auto de Fe celebrated in Mexico City. (114)

Briefly meditating on this last example might suggest to us just how multivariate are the issues raised in and around the converso (New Christian)/Marrano (crypto-Jew) complex. What, for example, did Alonso mean by confounding the Church with the synagogue when he allegedly forbade his wife to attend it during her menses? Was it an attempt to preserve Jewish customs in a world without *mikveh*s and synagogues? Or an effort to recapture the faded outlines of those customs from childhood memories or from the memories of previous generations? Or perhaps something entirely different: an effort at syncretism, a bringing-together of his new faith with the customs and prejudices of his old? And what did his wife think of this attempt? It would seem from the bare outline of facts given here that she was not herself a converso—indeed it is probable that she was not a European at all; at any event, did she perhaps testify against her husband to save herself from the Inquisition or to save their "mestizo son" (if he was theirs) from its fiery embrace? If so, was she successful? (Records on this matter are silent).

These kinds of questions are not dissimilar from the kinds of questions we are used to asking about the fraught, if not clichéd, issue of "Jewish identity": but when we raise them in this context, they reveal themselves to be different in structure, nature, implication. As my language above suggests, for example, the dominant metaphors U.S. literary critics employ to delineate the notion of hidden or secret identities are those of passing, derived from African American history and reanimated in African American cultural criticism, and the language of the closet, derived from the lesbian and gay male experience and put into discursive play by critics in queer studies. As we've seen, both these languages are apposite to the condition of metamorphosing, self-hating or just plain assimilating Jews as well—although, as we've also seen, when Jewishness enters these metaphorical domains, remarkably complex things happen to all concerned. But the problems of Marrano/converso identity, with its infinite vicissitudes of identity formation and reformulation, point in another direction: to the predication of a hidden identity that itself becomes a new order of being. The closeted gay man or lesbian woman still has a reference point for his or her dual sense of self, if only in the gap between desires and the sham performed in public; so, mutatis mutandis, does the passing African American. The Marrano, on the other hand, had after the second or third generation only the barest outline of contact with the beliefs and customs that nevertheless define what he or she feels to be the essence of his or her identity: such definitional material is accessible only through family narratives, carefully concealed from outsiders, or behaviors that, over time, have acquired the status more of obsessive-compulsive manias (turning pictures of Christ to the wall on Friday nights or hand-washing rituals) than of actual religious or communal practices. The identity of Marranos is Other to their community, but also, in a curious but palpable way, to themselves.

This form of being is intrinsically fascinating—so fascinating, in fact, that a number of contemporary philosophers and critics have attempted to use the Marrano experience as a metaphor for modernity itself. Thus Yirmiyahu Yovel has described Spinoza as the "Marrano of reason"—as an avatar of the Enlightenment in his intellectual separation from his own community that excommunicated him and the Christian community that he had no interest in joining—and traces Spinoza's philosophy of immanence and his privileging of reason to his status outside established communities of belief.[7] Similarly, Elaine Marks has deployed the Marrano experience as a metaphor not just for that of the contemporary secular Jew, but for that of the subject in modernity at large.[8] She takes her warrant from both Yovel and Jacques Derrida—himself a Maghreb-born descendent of the Sephardic Diaspora—who invokes Marranohood repeatedly, nowhere perhaps more eloquently than in his apotheosizing of "the universal Marrano" at the end of his 1994 meditation on death, truth, and knowledge, *Aporias*:

> Let us figuratively call Marrano anyone who remains faithful to a secret that he has not chosen, in the very place where he lives, in the home of the inhabitant or of the occupant, in the home of the first or of the second arrivant, in the very place where he stays without saying so but without identifying himself as belonging to. In the unchallenged night where the radical absence of any historical witness keeps him or her, in the dominant culture that by definition has calendars, this secret keeps the Marrano even before the Marrano keeps it. Is it not possible to think that such a secret eludes even history, age and aging?[9]

Like the invocation of passing or closeting that frames my discussion here, Marrano for Derrida becomes a trope of nearly existential proportions; a figure for what one might call (if it didn't sound so dizzyingly un-Derridean) an aspect of the human condition writ large, of a "secret" that transcends temporality but nevertheless gives content to it (death being the real subject of *Aporias*, the ultimate and indeed constitutive aporia, the unimaginable absence that paradoxically gives shape to absence itself). Indeed, for Derrida, Marranohood embodies not just the relation between secrets and individual beings, but between secrecy and Being itself. But eloquent though it may be, Derrida's apotheosis of the universal Marrano also brings into sharp focus a salient factor of that experience—and one that resists his, and Yovel's, and Marks's deployment of the Marrano as trope—namely, its unsusceptibility to any such universalization. "I am one of those *marranes* who no longer say they are Jews even in the secret of their own hearts," Derrida told Geoff Bennington in 1991, "because they doubt everything."[10] But, historically, many if not most crypto-Jews have fallen into a different category than that of Derridean dubiety; many, if not most, considered themselves to be Jews, despite all the pressure both from the Christian world, from which they perforce had to conceal their racial/religious origins, and from the Jewish community that frequently considered them apostates. As one historian beautifully put it, "the Marrano is a Catholic without faith and a Jew without knowledge, but a Jew by will."[11] And many, if not most, took advantage of any situation in which they could transform will into fact.

Consider Alonso: freed from the relentless oppression of the Inquisition in Spain, he emigrated to New Spain and began to disclose himself as a Jew, only to discover that the Inquisition had followed him there. Or consider Spinoza: despite his excommunication from the Jewish community, despite the rationalist tendencies of his thought, he never considered himself something other than a Jew. Or, to pursue an even more extreme case, consider Spinoza's contemporary, Juan (or Daniel) de Prado, also extensively treated by Yovel. A converso in Spain—where he conceived of himself in secret as a re-Judaizer, a discoverer of Judaism as the more authentic faith than Christianity—he went to Holland to preach this view to his fellow Jews, only to encounter their suspicion that his faith in their faith was heretical. Excommunicated not once but three times by his synagogue for his heterodox opinions, afflicted by spies who attempted to provoke him into the blasphemies that he was all too happy to utter, put to the question by Jewish authorities in ways that resembled in all but physical violence the Inquisition from which he had fled, he nevertheless consistently asserted that he was a Jew, finally leaving to pursue his faith in Antwerp and dropping out of the historical record.[12]

Obviously, matters become different for the Iberian Jews who did not make their way to Jewish communities in the Low Countries or the Mediterranean or the Near East, as many of them did. Nevertheless, remarkable is the continued maintenance, in the descendents of the descendents of the descendents of the Marranos, of their sense of themselves as Jews—even when their only access to that identity is a negative one, a general sense of otherness or difference from other townspeople, even when it has no formal relation to Judaism (on either side: conversos and even some Marranos often maintained their identity as Catholics; established Jewish religious authorities often disavowed even those Marranos who proclaimed themselves as Jews). Indeed, I want to claim, through a whole ensemble of means—in their syncretic, often improvised religious practices, in their housekeeping rituals, in their cuisine, and, most important, perhaps, in the narratives that got told by and about them—a new form of Jewishness was created: one that neither comported to the traditional

Judaism to which they no longer had access nor to the Judaizing of which they were accused by the Inquisition, nor to the heresy of which they were suspected by the parish priest and community alike, but rather to something much more resembling our modern (or even postmodern) notions of ethnic identity: of a people within a people who believe themselves to have a separate identity but whose identity as such is available to them only through improvised, often invented cultural practices and constructed (and often fictitious) narratives.

In what follows I'll be suggesting that these possibilities, and the kinds of narratives that follow from them, continue to ramify in the current literary and cultural scene, composing one of the most telling and significant imaginative outcroppings of the Sephardic Diaspora to the Caribbean, Latin America, and the U.S. I'll ultimately turn to two novels that explicitly deal with such complications: Kathleen Alcalá's *Spirits of the Ordinary* and Achy Obejas's *Days of Awe*. In line with the argument of the rest of the book, I want to use these novels not only to counter the dominance of certain kinds of narratives about the Jewish American experience but also to raise questions about the role that narratives of hidden religious identities and the cultural practices that stem from them play in the making of idioms of race and ethnicity themselves. And, more specifically, I'm going to be arguing that the discourse on the nature and fate of conversos and Marranos, New Christians and crypto-Jews in the Americas is of further significance: that it's used, as the idiom and history of Jews and Jewishness so frequently are deployed, as a metonym for ethnic otherness itself, especially as that discourse attempts to distinguish between race and culture as determinants of identity.

Conversos and Marranos in the American West: Crypto-Jews and the Fate of Ethnicity

Before turning to these texts, we need, I think, to consider the most recent historical outcropping of the Marrano/converso phenomenon, the rise of self-proclaimed crypto-Jews in the Americas, especially in the far reaches of New Mexico and Colorado—a phenomenon that demands to be traced to its roots in fifteenth-century Iberia. For the events leading up to and following the Expulsion of Jews from the kingdoms of

Spain and the imposition of exclusionary laws undertaken by Ferdinand and Isabella and the mass conversions undertaken in Portugal (1497) have been taken as more than just one particularly nasty incident in the doleful history of gentile oppression of Jews, opening instead an entirely new chapter in European constructions of racial, national, and religious identity. One can see why such an abundance of attention has been trained on this historical moment. For one thing, the long-standing community of Spanish Jews had, during the eight-hundred-year period in which Spain was ruled first by Arabs, then by Christians, established one of the most culturally advanced communities in the world, with respect not only to theology (Maimonides lived in Granada, under Moorish rule) and poetry (so did the finest Hebrew lyricist of the medieval period, Judah Halevy) but also medicine and science. Thus the tumultuous events of the century that preceded the Expulsion as well as the Expulsion itself—the wave of persecution unleashed first in the aftermath of a wave of Muslim fundamentalism sweeping from Northern Africa in the eleventh century, then the long effort at *reconquista* undertaken by Christians and climaxing in the conquest of Granada in 1491—take on the greatest intensity of meaning (all the more so at the present historical moment): if at various points in this history, Jews, Christians, and Muslims lived in relative peace and harmony with one another, then the failure of that serially triangulated *convivencia* and its fall into ethnic cleansing achieves a special poignance and power, and not only for Jews.[13]

Which leads to one other important significance that has been drawn from the tragic experience of Iberian Jews, one with indirect but powerful application to the cultures of the U.S: the claim that this moment in historical time represents the birth of racism in the modern sense. Boldly argued by Benzion Netanyahu and hotly contested by historians in his wake, the argument goes something like this: the crucial moment in the unfolding of the European imaginary was the adoption by Ferdinand and Isabella of the decree of 1492 prescribing *limpieza de sangre*—purity of blood—as a prerequisite for holding public office and advancement in the army. For that decree was not only linked to the Catholic state's increasingly intolerant attitudes toward Jews and Moors; it was most pointedly linked to the politics surrounding the increasing number and success of the conversos—the more than one hundred thousand Jews who had, under the impact of riots, spirited efforts at conversion led by charismatic priests, and ultimately the threat of the Inquisition, converted to Christianity, often to find spectacular success in gentile culture: as merchants, politicians, priests, authors, even inquisitors and saints.* The decree demanding *limpieza de sangre*, Netanyahu argues, was rooted in a backlash against the increasing social power and visibility of conversos and predicates something entirely novel: the notion that conversion itself was irrelevant as a marker of identity no matter how sincere one's acceptance of the Christian faith. This movement from the Inquisition's already nearly genocidal doctrine of *limpieza de fe*, the use of the Question to determine purity of faith, to state-sponsored demands for *limpieza de sangre* is precisely, according to Netanyahu, the moment at which long-standing prejudices morph into the typology of modern antisemitism, one in which Jewishness is defined in essentialist terms—as Sartre famously describes it in *Anti-Semite and Jew*, a quality "analogous to phlogiston or the soporific virtue of opium . . . a metaphysical essence [without which] the activities ascribed to the Jew would be entirely incomprehensible."[14] Or as Netanyahu puts it:

> Looking for a quality common to all Conversos, and at the same time so negative as to support the issuance of harsh, restrictive laws against them, the racial theorists believed that such a quality should be sought not in what the Marranos *did* or *believed*, but in what they *were* as human beings. This did not seem to be a difficult task. For what they were was determined . . . by their *race*. Since race, they maintained, formed man's qualities and indeed his entire mental constitution, the Marranos, who were all offspring of Jews, retained the racial makeup of their forbears. . . . All the Marrano's misdeeds, they stressed, had only one source: the Converso's race, his mental constitution, his urge to do evil to all men of goodwill, and the ruthless egotism that unscrupulously commands him to use his victims' assets for his own profit.[15]

---

*The Jewish population of Spain at the beginning of the Inquisition was roughly three hundred thousand (out of three to four million), historians estimate. Of these, one hundred thousand emigrated, largely to France, Holland, and the Balkans, one hundred thousand converted, and the remaining one hundred thousand stayed Jews, only to depart or convert at later times. The Inquisition is estimated to have executed thirty-three thousand, the majority of them alleged "Judaizers," most of them burnt alive (lucky ones were strangled by the executioner before the bonfire was lit).

No wonder that, as Werner Sollors reminds us in a different context, the very term *race* "in the physical, visible sense" may well have originated in the Castilian *raza* "used ... to describe (and expel from Spain) people 'tainted' by Jewish and Moorish blood."[16] *

Returning to this matrix, however, also complicates the ontology as well as the history of race thinking. As Sollors goes on to suggest, that "the list of people to whom the doctrine of purity of blood ... was applied included descendents of heretics and 'penitenciados' (those condemned by the Inquisition)" implies that "at this terrible beginning, 'race' was hardly based on perception of 'phenotypal' difference but on a religiously and politically, hence 'culturally,' defined distinction that was legislated to be hereditary, innate, and immutable" (xxxv). The catastrophic events of the fifteenth century, in other words, can be seen as creating the origins of what we have come to call ethnicity as well as the thing we call race: the Inquisition as it got unleashed on the conversos of Spain had the effect of defining those people, seemingly assimilated into the Spanish mainstream for hundreds of years, as a people within a people, a people apart, who cleaved to a separate identity via customs, cuisine, family ties, culture, whatever they retained of their religious affiliation: as, in short, what we today would recognize as a distinctive ethnic group. It was further heightened by their sense of corporate identity in the midst of their Diaspora: the free Sephardic Jews in Amsterdam, for example, referred to their sense of special, distinct belonging in terms we would recognize under the sign of ethnicity, not race, as "the Nation."†

---

* Both of Netanyahu's central propositions have proven to be enormously controversial. His denial of the persistence of marranism, it has been pointed out, depends on an all-or-nothing definition of Jewishness that in turn reflects an overreliance on the most hard-line rabbinical commentary and an underreliance on—indeed a refusal to consider—the abundant records of the Inquisition (historians like Henry Kamen suggest that the historical record would have been better served had these interpretive protocols been reversed). And critics have also pointed out that the Expulsion may well itself have been pushed by conversos eager to rid Spain of Jews to buttress their own position, that acceptance of the doctrine of *limpieza de sangre* was limited (one had to prove only purity to the generation of one's grandfather) and highly variable (often, it could be suspended for a court favor or ameliorated with a bribe), that it was frequently opposed by elements in the Church itself, many of whose most prominent figures were themselves conversos (e.g., St. Theresa of Avila and St. John of the Cross).

† A brief note on the etymology of the term *ethnicity*: the Greek *ethnos*, or "people," from which it is derived, translates in the Septuagint the Hebrew *goy*, or "nation," usually used

To be sure, proto-race and proto-ethnicity were utterly co-implicated with each other at this aboriginal moment. As Jonathan Schorch has powerfully argued, many Sephardic Jews accommodated themselves to emerging ideas of whiteness, defining themselves in contradistinction to the African or Caribbean peoples among whom they found themselves. If nothing else, then, returning to this moment in time can remind us of just how coimplicated are the racial and the ethnic, the phenotypical (and ultimately the genotypical) and the cultural have long been; the Sephardic narrative can thus serve to help us recognize that a similar dynamic—the intertwining between the cultural and the phenotypical in the discourse of race/ethnicity—plays out in the following centuries, with wildly uneven effects, in its long course of development from Herder through American cultural pluralism through the influential formulations of Glazer, Moynihan et al.[17] As we have seen, the main thrust of recent Americanist criticism has been to emphasize the insufficiency of the turn toward the cultural and/or ethnic in the face of a socially perdurable racialism. "In the years since the 1940s," writes Matthew Frye Jacobson,

> Race has been the larger body around which the concept of ethnicity has quietly revolved, as a moon around a planet. . . . In the early years of World War II, the culturally based concept of ethnicity may have seemed an alternative—a solution—to the biologically based race concept. . . . But race and its inheritances have been stubborn indeed; the mid-century's revision of race stopped at the color line, universalizing *whiteness* by lessening the presumed difference separating "Hebrews," "Celts" and "Anglo-Saxons" but deepening the separation between any of these former white races and people of color, especially blacks. . . . By the 1980s and 1990s, not only had ethnicity failed to replace race as an analytic category, but—since "race" had been so thoroughly etched into social practice and encoded in law—no concept of ethnicity could explain much if it failed to reckon with the undergirding structures of race.[18]

---

to designate nations other than the Hebrew people (e.g., the Canaanites), but also interestingly applied to the Hebrew people as well. Built into the term, in other words, is the dialectical alternation between in-group and other, Jew and non-Jew, that I am trying to parse throughout this book.

Jacobson's work both references and reflects the interests of, to cite work from a different field, Michael Omi and Howard Winant's *Racial Formation in the United States*. There, the emphasis is put almost entirely on the power of race in its direst formulations—in legal constructions of citizenship, property holding, marriage, and so on—and in its crudest manifestations— the black/white binary—to trump and manage the establishment of ethnic difference.[19] But, just to cite the seeming ubiquity of this tendency of thought, Walter Michaels, writing out of a different tradition and with an entirely different agenda in mind, makes much the same point: the valorization of culture wrought in the 1920s by figures like Horace Kallen and Waldo Frank, he argues persistently and powerfully in his own *Our America*, ultimately collapses into the very racialism that it is invoked to counter, producing a new conflation of the two—essentially a racialist nationalism— that is all the more insidious for its seeming celebration of pluralism. (Michaels has gone on, in his recent writing, to use the same critical position to attack identity-based analyses of all kinds.)

The persistence of marranism both as a phenomenon and as an imaginative resource, I want to suggest, can push this latest development in a centuries-long dialogue in a different direction. If, as I am suggesting here, the crypto-Jews' cleaving to an abjected, Othered identity even in the midst of persecution by their enemies and rejection by their own communities, combined with their eagerness to out themselves as Jews when it seemed socially or historically viable to do so, poses in the most acute form the question that bedevils critics who downgrade ethnicity in favor of race: why (other than for reasons of bad faith) do people choose to consider themselves ethnic, not only in the everything's-up-for-grabs world of the U.S. but also within the cultures of modernity and postmodernity at large? And, following on this, another, to my mind more consequential, question: what positive lesson (if any) can we derive from the experience of people who think of themselves in terms that we would recognize as "ethnic"? Plugging the Marrano into the race/ethnicity conundrum may seem like a recondite way of addressing these questions, to be sure. I do so not only because of what Sollors and Netanyahu see as the origins of the race/ethnicity problematic within the very conditions under which Marranos came into being, but because marranism represents (via, to be sure, the most extreme of possible contingencies) the possibilities I have been pointing to throughout this book: the improvisatory, *bricolaged*, revisionary structures of thought and representation that are, I want to assert, the chief contribution the ethnic/cultural perspective can bring to the social table.

All of these issues—the inseparability of race and ethnicity (and vice versa); the creative possibilities embedded in acts of revisionary identity-making—are crystallized within a recent historical controversy: the rediscovery (or, according to some critics, the "rediscovery") of their Jewish origins by contemporary Americans in the Southwest. Beginning in the 1970s and 1980s, a number of New Mexicans of Spanish-speaking descent emerged to tell historians, journalists—basically anyone who would listen—strikingly similar narratives of family practices that seemed mysterious or occult: an aversion to pork, killing chickens à la kashrut by slitting their throats and draining the blood, celebrating family dinners on Friday nights with the windows curtained to protect them from prying eyes. Sometimes these narratives lurched into the Gothic: a dramatic deathbed confession of Jewishness by a father, grandfather, or aunt, disbelieved at first by its recipient, who then starts putting together the pieces of a family puzzle (relatives with Jewish-sounding names, odd signs that look like Stars of David on gravestones, an aversion to the local priest, or Catholics in general)—all of which leads to a self-identification as a "Jew" that is as mysterious as it seems foundational.

These discoveries have led to the establishment of something of a cottage industry in the study of crypto-Jewishness. A number of historians, led by Stanley Hordes (formerly the state historian of New Mexico) have joined a host of anthropologists and sociologists in studying the crypto-Jewish phenomenon, as have more members of that community who have founded a Society for the Study of Crypto-Jews and Anusim with an excellent Web site hosting many of the narratives I have summarized above, held conferences to investigate the phenomenon, organized tours for interested onlookers, and so on. And, as one might expect, this flurry of activity has led to a vigorous counterresponse. Anthropologist Judith Neulander began fieldwork on the crypto-Jewish community only to find herself doubting many of their claims. While acknowledging that many New Mexicans of Latino descent were interested in proclaiming their hidden or secret Jewish past, she vigorously argued that much of the hard evidence for such a past—e.g., the presence of Stars of David on gravesites, the use of dreidels—and much of the soft evidence as well—family narratives of Friday afternoon housecleanings and Friday night Sabbaths, kosherlike dietary practices, etc.—can be explained either by the presence of

Ashkenazic Jews in twentieth-century New Mexico (dreidels are an exclusively Ashkenazic device) or by the influence of Seventh-Day Adventism, which exerted a powerful force in New Mexico at the turn of the century and borrowed liberally from Judaism's customs and tropes. Neulander's case was pursued by two reporters for the *Atlantic*, Barbara Ferry and Debbie Nathan, who aggressively questioned (as did she) not merely the conclusions of Hordes but also his ethics and methods. These critics and Michael Carroll, a sociologist, don't just critique the movement, but suggest an alternative explanation for it: a kind of ethnic self-hatred among New Mexico's Latino community. To fantasize a connection to a Sephardi past becomes a way for Latinos to connect themselves directly to Spain, asserting a white European rather than a mixed-race or Mexican-inflected identity.* As Ferry and Nathan pithily put it, "What better way to be a noble Spaniard than to be Sephardic, since Sephardim almost never marry outside their own narrow ethnic group?"[20]

The war of words continues. Hordes has recently weighed in with a book weaving together Inquisition records, personal testimony, and larger perspectives on the history of the U.S. West to produce a powerful circumstantial case for the crypto-Jewish phenomenon in New Mexico, based at its strongest on the presence of Jewish names mentioned in Inquisition records in early expeditions to what is now New Mexico and Southern Colorado.[21] Janet Liebman Jacobs has produced a fascinating ethnographic account of New Mexican women who claim to be descended from Marranos, arguing the crucial role played by gender in the maintenance of historical memory and group identity.[22] And ordinary Southwest

---

* If true, as Maria Cotera reminds me, this would be a deeply ironic development, since in Anglo America Spanish identities were shadowed by the so-called Black Legend, the belief that Spaniards were by their very nature intolerant, cruel, morally defective. (Even more ironic in this context is the fact that one piece of evidence adduced for this ascription is the rise of the Inquisition and the Expulsion of Jews and Moslems from Spain in 1492.) In some measure the phenomenon may reflect the particular ethnoracial dynamics of New Mexico and the American Southwest. More generally, it might also be a reaction to the rise of a multicultural agenda throughout the United States in the 1980s: putative crypto-Jews can claim for themselves a kind of indigineity no less than Chicanos celebrating their Mexican origins or black Americans their African "roots." But it's important to stress the other side of the coin—one must never forget that there would have been very good reasons indeed for people descended from converso families to keep their origins secret. After all, Jews in Latin America were persistently persecuted, stigmatized, burnt in public, for publicly proclaiming their faith.

Americans continue to come forward to proclaim their identity as Jews even though many of them are now fully practicing Catholics (including some priests): offering testimonies based on family histories, organizing houses of worship like the Iglesia de Dios Israelita (Israelite Church of God), even offering genetic evidence to support their case: a group of putative crypto-Jews from Albuquerque has performed genetic testing and discovered a high incidence of the genetic marker associated with the *cohanim*, the Jewish priestly class. But Neulander has yet more arrows in her quiver.[23] She has uncovered Seventh-Day Adventist roots for many of the Iglesia de Dios Israelita parishioners and has also turned to genetics to contest the claims of not only the would-be *cohanim* but also Hordes et al. Neulander is cited as coauthor of a genetic study on a population of New Mexicans and Colorodans published in the *Annals of Human Biology* that reaches the following ringing conclusion:

> Our results indicate that, other than a small American Indian component, the Spanish-Americans of New Mexico and southern Colorado are indistinguishable from Iberians in terms of paternal ancestry. Although Spanish-Americans undoubtedly have some Jewish ancestry, they appear to have no more than do Iberians. The crypto-Jewish scenario proposed by Hordes . . . is refuted by these results. The criticisms of Neulander . . . are well founded.[24]

The conclusions of the study, it should be noted, are somewhat less decisive than they appear for a number of reasons. Taken on its own terms, it suggests that there are many thousands of people of converso descent in the Southwest; if, by my rough population estimate, something like 10 percent of the people of Iberia are of Jewish descent—the great-great-great-great- (and so on for ten more generations) grandchildren of conversos and Marranos—then there ought to be close to ninety thousand such in New Mexico alone, although—and it's a significant omission—there's no way of knowing how many of these are descendents of crypto-Jews or not. (The claims of Hordes et al. don't come anywhere near this number.) Moreover, the genetic critique doesn't address a strong version of Hordes's thesis, which depends not on a horde of conversos making the trek from Veracruz or Mexico City to what is now northern New Mexico and southern Colorado (however romantic such a narrative might be), but rather on a number of descendents of these conversos being Marranos or, at the very least, being interested in thinking of themselves as descendents of crypto-Jews. This, it cannot be emphasized strongly enough, no amount of genetic testing can reveal. Indeed, the whole turn to the genetic seems oddly beside the point: the American Southwest could be teeming with descendents of conversos who have utterly lost any sense of connection to their ancestral past, and this would authenticate Neulander's thesis, *pace* Neulander herself. Conversely, there could only be a few hundred or so descendents of conversos out of the roughly 780,000 or so Latinos in New Mexico, yet, if every single one of them maintained some kind of connection with a Jewish past, this would more than authenticate Hordes's position.[25]

In either case, the turn toward the genetic—undertaken on both sides in the debate—is eerily and dismayingly appropriate, for it provides an echo of the historical circumstances whose aftermath it reflects. On one side stands a group of New Mexican *hispanos* who, on the basis of a do-it-yourself genetics kit, are convinced that they are descendents not merely of Marranos, but of the *cohanim*, the priestly class, the most exalted of all possible Jewish descents as well as one that has historically maintained the purest genetic lineage (albeit on the Y-chromosome and hence through the father, surely a problematic ascription given the matrilineal construction of Jewish identity that emerged in the early Talmudic period). On the other stand genetic scientists and Neulander, who cite data about descent not to suggest that matters are murkier and more complicated than they might seem to enthusiastic rediscoverers of their putative Jewish past— her skepticism, while somewhat maniacal, has been undeniably useful— but to deny any connection whatsoever between the *hispanos* of New Mexico and the Marranos of the Iberian Diaspora. In so doing, both show themselves captivated by the imaginary of *limpieza de sangre*, first demanding evidence of unbroken or unmediated descent as a warrant of identity, then misreading the ambiguous shards of such evidence as markers of identity categories that are ultimately cultural in nature and historical in determination. If nothing else, they authenticate an element of Netanyahu's thesis—that the turn toward *limpieza* in fifteenth-century Spain gave birth to a new style of thought about race as an essentialized and determining characteristic of identity—and remind us of just how powerfully the model of Jewishness persists as a paradigm for thinking about race itself.

But the questions raised in and around the Marrano at the center also opens up possibilities that are already (in deference to arch-Marrano

Derrida, I'm tempted to say: always already) circulating within the rigidities of race, which I would identify as one of the potentials raised in the discourse of ethnicity: ways of defining and negotiating a sense of belonging that are mobile, hybrid, polyvalent, and potentially recombinant with other identity categories. Indeed, it seems to me that whatever the merits of the Southwest Marrano argument in terms of empirical fact, the repeated claims by people for their status as descendents of Jews who have kept that identity as a family secret, and specifically the source of those claims in family stories, opens up the possibility that narrative itself can serve as source for this rooted yet flexible construction of social identification and cultural meaning. I mean this in two senses: first in the quite down-to-earth sense that the narratives that get told about and through the crypto-Jews of New Mexico bear a startling family resemblance to the narratives told by similarly isolated communities known to have more direct connection to their Jewish ancestors, stories that emerged into cultural prominence at roughly the same time that New Mexican crypto-Jews started to announce themselves as such. Such evidence is not uncontaminated, since many stories about the latter in particular began to emerge at roughly the same time as did the narratives of the Marranos of the American Southwest and may well have influenced them.[26] But I mean it as well in the more important way that, irrespective of the empirical "truth" of the background of the crypto-Jews of New Mexico, which can never be known, the narratives that emerge in and through their experience compose their own order of being with the power to shape and reshape both the sense of the past and that of the future. Indeed, one's sense in surveying these stories is that they are a structuralist's dream (or an empiricist's nightmare): that whatever the specific bodies and experiences in which it gets encoded may be, the story of the Sephardic catastrophe and Marrano persistence—the dual narrative of persecution, concealment, and the sense of new or bricolaged identities being composed out of it, the ancillary narrative of people discovering via deathbed revelations or other means their own hidden Jewish past with catalytic, if uneven, effects—quite literally has a life of its own, one with the capacity to create new shapes of experience for people who enter into it.

That is very much the use that narrative is put to, it seems to me, in the two novels to which I now turn. These fictions are set in very different locations at utterly different historical moments, and are written with very different intellectual and political agendas in mind, but—strikingly—they make the same structural use of the converso/Marrano story as a way of clarifying and complicating notions of ethnic belonging at large and of negotiating the fraught question of Latinoness specifically within the cultural framework of the U.S. In both, we can witness the continuing power of the marrano/converso narrative to create new possibilities of ramifying meaning as it enters into remarkably different discursive and historical contexts.

Spirits of the Extraordinary: Race, Spirituality, and the Crypto-Jewish Narrative

The first of these is Katherine Alcalá's 1996 novel, *Spirits of the Ordinary: A Tale of Casas Grandes*, set in Northern Mexico in the 1870s. Alcalá, a Pacific Northwest novelist born in California of Mexican parents, was active in the rise of multicultural writing in the 1980s and early 1990s—new wave American Indian writer Sherman Alexie, for example, included her work in an issue of the influential journal *Ploughshares* devoted to multicultural Northwest writers. She's also actively self-identified as a descendent of crypto-Jews, and her account of her experience fits in with many of the narratives of crypto-Jewishness we've been looking at:

> Growing up in San Bernardino, California, it was bad enough that we were Protestant, but the idea that we were also Jewish was too much to take seriously, especially given the Eastern European orientation of the Jews in our community. We were definitely brown, and they were definitely white, in a town that made much of these racial differences. Nevertheless, our mother, Lydia Narro, and her brothers and sisters insisted that this was the case, and went as far as to say that the brothers Narro were not only Jews, but rabbis.[27]

But, far more actively than most, she has done an enormous amount of work recovering her heritage. Following testimony given to her mother by her grandfather, she traced the Jewish strain in her family back to Saltillo, a city in Northern Mexico about 180 miles south of what is now Texas, thence to a family from seventeenth-century France whose name Narro has been historically associated with Sephardic Jews.

But that research has turned up other influences as well; the Narro strain is just one of many that went into the making of her family. Her grandfather converted, while studying in Michigan, to Protestantism and

> was subsequently disinherited and excommunicated by his family. At that time, he went in 1894 to live and work with his uncle, Oscar Narro, in Tucson, Arizona, where he met and married my grandmother, Rosa Martinez, shortly after her fifteenth birthday. She was the illegitimate daughter of an Opata Indian woman, Pastora Curiel, and an Irishman, George Voughan. Pastora later married a Mexican doctor whose last name was Martinez, so that my grandmother was married under the name of Rosa Martinez. They went on to have twelve children. My mother, Lydia Narro, was born in 1916 in Durango, Mexico.

Thus in line with many of the narratives of recovering crypto-Jews, Alcalá's choice to focus on her Jewish heritage here is a willed one. This U.S.-raised "brown" Latina could self-identify as Opata Indian, Irish, Mexican, or as mixed or mestiza in nature—in terms, that is to say, of any among a wide assortment of racial and national self-identifications—but, at least in addressing her fellow crypto-Jews, she chooses to know herself as a descendent of a group that includes two of these categories alone, the Mexicans and Jews: the Marranos. (She has written novels, it should be emphasized, that explore Mexican and Opata Indian histories, each as relevant to her background as her Jewish ancestry.) It should be noted that, even if it were accepted by the Jewish community—which it is not—the part of her self-identification that figures her as a Jew is hardly halachic in nature, since it's carried (if it is carried) on the patrilineal line by a convert from Catholicism to Protestantism. And the evidence for it is not unshaky. Other than family narrative, the discovered existence of some Jews named Narro as well as the presence of the name in records of Sephardic families, the only piece of concrete evidence Alcalá can produce to substantiate her Jewish origin is the undeniably suggestive but ultimately irrelevant fact that her grandfather studied Hebrew.

What's important to stress here is that a tenuously established but nevertheless tenaciously held sense of residual Jewishness seems to trump these various possibilities, to take over from among the welter of possible differences the burden of difference itself—of difference from the white community *and* the Mexican American one. Or perhaps it would be better to say that it serves as a trope for that sense of difference and can give us some sense of its vectors and intensities:

> Because of the conversion, many of the traditions associated with Catholicism had been left behind as superstitious or idolatrous. My family did not drink, smoke, dance or play cards. Although steeped in religion, we did not wear crosses. The worship services of my relatives did not have crosses in front of the church, and were organized along the lines of the early Christians, with elders giving the sermons or serving the communion. Mostly, we did not eat pork, but I understood that to be for health reasons. When my grandfather's conversion was recounted by family members, it was always accompanied by the phrase, "no se pagó el catolicismo." Only in researching my novels did I realize that the Catholicism didn't stick because it had been pasted on over a Jewish heart.

Perhaps so: Neulander et al. would certainly disagree. What they would not contest is that Jewishness provides a language for describing the sense of otherness that pervades the experience of the Narro clan both as Protestants in Mexico and then as Latinos in the United States. Whether the ascription of Jewishness is a cause or an effect of this sense of otherness seems beside the point, and it seems almost churlish to raise the question: it is clearly, for Alcalá, the means by which her persistent sense of alienation in both Mexico and the U.S. is negotiated or understood. For her it is a "Jewish" heart that beats under the surface of all these various alterities, that gives them bodily life and meaning.

That complex work done by the ascription of Jewishness is put display in *Spirits of the Ordinary*, for there the standard narrative structure of crypto-Jewishness I outlined above—the story of catastrophe, hiddenness, bricolaged new identities that respond to the persistent sense of otherness—plays off narratives of Mexican identity to produce a powerfully dialectical effect. Indeed, as the novel layers these two narratives against each other, it seems to be posing the first—the Marrano narrative—as a kind of mystery story, a tale of secret origins and hidden identities, of mysterious quests both physical (for gold) and metaphysical (for mystical knowledge), and the other—the Mexican narrative—as a more straightforward one, as a narrative of people trying to come to terms with the vagaries of existence in the face of such strangely compelled people. But, as the novel continues, the two positions, the odd or othered or ethnicized and the normative, seem to shift about, so that by the end of the novel it's the Marrano identity that seems stable and secure and that of the Mexican revealed to be unstable, more tenuous, its meaning hidden or obscured under the surface of official culture—to be, in sum, more like that of the Marrano. And here the role of Jewishness becomes even more prominent. In the novel's conclusion, the mythoi of Marranohood take over the novel entirely and lead it to its utopian conclusion in which, among other things, a new revelation is generated not only for Marranos and Mexicans but for the Americas themselves.

The novel tells two intertwined tales: that of a descendent of a Marrano family named Zacarías Caraval and that of his Catholic wife, Estella. Zacarías's father Julio, an apothecary, is a barely concealed crypto-Jew, ostensibly a Catholic but known to his fellow townspeople as a Jew; he devotes his life to the study of kabbalistic texts that have been handed down for generations, there searching for the mysterious multiple names of God and other pieces of hidden knowledge with both mystical fervor and the obsessive eye for detail that make him such a good mixer of potions and medicines.[28] Zacarías's mother Mariana is also a *judía* whom Julio has married because her origins would guarantee that his child would be halachically a Jew, but whom he has grown not only to love but also to admire. For, although she is mute since an attack on her by antisemitic schoolmates, she has dreams and visions that far exceed his; she sees angels, is able to access distant events, foretells the future. Most important of all, she has a "knowledge of the heart" that complements and completes Julio's heady mysticism and nourishes him and her son even in the face of the tension between the two. For although Zacarías is the first child of the family to bear a Jewish name since the mass conversion of Mexican Jews in 1596, he is rebellious against "the name he bore" and all that it entails: "hunched under the weight of thirteen generations ... had no love of books, of tradition, or of enclosed places" (23). Zacarías renounces his family's crypto-Judaism when he marries the beautiful and wealthy gentile Estela (who, again like all the townspeople, knows full well of his *judío* background, yet chooses him out of love); but even this act of familial rebellion is not enough to quell his urge to assert his sense of specialness. He remains, at heart, a "wild stranger," driven to pursue dreams of wealth rather than work as an apothecary like his father or a store clerk like his uncle. Disappearing for weeks at a time (frequently, Estela notes, on Christian holidays), he seeks "minerals in the hills as though they were the Holy Grail, the Seven Cities of Cíbola, the voice in the wilderness" (24). As that syncretic vision—at once Christian, conquistadorial, and Jewish in nature—suggests, his desire pushes him to the edge of all the established identity categories in nineteenth-century Mexico, indeed, it impels him to wander off into Indian lands, where, after a disastrous encounter with spoiled water, he is rescued by an Opata chief.

Needless to say, his marriage is quickly strained by his sustained vagrancy, and when he returns with gold taken from a mine he calls Esmeralda, Estella hears his calling of that name in his sleep as sign that he has taken up with another woman and cuts him off financially. Impelled by increasingly frequent visions—he is indeed his mother's son—Zacarías departs for the mountains again. Led by his Indian friends, his travels take him to Casas Grandes, a place in the mountains in which the indigenous peoples have established a utopian community, free from involuntary servitude, state repression, and the tender mercies of the military. There he becomes something of a biblical prophet, like his namesake (although he also takes the name of El Tecolete, the owl), drawing more and more of the poor, the oppressed, and especially the *indígenas* to that site:

> Word of Zacarías' visions spread rapidly, and more and more people came to Casas Grandes from the surrounding countryside, from Cuidád Chihuahua, Juárez, and even from as far away as Pitíc and places in Texas and Arizona. The Conchos, the Jova, and the Pima Bajo Indians came; so did the Opata, Guazapar, and the Vorohío, as well as the Temori and the Tepehuan . . .
>
> Hearing of his visions of the ancient deer dancers, the men brought out their old rattles, concealed in caves in the mountains, and re-created masks and headwear in the tradition of their forefathers. Women brought herbs and healing songs passed down from mother to daughter. Ceremonies thought to have been lost were revived and re-created from the memories of old ones . . .
>
> Most of all, people brought their faith—in the old ways, the new ways, the Virgin Mary, Christ the King, Father Sun, Mother Moon, healing signs, heavenly bodies and potions.   (184)

Predictably, Zacarías comes to be treated as a combination Old Testament prophet, Christ figure, and shaman (he prays "in three languages," Hebrew, Spanish, and Opata, over a sick Apache child, who is healed—although Zacarías knows that it is a result of native Indian medicine, not his incantations); he finds himself increasingly, and disturbingly, deified by the people. Fearing that, as it had previously in volatile Mexico, the rise of a people's prophet will lead to insurrection, the Saltillo-based army attacks the growing Casas Grandes community, massacring those who have come there. Zacarías escapes and returns briefly home, to encounter the son he fathered during his last visit. He circumcises the child with a kitchen knife, definitively for the first time proclaiming himself (and his son) a Jew ("I have promised him to God... the way my father promised me. It is a covenant.... It is a sign that we are apart," he cries [212]), then disappears for parts unknown. The townspeople, incited by the local father, stage a minipogrom, burning down Julio and Melissa's house. At the end of the novel Julio and Melissa have fled to Mexico City, Estela soon follows them, and Zacarías becomes even more a wanderer, "a phantom, a name carried by the wind, a set of letters that did not necessarily add up to a person" (232), moving northward until somewhere, on the American side of the Rio Grande, he encounters another Marrano, with a fountain in his garden exactly like Julio and Melissa's Saltillo home. The novel concludes with his and Estela's son Gabriel, who has been converted to Protestantism in college, returning to Saltillo to read his father's diaries and vowing to rebuild the fountain in the garden of the home of his grandparents.

Spirits of the Ordinary is, like Zacarías's visionary experiences, deeply syncretic, a blend of Marquezian magical realism, Jewish mysticism, and intensely researched Mexican and Southwestern U.S. history. Its narrative is syncretic as well. It sustains and fleshes out the Marrano narrative I have been adverting to throughout this chapter; but it layers that narrative with an ensemble of other texts, creating the effect of a literary echo chamber. It's profoundly reminiscent of Cather's *The Professor's House*, for example, with its evocation of a dead, utopian Indian community that lurks behind the Casas Grandes portions of the book. Its use of Indian narratives echoes the invocation of Indian indiginity in multiculturalist fictions of the 1980s and 1990s, like Barbara Kingsolver's *Animal Dreams* (1990); its interest in positioning these narratives as part of a larger indigeneous apocalyptic movement echoes Leslie Silko's *Almanac of the Dead*

(1991). And for its representation of Jewish family dynamics it mines hundreds of Jewish American fictions: think *The Jazz Singer*, with Julio, the Marrano Kaballah-reading father, standing in for Cantor Rabinowitz, and Zacarías cast as the rebellious, Westernizing son who loves a goy but returns to the faith (although, in this case, sans *shikse*). In its evocation of kabbalistic lore about Eden and angels put in the service of a vague revolutionary apocalypticism, it resembles nothing so much as *Angels in America* (and, in its subplot about a cross-dressing female photographer, Corey, *Yentl*).

I don't mean to sound dismissive of *Spirits of the Ordinary* but rather to suggest that it takes its narrative warrant from the plethora of fictions about Jewish Americans of the last century in order in order to address what the novel sees as a significant lacuna: its correlative inability to find a narrative frame for the question of Mexican—and hence ultimately U.S. Mexican-American identity. To put it simply: to be a Jew, even a crypto-Jew, is something for which there exists a narrative structure, even (or especially) if that structure is one that expresses a hidden or a secret identity. But to be a Mexican, and hence a Mexican American, is for Alcalá a far more mysterious multiple thing—something that can best be glossed by the abjected and repressed figure of the crypto-Jew.

For Mexicanness as this novel understands it is a complex and unstable amalgam of various different races, religions, and nationalities roiling underneath the superstructure of a nation still in the process of being made. We are asked to witness this complexity throughout the novel, but, as the English-speaking audience to whom the novel is addressed, we never see it more thoroughly than when it's rendered through the eyes of our surrogate, the gender-bending photographer Corey, one of the many characters who is woven in and out of the novel's central concerns. When she travels south of the border, she

> found herself looking into dark faces with blue eyes, blond, green-eyed children speaking Spanish together with darker siblings, a pale, refined-looking woman holding a child Corey would have taken for pure Indian.... There was a family with kinky red hair and pale, freckled skin, but negroid features. She was continually startled by types she expected to speak the King's English opening their mouths to use Indian and Spanish dialects, or some combination of all three. (109)

And we are asked to witness the moral problematics even more acutely resulting from this complexity in a carefully staged debate between the promiscuous Irish priest and Magdalena, the beautiful daughter of an Indian family sold (without her knowledge) to a white plantation owner who takes over after his death and manumits his slaves. Magdalena is quick to note the continuing racial oppression faced by blacks in Mexico, even after the outlawing of slavery (and the defeat of the South, just a week's journey away, in the Civil War); the white priest, Father Newman, is equally quick to defend slavery on the grounds of natural law and practical necessity, to remind her that her fortune was built on the backs of slaves, and that the treatment of Indians is not necessarily better than the treatment that blacks received.

What's important to note here is not this debate per se but rather the degree to which Alcalá, by staging it, is anticipating some of the important recognitions that are going to mark the reconfiguration of discourses in the academic and political sphere in the years following the publication of her book. Writing in 1995, she anticipates the critical turn that José Aranda has called the new Chicano studies—the work of critics attending to issues of gender, sexuality, and especially race in the making of Mexican and hence Mexican American identities.[29] Aranda argues that, breaking with the politically efficacious but historically problematic founding mythos of Aztlán—the mythical homeland of the Mexican American peoples—and breaking more ambivalently with the equally powerful figuration of the borderland offered by the late critic, artist, and poet Gloria Anzaldúa, anthropologists, historians, and literary and film critics in the 1990s and early 2000s sought to reconfigure the notion of Mexicanness around a fluid continuum of locations, identities, and discursive possibilities that foregrounded race, gender, and sexualities. With respect to race in particular, work like Martha Menchaca's *Recovering History, Constructing Race: The Indian, Black, and White Roots of Mexican Americans* has brought to the fore the full range of racial components that went into the making of Mexicanness—in addition to the three referenced in the title, she focuses on the *mestizo* (white/Indian) and the *afromestizo* (black/Indian), with particular emphasis on the last of these, the repressed black component evident in the descendents of the two hundred thousand or so slaves imported by the Spanish colonial administration in the sixteenth century.[30] With encyclopedic zeal, Menchaca traces the mixed and multiple origins of all three groups that form her essential narrative back to their prehistoric origins in Spain, Africa, and the U.S. and forward to their collisions in eighteenth- and nineteenth-century Mexico and the Southwest United States.

Oddly, though, Menchaca doesn't include Jews in the roster of races and ethnicities making up Spanish and Mexican populations. This exclusion from the account of Spanish whiteness—whose makeup Menchaca traces back to the Visigoths and in which she includes Greeks, Basques, and Muslims—might seem puzzling. But there are good if doleful reasons for such an act of historical forgetting. It's a sign of just how successful was the suppression of Jews, both by the popular pogrom and by Church and state, first in Spain, then in Mexico, and by the equally successful self-suppression of the conversos and Marranos who melted into the fabric of Spainsh and Mexican life. Menchaca is hardly alone in this excision; although it's not my primary field of expertise, I've found little mention of the converso/Marrano presence in contemporary Latino studies circles, although when I've given talks before ethnic studies audiences, my speculations have been greeted with enormous interest and frequent reference to secret or long-lost Jewish relatives. Alcalá's novel aims at a similarly cathartic effect. But it has greater uses still; what she does complements and completes, rather than contests or invalidates, the perspectives on race that mark the New Chicano studies in general, and Menchaca's book in particular.

To be sure, Alcalá's work comes from a different place than Menchaca's: it grows, as I suggested above, out of the multicultural literary movement in the United States—and particularly, to localize it a bit further, out of the group of West Coast, especially Seattle-based, writers that flourished in the 1990s. But it's quite similar, I think, in stressing the multiplicity of determinants that go into the making of Mexicanness, specifically the compelling role played by regimes of race in their construction as such. Indeed, in many ways, Alcalá moves beyond Menchaca, since the novelist's license gives her the ability to focus more intently on the makeup of individual categories and to suggest the complex interplay of culture, race, and nationality in their construction. We've already seen the attention she pays to the African and the *afromestizo* in the complex racial stew that composes the peoples of northern Mexico. Alcalá's taxonomies go even further: among whites, for example, she's interested in the presence and propagation of the Irish as well as Spaniards and of the cultural influence of the French even after the fall of Emperor Maximilian. (Indeed, in one of the most interesting moments of the book, the converso Zacarías chides his daughter for wearing fashionable French low-cut blouses and dresses: "We [Mexicans] shed the blood of brave men to get out from under Spain's thumb and that crazy Hapsburg so that we can imitate the French?" [18]; that the son of a family persecuted by Mexicans and whose family is about to be attacked by a Mexican mob identifies himself with their national project has much to say about the complexities of belonging in this particular milieu). She even extends the ethnoracial canvas to include Muslims—in this case, a trader with whom Zacarías and Magdalena do business as they build their bakeries.

But, most important of all, Alcalá uses the marrano narrative to put *symbolic* weight on the religious variegation as a crucial element in the makeup of 1870s Mexico. This is the case on the Christian side, in which Father Newman preaches sermons in favor of racial and gender hierarchy— of the order that was established at the Creation and must be maintained thereafter (in this sense, his name is deeply ironic; his message is very old indeed). And it's true as well in the detailed inspection of religious feelings and practices lying just under the Catholic surface, constantly threatening to rise up from below to challenge or transform the state-sanctioned religion and the power of its priests and potentates. Thus in Casas Grandes, not only do Indian, Catholic, and Jewish mysticisms meet and turn each other inside out; new belief systems get created. People bring their faith in the "old ways" and in the "new ways" and (in a verb repeated twice in the passage I have quoted above) "recreate" the rituals and practices that they abandoned under the ministrations of missionaries and priests; Zacarías tells the people he encounters the stories he remembers from his father's kabbalistic inquiries (even though as a Marrano, of course, he has no direct access to an established Jewish community of worship or even to the Torah and Talmud); they respond with their own folk narratives; he ends up speaking his parables back to them in three languages, a mixture of Spanish, Hebrew, and the trade argot of the indigenous peoples. But more is at stake here than mysticism. The appearance of such holy men, the army captain correctly thinks, was often correlated with the rise of political insurrections of particularly dire quality. "People whipped up by these quasi-religious leaders were willing to fight to the death," he muses, then ominously uses that sense as a justification for genocide: "And in order to defeat them, one had to fight the same way" (187).

We can see, then, why the Marrano presence is so important for Alcalá: it's a metonym for a wide variety of secret identities and hidden practices, forbidden and feared by Church and state alike, that lie roiling under the surface and bubble up at moments of political or economic stress to contest them. And it's a trope as well for the possibility of a recreation of spirituality itself: for a return not so much to indigenous religious faiths, but rather to what Alcalá insists is a generative remaking, a reanimation that brings old ceremonies and new visions together into a new syncretic whole just the way that Marranos were persistently forced—or is it enabled?—to do. Such a vision, it should be added, is hardly Jewish anymore—Zacarías's visions and the mysticism on display here are more New Age–like than anything recognizable from the Jewish tradition But, in Alcalá's hands, this created, invented form of spirituality is put to a greater, deeper use. It helps her create her own syncretic vision to offer a new Creation myth, not just for Mexicans, or Mexican Americans, but for the Americas themselves.

This project is undertaken throughout the novel in its persistent allusion to the narrative of Adam and Eve and to the notion of a successor to them who might redeem their fallen state. Its thematic is interlaced throughout the book—in the name, for example, of Father Newman, who represents the ironic negation of that hope, or in the way that Zacarías is continually described as covered with dust, that which Adam is made of, that which he, like all men, must return to, crossed with the ways in which his trajectory through the novel imitates that of Christ (with, of course, the difference that this imitation brings him back to his Jewishness). It's most fully expressed in the symbology of the garden with an ever replenishing fountain behind Julio and Mariana's house, one that falls into ruination, first through Julio's desire to reshape it in a potted scheme to bring Zacarías back home, then when it's destroyed by the pogrom-mad mob at the end of the novel. But the final image with which Alcalá leaves us is a dream vision of the garden restored and redeemed, and with it all the characters of the extended Caraval clan:

> I could almost see them walking towards me, Mariana with a bunch of wildflowers clutched in one hand, Julio with dust on his shirt, tie askew. They were surrounded by children—my father Zacarías, my mother Estela, her sister Blanca and their beautiful brother and sister Manzana and Membrillo—all of them children, and mixed together with them my own sisters and cousins [and children].
>
> . . .
>
> I understood that this was an hallucination of sorts, no doubt brought on by my strenuous journey and the heat of the afternoon.

> Nevertheless, I recognized the curly black hair and hawk noses of my family, the air of otherworldliness that marked and set us apart. They seemed not to fear the place, or at least, not to know it. (243)

Here the narrative syncretism and the familial conjunctions merge into each other: mystical visions and biblical echoes fully define Mariana as the new Eve (but also the type of Mary), Julio (his name, we now realize if we haven't before, is one letter away from *judío*) as a new Adam, both of them the progenitors of a new race of religious mestizos: part Christian (the amalgam provided by Estela, Blanca, and their relatives), part Jewish: all, in the end, however, defined as definitively the latter, by the "curly black hair and hawk noses" that are racial markers of Jewish otherness as much as the sense of being "set apart" is a sign of the Jew's ontological difference. (That Jews defined as such are so phenotypically close to Indians only enhances the syncretism of this final vision of omnibus difference, but it also reminds us that all categories of otherness here are organized through and refer back to the Jew.)

There's much more to be said about this amalgamating move in the context of the Hordes/Neulander controversy: it brings to the fore, if nothing else, the ways that Jewishness is a metonym for otherness of all sorts, which then morphs back into Jewishness in an oscillating pattern of identity-blending crisscross. But I want to close with what I see as the grandest ambition of this conclusion. This scene of the new redeemed family set in the ruined garden resonates, for a U.S. audience at least, with the familiar topos of the American Adam—the idea, as explicated half a century ago by R. W. B. Lewis, that nineteenth-century writers north of the border were obsessed with of a new, redeemed Adamic beginning on these shores compensating for, or even annulling, the dramas of fallenness and corruption that were associated with Europe and the Old World.[31] Here with its clear allusion to the language of a second birth that comes out of the both the Christian tradition and the secondary echoings of the Jewish immigrant narrative that tropes that tradition, Alcalá offers her multicultural audience of the 1990s an alternative mythos of American new beginnings to the ones that have predominated in the U.S. tradition. Most important, this vision redefines the American Adam as a secondary figure—as following behind Eve, identifies both these figures as Mexicans, identifies them, moreover, as crypto-Jews, deviants, Others even in this tradition, and recognizes them as progenitors of a visionary who speaks to

Indians and whose mystical visions conflate his, theirs, and those of Christian spirituality.

This conclusion is not unproblematic—the topos of the American Adam and Eve as indigenous or Other is a foundational and quite familiar piece of European mythmaking about the New World, one with a particularly gruesome relation to the genocidal realities it masked. But what is crucial, and unique, and original about Alcalá's text, as I've been arguing throughout this section, is the specific narrative means by which this work is done—the narrative of the crypto-Jew sloughing off his or her hidden identity, discovering and proclaiming his or her origins no matter what belief system he or she currently subscribes to. Here, again, what's important to stress is the use that Alcalá makes of this narrative, especially at the end of the novel. Gabriel travels south to encounter the fountain that signifies Edenic life (like the Bethesda fountain in *Angels*) and the underground continuation of the wellspring of Jewish identity in the parched lands of Catholic Mexico; his father travels north to discover exactly the same thing on the opposite side of the border. Their crisscross enacts the cross- or transborder identifications that Alcalá uses to lock the U.S. and Mexico into a common fate, a shared destiny. Jewish and Christian, white and brown, colonized and colonizer: all are caught up in a larger identity linking exploiter and exploited, people who articulate orthodox religious beliefs and those who cleave to subordinated or repressed ones, in an ethnoreligious as well as a racial *mestizaje*: one that can only be organized and encoded through the repressed but ever resurgent narrative of the hidden, othered, crypto-Jew: the universal Marrano.

Found in Translation: *Days of Awe*

Achy Obejas's 2000 novel, *Days of Awe*, too, begins with an invocation to an Eve of the Americas, but one that gives that figure an entirely different spin: "Revolutions happen, I'm convinced, because intuition tells us we're meant for a greater world. If this one were good enough, we'd settle, happy as hens, and never rise up.... Even Eve—or was it Lilith?—felt the pang of desire for something else well before she was officially bestowed the mortal right to yearn."[32] Here she not only invokes Eve as the muse of yearning—a familiar enough story, one hallowed in Christian as well as Jewish theology—but also shadows her with the midrashic story of

Lilith invented by the rabbis to explain the inconsistency between the two creation stories in Genesis. Lilith is a dark-completed, black-haired sprite, not just an affront but a block to heteronormativity, for, in traditional Jewish cultures, she is thought to steal babies at birth, so much so that three *mezuzas* are often placed above the cradle to ward her off. As such, she serves as an appropriate muse for Obejas. Her protagonist Alejandra is a bisexual Cuban émigré in the United States struggling to come to terms with her multiple roots. But the way Lilith surfaces in the text—hidden syntactically behind or even occluded by Eve, yet peeping out from her secondary position—frames her as the dark shadow of a figure whose narrative is shared by Christians and Jews: Lilith as Eve's all-Jewish avatar, perhaps, or even her "true" aspect. Taken together, the two form a perfect emblem of that with which Alejandra—and the novel at large—are obsessed: the phenomenon of crypto-Jewishness.

For a similar doubling hiddenness, or a hidden doubleness, shapes the fates of virtually all the characters in the book in many dimensions: political, sexual, national, and affectional as well as ethnoreligious. In all these cases it is a confrontation with Jewishness that brings these multiple affiliations into the light of day. Obejas's remarkably layered narrative tells no fewer than six interlocked stories. First, it recounts that of its first-person narrator Alejandra San José (also known by her nickname Ale), a contemporary Cuban American who works as a legal translator and who discovers in Cuba that both her parents, in fact, were born of Marrano roots, a matter of little consequence to her mother but of the greatest moment to her father. It therefore also tells the story of her father Enrique, an exiled professor of Latin American literature and a brilliant translator of South American and Cuban poetry and prose, who has essentially become a contemporary Marrano by renouncing his Jewish origins, marrying a beautiful Catholic woman (or so she seems) to live as a fully assimilated gentile. Enrique persistently denies his origins to his inquisitive daughter. For example, after she learns that the name of her grandmother is typically a Jewish one (a familiar trope in the literature of Marrano self-discovery), she asks him directly about their Jewish heritage; he replies with the disingenuousness of the true crypto-Jew by speaking words each of which is perfectly true but whose collocation gives an impression that is palpably false: "We're Spaniards, we're Catholics . . . we're like everybody else in Cuba" (115). For all this denial, however, he also disappears into his study to pray and bind himself with phylacteries in a ritual of secret Jewishness that is almost sexual in its combination of ecstasy and hiddenness. Complicating their relation further, when the young Alejandra peeps in the basement window to voyeuristically observe her father's secret ritual, she shatters the window, cascading shards of glass all over him. The scene resonates with intensities that extend the psychosexual dimensions of this secret act from Enrique to Ale and from Jewish to Christian in an intricately chiasmic series: his bleeding hands conjuring hints of Christ's stigmata, her fascinated, voyeuristic vision conveying hints of the primal scene. Sex and religion, Christian martyrdom and Jewish self-identification, even male and female (she gazes, he bleeds) mix and match in a fascinating blend that is as compelling as it is overdetermined.

To continue with the parade of narratives: the novel also charts, via Alejandra's researches, the story of her family: of Enrique's Marrano mother Sima and his somewhat irrelevant father Luis, who choose to stay crypto-Jews in the provinces, and most important, the maniacally self-asserting Ytzak, a one-legged descendent of a Marrano family (he lost his limb fighting in 1898) who, Abraham-like, decides more or less ex nihilo to proclaim his Jewishness, leaving his suffering wife not once but twice, circumcising his grandson Enrique and heaving off with him to Havana—"his city, his Zion, his place of salvation" (348)—where they can live as Jews. It is also the story of Ale's mother Nena, whose ancestry the industrious Alejandra traces back to the Abravanel family, a converso clan one member of whom had been counselor to the captain general of Havana in the 1600s who had inadvertently betrayed the city to the Dutch by an indiscreet word to his *mulata* mistress.

Nena is uninterested in her own converso roots; she is happy to pursue the admixture of the (quite lax) Catholicism and Santaría that is the true heritage of her family: the Abravanels' "Catholicism [becoming] as corrupted as [their] initial Judaism" (47). The same, however, cannot be said for the last significant group in the novel, in many ways its most significant next to that of Ale and her father: the story of her father's childhood friend and next-door neighbor Moisés Menachs and his family, whom Alejandra discovers when she makes aliyah to her family home in Havana and with whom she becomes involved as friends and even, in the case of the son of the family, Orlando, lovers. Indeed, she first discovers her passion for Orlando in a powerful echo of the primal scene of discovering her father's Jewishness: here too she gazes on scene of hidden passion from a window—this time, the bathroom, from which she spies Orlando pouring milk on the vagina of a beautiful fifteen-year-old gentile neighbor and then performing oral sex on her. And here too the implications are multiple: she yearns for the neighbor (at one point even thinking that she has glimpsed an image of her naked body in a *Playboy* spread on the girls of Havana) while enjoying passionate sex of her own with Orlando, who becomes not just a lover but also a tour guide, expositor of all things Cuban, even friend. So too, in a less dramatic fashion, with the rest of the family, who provide for her a quarrelsome but closely knit ethnic unit, at once deeply "Jewish" and profoundly "Cuban," that stands in stark contrast to what she sees as her rigorous, repressed father and her self-contained mother.

Each of these narratives is allowed its own integrity; each resonates in a different way with the novel's thematics of dislocation and translation—between languages, communities, identities—and its probing dialectic of belonging and alienation. But each comes back to the mysterious conundrum of the crypto-Jew, not so much as an explanation or a metaphor for the multiple allegiances that Obejas's characters aver, but as the clearest example, even the quintessence, of the problems and possibilities of such multiplicity. Thus, to cite Alejandra herself, her multiple affiliations—as a bisexual woman, as a Cuban American, as the daughter of a closeted Jew who is only beginning to come to terms with the effects of his self-silencing on her own life—come into focus when she breaks up with her dull but sweet Jewish boyfriend Seth and embarks on a passionate affair with a Jewish woman, Leni Bergmann. Leni can be best described as a particularly American version of the crypto-Jew, the kind that the Jewish community labels a self-denying or self-hating American Jew. Leni doesn't take her own Jewish heritage terribly seriously; indeed, she associates it with the suburban complacency and reactionary politics of an older generation, including Zionism and "all that matrilineal shit." "I'm not Jewish," she tells Alejandra when they first meet, "my parents are" (177). Like so many American Jews, Leni is dark complected; she thus passes—and enjoys passing—for another Other, a free-floating exotic whose Levantine looks allow her to escape white suburban normativity: "with her big dark eyes, full lips, and cinnamon skin, she was always mistaken for Moroccan or Greek, sometimes Brazilian or even Cuban" (179). In this sense she is the reverse of Coleman Silk: a Jew who passes for a Levantine or South American as a way of denying her identity as a white woman. But not fully: in a catalytic moment for Alejandra, Leni explodes in rage when she is recognized as a Jew by an African American woman on a CTA bus who wishes her "Happy Hanukah." Leni, Alejandra realizes, wants to be "anonymously American, unfettered and free": in a word, a person without an ethnic identity (182). Leni's desire to be rootless forces Alejandra to confront her own yearning for that which Leni possesses but rejects, a simple connection to a historical past, a sense "of the inevitability of [her] Jewishness," one she spends the entire book seeking to overcome (182) "The height of denial," Leni says of herself. "The real denial is mine," muses Alejandra (180).

Contrasting with her increasing closeness to her Cuban family and friends, her tormented affair with the faithless (in all senses) Leni reflects Alejandra's own crypto-Jewishness back to her and fuels her attempts to overcome it. These attempts also bring to the surface that for which crypto-Jewishness also serves as a particularly resonant figure, the Cuban American. "With Leni, I could be as free as I wanted about my cubanidad because she never challenged my authenticity," muses Alejandra. Leni's embrace of her identity as a free-floating swarthy-skinned exotic invites Alejandra, too, to get in touch with her "own darkness" (179). But, with consummate irony, Cuban American Alejandra can pass as a normative white Christian American, even a Midwesterner, far more easily than can the Jewish American Leni—a lovely turn on the familiar trope of the Jew's whiteness of which the politically engaged Leni and Alejandra are also quite aware: "While I could talk eloquently about how negative Latino media images affected us all, I could also—with my white Cuban skin, my perfect English—enter any retail store with the assurance that I could wander the aisles at liberty, sure to be perceived as the descendent of an Italian dancer or, perhaps, a French winemaker, if I had any ethnicity at all" (179). The exact nature and properties of her *latinidad*—the "us all" in the above quotation—is called into question by her *cubanidad* or, more accurately, her status as a white Cuban exile in the U.S, which allows her to pass as a European. But—just to nail these ironies down and to suggest their relevance to the Jewish—she so appears because she is the member of a family who are "direct descendents of fifteenth-century Jews from Seville, where there was a particularly vibrant Hebraic community prior to Ferdinand and Isabella's orders" (35). Precisely because she is the daughter of crypto-Jews, Alejandra is able to pass as a crypto-Latino.

Alejandra's progress toward an affirmation of her own Jewishness thus serves to disarticulate a whole set of identity categories, to suggest how historically layered and internally contradictory such categories are, and to trace what new configurations can be made of them. The central example of these process is the interplay between Alejandra's Jewishness and her increasing sense of *cubanidad*. On the one hand, the identification is natural: Cubans are the Jews of the Caribbean, she muses at one point, diasporized yet clinging to their sense of home at one and the same time, model minorities in the U.S and frequently able to pass there for white. But, as Alejandra discovers when she returns to the island, her American-Cuban assumptions (even those of a good tormented leftist, critical of America but also of the imprisonments and persecutions and silencings of Fidel's Cuba) are a far cry from the always-already multiple realities on the ground, where faith in the fading example of the Revolution and its manifold absurdities vies with a yearning for freedom in America; where Castroism and Che worship (however commodified) contends with Catholicism, Santería, and even a residual and attenuated Jewishness as a belief system. And this polysemy is expressed through Jewishness itself. On the one hand, Jewishness is a figure for revolutionary zeal: her Cuban relatives and friends are firm but ironic adherents of the Revolution in just the same way religious Jews are firm but ironic adherents of the possibility of the return of the Messiah. Moisés persistently defends its absurdities or excesses with a whimsical shrug of the shoulder; while they criticize the government in private, his children volunteer to paint over anti-Castro graffiti and beat up a friendly neighbor who taunts them on his way out on a boat. On the other, their true sentiments, by the end of the book, seem as unclear as the fate of the revolution itself. "Next year in Miami," cries out one of the Menachs on the way to services 316); Deborah, one of the granddaughters, stages a subversive play in tandem with a performance artist in Miami that shocks the family. Similar perturbations occur elsewhere in the small Jewish community of Havana. Enrique's grandfather Ytzak is a committed leftist as well as a fervent Jew from his youth; nevertheless, he dies in a crowd of would-be émigrés trapped for weeks by the police in the Czech embassy, confined there by Castro's dreaded police.

This last moment, in particular, resonates with multiple meanings. Is Ytzak's own affiliation as a faithful Cuban patriot undone, finally, by the weight of his perpetual desire, the yearning for exile, his version of the urge to diasporize that drives his grandson Enrique to assert his own wandering itinerary? Or is he really a crypto-counterrevolutionary or someone, like so many of his fellow Cubans, undone in his commitment to Revolution (that quality is invoked in the first pages of the text, doubly associated with Eve and Lilith) by revulsion at what the Revolution has become? Or is he simply caught in the wrong place at the wrong time—a ninety-year-old man trapped in a mob of people, then crushed by them? The text has no answer for these or the other ambiguities generated by the example of the Revolution; all we can say with certainty is that, as it has done with *latinidad* and *cubanidad*, it figures the Revolution in two ways, both deeply suffused with Jewishness: as an image for a faith in an unrealizable ideal—Havana as the potential new Zion—and as a figure for the inevitability of loss—Cuba as a site of nostalgia for a way of life that has passed, killed by a revolution that has run its course.

The same thing, in the end, is true of Jewishnessness itself, which ramifies with increasing intensity the closer Alejandra gets to it. Seemingly, the novel tells a fairly conventional story—doubly so in the context of the narratives of crypto-Jews: one in which someone comes to discover her hidden Jewish heritage and moves forward to identifying themselves with this hidden identity, no matter how disjunct from their current sense of self it may be. And the narrative follows this trajectory faithfully: Alejandra learns of the crypto-Jewishness of both her parents, investigates its origins, has her heart broken by a Jewish woman, learns Hebrew, celebrates the High Holidays, and, in the end, finally identifies herself as a Jew, despite her own crypto-Jewish reticence in doing so. (She only publicly proclaims herself a Jew when she encounters irritatingly persistent Christian missionaries in an airport, in ironic but powerful contrast with Leni's response to the same situation on the bus.) But things rapidly become more complex: the closer Alejandra gets to her Jewish "roots," the more plangently she learns that there are none. We see this most clearly, perhaps, in the kaleidoscopic itinerary of origination that Alejandra's narrative traces. In the opening pages of the book, Chicago, where she is raised and where she lives, has already receded as a spot of origin to Miami, where, in a wonderful parody of the Exodus story, the San Josés first arrived in America. But Miami soon gives way as a place of origin to Havana, with all its attendant ambiguities—a place where the Revolution still lives, a place where Jews have long been able to be Jews, as they are not in the rest of Cuba. But, as she learns more of the family narrative, Havana gives way as a site of origins to Oriente, the mountainous eastern province of Cuba, where the family originally arrives, from which her great-grandfather makes a treacherous journey to Havana, and to which she returns to trace the roots of her great-grandmother and the side of the family that choses to remain there as Marranos. (Oriente serves as a site of historical as well as familial origins: it's the part of Cuba where Europeans first landed and the site from which Fidel, who makes a guest appearance in the novel complete with a knowing reference to rumors of his family's own crypto-Jewish roots, also originates.) Further, she learns more about the history of crypto-Jews (including, as well, it turns out, her mother's family); even Oriente gives way to Seville as a place of primal origins and organic wholeness—it is the place that her father, whatever his Cuban roots and his American identity, claims as his own spiritual home. But the wheeling of origination doesn't stop here. Ultimately it passes back to Jerusalem, a place at once real and fantasized, fictionalized, or forgotten, yet serving, as it does for every Jew, as a trope (and for many more than a trope) for origination and identity. But even in its invocation of Jerusalem, the novel pushes beyond any rooted place as a stable site of origin, This process is performed by the text's persistent and consequential allusions to the work of Judah Halevy, the great poet of the Jewish-Spanish Renaissance who set out for Jerusalem and died (Moses—or is it Moisés?—like) before he could get there. It is no coincidence that Halevy is Enrique's favorite poet, "possibly," Alejandra writes, "the most eloquent voice ever on the subject of exile (in both Ladino and Hebrew)" (91)—that is to say, in both the language of the place of origins *and* that of diaspora. And it is equally significant that the novel ends by Ale's quoting in lieu of Kaddish for her father one of Halevy's most beautiful lyrics, a meditation on the sea—the feared but also beautiful avenue of physical translation that leads Halevy to the edge of Jerusalem. What Ale finds, in short, is that there is no *place* of origin but rather that the persistent expression of a yearning for origination, a yearning that, like the secret identites and bricolaged practices of the crypto-Jews, can become a source of meaning, beauty, value in its own right.

Which is not to say, to give the argument one last turn of the screw, that Ale's discovery and articulation of crypto-Jewishness or irrelevant or unmeaningful—to the contrary. For what's important about it, as I've been stressing throughout this chapter, is its ability, out of its voiding of the past yet its continual referring back to it, to generate narratives, stories that engender in turn other narratives—stories, here, of ethnicity, race, politics, sexuality. The most important of these, though, is the narrative that drives the novel forward: the story of Alejandra's coming to terms with her father's own chosen, indeed willed Marranohood or, rather, the story she learns about his Jewish past and his decision to conceal it. This choice asks to be read, like everything else in the novel, in multiple ways. On the one hand, his decision to re-Marranize himself offers him the chance that every person seeks as part of the process of individuation: to, as it were, translate one's own identity from the language by which one has been written into one more fully satisfying, a language one might even have some role in shaping oneself. Having been circumcised by his grandfather, carried away from his own Marrano parents (his mother, in a moving moment near the end of her life, comes to Havana to worship with Ytzak when she thinks he is dying, but returns to Oriente to die a Catholic), and raised as a Jew, Enrique's choice to pass as a fertile is oddly, but distinctively, self-affirming. But he has not fully done so without cost or pain: indeed, at the end of the novel, Ale learns, somewhat melodramatically, the true reason that, unlike Moisés or Ytzak and his other relatives, he chose to deny his Jewishness—a primal moment of humiliation by fascists in 1930s Havana, when, to escape a beating, he pretended as a fascist sympathizer, led him to adopt that stance of perpetual abjection. Alejandra is right to understand that this duality torments him, as expressed not only in his secret phylactery sessions in the basement but also in his extravagant and protracted mourning for his parents, especially his mother: lacking the proper venue for ritual enactments of his grief, like the saying of Kaddish or the lighting of *yahrtzeit* candles—for this would demand that he out himself as a Jew—he can mourn only in private, howling like an animal. As he lays dying, Alejandra wants to help him heal his wounds, help him proclaim himself as the Jew he once was and has pretended not to be—to perform with her the acts that he has been performing in private one last time before he dies. And she does so: in a moving scene, she brings his phylacteries from his study to his deathbed, helps him stand and binds him with them, then says his prayers with him until he collapses back on the bed, lifeless.

The scene is yet another example of the Gothic melodrama to which the crypto-Jewish tends; indeed, it is a particularly triumphant example of it. But crypto-Jewishness is given yet another spin in the text, in which it becomes the ground of a more positive form of identity. In his will, he makes a most unhalachic request, one that drives Alejandra into a state of rage: although he asks her to say Kaddish for him, he does not wish to be buried as a Jew: rather, he wishes her to scatter his ashes in his beloved Cuba. He is asking her, it must be stressed, to do two contradictory things. It is the injunction of every good Jew to say Kaddish for the dear departed dead; her doing so, then, would be a way of enfolding him into the Jewishness about which he is so ambivalent. But in traditional Judaism there are equally strong injunctions against burning the body, much less scattering the ashes; in Judaism bodies are merely lent to the men and women who inhabit them, to be returned to the earth as quickly as possible.[33] Enrique's gesture, then, not only expresses his own profound ambivalence but also binds Ale into his own insistently multiple structure of identity and being. In essence, he is trying to give his daughter the gift not of his Jewishness—she already has that—but of his marranism.

What, finally, is that gift, we can ask not only of *Days of Awe*, but of the entire set of texts and traditions I have been surveying in this chapter? It is first and foremost a gift of narrative, a trove of stories, hidden and reanimated, "real" and fictive, that simultaneously liberate and enchain, just as the narratives of Ale and her father do to and for each other, just as the stories of the crypto-Jews in New Mexico do for those who come to hear and understand them. It is also, however, the gift of syncretism—of the conflation of experiences, traditions, and religions that crypto-Jewishness doesn't just allow to come into being, but actively produces. Here, it's important to note Enrique's vocation as a particularly gifted translator, one who doesn't just relocate words from one language to another but who is able to shuttle back and forth between the worlds they originate in and conjure forth: "Most translators work best into, not from, their native language, using instinct to access the vernacular, the familiar. But my father did it both forward and backward, into and from his native Caribbean Spanish into a pure, songlike American tongue" (262). Unlike less successful translators, Enrique is dislocated from the first—at once part and not part of the Catholic Cuban culture from which he comes—and uses the dislocation of his crypto-Jewishness as the ground of his profession (in all senses of that charged word). But to conclude the paradoxes, to bring them, as it were, back home, this act is defined by the novel as a profoundly Jewish one, which is to say that the more he tries to evade his past, the more Enrique affirms it. "I told him once," says Ale, "that the rabbis quoted in the discussions in the Talmud are known as amora'im, Aramaic for translators, making his entire career an inadvertent but quintessentially Jewish act." "What does that say about you?" he replies (91).

The same question might be posed not only to Ale, or even the reader of the novel, but to those of us engaged in thinking about ethnic difference in the context of contemporary U.S. (and for that matter world) culture. *Days of Awe* can serve as a powerful reminder of just how much we might gain from thinking about difference through the image of crypto-Jewishness. The book's persistent invocation of the crypto-Jewish experience as a trope for ethnicity (*cubanidad, latinidad*), itself implicated in gendered and sexual experience, asks—demands—that we dislocate fixed notions of cultural identity and origination and replace them with ones organized by a wholly different logic. As such, the book offers a powerful counternarrative to that offered either by ethnic enthusiasts (like the multicultural fiction of the 1990s, which Obejas's emphasis on the layering or multiplicity of irreconcilable identity claims implicitly critiques) or by those contemporary Americanists for whom ethnicity is a ruse at best, a pernicious snare at worst. Following her example, rather than those of Jacobson, Michaels, Omi and Winant et al., would emphasize the powerfully productive role played by cultural syncreticism and the proud or shameful generation of the counternormative in the ethnic narrative—and a rich promissory note for what such narratives can offer us by way of critical and hermeneutic resources. In this Obejas comes close to the alluring but problematic example of Derrida, who elevates the Marrano into something of a concrete universal, a condition of (alienated) being. But, with its insistent focus on the layering of the local, *Days of Awe* seeks at one and the same time to forestall the universalizing gesture and to make us attend precisely to the particular blend of othernesses that lie within the drama of the Sephardim and their converso and Marrano manifestations. The goal of invoking the book as a paradigm of ethnic belonging, then, wouldn't be to ascribe its particular dynamics to ethnicities across the board—to the contrary!—but rather to remind us to pay closer attention to precise patterns of silencing and expression, cultural remakings and cultural forgettings, of religious gestures and combinations that can be articulated through the multiple, and intertwining, dramas of ethnic (as opposed to its dark twin, racial) belonging.

Indeed, at its most powerful and consequential, Obejas asks us to redefine ethnic belonging and even belonging itself as an alluring but impossible project, as leading not so much to a state of being, as to a persistent condition of longing, a shuttling between locations and sources of origination that never cohere with their place in cultural memory no matter how often that memory is appealed to. In so doing, *Days of Awe*, like so many of the narratives of the crypto-Jews, thus reminds us how rich and consequential are the stories we make out of the cascadings of diaspora, how triumphant are the results as well as how painful are the causes of the syncretism it nourishes, how meaningful are the acts of cultural shuttling we call translation, and how consequentially all these can extend and complicate the kinds of difference we invoke with the inadequate yet irreplaceable term *ethnicity*.

6. TRANSGRESSIONS OF A MODEL MINORITY

There they are, nice Chinese family—father, mother, two born-here girls. Where should they live next? . . . For they're the new Jews, after all, a model minority and Great American Success. They know they belong in the promised land.

Or do they?
—Gish Jen, *Mona in the Promised Land*

In the final analysis, the Jew is actually an Asiatic, not a European.
—Adolf Hitler

THE PROCESS OF THOUGHT leading to this chapter began nearly a decade ago at my favorite Chinese restaurant in New York, Hop Li Rice Shop, 17 Mott Street. I was taken there by my wife Sara to meet for the first time her sister Koren, a high-powered attorney, one Friday night. While I was undergoing Koren's friendly cross-examination—I am happy to say that I seem to have passed muster—I saw at the table next to us a striking fivesome: a very well dressed white man, his father, his Chinese American wife, their two biracial children. When the dinner came, they all pulled out yarmulkes and a kiddush cup and said Shabbat prayers. The ceremony concluded, they dived into their meal—a Hop Li specialty I had also ordered: hot pot pork with shrimp. I said to Sara and Koren, "Gosh, I love being a Jew."[1]

Eight years later. I am interviewing a young Korean American writer, Min Jin Lee, for this project. I had known Min Jin at Yale, where she been an undergraduate and where I had my first job; she became famous there for protesting the ethnocentric teaching of Korean American history. We had been corresponding about the attitudes of contemporary Asian American writers toward the Jewish example—Min Jin had brought herself to my attention by saying that her current project, a multigenerational family saga recently published under the title *Free Food for Millionaires* (2007) took as one of its models Herman Wouk's *Marjorie Morningstar*.* Naturally, I took her to Hop Li. The waiter was surly—usually, they are merely indifferent—but the food was, as always, spectacular. As we were walking off our meal on nearby Hester Street, she said to me: "If you had been an Asian man or if I had been a white woman, we would have gotten better service." This time, I had no snappy response.

These two vignettes define some of the many potential crossings between Jewish and Asian American experience and identities and trace shifting possibilities of identification and distance, affinity and suspicion. Defined variously and problematically as "people of the book"—or of the restaurant, constructed in strikingly similar ways in terms of gender (the men as hyperphallic or emasculated, the women as exotic seductresses or overpowering mothers) and socioeconomic role (merchants, hagglers, bargainers, gamblers), the stereotypical Jew and the stereotypical Asian have long borne a striking resemblance to each other. And the resemblance goes deeper still. The heterogeneous groups composing the categories Jewish and Asian American are each made up of a diverse set of peoples, of a wide range of national origins and cultural practices, who have come to be ambiguously marked as "ethnic" others within the binary black/white logic of American race thinking. And not entirely without reason. Jewish and Asian Americans have been shaped by a number of similar but not identical events: imperial adventurism, revolutionary ferment, genocide. Each group, as a result, is composed of émigrés, seekers of economic opportunity, refugees, victims of racist anti-immigration laws, or their progeny. And both have been installed, at divergent times, as so-called model minorities, embodiments of the habits affiliated with ethnic success: dedication to education, willingness to delay gratification, entrepreneurship, and so on. Indeed, at the current moment, it would seem that we simply can't tell the story of ethnic success and its perils in America without invoking the example of Jews and Asians.[2]

---

*I am reminded by Joshua Lambert that Chinese restaurants play a particularly consequential role in *Marjorie Morningstar*, serving, as Lambert put it, "as a fairly central marker in the title character's *bildung*." Much ado is made, early in the novel, by the young Marjorie when she first eats with her older, sophisticated friend Marsha at a Chinese restaurant; the waiter has to assure her that there is no pork in the dishes she is ordering. The scene of boundary-crossing foreshadows another when, just before she decides to have sex before marriage, she makes herself eat take-out Chinese pork. See Herman Wouk, *Marjorie Morningstar* (New York: Doubleday, 1955), pp. 46–53 and 341–342.

Looking at the *longue durée* of the historical crossings of Jewish and Asian Americans—or, to be more precise, the shared discursive matrices out of which Jewish and Asian identities were shaped in nineteenth- and twentieth-century America—may serve to give some texture to their encounters and complicate the relatively simple stories told about both. It might serve, at the very least, to remind us of the many things that get left out of the dominant narrative—the "good ethnic" story told about both communities—and begin to suggest new identities for each community fit for the more complex ethnoracial environment of the twenty-first century. Whether or not these possibilities can be realized in theory or in practice is an open question, to which I'll turn at end of this chapter.

The Jewish Oriental/The Oriental Jew

> Mischa, Jascha, Toscha, Sascha—
> Temp'ramental Oriental Gentlemen are we,
>   Fiddle-lee, diddle, dee.
> Shakespeare says "What's in a name?"
>   With him we disagree.
>   Names like Sammy, Max or Moe,
>   Never bring the heavy dough
>   Like Mischa, Jascha, Toscha, Sascha—
>   Fiddle-lee, diddle-lee, dee.
> —Israel and Jacob Gershowitz, aka Ira and George Gershwin

That story might well begin on the Lower East Side of New York, in the late nineteenth century. That area, of course, was the home both to one of the larger Chinese communities in America (albeit a minuscule one, numbering in the thousands)* and, more prominently, to hundreds of thousands of Jewish immigrants from the Russian, Austro-Hungarian, and

---

* According to the 1890 census, there were 6,321 Chinese in New York City, the vast majority of them living in Chinatown. Other estimates of the time put the number substantially higher—13,000, according to Louis Beck in his *New York Chinatown* (1898), with 17,000 in the metropolitan area. (The majority of these were employed in Chinese-owned and run laundries—there were up to 4,000 of these in New York, according to Beck.) The Lower

Ottoman Empires. Hasia Diner properly reminds us that, contrary to the reification of the Lower East Side as synonymous with "eastern European Jewish" (or just plain "Jewish"), that area could be better defined as a "multiethnic" space, a "broad urban borderland, a sprawling zone where pockets of Jewish life functioned alongside areas shaped by other peoples"—mainly Italians, Slavs, and the Irish.[3] Diner does not note—nor is there much note taken in the historical literature—the interactions between Jews and Chinese, but many contemporary accounts suggest that these need to be included in the roster of such interactions as well. Although the Bowery marked the official point of demarcation between Chinatown and "Jewtown" (as Jacob Riis named the latter, in imitation, one presumes, of the former), the interpenetration of peoples that marked the Lower East Side frequently brought the two together. "We were near Chinatown," Michael Gold writes in his remarkably frank, unsentimentalized memoir of the Lower East Side, *Jews Without Money* (1930), but

> at various times Chinese lived in our tenement. Once a group of fifteen chop suey waiters moved into one of the flats. They were a nuisance from the start. They never seemed to sleep. All night long one heard a Chinese phonograph whining and banging horribly. The waiters held long explosive conversations all night. They quarreled, played cards, cooked queer dishes that filled the tenement with sweet, nauseating smells. An opium den, some of the neighbors said. A gambling house, said others. One morning there was a crash. Then the police came and found the house in wreckage. The young Chinese had disappeared. The nude body of a white girl lay on the floor. She had swallowed rat-poison.[4]

Sensational as it is—indeed, it resembles nothing so much as one of the many hystericized newspaper stories of the time or Cecil B. De Mille's film *The Cheat* (1915), which just narrowly deflects itself from precisely this tragic outcome in the final reel—Gold's anecdote points to the extensiveness of the interplay between these two communities.[5] And there are

---

East Side Jewish population at the same time—doubtless also undercounted—was roughly 500,000.

tantalizing hints of other such connections, particularly on the level of vice habitually associated with images of Chinatown and too frequently airbrushed out of accounts of the Lower East Side. For example, the madam of the largest brothel on the Lower East Side—one servicing largely Jews—was named Mamie the Chink, although it's not clear whether she was Chinese American or a Jewish American (perhaps one of the "Mongolian" Jews, or Jews from Russia and eastern Europe whose physical appearance was shaped by the aftermath of the Mongolian invasions). And one of the most famous "hot spots" in Chinatown was Salter's, on Pell Street, run by "Nigger Mike" Salter, a Jew from the Lower East Side—a saloon on the first floor, an opium den upstairs—where a singing waiter named Isadore Bailen was discovered and began his glorious career under the name of Irving Berlin. Other Chinatown clubs provided employment for such figures as Al Jolson and Eddie Cantor at the beginning of their careers.[6]

But there's more resonant imaginative interaction between Jews and Chinese on the Lower East Side than the fairly standard invocation of venues of vice and entertainment. Perhaps the best example is provided by one of the greatest texts to emerge from that matrix, Henry Roth's extraordinary 1930 novel *Call It Sleep*. At one powerful point in the narrative, Roth's protagonist, the sensitive nine-year-old David Schearle, muses over a complicated stew in front of a Chinese laundry on the corner of Tenth Street and Avenue C—his mother's failure to return from the laundry with her customary supply of "Chinese nut" candy, his salty Aunt Bertha's impending marriage to the Russian-born Jewish Sternowitz who promises to open a candy store, whom his mother describes as "yellow" and, later, "sallow" (perhaps a trace of Mongol blood? [177]). These bits of experiential flotsam and jetsam lead him into one of his characteristic stream-of-consciousness swirls in which the recognition of sexuality, and specifically his anxieties vis-à-vis his own masculinity, is conflated with the recognition of ethnic difference:

> He shifted the mind's trinkets, searching for one elusive. Was wondering. Birds. Not birds. Bad words? No. Before that. When? Aunt Bertha, the new man? No. Can't find. Funny. Maybe his name. Mr—Mr What. Yes. Maybe. No—But—Approaching the laundry, he gazed up at the low sign, the dull black letters against the dull red. C-h-Chuh-Ch-ar-ley. Charley, American name. Just like Charley in school. But something else maybe, like Yussie is Joey. Gee, forgot. Yussie! L-i-ng.

Ling. Ling-a-ling. Is Jewish. Can't be. Ling. Don't like. How it hangs in the butcher shop. Mister Ling.[7]

Reminding himself of suitor Sternowitz's name leads David to a meditation that conflates the mysteries of phallic male sexuality—"the new man" who will marry his aunt, which leads, by free-association, to the reflection on "how it hangs in the butcher shop"—with those of ethnic identity. The linkage between the two poses the most essential question of the book—its version of the question that we saw at the center of *Yekl*: how are "new men" in America, like David's brutal working-class but western European father or the upwardly mobile but Russian-born Sternowitz, to negotiate their maleness in America? Are they to be fully active agents in that culture or emasculated by it, limp sausages hanging in the butcher shop? Both the status of their masculinity and that of their backgrounds and class aspirations are mysterious, at least to David; they are matters very much of moment to him, but that he can't begin to resolve. Or at least he can't without invoking the example of the Asian, the Chinese laundryman Charlie Ling. Like David's friend Yussie, Ling has two names, one Americanized, the other foreign; he thus has two identities, one assimilable to Americanness, the other not. But, as opposed to Yussie, or Sternowitz, who "is Jewish," Ling "can't be" because he is Chinese; Ling's Chineseness anchors, by the logic of difference, Sternowitz's Jewishness (Sternowitz may be a "sallow" Russian Jew, but at least he is not a "Chinaman"). And it does his masculinity as well: although Sternowitz's maleness is somewhat questionable, at least in the light of that of David's father Albert, Ling's is unambiguously ambiguous. "Like a lady he looks," says David's friend Izzy, who dares David to go into the shop and ask for the candy. "Wod a big tail he's god on his head" (172).

But matters here are yet more complex. The juxtaposition of Jew and Asian in this passage leads as much to the establishment of common ground between the two as to discrimination between them. Sternowitz, like "Mister Ling"—and unlike odd-job worker Albert—becomes a small business owner, not someone who works for others for a living. Ling, like Sternowitz, provides candy to his clientele; via the association with "Chinese nuts," both are linked to a commodity—a candy—that indexes castration both in its name (David, in fact, takes to thinking of it as "Chinee-nuts" [172]) and in its physical properties: hard on the outside, the candy is gooey, soft, viscous on the inside. Since Sternowitz has earlier been described as "yellow," it would seem the conundrum that's really being faced here is the racial equivocality of this Jew, who, like the Asian man, is constructed in nonmanly ways (he, too, has "Chinee-nuts"), or, to be more precise, the interplay between class aspirations and national origins (*Ost-Juden* versus western European) that reticulate Jewish American identity. Ling's Asianness, in other words, rhymes with rather than confutes Sternowitz's eastern European Jewish alterity, and confuses rather than clarifies young David's musings on Jewish masculinity. Indeed, things soon become impossibly complicated when Sternowitz, for all his seeming sweetness, turns into an emotionally distant and abusive husband—a different version of David's father, but recognizably akin to him. Ultimately, then, Ling's seeming status as a castrated man anticipates neither Albert's nor Sternowitz's version of masculinity but rather David's itself, at least at the end of the novel, when David suffers an accident resounding with castrating implications (he's immobilized, nearly electrocuted when he throws a large rivet onto a live el tracks).

What David Eng would call the racial castration of the Asian man anticipates, tropes, and represents that of the Jewish American man—and, as we shall see, vice versa. But this is not the only discursive crossing between Jewish and Asian Americans at which race, masculinity, and Americanness are at stake, and, of equal importance, this nexus is not just a matter of concern to Jewish American writers. Indeed, what I find most fascinating in the literature and culture of the U.S. at large, in the mainstream as well as in the precincts of "ethnic writing," is how persistently the Jew and the Asian are brought into contact with one another, frequently on the charged discursive terrain of masculinity. This process, initiated in the late nineteenth century and continuing to the present moment, grows out of and delineates both Jewish and Asian difference in terms of the bundle of responses, clichés, stereotypes, and acts of imaginative projection that we have learned to call, after Edward Said, Orientalism.

To begin with the Jewish side of the coin: as Said himself argues, that discourse, with all its assumptions (the opposition between an exotic East and a rational West, the sense of the former as sexualized and feminized and of the latter as austerely masculine), was one of the ways of describing Jews throughout the eighteenth and nineteenth centuries. Since Orientalism originated to limn the exoticism of the *Near* East, extension to the newly arriving eastern European Jews was perhaps inevitable, but we might want to pause over its oddity, both historically and geographically.

In many ways it was part of a process of cultural head-scratching. These odd, jabbering figures scuttling about the Lower East Side must in some way be connected to the peoples of the Near East, gentry observers reasoned. As social reformers like Hutchins Hapgood and Jacob Riis inspected the new ghettos of the Northeast, their accounts foregrounded the exotic, Eastern—and androgynous—quality of the men's flowing daily dress or prayer shawls, and they frequently described Jewish women in terms more reminiscent of Flaubert's *Salammbô* than gritty urban realism. "Men with queer skull-caps, venerable beard, and the outlandish long-skirted kaftan of the Russian Jew, elbow the ugliest and the handsomest women in the land.... The old women are hags; the young, houris," writes Riis in *How the Other Half Lives*.[8] Similarly, Hapgood's ethnography (his informant was none other than Cahan himself) stressed the Westernized qualities of the dress adopted by Russian Jewish immigrants, but was illustrated with brilliant woodcuts by Jacob Epstein that also emphasized the prayer shawl or the exotic garb worn by what Oliver Wendell Holmes called in the poem I discussed in the introduction "Orient-eyed" girls. Indeed, the last of these qualities comes to define Jewish physiognomy tout court, at least in Hapgood's text. "A big and ugly nose," writes Hapgood of Epstein, "is not the enthusiastic artist's idea of what constitutes a downtown Jew. The Jew, to him, is recognized rather by the particular melancholy of the eyes."[9] A philo- rather than an antisemitic stereotype, this quality marks the Jew as a person of feeling, not the rational calculation or rapacity that characterizes the Jew in most American discourse of the era, but this is feeling given, as it is in Holmes's poem, an exoticized, Orientalized cast.

In the 1880s, however, these Orientalist descriptions both augmented and took on a different tinge. When Joseph Seligman was barred from the Saratoga retreat on the grounds of his Jewish "'ostentation' and lack of 'civility,'" it was the "barbaric and coarse" quality of the Jew's "Oriental passion for brilliancy of costume" that the otherwise sympathetic *Nation* cited in partial extenuation of this exclusion.[10] Not just manners, but actual qualities of mind, temperament, and character that depicted the Jew as essentially Other to the Anglo-Saxon temper were ascribed to that figure's Oriental cast of being. In "The Russian Jew in America," for example, Abraham Cahan quotes a contemporary minister describing the Jew's "essential oriental quality of mind and character ... reflected in a deep intensity of feeling, high imagination, and quickly varying emotions."[11]

6.1a, b   Some of Jacob Epstein's East Side Jews from Hutchins Hapgood, *The Spirit of the Ghetto* (1902).

And, significantly, this characterization rapidly entered the Jewish self-imagination as well as the gentile one. It may not be too surprising to find it in non-Ashkenazic writers like Emma Lazarus, who spoke of "the fire of our Oriental blood" or "the deeper lights and shadows of [Jews'] Oriental temperament" in her tract, *Epistle to the Hebrews*.[12] But this linkage also shaped such texts as the American-born Russian Jewish Gershwins' song that forms the epigraph to this section (their list includes, I might add parenthetically, the sons of klezmer fiddlers who became famous classical musicians, namely, Jascha Heifitz and Mischa Elman): note how the *Oriental*ness of the Jew is paired with the adjective *temperamental* or, in another transcription of the song, *sentimental*. (And note as well how their Oriental exoticism is the ground of their popularity, in comparison with Americans like "Sammy, Max and Moe.") Such a conflation is even more evident in the work of Ashkenazic writer Anzia Yezierska, whose *Salomé of the Tenements* uses exactly this language to limn the "overcharged ... emotionalism" of its heroine ("Sonya and [her gentile husband Manning] ... were the oriental and the Anglo-Saxon trying to find a common language. The over-emotional ghetto struggling for its breath in the thin air of puritan restraint").[13] And Yezierska goes one step further in building the chain of racial association; she identifies the racialized quality of Jewish affect, or "over-emotionality," as one that tends to melancholia, the "Weltschmerz" that is part of "our race" (*Salomé*, 37). So too Cahan, in his crucial novel

The Rise of David Levinsky, identifies the racial essence of the Jew in terms of "Oriental" emotionality that tends toward the melancholic: "There is a streak of sadness in the blood of my race," muses Levinsky at the very opening of the novel, while recounting without emotion his memories of his father's burial. "Very likely it is of Oriental origin. If it is, it has been amply nourished by many centuries of persecution."[14] Indeed, Levinsky's whole problem in the book—his odd self-alienation, the distance from which he narrates his own tale of social rise and moral decay—can be said to stem from this moment, from the necessity, in becoming an American, to detach himself from a melancholia that is deemed racial—"Oriental"—in nature and expression.

The point to be made here is that the familiar fin de siècle conflation of the Jew with the hysteric—with the person ruled by spasms of emotion—has throughout the period not only an explicitly racial component, but an origin with a specific (or, rather, vague) geographic cast: the hysterical Jew, we might say, is also the Oriental Jew, and vice versa. Indeed, this was more or less what popular commentators of the time said: "[Jews] have a nervous make-up that is not easily susceptible to the formation of habits of body or thought, and it would often appear that their mental processes were not of the western order, but, after all, the Hebrew is only a more or less modified Oriental still."[15] It's no wonder, then, that when in 1897 the conservative *New York Sun* wished to find a breezy way to describe the disastrous trip of a mayoral candidate, Benjamin Low, to the Lower East Side, its headline read: "Low Invades the Orient," and the story goes on to stress the absolute gulf of communication between the gentile reformer and the frenzied inhabitants of the ghetto.[16] I cite that allusion to bring attention not to the exceptional but rather to the commonplace quality of the ascription. For much of white New York, and for that matter white America, the Lower East Side—and hence by extension the Jews who lived there—was quite literally understood as the East in all of its connotative power: a place of mystery peopled by mysterious, hyperemotional, jabbering, sexually ambiguous others.

Indeed, it is this last quality—that of sexual non-normativity—that most interestingly lingers in WASP discourses about Jews. Thus, for example, the house organ of gentry progressive reform, *McClure's Magazine*, published in 1909 an article by George Kibbe Turner limning the so-called white slavery trade, a business run, in Turner's account, by malign Jews. Not only does the very notion of the Jew-run white slave industry correspond with classic Orientalist preconceptions, but the very figure was explicitly Orientalized by Turner's bizarre naming of the Jewish pimp as "the *kaftan*"—metonymically associating that figure with the "outlandish long-skirted garb" of the traditional Jew that Riis highlighted in his description of the East Side Jew. And more: the *kaftan* (the pimp, not the garment) is for Turner a conduit between the ghettos of the West and the brothels of the East—and one whose arrival in New York bodes ill for America itself:

> The ancient and more familiar white slave trade was the outright sale of women from Eastern Europe in the Orient through the big general depot of Constantinople.... Out of this racial slum of Europe has come for unnumbered years the Jewish *kaftan*, leading the miserable Jewish girl from European civilization into Asia.... To this day he comes out of Galicia and Russian Poland, with his white face and his long beard—the badge of his ancient faith—and wanders across the face of the earth. Occasionally, [now] members of the fraternity come into New York: men of seventy, sometimes, with gray beards, following their trade through life to the very end.[17]

A similar sense of the malevolent presence of the Oriental/Asiatic Jew on the American scene can be found in *The International Jew*, a compendium of antisemitic aspersions culled from Henry Ford's *Dearborn Independent* to which I have had occasion to refer throughout this volume. Here, the putative Orientalism of the Jew is used to imply a corruption of high culture and mass culture alike. In its chapter on jazz, for example, *The International Jew* fulminates: "The insidiousness of [this] Jewish menace to our artistic integrity is due partly to the speciousness, the superficial charm and oriental persuasiveness of Hebrew art," and Henry Ford himself deploys this same language in his autobiography to indict the Jewified culture industries:

> There had been observed in this country certain streams of influence which were causing a marked deterioration in our literature, amusements, and social conduct; business was departing from its old-time substantial soundness; a general letting-down of standards was felt everywhere. It was not the robust coarseness of the white man, the rude indelicacy, say, of Shakespeare's characters, but a nasty Orientalism

which has insidiously affected every channel of expression.... The fact that these influences are all traceable to one racial source is a fact to be reckoned with.[18]

To be sure, Ford represented the extreme wing of anti-Jewish opinion, but the prevalence of the associations he and *The International Jew* play off can be gauged by the omnipresence of the term for the Jewish studio heads of the 1930s, the Hollywood *moguls*—a term derived first from the Indian moguls, or rulers, of course, but a term itself derived from the Persian for "Mongol," as the Indian moguls originally were. Even as far as the press and public were concerned, in other words, the Oriental barbarians were literally within the U.S. cultural gates—a sense that was heightened by the gaudy Oriental-style movie palaces they built (Near Eastern neo-Moorish or East Asian exotic, like Grauman's Chinese) and by the Orientalist fictions their studios purveyed.[19]

Throughout these discursive arenas, then, the Orientalization of the Jew thus tends to wander both geographically and ontologically, ending up hypostasizing a putatively "Oriental Jew"* (a better term might be "Orientalized Jew") who may have emigrated from Russia, Romania, or Syria to the Lower East Side, but who, whatever his or her origins, comes by the 1920s and early 1930s to be banefully lodged at the center of social, intellectual, and cultural life. Prostitution, jazz, the movies: all these betokened what could only be called the Orientalization of American society, a metastasizing growth within the body politic created by the malignant presence of eastern Jewry. Meanwhile, indeed at the same moment, the Orientalizing process began to churn with respect to East Asians. As critics like John Tchen, Henry Wu, and Robert Lee have reminded us, with the "opening" of Japan in 1854 and the Boxer Rebellion of 1900, Japanese

---

*A terminological note. The term *Oriental Jew* has come to denote those Jews who come from the lands of the Near East. Different from, if sometimes conflated with, Sephardic Jews—the Jews of the Spanish Diaspora, post-1492—these are also known as Mizrachi Jews—the term *mizrach* being the Hebrew for Orient or East. Mizrachi Jews have by and large fled their homelands post-1948 and made their way to Israel, where they have, in recent decades, risen to challenge the Ashkenazic elite (the former minister for defense, Shaul Mofaz, is an Iranian-born Jew; the current minister of defense, Amir Peretz, was born in Morocco). For more on the Mizrachim and their denigration by the Ashkenzim in the early development of Israel, see Ammiel Alcalay, *After Jews and Arabs: Remaking Levantine Culture* (Minnneapolis: University of Minnesota Press, 1992).

and Chinese otherness was very much on the mind of the same gentry Western critics, who redirected the language of Orientalism to limn this different form of Asiatic (or, as ethnologists also called it "Mongolian," and sometimes, with inevitable resulting confusions, "Mongoloid") difference. These expressions took on many, and contradictory, guises. On the one hand, the debased and racist attacks on Chinese that led to the Chinese Exclusion Act of 1882—the first and in many ways the model attempt to limit immigration to the U.S.—were heightened by further, deep prejudice against Asians who were associated with rats, disease, opium dens, sexuality, etc. Indeed, many of the same fears we have seen processed with respect to the Jew—especially that figure's unassimilability, due to his systemic, constitutionally nonrational, "Oriental" makeup—were present with respect to the Chinese, especially in the discourse of scientific racism. As one historian has summarized early twentieth-century racial ideology, "'Oriental blood' determined the 'Oriental thoughts' and 'Oriental habits' which precluded any possibility that the Chinese could be 'Americanized.'"[20]

But, intriguingly, underneath the discourse of an inherent unassimilability due to "'Oriental blood' ... 'thoughts' ... and ... 'habits'" lay moments when precisely these qualities were envisioned in ways that distinguished that figure from other Others like African Americans, Mexicans, and, most crucially, the Irish, and that brought Asians into closer contact with that of the stereotypical Jew.[21] This was particularly true in responses to the first major group of Asian immigrants to the United States, a group that formed the template for reactions to subsequent Asian immigrants—the Chinese. "The Chinese are born traders," wrote the *Atlantic Monthly* in 1900. "No Jew can smell out [sic] with keener instinct an opportunity where money can be made to grow than can a Chinaman."[22] To be sure, this metonymy may be nothing more than a commonplace—Jew and trader (with more than a hint of racialized condescension) being virtually synonymous from the sixteenth century forward. But the association shapes genteel Americans' encounter with both at the crucial Progressive-era moment of confrontation with urban poverty. In the most influential text of that period, *How the Other Half Lives*, Jacob Riis implicitly works out the analogy. Echoing the most common of nineteenth-century antisemitic animadversions, he writes of Jews that "money is their God. Life itself is of little value compared with even the leanest bank account. In no other spot does life wear so intensely bald and

6.2. "The Difference Between Them." *Puck*, 1881. Courtesy of the University of Michigan Library.

materialistic an aspect as in Ludlow Street" (71–72). A chapter earlier, we have learned that what is figuratively the case with the Jew is quite literally true of the Chinese: "Between the tabernacles of Jewry and the shrines of the Bend," Riis's chapter begins, "Joss has cheekily planted his pagan worship of idols, chief among which are the celestial worshipper's own gain and lusts. Whatever may be said about the Chinaman being a thousand years behind the age on his own shores, here he is distinctly abreast of it in his successful scheming to 'make it pay.' It is doubtful if there is anything he does not turn to a paying account, from his religion down, or up, as one prefers" (62). Indeed, so materialistic are the Chinese that they literally worship money. "There was [in the temple] another inscription overhead that needed no interpreter. In familiar English letters, copied bodily from the trade dollar, was the sentiment: 'In God we trust'" (68). No wonder that, when Riis actually quotes a Chinaman, that figure speaks in a language that sounds as much Yiddish as Chinese: "The stranger who enters [a Chinese store] through the crooked approach is received with sudden silence, a sullen stare, and an angry 'Vat you vant?' that breathes annoyance and distrust" (64).

This conflation of Jew and Chinese as economic players has a long history. Jay Geller reminds us that Herder explicitly compared the Chinese to the Jews not only on such matters as "a prideful refusal to intermix and interbreed with other nations" but also on the grounds of their "cunning industriousness and their talent for imitating anything their greed finds useful."[23] There's good reason for his conflation. Like Jews, Chinese merchants were traditionally active throughout East and South Asia and faced—again like Jews—resentment, discrimination, and even the occasional pogrom as a result. And, perhaps not coincidentally, a similar mixture of industriousness and avarice runs throughout the representations of both groups, even as it is, in both cases, accompanied by language that stresses a debasing sense of their dirt, filth, sexual deviancy. Thus (to stick with the Chinese example) the satirical magazine *Puck* may have visually associated the Chinaman with the rat, as John Tchen has convincingly argued.[24] But the journal also persistently associated the Chinese with economic diligence, not always in uncomplimentary ways. A November 1881 cover called *The Difference Between Them,* for example, defines the Chinese against the Irish by parading the latter as potential convicts or worse (their signs define them as future aldermen, coroners, congressmen) and the former as hardworking exotics ("wantee washee-washee for Melican Man") who are working hard at menial tasks in order to return to China rich ("Wantee Plentee Monee to Takee Homee" is the inscription on the box on which one Chinese sits). The main point of the cartoon is to contrast the Chinese with the Irish—the former will only plague us temporarily, the latter are here forever—but along the way, it casts the Chinese in the same role in which the culture had traditionally placed the Jew: as hardworking if money-mad, entrepreneurial, if maniacally obsessed with the economic at the expense of other human relations.

As early as the 1870s, then, we can see emerging a discursive terrain that Jews and Chinese—and thence, ultimately, the Asian American—shared, however contingently. And it is one, moreover, where their economic appetencies and entrepreneurship bring them dangerously close to being located at emerging and contested centers of cultural value. But this pattern

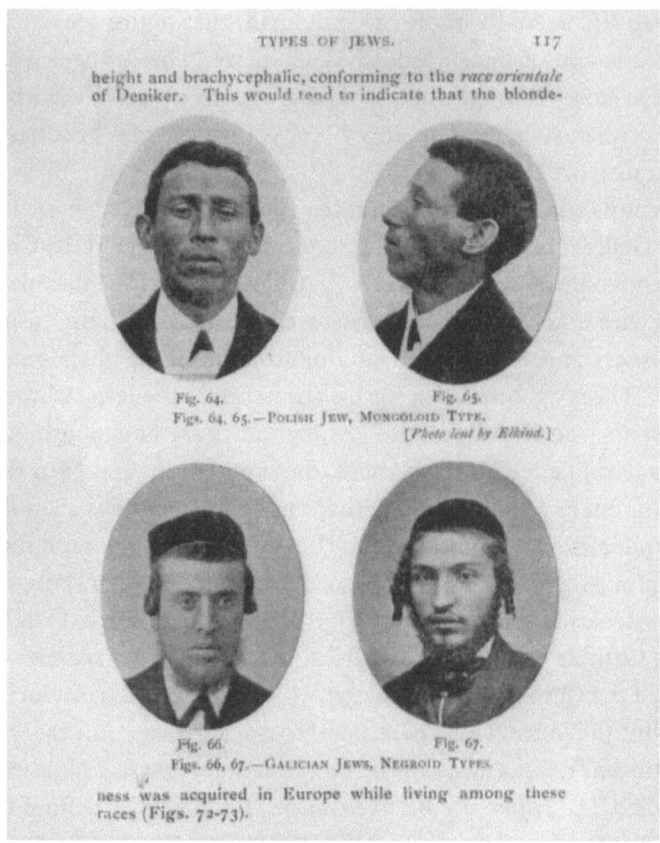

6.3. Jewish Others: Polish Jew, the Mongoloid Type; Galician Jew, the Negroid Type. Maurice Fishberg, *The Jews: A Study in Race and Environment* (1911).

of response is accompanied by another striking similarity: the shared perception of Asian and Jews, especially Asian and Jewish men, as sexually equivocal in some complicated and ill-defined way: not only perverse, but also perverting; not only feminized but hystericized. The exact relation between these two is shifting and mysterious; in addition to there being a heritage of the discourse of Orientalism that shaped perceptions of both groups, it seems, their similar construction might have something to do with a sense that the *ways* that Jews and Asians made money (from commerce, speculation, and the like) were illegitimate. These were perceived as being less than fully manly, at least in the early years of the twentieth century when Rooseveltian rugged masculinism and working-class consciousness both privileged the vital, active male body as a locus of value—as opposed to that of the shopkeeper, like Cahan's Bernstein or the sullen storekeeper Riis confronts in Chinatown. But, whatever the source, their connection with the economic ethos makes both Jews and Asians, I think, distinct, in similarly distinctive ways, from the other racial minorities of the time: from African Americans, obviously, but also Irish, Italians, Slovaks, Mexicans, etc., each of which was given a strikingly different stereotypical definition. And it also serves, as we shall see, as the ground of the twentieth century's construction of both Jews and Asians as "model minorities," as ethnic people whose entrepreneurial ethos, ability to delay gratification, and devotion to savings, education, and self-improvement lead to their success in an America where mental, not manual, labor is the way to wealth. Indeed, not only does the construction maintain itself, so does the contrast with other racial and ethnic groups. The Irishman represented by *Puck* as a plague on the body politic will become, a century later, the undeserving African American and Latino in need of welfare assistance and affirmative action consideration in college admissions even as, mutatis mutandis, the Asian—like the Jew before him—will become defined by work, family, and economic self-sufficiency. Even in—or precisely in—images of exclusion, in other words, we can see the grounds for moral and economic inclusion in normative Americanness, model minority style.

Discursive Bleeding, the Jewish Asian Supervillain, and the Making of the Model Minority Mythos

But before turning to that labile construction I need to be clear about what I'm arguing here. I'm not suggesting that the culture at large proposed an outright identity between Jews and East Asians—although, before moving forward, we should pause to note that there were numerous and not insignificant attempts to do so. As Robert Singerman has helpfully noted, commonplace identifications of Jews *as* Asians could be found throughout the 1920s, made by gentiles and Jews alike.[25] In his seminal 1911 *The Jews: A Study of Race and Environment,* Maurice Fishberg relied on German ethnological work to identify a substantial proportion of Jews (23 percent, to be precise) as belonging to "the Mongolian type," a type he found to be prevalent on the Lower East Side as well.[26] And Fishberg was also a proponent of the thesis—one as old as Renan and one Joyce was to echo in *Ulysses* (Joyce possessed a copy of *The Jews* in his library and seems to have consulted it in his representation of Leopold Bloom)[27]—that many Ashkenazic Jews were descendents of the people of the land of Khazaria, a kingdom centered on the area between the Black and the Caspian Seas whose rulers had converted to Judaism in the ninth century and whose elite remained Jews until they were conquered by the Rus people in the eleventh century, after which they mysteriously disappeared from the historical record. While no one knows what they looked like, some claimed that the Khazars were predominantly Mongol in appearance and hence identity.* This thesis entered political discourse in the 1920s via anti-immigration activists like Madison Grant (author of *The Passing of the Great Race*) and Lathrop Stoddard (author of *The Rising Tide of Color*). The latter, for example, claimed that the "dwarfish stature, flat faces, high cheekbones and other Mongoloid traits" of the eastern European Jew could be traced to their Khazar/Mongol origins and hence implicitly distinguished that figure from the less debased western European Jew. And it should be added that the myth of the Khazar/Mongol origins of the Jew has remained a part of the politics of Jewish identity. Arthur Koestler pursued the Khazar thesis with his 1965 book *The Thirteenth Tribe*, a work intended explicitly to disarticulate the Ashkenazim of Europe from the Semites of the Near East and so critique the racialist (as opposed to culturalist) claims of Zionism. And the anti-Zionist implications of the Khazar thesis continue to keep it alive and well; it remains a staple of antisemitic and anti-Zionist websites and broadsheets to this day.[28]

But as intriguing as these identifications might have been, they were not predominant in the discourse of the era, which was obsessed with rendering both Jewish and Asian difference in the familiar American idiom of black and white. More important for our purposes is a certain habit of mind in which these two immigrant groups were glossed, interpreted,

---

* The Khazars are currently classified as a Turkic-Mongol people, which doesn't settle the matter, since that's simply a classification for the many nomadic peoples of Central Asia. The Mongols conquered most of these in the eleventh century—i.e., after the fall of the Khazars to the Rus people; and they assimilated as much to—as they learned from—the Turkic peoples they ruled as the other way around; so the classification is not only a guess but also an anachronism.

compared, and contrasted with each other—sometimes in ways that linked the two, at others that set them in contrast with each other, as they were both compared to a dominant WASP cultural ideal. This tendency is all over the discourses of the era, in high culture and low, in the political arena and the public sphere alike. In 1881, for example, the satirical publication I mentioned earlier, *Puck*, was taken to task by the conservative New York *Jewish Messenger* for illustrating a sympathetic piece on Jews with an antisemitic caricature, and *Puck* responded to the critique of its palpable ambivalence with a comparison intended to set the record straight:

> Our Hebrew friends must not be so sensitive; and like sensible people as they are, must take a joke as their neighbors take one. If they do not wish to be made fun of, they should not intensify the traditional peculiarities that so often make them subject to ridicule. They are clannish, and cling to their antiquated puerile Oriental customs and manners as a Chinaman clings to his pigtail. They should become Americans. Let them mix, marry and associate—we will not say with Christians, as there are few real Christians nowadays—with non-Jews or Gentiles and get rid of the silly idea that their race and religion are immeasurably above all others. If this were done, there would, in time, be no more reason to caricature the peculiarities of a Jew, as a Jew, than of a Quaker, a Swedenborgian, a Shaker, or an Episcopalian.[29]

The obvious point of this passage is to suggest that Jews are unlike the Chinese with whom they might best be compared on the grounds of their potential assimilability. But, in so doing, it reinforces the similarity between the two, one that is grounded in their common (putative) sense of racial superiority as well as the sense (more or less a constant from Herder and Hegel forward) that both have been superannuated by Christian culture—a culture that, as *Puck*'s nervousness on the subject suggests, is itself in danger of being rendered irrelevant by an increasing secularism. In these cases, and more, the Jew and the Asian are implicitly weighed against each other even as—or especially because—they or the qualities associated with them (mercantilism, secularism, or at least tolerance of multiple religious traditions, exoticism, cultural heterogeneity) are seen as moving closer to the center of a culture normatively white and Protestant in its orientation.

A similar cultural dynamic can be seen throughout the multiple juxtapositions between Jews and East Asians and South Asians that, as I have suggested, bubbled throughout U.S. culture throughout the late nineteenth and early twentieth centuries. An excellent example is provided by a fascinating 1911 story by Willa Cather, *Scandal*. There, a villainous Jew, Sigmund Stein, whose cheeks denote a "Mongolian" cast of appearance, plots to publicize a relationship with the most renowned soprano of his time, Kitty Ayrshire, a woman at once intensely aware and intensely weary of the split between her public and private selves. His first gambit is to hire an immigrant worker who resembles Kitty to impersonate her and accompany him to concerts, openings, extravagant dinners. When this fails to make the gossip pages, he invites Kitty to a dinner party and maneuvers her to make sure that she appears in the press alongside himself and his parvenu wife. His non-American exoticism is, however, oddly isomporphic to that of Kitty herself, who lives in a hotel suite full of Japanese and Chinese curios and appears at one moment posed as one such herself—indeed, as a veritable symphony of Orientalist appurtanences and images as rendered by a Whistler or an Alma-Tadema:

> Her costume was folds upon folds of diaphanous white over equally diaphanous rose, with a line of white fur about her neck. Her beautiful arms were bare. Her tiny Chinese slippers were embroidered so richly that they resembled the painted porcelain of old vases. She looked like a sultan's youngest, newest bride; a beautiful little toy-woman, sitting at one end of the long room which composed about her—which, in the soft light, seemed happily arranged for her. There were flowers everywhere: rosetrees; camellia bushes, red and white; the first forced hyacinths of the season; a feathery mimosa tree, tall enough to stand under.[30]

Kitty's multiple Orientalism—at once East Asian and Near Eastern—is not only contrasted with that of the upwardly mobile Jew; it is also at one with it. Early in the story, Stein has created a double of an artist who not only creates doubles of herself on stage or in her room (where she is clearly dressing for effect) but also encounters, in the paragraph just after the one I quoted, a representation of herself in a painting; later in the story, we learn that she does nothing to halt the taking of her picture at Stein's gala (on the principle, apparently, that no publicity is bad publicity): in both cases her faux Orientalism is, appropriately enough, a version of his perniciously real kind. This is not just a story about a parvenu Jew who is able to use the organs of the publicity and the press to worm his way into the sphere of high culture, but about the complicity of that sphere with the Jew who seeks admission to its realm. Cather's ultimate aim in emphasizing these doublings and poses and self-representations is to suggest just how fully what Henry Ford would call the Orientalization of American society has affected its culture industries—and her vehicle for doing so is the nexus between the Mongolian-appearing Jew and the Asian-appearing WASP.*

What marks the discursive relation between Jews and Asians in all these cases, is a phenomenon I would call discursive bleeding—the seeping, usually at a level somewhere below full consciousness, of associations from one racial and ethnic group to another, in this case from the long-established patterns of response to Jews to newer ones being crafted to explain and understand Asian difference, the result being that the terms used for both began to blur into each other. This phenomenon was particularly marked in terms of the negative ascriptions that Jews and Asians faced in the increasingly troubled period of the later years of the nineteenth and earlier years of the twentieth centuries. Consider the ways in which the "white slavery" hysteria of the 1910s and 1920s oscillated between identifying as its villains Jewish Orientals and Asian Orientals. Or consider the ways that the same actors frequently played both Jewish and Asian characters—the most notorious of which being Warner Oland, a high-cheeked Swede who claimed that he "owed [his] Chinese appearance to the Mongol invasion."[31] Oland played the notorious Fu Manchu, a passing-for-white Chinese white-slaver in a film called *Old San Francisco and* Cantor Rabinowitz, father of Al Jolson's jazz singer—all in the same

---

* The cultural otherness of the Orientalized Jew clearly interests Cather in a number of contexts. Here's her description of Israel Zangwill, whom she encountered as a journalist during his American lecture tour of 1911: "Handsome he certainly is not, but neither is he a freak. I was rather pleasurably surprised, indeed, when this slender, pale gentleman stepped before us. His physiognomy is typically Semitic; the bold nose, the pale, olive skin, the full lips, the heavy dark eyes, the shaggy black hair, suggested not only the Jew, but Oriental Jew." Zangwill's Orientalism is of course of the familiar Near Eastern variety rather than the East Asian sort with which Stein is contaminated; but the mixture of fascination and repulsion on Cather's part seems similar. See Loretta Wasserman, "Cather's Semitism," *Cather Studies* 2 (2003): 6–9.

year, 1927. Or consider the ways that Oland's most famous role, as Charlie Chan, was succeeded by a cycle devoted to another Asian detective—Mr. Moto—played by German Jewish refugee Peter Lorre, indeed quite literally; when in 1938 Oland died during the making of *Charlie Chan at the Ringside*, that film was quickly rewritten for Lorre as *Mr. Moto's Gamble*, with all the extant footage easily incorporated for a faux Japanese, rather than a faux Chinese, detective. Or—on a much more consequential note—consider the fact that when the notorious *Protocols of the Elders of Zion* was published in England in 1920 and widely circulated in America, it was given a title that alluded directly to the public hysteria about rising Asian power and immigration: *The Jewish Peril*. Indeed, that phrase—"the Jewish Peril"—headlined a notorious June 19, 1921, *Christian Science Monitor* editorial that repackaged the calumnies of the *Protocols* for a mainstream, respectable, middlebrow American public.

Or consider a third case. In 1895, a British magazine illustrator of French ancestry named George Du Maurier published *Trilby*, which featured Svengali, a supremely talented musician of eastern European Jewish descent, portrayed with high cheekbones, hypnotic eyes, and magical musical powers, all of which he uses to seduce an innocent *grisette* and achieve world prominence. A triumph in England, the novel found its most receptive response in America, where it was serialized in *Harper's Monthly*, shot up to number one on the *Critic*'s bestseller list, spawned numerous theatrical companies, and was ultimately remade into a number of films. In 1921 an English journalist of Irish ancestry, Arthur Henry Ward, took the name of Sax Rohmer and published *The Rise of Fu Manchu*, featuring an Asiatic villain with high cheekbones, hypnotic eyes, and "one giant intellect," all of which he uses in the attempt to achieve world domination.[32] A minor success in England, this and subsequent works in the series were runaway successes in America, where they were serialized in *Collier's Magazine*, released in numerous cheap book formats, and made into a number of highly popular films. To be sure, these two evil figures are divergent in many respects—the former dies, the latter seems to live forever; the former is as "bad as they make 'em," the latter even worse; the former is compared to an insidious spider, the latter to a cat or a tiger, and so on. But they have in common their connection with mysterious wellsprings of intellectual and cultural attainment—Svengali is the greatest musician of his time, Fu Manchu an omniscient genius. Both, moreover, are contrasted with icons of male normativity: their frames and features define them as other to the manly masculinity of their English antagonists.

The Svengali/Fu Manchu doublet vividly exemplifies the process of bleeding between Jewish and Asian stereotypes in the early years of the twentieth century. But it also suggests how labile and contradictory are the results, how multivariate are the associations created in the contact zone between Jewish and Asian American alterities. While both are obviously villainous in some crucial way, both Svengali and Fu Manchu are connected to qualities that the culture is to find valuable—transcendent cultural abilities, intellectual acuity. And here too in ironical and unexpected ways, in the very depths of their villainy we can see the grounds of the common constructions that will enwrap both Jews and Asians a century later. For precisely the correspondence of the combination of mental dexterity and otherness to WASP ideals of physical assertiveness that Svengali and Fu Manchu exemplify becomes, in ironic ways, a crucial building block of the most significant intersection of the Jew and the Asian, the model minority stereotype.

The process, of course, began with the Jew, particularly those urbanized Jews whose putative combination of intellectualism and physical deficiencies were the subject of much early twentieth-century worrying. Indeed, as Sander Gilman has reminded us, the two had long been linked; in the discourses of the late nineteenth and twentieth centuries—culminating in, or at least continuing through, the films of Woody Allen and the novels of Philip Roth—a putative male "Jewish intelligence compensates for [alleged] Jewish physical inferiority."[33] As we've seen, in the 1950s this model flipped around, as the demasculinized—or at least *schlumpy*—Jewish intellectual became something of a cultural icon not despite but because of his difference from robust WASP norms of masculinity. Albert Einstein may have been something of a sexual scoundrel in real life, but in the media he was portrayed as a baggy-sweatered neuter; as we have seen, Arthur Miller may have married America's most desirable woman, Marilyn Monroe, but it was his artistic genius, not his physical prowess, that won her—and from a baseball player yet. Similarly, the qualities for which Jews were formerly critiqued (economic stringency, clannishness, etc.) got revalued in the work of (largely Jewish) social scientists in the 1950s and 1960s to become criteria of value, indeed more: as models for the process of ethnic assimilation itself. Thus, as a number of critics have powerfully argued, Milton Gordon's classic *Assimilation in American Life* (1961) took the experience of Jewish Americans as paradigmatic of the experience of immigrants tout court. And this process applied to the inner as well as the outer: in his analysis of the immigrant *mentalité* Gordon reified the psychology of the first- and second-generation immigrant (as Barbara Kirschenblatt-Gimblett puts it) as "a psychosocial portrait of 'the Jew,' the prototypical marginal man and model for the sociological concept" itself. Indeed, as Krishenblatt-Gimblett implies, in Gordon's hands the immigrant's psychology is limned in terms of that of the Jewish man—a Woody Allen (or Milton Gordon?) *avant la lettre*: "Frustrated and not fully accepted... ambivalent... he develops according to the classic conception, personality traits of insecurity, moodiness, hypersensitivity, excessive self-consciousness, and nervous strain [but also] greater insight, self-understanding, and creativity."[34] According to Jewish intellectuals like Gordon, in other words, the quintessential immigrant was a Jewish intellectual like Gordon—or at least ought to have been.

Both the model minority myth and its implications in terms of masculinity have been central as well to the development of Asian American identity. Consider, for example, the stereotype, essential to the "model minority" mythos, of the "smart Asian." Like that of the hyperintelligent Jewish man, the stereotype has fin de siècle origins, as one strain in the many contradictory impulses defining the Yellow Peril. Not only is Fu Manchu a supergenius—and one with a Western college education—so were many of the supervillains of the fictions that preceded him: Kiang-Ho, the villain of the dime novel *Tom Edison Jr.'s Electric Sea Spider, or, The Wizard of the Submarine World* (1892) sports a degree from Harvard; Quong Lung, of Dr. C. W. Doyle's *The Shadow of Quong Lung* (1900), graduated Yale.[35] The threat posed by the Asian supergenius is that of superior intelligence married to Western knowledge, a combination that proves well-nigh fatal in the ability of the supervillain to use Western technology against its source. Whatever the vicissitudes of the subsequent years, this image of superior Eastern intelligence persists in popular culture, in venues like the Charlie Chan and Mr. Moto series I adverted to above: the salient point here is that both Chan and Moto possess intellectual powers that confound the Western police forces with whom they are working. Although this stereotype may have gone underground in mid-century, it reemerges with a vengeance in the 1960s and early 1970s with the stereotype of the "smart Asian": the sense that Asians are superior at mathematics, science, abstract thinking, and (like Svengali) classical music, although, as many nineteenth-century antisemites claimed of the Jew, incapable of original thought.[36] That construct, so crucial to the life of the model minority myth in the 1960s and 1970s, reaches consummation—and achieves direct communication with the stereotype of the Smart Jew—in that grab bag of pseudo-scientific misinformation, Charles Murray's *The Bell Curve*, in which "Ashkenazic Jews" and peoples of Asian descent are both assigned superior mental abilities as opposed to members of other, "dimmer" races.[37]

The myth of superior Asian intellectual endowment has another point of contact with constructions of the Jew: accompanying it is an understanding of the Asian man as being less than manly. Asian American critics of the 1960s—Frank Chin in particular—reminded us that a demasculinized version of Asian American manhood accompanied what we might term the model minority model. As Chin has famously (and hilariously) written,

> Devil and angel, the Chinese [man] is a sexual joke glorifying white power. Dr. Fu [Manchu], a man wearing a long dress, batting his eyelashes, surrounded by muscular black servants in loin cloths, and with his bad habit of caressingly touching white men on the leg, wrist, and face with his long fingernails, is not so much a threat as he is a frivolous offense to white manhood.[38]

Asian American criticism has continued to mine this vein. Robert Lee and David Eng analyze model minority discourse in terms of the feminization (or outright castration) of the Asian American man. Tellingly, as they have done so, they frequently use language quite familiar from discourses on either Jewish masculinity or its application to immigrant identity itself. To cite but one brief example: when Eng addresses the question of the model minority, he stresses the psychic as well as the sexual alienation of that figure, which he calls, alternatively, "male hysteria" and "internal exile"—terms that resonate, to put it mildly, in the analysis of the psychology of the Jewish man. (Eng cites Sander Gilman's and Daniel Boyarin's analyses of Freud's Jewishness in the notes, but not the text, of his book.) And, when he addresses the "psychological toll" exacted by the "resignified dominant perceptions of Asian Americans from yellow peril to assimilated mascot in the span of a few short decades," Eng quotes an Asian American social scientist, Bob Suzuki, whose analysis bears an uncanny resemblance to none other than Milton Gordon's. The "over-anxious attempts by Asian Americans to gain acceptance," Suzuki writes, "have stripped them of their dignity and have caused them to suffer from severe psychological disorders characterized by lack of confidence, low self-esteem, excessive conformity and alienation."[39] The alienated, melancholic Jewish intellectual that Gordon pressed into service to model the immigrant man lingers on as the double of—if not prototype for—Eng's (stereotypical) hysterical, self-alienated, castrated Asian American male.

JEWS AND ASIANS BEYOND THE MODEL-MINORITY MISHEGAS

There exists, in short, the grounds of a fascinating dialogue between Jewish and Asian American studies. One might pursue, in the cases of each, the results of the common ground of Orientalization—and especially its concomitants on the field of gender construction (what, after all, is Woody Allen but a "frivolous offense to white manhood"?). Or one might interrogate further Jews' and Asians' similarly ambiguous status as off-white peoples, as a "middleman minority in a racially stratified society" (to quote Lee on the Chinese Americans) whose collage of alleged attributes—ranging from verminous and swarming to industrious and intelligent—tended to bleed into one another.[40] Or one might assay in greater detail the ways that each morphed from supervillain to model minority. But, sadly, neither Jewish nor Asian American critics have entered into this dialogue. Indeed, Jewish neoconservatives were prime movers not only in crafting the narrative of Jews as model immigrants but of Asians as "the New Jews."[41] And Asian American critics have responded, not inappropriately, by conspicuously ignoring the Jewish example. One can read the most important work in Asian American studies of the last generation, Lisa Lowe's *Immigrant Acts* (1995), without encountering the once inevitable conjunction between the terms *Jewish* and *immigrant* at all. Similarly, Gary Okihiro's very fine *Common Ground: Reimagining American History* (2001), an attempt to rethink the basic structures of American experience by taking Asian American difference into account, positions Asians as an in-between people, fitting into none of the available dichotomies that govern U.S. historical experience: black and white, male and female, gay and straight, and so on. Although I'm sure Okihiro wouldn't be hostile to it, there's little mention in his book of a similar analysis of Jews as men/women, occupying a liminal position between black and white ethnics, sexually androgynous creatures, and so on, that proliferated throughout the 1910s and 1920s (and well before) and that's served as the basis of extraordinary analysis from Sander Gilman, Daniel Boyarin et al.

I've suggested some of the reasons for this lacuna above, on the level of discourse and ideology. There are material reasons as well. The post-1965 wave of immigration spurred by revision of the immigration laws and accelerated by the aftermath of the Vietnam War and the rise of globalization has brought millions of people from Asia (over seven million between 1971 and 2002, according to the most recently compiled statistics—more than a third of all the immigration in that period). And, by and large, this immigration has included not only trained professionals but new groups of economic and political refugees—and peoples increasingly drawn from a wider variety of national backgrounds: Laos, Vietnam, Pakistan, the Philippines. With this immigration has come new patterns of response. The class reticulation of Asian Americans—particularly earlier arrivals, strikingly successful, and many, particularly later arrivals, increasingly proletarianized—combined with the rise of a distinctive Asian American cultural formation, including the literary culture I have been foregrounding here but extending well beyond it and other traditional forms of cultural aspiration (e.g., Western classical music) into rock, hip-hop, independent film; combined with the rise of Asian American studies programs and omnibus forms of political activism—all these have led to an explicit a rejection of the model minority paradigm that never worked as fully as advertised and seems less applicable than ever to proletarianized "new immigrants." And going along with that rejection is a sense of the perdurability of class and race barriers even for those who excel in college. As Deborah Woo has demonstrated, to cite but one example, Asian Americans are underrepresented in managerial positions as well as at the top echelons of major U.S. corporations, an underrepresentation she attributes to perceptions, on the part of such white-dominated institutions, of Asian Americans as culturally and socially "foreign."[42] To be sure, as sociologists and anthropologists have shown, there remains a significant attachment to the values of education, family, and self-sacrifice among Asian Americans, especially Chinese and Korean Americans, although it is structured in ways that often complicate the model minority paradigm (one reason that many younger Chinese Americans identify so strongly with the imperative of educational success, argues anthropologist Vivian Louie in her resonantly entitled ethnography, *Compelled to Excel*, is that they believe that a racist American society demands that they outperform their white peers).[43] And there's also a good deal of evidence in these studies that success-oriented Asian Americans track themselves against Jewish Americans, usually although not universally in positive ways—recognizing, for example according to Nazli Kibria, that Jews are relatively unique among white ethnics as objects of long-standing discrimination.[44] (It's telling, I think, that when one of Kibria's informants proposes a hypothetical situation of workplace discrimination in which a white ethnic is promoted instead of him, the ethnic he chooses to illustrate his situation is an Italian, not a Jewish American.) But the precedent is far from authoritative: references to Asians as "New Jews," *pace* Eric Liu, are rare even among Asian Americans who are pursuing the education-and-family path culturally linked to Jewishness.

In such a volatile context it's no wonder that Gish Jen's ironic words that serve as an epigraph to this chapter (which are themselves, in the novel, posed as already anachronistic, rendered moot by the spirit of the 1960s) ring hollow for many in this generation. That having been said, however, it also might be asserted that the case for the parallels between Jews and Asian Americans has never been stronger. The volatile admixture of economic and political immigration in mass numbers, the sweatshop conditions that await many who make the journey to a seeming promised land of freedom and economic security: I could be referring here either to Jews on the Lower East Side in 1907 or Cambodians in L.A. in 2007. Charges of illegitimate influence peddling wielded by sinister foreign-born elements: these could have come from either the Republican–inspired pseudo-campaign finance scandal of the 1990s or the pages of *The International Jew* in the 1920s. Charges that scientists spied for foreign governments to whom they owed "true" allegiance despite many years of faithful-seeming U.S. citizenship: these might be located in the Wen Ho Lee witch hunt of 2000 or the persecution of Robert Oppenheimer in the 1950s. And of course so is the flip side of model minority discourse, the charges that Asian Americans are somehow unfairly competitive in the college classroom, largely through overstudying and inattention to other forms of socializing: these constituted one of the bases for the quotas placed on Jewish students at Ivy League universities in the 1920s.

To note these parallels is not to stress the inevitability of the comparisons. The point of this chapter has been to illustrate the claim that Asian and Jewish destinies in the U.S. have been converging and diverging for the past hundred and fifty years, and these points of convergence may well be overtaken by the divergences in the next millennium. Moreover, as a Jewish American, it's not for me to tell peoples of Asian descent how they might respond to their situatedness in the current ideological moment, beyond pointing out that there may be some salient lessons (both positive and negative) to be gleaned from the Jewish experience in the U.S. and urging readers of Asian descent, or those engaged with the critical reconstruction of U.S. culture from a point of view that foregrounds Asian difference, actively to engage with that precedent rather than shunting such engagements to the footnote page or not mentioning them at all.

But it *is* appropriate for me, I think, to pass on to what I think may be the lessons that might be applicable to Jewish American self-constructions. One of the things that the crossings between Jews and Asians I've been surveying foregrounds is another way of talking about the racial dimensions of assimilation than the now formulaic language of whiteness: a way of describing it as involving what educational scholar and theorist Isaac Berkson described in 1927 as "the complete de-orientalization of the American Jew."[45] For if, as we have seen, it was the matrix of contradictory Orientalized identifications that defined Jews *as* Jews in the crucial 1880–1924 period—as exoticized, hysterical, emotional, melancholic, jabbering, money-mad, sexually aberrant, neocastrated, sallow-faced, nonwhite, nonblack others—then one of the things that American Jews did in the period that followed it was to distance themselves from those Orientalizing constructions in every conceivable way. They sought to redefine themselves as definitively European rather than Middle Eastern or Mongol-Russian-Oriental in origin and appearance and most importantly as conservative in behavior, as unecstatic in religious practices (if religious at all), as sober-minded professionals—doctors, lawyers, professors—rather than ragpickers, haggling merchants, or even movie moguls. Understanding the process in these terms would help us, I think, capture the true dialectical quality of the encounter between Jewish self-understandings and broader cultural processes in the crucial period of high immigration followed by acculturation—an acculturation as much involving, it seems to me, gentile culture's lurching attempts to define and encompass Jewish difference as it does that of Jews to the people among whom they found themselves, which perforce responded to those constructions with reaction formations of their own. Think as an emblem of the former of a powerful shot in *The Jazz Singer* in which the spirit of Cantor Rabinowitz, having just passed away while hearing his son sing *Kol Nidrei*, lays his hand on Jackie dressed in full, exoticized, traditional regalia: at once imparting his Orientalized otherness onto Jackie and enacting its generational extinction. Think of the latter in terms of the fact that the actor who played Cantor Rabinowitz also played Fu Manchu: that, as we've seen, labile stereotypes of the Jew as Oriental in the most insidious sense flip around to create the lineaments of the model minority stereotype to which Jews fitted themselves in the 1940s and 1950s.

Most important of all, however, is the fact that bringing this context back into play helps us recognize, and appreciate, the cultural developments of the current moment that I've been attempting to foreground throughout this book. Another way of thinking about what I've been calling queer diasporism or radical Jewish culture—two different sides of the same coin—is that both endeavors involve what we might want to call the re-Orientalization of American Jewish cultural life, a reorientation (the pun is unavoidable) toward cultural formations and experiences that bring back all the things that got repressed in the march toward respectability that governed Jewish acculturation in the period between 1930 and 1990 or so. To a certain extent, I mean this literally: the revival of Sephardic/Mizrachi music production that I have been stressing throughout, for example, is a striking and unanticipated aftergrowth of the klezmer revival—and eventuates in the musical revisionism not only of Uri Caine and Aaron Bensoussan but also of a wide variety of musicians.[46] But I also intend it more broadly as well: one sign of it has been the revival of ecstatic mysticism, the cult of kabbalah (under the sign of which even Madonna can become Jewish: surely an unanticipated confirmation of Malamud's famous assertion that "every man is a Jew, though he may not know it").[47] So, too, in an even broader sense is the reconstruction and celebration of the queer Jewish paradigm, whether represented by the Klezmatics, Daniel Boyarin's *femme*-inized Jew, the various avatars of Kushner's Louis: a recovery, indeed a proud proclamation, of sexual non-normativity. And as we'll see in more detail in the following chapter, the writing of new immigrants from the former Soviet Union recaptures the sense of oddity, queer-

6.4 The (Orientalized) Cantor—and his (Americanized) Son, the Jazz Singer. Warner Oland passes the torch to Al Jolson, 1927.

ness in all senses of the word, that attends to the entry of these new Jews to the American scene—themselves constructed as ethnics in the land from which they came in ways that don't comport to the U.S. model.

But, whatever one calls it, these recent developments represent a striking return to a previous cultural dispensation not so much in the much reviled return to roots in the classic 1970s or 1980s sense—the *Sunrise, Sunset!* moment in Jewish self-definition—but a moment of creative ferment in Jewish life, and American cultural life across the board that preceded it, that chimes with the radical experimentation that marked cultural life in the 1910s and 1920s, the literary and cultural ferment we metonymically associate not only with the Yiddish poets on and beyond the Lower East Side but also with avant-garde writers in Greenwich Village, tunesmiths in Tin Pan Alley, and directors and producers in Hollywood. What marked that moment, other than the common cultural description of eastern European Jews as jabbering Orientalized overemotional others, was a radical set of experimental practices and possibilities that was explored among first-generation eastern European Jews and an extension out of those practices and possibilities by second- and third-generation ones into literature (not just by writers but also via modernist-friendly Jewish-dominated publishing houses like Random House and Boni and Liveright), music (not just Gershwin and Berlin, but also Bernstein, Copland, Diamond), film (not just the moguls, for example, but the countless actors, directors, set designers, etc., who began in the Yiddish theater), comedy, and so on. The experimental art of our moment promises to do something of the same, as it were in reverse; not to slough off the Jew-as-Other model, but rather to embrace it, and with it new possibilities of racial and ethnic crisscross. Standing outside the assimilative patterns of the past generations, and taking particular aim at the model minority model of economic success and cultural achievement, these new predications point toward a more capacious set of possibilities not only for Jewish Americans but also for culture at large. As such, they pose both a challenge and an opportunity for other contemporary ethnic artists struggling with the model minority model—and with the problematic burden of the massive Jewish entry into the cultural scene, as we'll see in detail in the next chapter.

7. ASIANS AND JEWS IN THEORY AND PRACTICE

IN 1998, a second-generation Chinese American, Eric Liu, published a series of essays entitled *The Accidental Asian*. Graduate of Yale and Harvard Law School and a former presidential speechwriter, Liu would seem to be the very model of the model minority, and, not uncoincidentally (as my argument in the preceding chapter would suggest), he is readily at home with Jews and Jewishness. Liu, after all, grew up alongside many Jews in Poughkeepsie, a middle-class town in upstate New York; attended universities like Harvard and Yale chock-full of accomplished Jews; served in the most Jewish-friendly administration in history, that of Bill Clinton; and is married to a Jewish woman. Throughout the book he not only uses the model of assimilation derived from Jews and Jewishness to gloss his own experience, he also frequently adopts its very tropes.* So it is all the odder that, in an essay entitled "The New Jews," the tonalities of Liu's otherwise fluid and supple prose become contorted, strained. Jewish Americans, Liu writes, possess a historical narrative about themselves that allows them a coherent group identity; Asian Americans do not. While Jews compose 2 percent of the population as opposed to the Asians' 4 percent, they have managed to amass a considerable degree of political power, but Asians have not. Jews have the ability to pass as white; Asians do not. And, most poignantly, Jews have managed to transform American culture even as they entered into it and, as for Asians, well . . .

---

*At one point, for example, Liu refers to his status as an "ABC"—an American-born Chinese—with the term *greenhorn*, one that Abraham Cahan brought into common English parlance from the Yiddish *oyshgreen* in both *Yekl* and *The Rise of David Levinsky* as a way of describing a just-off-the-boat immigrant to America. But, in his eagerness to affiliate his experience with that of American Jews, he makes an interesting slip: to be a greenhorn is to be foreign-born and, obviously, to be ABC is not.

A novelist from England speaks of "the Great Jews"—Bellow, Malamud, Roth and so on—who articulated the inner life of midcentury America. It was a Jewish playwright named Israel Zangwill who immortalized the phrase "the melting pot." And what was Hollywood, asks author Neil Gabler, but the invention of Jews who wanted so badly to invent another America? Listen now to television, or the radio, or a conversation on the bus: the Jews gave us another voice. *What, you need an example?* The Jew changed the very inflection of an American question. The Jew changed our food, our images, our language, our humor, our law, our literature.

The Asian, so far, has changed our food.[1]

Given this last, and not unrepresentative, turn, it's no surprise that Liu's work has been the subject of a good deal of critique from the Asian American community. To be sure, the book was quite positively received by Michael Omi, who along with Howard Winant has done the most to transform notions of race in ways that have been catalyzing for radical scholars of race and ethnicity. In a short review Omi praises Liu for his recognition of the variability and contingency of racial identifications and describes sympathetically Liu's "Kodak" moment of ethnic self-recognition in the face of anti-Asian hysteria during the overhyped "campaign finance scandal" of 1996.[2] But Liu's claim that his race is an "accidental" integument of his identity, combined with his desire for the kind of assimilation into normative Americanness, has also provoked strenuous critique. David Li writes:

> Rather than tracing this entrapment of the Asian American to the fundamental contradiction of American citizenship, to the ways in which the white body has been postulated as the American universal in and by itself, Liu seems more than willing to sacrifice ethnic morphological visibility.... "[A] hairless, skinless, bloodless universalism" has finally come to "unstick" the accidental Asian, justifying the natural extinction of racial difference in apparent national synthesis.... [Via intermarriage], Nature eventually proves omnipotent to do what culture cannot.[3]

What may ultimately be most interesting about Liu's work, however, is the slippage it displays between these two responses—between Omi's hailing of the historical variability of racial inscriptions and Li's desire to cleave to the concept of "ethnic morphological visibility," if only as an alternative to an assimilation understood as accession to a bland, all-inclusive whiteness. Or, to be more precise, what may be most interesting about Liu's response is the way that he negotiates this contradiction—by appealing to the highly anomalous yet highly charged example of Jewishness. In Liu's account, the Jew becomes the paradigm of successful assimilation, but it's not assimilation in the sense in which Li means the term. Rather, from Liu's perspective, dominant white culture has assimilated to Jews rather than the other way around: "the Jews gave us [Americans] another voice," changing nothing less than "the inflection of the American question." Jews may or may not be white—racial categories, perhaps problematically, aren't all that important for Liu. In Liu's account, however, the normative national body itself has been transformed in an equally significant locus, the vocal chords. Liu's position in this drama of transformation is ambiguous. Note his pronoun: he includes himself as an American insofar as, like all Americans, he speaks with a Jewish voice. But when his Asianness foregrounds itself, he falls into a fit of writerly sputtering, speaking simultaneously from two subject positions: the "Asian" (like himself?) has changed [only] *our* food" (my emphasis). The only way to resolve this contradiction would be to achieve the cultural power and social éclat that seems to have come, after many centuries of obloquy and persecution, to Jews in America. It's a self-Jewifying program, rather than the desire for whiteness of which Li accuses him, that marks the contours of Liu's assimilationist politics: Asians should aim not to be "white" or WASP in their endeavor to join "the national synthesis," but rather trade in one kind of alterity for another.

This complex admixture of affect in the face of Jewish difference—desire and envy, aspiration and anxiety—and the ways in which they are negotiated, finessed, transformed will be my subject in this chapter. For Liu's response is not unique or idiosyncratic, especially when considered in the context of Asian American fiction of the last twenty-five years or so. Emerging just after the first generation of Asian American writers to achieve mainsteam success (the generation, that is, of Frank Chin, Maxine Hong Kingston, and, in a more popular vein, Amy Tan), a new cohort of East and South Asian writers entered the field of literary achievement and combat with precisely the experience, burdens, anxieties, and aspirations that Liu evinces. Like Liu, this generation—in which I would include such enormously talented and successful authors as Chang-Rae Lee, Vikram Seth, Bharati Mukherjee, Gish Jen, Jhumpa Lahiri, David Wong Louie, Don Lee and (as part of a slightly younger cohort) Susan Malka Choi, Lan Samantha Chang, Christina Chiu—is largely but not exclusively mainstream in orientation; their fiction, while frequently quite audacious, is not overtly experimental or paradigm shifting in the mode of, say, Filipino American writer Jessica Hagedorn or MacArthur-winning playwright cum novelist Han Ong. Like Liu, these mainstream writers have by and large been products of a first-rate education. Jen was a student at Harvard; Chang-Rae Lee, Lan Samantha Chang, Susan Choi, and Min Jin Lee graduated Yale. Many had professional training of other sorts: Gish Jen attended Stanford Business School; Jhumpa Lahiri has a Ph.D. in renaissance studies. And most were credentialed by the top-rated writing programs in the country, including Columbia (Christina Chiu), Cornell (Choi), and, of course, Iowa (Jen, Mukherjee, Chang—the last-named of whom has just been appointed its new director). Again like Liu, these writers enter a field they recognize, willingly or not, as massively shaped by the Jewish example. "Perhaps not since the mainstream 'discovered' Jewish American fiction in the 1950s has such a concentrated, seemingly 'new' ethnic literary wave come our way," wrote *Publisher's Weekly* in 1991 of Maxine Hong Kingston, Amy Tan, Gish Jen, Gus Lee, Frank Chin, and David Wong Louie's "arrival" on the literary scene, the phrasing doubtlessly irritating many it named.[4] And the same situation applies, as I will show, to the generation of Asian American writers who, rebelling against the minimialist protocols that dominated fictional practice in the 1980s, turned back to the Jewish "ethnic" writers, especially Malamud, for inspiration.

Like Liu's, the response of many of these writers to the cultural achievements of Jews is at once powerful and overdetermined; they, too, frequently register the sense lingering behind his language of an occulted Jewish cultural power to which Asians need to aspire. But they are able to mount an effective counterresponse to the Jewish presence in the literary field, and it is their response that is the subject of this chapter. Mingling respect and even imitation with revisionist energy, mixing envy with critique, they engage in what Jonathan Dollimore has nicely called, in an entirely different context, "transgressive reinscription," the rewriting of previously established narrative modes so as to turn them to alternative ends.[5] Where they succeed, and where they fail, and, more important, what alternative vision they project of the charged issues I've been dealing with throughout this book—the immigrant narrative with its ancillary agendas of assimilation and acculturation, the complicated interplay of race and ethnicity and of both with the reshaping powers of sexuality, and, most powerfully of all, the ambiguous force of the model minority paradigm—will be my subject in what follows.

The Discourse of Diaspora and (Versus) the Anxiety of Influence: Bharati Mukherjee

A fine case in point is is provided by the early work of Calcutta-born novelist Bharati Mukherjee, now professor of English at the University of California, Berkeley, author of a number of novels about the translocational experience of exiled, hyphenated migrants in a world of loss, exile, political revolution, terrorism: in short, the world we have always lived in, and now, post–September 11, know we live in. Particularly in the early phases of her career, Mukherjee frequently defined her writerly ambitions "in the tradition of other American writers whose parents or grandparents had passed through Ellis Island," as she writes in the introduction to her first collection of stories, *Darkness,* "The book I dream of updating, is no longer *A Passage to India*—it's *Call It Sleep.*" *Darkness* is dedicated to Bernard Malamud (a teacher of her husband, the Canadian novelist Clark Blaise),* and she consistently mentions Malamud as a prime influence on her work, the one who gave her her new, true subject, the lives of immigrants:

> I see a strong likeness between my writing and Bernard Malamud's, in spite of the fact that he describes the lives of East European Jewish immigrants and I talk about the lives of newcomers from the Third World. Like Malamud, I write about a minority community which escapes the ghetto and adapts itself to the patterns of the dominant American culture. . . . Immersing myself in his work gave me the self-confidence to write about my own community.[6]

---

*Indeed, their son was named Bernard, after Malamud.

This act of affiliation has led to strenuous criticism of Mukherjee, particularly from postcolonial critics suspicious of both dramas of assimilation she is both enacting for herself and "newcomers from the Third World."[7] Gestures of literary affiliation are, however, complicated amalgams of appropriation and appreciation, and Mukherjee's are especially so: this is, after all, a woman who has expressed the desire to supplant first Tagore, then Forster, then, in her 1993 novel *The Holder of the World*, Hawthorne. So it should come as no surprise that Mukherjee invokes Malamud's example in order to challenge it. In the same interview she is asked how her writing differs from his and responds: "When you are from the Third World, when you have dark skin and religious beliefs . . . mainstream America responds to you in ways you can't foresee. My fiction has to consider race, politics, religion, as well as certain nastinesses that other generations of white immigrant writers may not have had to take into account" (650–651).

Fair enough—and, as we shall see, not only Mukherjee, but also Gish Jen uses the example of Jewish American fiction to measure the ethnoracial and religious nastinesses that dark-skinned, non-Judeo-Christian immigrant communities face. But there's another moment in this interview that suggests just how complex is Mukherjee's engagement with the Jewish American tradition. Mukherjee claims that the title story of her signature collection, *The Middleman,* developed as follows: "While I was working on [an uncompleted novel], a character with a minor role, a Jew who has relocated from Baghdad to Bombay to Brooklyn, took control and wrote his own story. He attracted me because he was a cynical person and a hustler, as many immigrant survivors have to be" (648). As this language may suggest, Mukherjee's character Alfie Judah is about as far away from Malamud's protagonists—and, more important, those common to Jewish American writing—as can be imagined. (Bellow's Augie March may be a hustler, but he is far from cynical.) From Henry Roth's David Schearle to Saul Bellow's Herzog to Philip Roth's Alexander Portnoy, the archetypal Jewish American narrative has been of the assimilation of a sensitive Ashkenazic man, tied to the world of his parents but struggling to find his place on the bustling, commercial American stage upon which he is too fine by nature to flourish. That Jewish man, moreover, is defined by a powerful sexuality but loaded with guilt for his expressions of it—largely because that guilt is incestuous, or miscegenating, or both, in nature. And, finally, that figure is frequently, if not triumphantly, victimized by those less morally scrupulous than he, a victimization that grants him a moral superiority even as it denies his practical efficacy.

Alfie, however, is the polar opposite of the Noble Schlemiel. "Alfie Judah, of the once-illustrious Smyrna, Aleppo, Baghdad—and now Flushing, Queens—Judahs" is neither ethnoracially nor behaviorally normative.[8] He is dark-complected—a fact that makes him acceptable to the Central American revolutionaries among whom he finds himself: he may be a Jew but at least he is not a gringo (19). And, rather than assimilating, he is in flight from America by virtue of some shady deals that have landed him on the wrong side of the law. Alfie is deeply amoral, both in his business practices ("there's just demand and supply running the universe," he muses [14]) and, perhaps more pointedly, in sexual ones as well: indeed, he is remarkably free of the sexual guilt that defines the Jewish American quasi hero. "I must confess my weakness. It's women," announces Alfie, and the story details his dangerous, and adulterous, lust for Maria, the consort of his American host, Clovis T. Ransome, and former mistress of an unnamed country's president. Alfie's amoralism crosses between his business and his bedroom practices, as does Maria's (4). Indeed, she uses him to help her deliver some of the supplies to the guerrillas, led by her lover Andreas ("I have no feeling for revolution," Alfie notes, "only for outfitting the participants" [15]), then rewards him with sex. Afterward, Alfie listens to Maria detail the multiple violations of her life, responding with pragmatic comfort. At the end of the story, Maria kills Ransome in the midst of a guerrilla intrusion led by Andreas, then briefly points a gun at Alfie before turning it aside, lighting out for the jungle with her lover. Alfie realizes that only his intimacy with her—his compassionate response to her in bed—has saved his life. The story closes with Alfie plotting his next move: "Someone in the capital will be happy to know about [the guerrilla attack]. There must be something worth trading in the troubles I have seen" (21).

A more un-Malamudian/Rothian/Bellovian Jew I cannot imagine.[9] Indeed, Alfie is not just unlike, but the very converse of, the sensitive Ashkenazic Jewish man: he is the embodiment of the worst nightmares of the generation that produced that figure. After all, the specter haunting assimilating American Jews of this period was not only the Holocaust but also the antisemitic projections of the Jew as the horny trader standing outside national and moral borders alike. Memorialized not only by antisemitic pamphlets of the 1890s, but by the spirited endeavor of Henry Ford—and high-art literature by the likes of T. S. Eliot and Ezra Pound—the concept of the hyper-phallic, dark-complected Asiatic or non-European Jew as morally corrupt and corrupting cosmopolitan, frequently associated with exotically corrupt (and hence covertly attractive) sexual practices, suffused both Middle America and high-art modernism. (Mister Eugenides, one of Eliot's more sinister Jews, is a "Smyrna Merchant," just like Alfie.) If Alfie Judah seems like a literal embodiment of such a figure it is surely not because Mukherjee wants to revive the Ford- or Eliot-sponsored antisemitic notions of the Jewish man, but rather because she wants to invoke—if not make her own—all the ethnoracial cultural sexual stuff that Jewish American fiction had to expel in order to make its successful march into respectability.

In this light, Mukherjee's desire to "update" *Call It Sleep* takes on a new salience. She doesn't so much bring its immigrant narrative into the contemporary scene as suggest, from a contemporary perspective, all the things that were missing from that narrative in the first place. I will have more to say about this effect and its implications further on in this chapter; for now I want to suggest what Mukherjee gains from this transaction. For she gathers not only a revisionary purchase on the tradition she is "updating," but a base upon which to build her own career. Just as Alfie Judah takes over, and starts to write, "The Middleman"—becomes, in short, Mukherjee's muse of the transcendently transgressive—so he does in her career, which received its greatest boost in the creation of a character who matches Alfie for amoralism. I am thinking of her most commercially successful narrative, *Jasmine,* in which—to be more accurate—Mukherjee creates a character who combines the qualities she identifies in Alfie with those she sees in Maria: the novel's morphing protagonist, born Jyoti, transformed variously over the course of the novel into Jase, Jane, and Jasmine. In the plot arc of the novel she constructs a woman who, like Maria, becomes empowered, sexualized, and amoral. Over the course of her trajectory from small town Indian girl, Jyoti/Jane/Jasmine kills the rapist who transports her to the United States, seduces, marries, and then dumps the crippled Midwestern banker who dotes on her, and lights out for the territory with her lover—here, California instead of the Central American jungle. But as she does so, Jyoti/Jane/Jasmine also follows Alfie Judah's path: although her motives may vary, her actions increasingly resemble less those of an Indian villager and more those of an Alfie-like hustler, continually looking for and finding something to leverage in the multiple troubles she has seen.

In Mukherjee's 1980s work, I am suggesting, the discourse of diaspora manages what might be best described in Harold Bloom's tropology as the anxiety of influence: it allows her both to place herself in a powerful tradition and to remake it.[10] And, as Bloom's paradigm would suggest, Mukherjee seems to have successfully internalized and then moved on from the tradition of Jewish American immigrant writing she invoked early in her career; her most recent fictions, like *Dutiful Daughters* (2001), juxtapose Indian and American destinies in the transnational, postmodern, globalized economy stretching from Silicon Valley to Bombay. But her path in the 1980s, it seems to me, has important salience for a new generation of Asian American writers, not only South but also East Asian, not only immigrants, but also first- and second-generation Americans, many of whom engage themselves in rewriting the immigrant narrative in ways that deal with Jewishness with the same revisionary energy that Mukherjee so fiercely displays.*

---

*And for which she has been so roundly criticized. Here is a sample from postcolonial intellectual Amritjit Singh:

> Possibilities of connection and coalitions with other Americans of color are lost, for instance, in the vestigial colonial ventriloquism of Dinesh D'Souza and the celebratory assimilationism of Bharati Mukherjee. In a novel like *Jasmine* and writerly statements such as "Immigrant Writing: Give Us Your Maximalists!" Mukherjee's cheerful, forward-looking attitude towards the possibilities of assimilation is achieved through a reductive and stereotypical representation of South Asian realities, a fantastic view of human psychology and individual consciousness, and debatable generalizations about immigrant and expatriate writing.

Quoted in Jon Stratton, *Coming Out Jewish* (London: Routledge, 2000), p. 270.

What's noteworthy here, as Stratton implicitly suggests, is the claim that Mukherjee's frame for viewing the South Asian diaspora is too "Jewish" in the Malamudian sense: fantastical as well as pro-assimilation. For to expect realism from Mukherjee—or Malamud—vis-à-vis "human psychology and individual consciousness" is to commit a category error. The comparison with arch-conservative Dinesh D'Souza strikes me as an ad hominem slur.

"The New Jews" in the Promising Land: Gish Jen

The classic example of this tendency is the work of Scarsdale-born, Harvard-educated Gish Jen. Jen often speaks of the mixed generic and experiential relation between Jewish American fiction and her own. Sometimes this expresses itself as a kind of a benign inspiration: "The biggest influence on my work has come from Jewish American writers.... It's partly Scarsdale and partly the sympathy I see between the Jewish and Chinese cultures." Sometimes, on the other hand, her attitude seems to be touched with irritation: "What we [Asian American writers] don't want is to be lumped together, ghettoized. I hope that twenty-five years from now, we'll achieve the kind of standing that Jewish American writers have—that is, we'll just be judged as writers." Throughout, there is a sense that both as a writer and as an *ethnic* writer—especially one who has parsed the interconnection between Chinese American and Jewish American identities in *Mona in the Promised Land*—the relevant judges of her work for better or worse are Jews: "I was very happy when Cynthia Ozick reviewed [*Mona*] and presented, really, a banner take. I was thrilled just to have attracted the notice of a writer whom I admire as much as I admire Cynthia Ozick. But in addition I was thrilled to have passed muster with her."[11]

This mélange of conflicting affects—admiration, resentment, competitiveness—structures Jen's fictional response to her Jewish American predecessors as well. Her first novel, *Typical American*, as Rachel Lee has nicely noted, draws "upon a hodgepodge of eighteenth- and nineteenth-century literary references"; "[her protagonist] Ralph Chang emulates Benjamin Franklin, believes in Emersonian Romantic individualism, encounters a Melvillian confidence man, and lives a rags-to-riches life made familiar by Horatio Alger."[12] But, on the structural level, it seems most deeply engaged with fictions like Saul Bellow's, particularly that of the classic phase of the 1950s and early 1960s (the period *Typical American* describes; the period in which Gish Jen grew up in Scarsdale). The plot of *Typical American* is familiar from Bellow's great picaresque fiction *The Adventures of Augie March* (1956). A callow, relentlessly optimistic outsider on the fringes of American society undergoes a number of comic misadventures on the way to becoming a fully credentialed—a typical—American. In Jen's novel, as in Bellow's, these adventures turn on the protagonist's encounter with a number of ambiguous, and at times outright hostile, mentors. In Bellow's early work these are as likely to be women as men; in Jen's (as in Bellow's later work) they are almost always older and male. The first in *Typical American* is, significantly, a thoroughly assimilated Jew: his aristocratic, cane-carrying, mansion-inhabiting thesis adviser, Pinkus, who having heard an erroneous rumor about his student, transforms poor Ralph into a walking version of the Yellow Peril, even to the degree of accusing him of stalking Pinkus's daughter. (The irony here, of course, is multiplied by the fact that precisely this language and these allegations—that they lusted after "white" gentile women—were made against Jews as well as Asians as late as the 1930s.) But, tellingly, Pinkus is less important to Ralph's fate than two Chinese American men: Old Chao, a slightly senior colleague, and, even more important, Grover Ding, a rascally entrepreneur. Both, in some sense, cuckold Ralph as they help advance his career. Old Chao, although married, is in love with Ralph's beloved sister Teresa. He uses her concern for her hapless brother to seduce her: feeding her information that helps him earn tenure as he advances, inexorably, toward a sexual relation with her. Cuckoldry is more explicit still in the relation between Grover and Ralph. Grover is a classic self-made entrepreneur cum petty crook who fills Ralph's head with Dale-Carnegie-like nonsense, enmeshes him in criminal schemes, and even sells him a building for his restaurant that is quite literally falling apart—all in the hopes of seducing Ralph's beautiful, sensible wife Helen, as Grover ultimately does.

Even more than her plots, then, Jen's dramatis personae fit into the pattern of Jewish American writing, most specifically that perfected by Bellow not only in *Augie March* but also in *Herzog* and *Humboldt's Gift*. Crucial here is the character-type of the schlemiel—the bumbling but endearing loser—encountering near-criminal rascals who teach him valuable lessons about life in America even as they bamboozle him.[13] Bellow's term for these latter figures is "reality instructors, [those who] want to teach you—to punish you with—the lessons of the Real," and in Bellow's case, as in Jen's, these figures frequently cuckold the protagonist not only as an act of sexual domination, but as part of the latter's reversal of the Horatio Alger story ("how I rose from humble origins to complete disaster" is Herzog's description of his own life, one that more or less applies to Ralph's as well). In Bellow's case this narrative turns quite rapidly to the comic in the deepest sense of the term. Augie concludes the story of his life with the deep, affirmative laugh of what Bellow calls the *"animal ridens"*;

Herzog ends, purged of anger and hate, in his house in upstate New York, there to revive his life beyond the neurotic if brilliant kvetching in which he has been indulging for most of the novel. Ralph Chang, too, is by and large a comic character, one whose own bumblings are orchestrated by his seeming friend, Grover, and part of the fun of the novel is to witness his sublime cluelessness as Grover leads him into one harebrained scheme after another while his wife and sister attempt, loyally, to clean up after him. And, near the end of the novel, Ralph snaps much as does Herzog (who stalks his ex-wife and her lover with a gun). Ralph drives off with his wife, threatening her until she confesses her relation to Grover. Returning to the house, Ralph attempts to run down the dog he has named after Grover but hits his beloved sister Teresa instead.

Jen claimed in an interview that this swerve from the comic high spirits of the rest of the novel to its sober conclusion (Teresa remains in a coma in the novel's final chapters) has much to do with the miscarriage she suffered while writing it.[14] But it seems to me also a willful swerve (in Bloomian terms, a *clinamen*) from the kinds of narrative and ideological structures that Bellow's text exemplifies. For, in Bellow's novel, the ultimate service of the reality instructors is to return Herzog to his roots, restore him to his family, and ultimately bring about comic, or at least affirmative, closure. After he is arrested and his gun—significantly, his bootlegger father's weapon—has been confiscated, Herzog calls on his estranged brother to bail him out, reestablishing a relation that he had severed long before. In *Typical American* the situation is precisely reversed. Ralph's murderous rage at his wife and Grover leads him to eliminate neither of these two tormentors, but rather his own sister who has, in stereotypical immigrant style, been living too closely with the family for anyone's comfort.

Swallowing up the Jewish American example, in other words, Jen proposes a tragic variation on it: she uses the comic plot of transcendent schlemielhood to tell story at once more sinister and more troubling than the one that Bellow has to narrate. Ties to the traditional family have to be severed, however violently; the "reality instructors" pass over the edge into outright criminality and threaten to bring the assimilating outsider with them; the bumbling protagonist actually does harm. Jen's lesson would seem to have as much to do with the inadequacy of the Jewish immigrant narrative to her Chinese American protagonists. That narrative, however ironically represented (as it surely is in Bellow's hands), has become just one more fallible American construction, like Emerson's or

Melville's or Dale Carnegie's, that exists as a bane and a lure the Changs must overcome—as, one senses, must Jen.

A completely different take on this issue is suggested in Jen's next novel, *Mona in the Promised Land* (1996), which offers a delightfully comic series of riffs on the Asians-as-the-New-Jews topos (Jen invokes it directly on the first page of the novel, in the lines I have taken as an epigraph to the previous chapter). But here Jen's thematic interest is in complicating the idea of ethnicity tout court. When a teenager in Scarshill, New York named Mona Chang converts to Judaism, that act puts into stark relief not only the complexity of Jewishness but also, as her rabbi suggests to her, that of her own Chineseness. To a certain extent, of course, Jewishness in the New World is put under interrogation by Mona's conversion, her becoming "Mona-also-known-as-Ruth, a more or less genuine Catholic Chinese Jew," and in multiple ways.[15] Vis-à-vis the Jews among whom she lives, her conversion calls into question *their* authenticity rather than her own: Mona's desire to become Jewish highlights the novel's Jews' desire to become something—anything!—other than what they are. (As her best friend Barbara Gugelstein puts it, "a little Jewish fine, but my mom says too much is too much.... Some people are too Jewish even for other Jews" [222]). Her "authentic inauthentic" Jewish boyfriend Seth ("more ethnic than religious" he explains [112]), for example, not only falls in love with Mona because (as Seth's ex-, Barbara Gulgelstein, says) "he wants to be with a shikse"(74), he also decides in a classically sixties way that he wants to become an Indian, and so sets up a teepee in the back yard. (Tellingly, it's at that site of "playing Indian," in Philip Deloria's sense—of whites renegotiating the terms of their identity by adopting the guise of natives—that Mona loses her virginity, the site of Indianness being for her the place of libidinal freedom and exogamous desire.)[16] And, at the end of the book, he's exploring Zen and other Asian mysticisms as an alternative form of self-identification. But the urge to escape their Jewishness has special salience for Mona's Asianness; her conversion brings into sharp relief her own Chinese identity. "Now that she's Jewish," Mona wants to tell the hip if not hippie Rabbi Horowitz, "she feels like more of a Chinese than ever" (66), by which she means many things: that she has come to recognize her own ethnic identity by affiliating with that of this historically charged category of otherness (as she certainly does when she comes into contact with antisemitic and racist WASPs, the Ingle family); that has discover her own difference *from* Jews by affirming religious solidarity *with* Jews; that being

Jewish means being something—anything at all—in a culture that enthusiastically deracinates its participants. As Mona says fliply, at one point: "American means being whatever you want, and I happened to pick being Jewish" (49).

But most important of all, perhaps, he conversion brings into sharp outline the lineaments of the Chinese experience. On the one hand, the recollection of the Holocaust that hangs heavily over only one or two of the Scarshill Jews—Seth's mother survives the death camps, but dies in America in an auto accident—resonates in the Chinese experience of Japanese war atrocities, especially as Mona discovers those memories shaping the experience of her own parents who of course do not speak of them (except when in the eighth grade Mona makes out with a Japanese boy, Sherman Matsumoto, to their horror). On the other hand, the "whole endless history that spirals up to [the Holocaust] like a staircase in a nightmare" casts into shadow the privileged past of Mona's family: as opposed to the Jews, "their group hasn't always been the oppressed. [In China], they used to be the oppressors; and that makes them, as a minority [in America], rank amateurs" (36).

In these ways and more, Mona works out the dialectical pattern of interplay between Jewish and Asian (specifically Chinese) experiences we saw, in the previous chapter, as a constant in U.S. history from the 1870s to the present day, dissecting the full complexity of that interplay with scalpels of wit, satire, parody. Indeed, it is the last of these that seems to me the most salient representational device of *Mona*, as it was in *Typical American*; here Jen turns to a different representational structure, to Shakespearean comedy, with its rapid-fire transformations of costume, identities, and affiliations. What Shakespeare does with and to gender, it might be said, Mona does to ethnicity—a nexus made clearest at the end of the novel when, after they have broken up, Seth successfully woos Mona in the guise of Sherman, a feat worthy of one of Shakespeare's trickster heroes. The world she thereby renders is a thoroughly comic one in the Shakespearean sense: not for nothing does it end with a wedding in which the older generation, in the persons of Mona's hostile mother and feckless father, are reconciled with their daughter and Seth (and their lovely granddaughter, Io). Given this benign end, it would seem that not only are Jewish and Asian identities enfolded into this harmonious vision of ethnic masquerade leading to social integration, but so are ethnic identities across the board. And, in so doing, in its very form, the novel offers itself as a triumphant literary enactment of the multicultural ideal of the 1980s.

But, despite the novel's comic tone, representational structures, and conclusions, matters in it are not so simple; indeed, they become impossibly complicated when race gets factored into the ethnic mix. Near the end of the novel, Mona says to Seth/Sherman that she's having trouble figuring out what it is to be "not wasp, and not black, and not as Jewish as Jewish can be; and not from Chinatown, either." Seth/Sherman responds in classic American terms, telling Mona that she's best defined as an individual ("a sore thumb . . . sticking out by yourself"), but the point remains as true in relation to ethnoracial as it does to individual identity: Chinese Americans like Mona fit into none of the available boxes our culture has created; neither white nor black nor "Jewish as Jewish can be"—and not even, for that matter, Chinese American, at least in the terms in which the cultural imaginary creates Chineseness (231). But this is not to say that Mona isn't Chinese American in some compelling and important way; it is to suggest, rather, that that Chinese Americanness is defined only in differential terms, in relation to all these other, equally factitious, identity boxes. Thus, to cite one loaded example, Mona confronts her own sense of inhabiting a racialized body when she begins to think about her nose, eyes, skin color, and breasts as ethnic markers alongside her Jewish friends discussing their own nose jobs: their desire to mutilate their bodies in order to pass as gentiles brings into sharp relief her own nongentile, nonwhite, non-Jewish physiognomy.

But the exact meaning of Mona's Asianness is also up for grabs in the novel. Set in 1968—the moment at which Asian American identity is beginning to be defined as such—Mona is aware of the inadequacy of that category in the face of long-standing national antagonisms, like that between Japanese and Chinese. Moreover, the place of Asian difference, however defined, in the American ethnoracial cavalcade is uncertain. Her increasingly Chinese-identified sister's Harvard roommate, an African American woman, identifies Mona as a person of color—"yellow," not white—an identification Mona first accepts, then edges away from (170). But other, angrier African Americans like Alfred, the cook in her parents' pancake house, identify Mona as white, much to Mona's chagrin. While Alfred may be wrong in the sense of skin color, he is clearly onto something when he twits Mona for being from a family that keeps a black gardener and relegates all the African Americans in their restaurant to the kitchen.

On the other hand (and nothing in this novel can be said to be one-sided), Alfred and his friends enforce racial essentialism in its crudest form after Mona announces her conversion; they chant, "Grow your nose, grow your nose," an aspersion at once anti-Asian and antisemitic in its implications. (While Barbara Gugelstein, whose nose job is in part at stake in this byplay, may join in, as much out of a desire to be accepted as Jewish self-hatred, Mona quietly observes, "I think you guys are stereotyping" [136]).

Race in its crudest, most American-inflected aspect—the black/white binary and all that comes with it (including the long history of intimacy and tension between African Americans and Jews)—thus halts the unfolding of the novel's Shakespearean masquerade in its tracks in exactly the same way that *Typical American's* rollicking immigrant picaresque is brought to a premature conclusion by a neo-Bellovian intimation of mortality. This isn't to say that Jen doesn't devote a significant amount of narrative energy to overcoming this challenge to her comic vision: to the contrary, she attempts to write her way out of it. Much of the second third of the novel is taken up with a subplot involving Alfred, a protracted episode in which Mona and her friends hide in the wing of Barbara Gugelstein's family house—more like a mansion, complete with a gardening staff; they bring him food and other supplies through a tunnel running into the wine cellar they name "the Underground railroad." And they go through elaborate mechanisms to keep Alfred hidden from Evie and her parents, mechanisms that are frustrated when it turns out that Evie and Alfred have discovered each other and become lovers. Here, too, the implications of crossracial love may be a comic turn on a Shakespearean riff (Mona studies *Othello* in high school but thinks the scenario exaggerated), but the resonances are specifically American. Indeed, the whole episode echoes the last third of a crucial text in the American racial imaginary, *The Adventures of Huckleberry Finn*. At the end of that novel, Huck and Tom notoriously and problematically keep Jim hidden in a shed on the Phelps estate in order to stage a rescue of him, despite Tom's knowledge that Jim has already been freed. Here, Mona, Seth, and Barbara play Tom-and-Huck-like games with Alfred, and with something of the same romance-inspired self-consciousness (Tom thinks of the *Count of Monte Christo* when he puts Jim in a hole under the shed; Mona and her pals riff on *A Cask of Amontillado* and the talking trees of *Babes in Toyland* as they navigate the underground passage with Alfred). But Alfred reverses this narrative of romance-derived game playing that reinforces established structures of power and knowledge. Just as he and Evie undo the Othello example—they remain together and even marry at the end of the novel—so he reverses the Huck precedent and acts as if he needs to be hidden from Evie well after the need for subterfuge has passed.

Alfred and the race plot continue to resist incorporation into the narrative frame. A group of his friends come to the Gugelstein house to smoke dope, do yoga, and hang out with Mona and her friends; they accuse his friend Luther of stealing Mr. Gugelstein's silver flask; Luther then launches into an antisemitic rant and the group is forced to leave, upsetting both Alfred (who stays behind to be with Evie) and Seth (who, despite his aspirations to Indianness, is really at heart, Mona thinks, "an Old World scholar boy, the kind with cuff links and green skin and no appetite" [207]). And things go from bad to worse: Alfred and Evie are on the verge of splitting up when Mrs. Gugelstein, returning home, finds her photographs of them in bed together; Evie is shipped back to Minneapolis and Alfred fired, to which he responds with a lawsuit for racial discrimination. Although all is (barely) made well at the end of the novel,* the energies unleashed in this section of the book aren't so easily resolved by Jen's comic method; indeed, Luther is severely beaten at a civil rights rally, and even Alfred's response ("that Luther's always all right in the end" [292]) doesn't seem adequate to this intrusion of historical reality into the comic orbit of the novel. For Jews—and, at least for Mona and her family, for these Asians—"the Promised Land has turned out more or less as promised" (135). But not necessarily, it would seem, for Alfred and Luther—a discordant note that remains to complicate the novel's comic celebration of a new, multicultural America.

In *Mona*, then, Jen moves in and through her encounter with Jewishness so as ultimately to pose hard questions of upwardly mobile Asians well as assimilating Jews. And these questions continue to fructify in her work in ways that push her beyond the delightful comedy that marks the first two-thirds of *Typical American* and the vast majority of *Mona*. To

---

* And somewhat problematically too. Luther is also accused of stealing Mr. Gugelstein's silver flask; it was actually taken by a Latino cook at the Pancake House, Fernando, who may also have been the mysterious man who attacked Mona earlier in the novel. Fernando's crime clears Alfred, but it's not necessarily clear that the racial problematics are resolved in a more enlightened way as a result.

make that push, she engages with Jewish fiction making in a subtler, if ultimately more complicating, way. I am thinking here of her acclaimed story "Birthmates," first published in 1995 and included not only in the *Best American Short Stories* volume for that year but also in John Updike's selection of the *Best American Short Stories of the Century* (1999). Jen's protagonist is Art Woo, a fifty-one-year-old traveling salesman for a company in an unnamed "dinosaur" industry. Ambitious but frustrated, facing racist taunts by his boss (who blames the "Japs" for everything wrong in the industry but then consoles Art by telling him he knows he's a "Chink"), worrying obsessively about a white colleague, Billy Shore (who shares his birthday but seems to be doing better at the firm than he), mourning the loss of his girlfriend and of the fetus they aborted, Art is mistakenly booked into a welfare hotel next to a convention he is working. Entering the hotel, he is first greeted by an enormous black man at the desk, then mugged by a crowd of children as he goes up to his room. He wakes up while being tended by an African American woman, a nurse turned heroin addict named Cindy, who keeps him safe from the crowd outside. After feeling a pang of desire for her, he returns to his work, only to find that his birthmate/competitor has moved on to a more promising job in California. His sense of loss and his confrontation with his own mortality combine at the end of the story, where he too contemplates a move West, and, seemingly for the first time, he expresses his sense of loss of both his lover and their almost child, aborted, we now learn, because it would not have been viable outside the womb.

There are no explicit references to Jews, Jewishness, or the canon of Jewish literature in the story, but in many ways this is the one work of Jen's that engages most intensely, and with the greatest degree of contestable energy, with that tradition—and in such a way, I think, as to make us read it differently, just as Mukherjee does. The tale of the failing salesman who is being passed over by the home office, for example, inevitably recalls Arthur Miller's *Death of a Salesman*, a text rich in family dynamics that resonate, ironically, against the context of Art's familylessness. Even richer effects are created by the story's echoes of Grace Paley's "The Long Distance Runner." In that text Paley's pseudonymous protagonist Faith goes for a run in the Brooklyn neighborhood where she grew up and returns to the apartment house in which her family lived, now inhabited by African Americans, as is the entire neighborhood. There, she is at first an object of curiosity, then an object of anger and potential mob violence until she is rescued by the woman who occupies her former apartment, Mrs. Luddy, who hides her under the bed until the crowd disappears. Faith stays with her there for many weeks, becoming almost a part of the family unit, until finally she returns to her own comfortable suburban home—where her own grown children have barely noticed her long absence.

The echoings of Paley's story in Jen's are subtle but unmistakable: the plot arc is the same, the incidents chime with each other. But the effect of those echoings, as it is in the explicit invocation of the black/white divide in *Mona*, is to suggest how complex the position of Asian Americanness is on the American terrain of race. The point of "The Long Distance Runner" is to emphasize the curious admixture of intimacy and distance that exists between Jewish characters and those African Americans who inhabit their former terrain. When a Chinese American like Art Woo enters a welfare hotel—already a significantly different space from an apartment—he is treated, like Faith, as if he were white by the hostile African American inhabitants, even though at work he is treated as if he were not by his complacently racist bosses. And, when he encounters Cindy, these shifting definitions collide:

> "This ain't no place for a nice boy like you," [she says]. That stung a bit, being called *boy*. But more than the stinging, he felt something else. "What about you? It's no place for you, either, you and your kids."
>
> "Maybe so," she said. "But that's how the Almighty planned it, right? You folk rise up while we set and watch." She said this with so little rancor, with something so like intimacy, that it seemed almost an invitation of sorts.[17]

As in *Mona*, but with a tragic rather than comic twist, Art is caught in the shifting definition of his ethnic identity when confronted with the all-American idiom (and experience) of race. His response to the African American Cindy's use of the term *boy* resonates with racial ambiguity: does being called boy sting because it reminds Art of the racist condescension of Billy Shore and his boss? Or because it is an African American woman who puts him in the position of a racialized subject—along with her? But this response rapidly shifts into a more complex, if unnamed, one ("something else") that in turn leads to her placing him in the familiar position of the upwardly mobile—the trajectory commonly ascribed to Jews and Asian Americans, but not available to African Americans: "You folk rise up while we set and watch." And it's at this moment of racial identification that Art feels that her tone, "something so like intimacy," is offering something more, although exactly what her "invitation" might be, and whether it's in his mind or hers, is left thoroughly open by the text.

Complex as the moment may be in terms of defining the shifting racial identification of Asian Americans vis-à-vis African Americans (a dynamic that resembles in many ways the half-racialization of Jews in the first decades of this century), it gains further intensity through Jen's echoes of Paley's story. As with Faith and Mrs. Luddy, a kind of intimacy seems to be established between Art and Cindy; as with Faith, Art moves out to some kind of reconnection with his own would-be family, even if that family consists of his ex-girlfriend, whom he thinks at the end of the story to call and invite to move with him to California. And, as with Faith, this act would seem to happen through his encounter not just with an African American but with the complex historical and ontological facts of black experience itself. But the point of the echoings in the story is also to measure the difference between Art's and Faith's experience. Paley's story defines the long distance that Jewish Americans have run from their ghettoized past. Jen's suggests that, just as Art has not come to terms with his personal traumas, Asian Americans have not yet come to terms with the equivocal racial position they occupy—and the racism they continue to confront. The pointed contrast becomes clearest at the end of the story, as his rivalry with his jocular birthmate Billy Shore, and the inability to imagine a new life for himself symbolized not only by his dead child but also by his failure to mourn for that child, continue to press on Art, even if he seeks to solve the problem by moving to California. Faith can return from her ghetto experience to her family; Gish Jen measures Art's greater alienation by having him (like Mukherjee's Jasmine) light out for the territory, assimilating to Americanness only in his desire to flee from the site of trauma. The downwardly upwardly mobile Asian American has no language with which to limn his own situation—except the residual, shadowy language of the Jewish American, which applies only fitfully and ironically to his condition.

Lan Samantha Chang and the New Immigrant Narrative

Jen's persistent but progressive engagement with the Jewish Asian metonymy, and her working through of the Jewish American fictional example, then, leads her to a position where she interrogates, from within, the model minority narrative that has constricted as it has constructed the dominant discourse on both groups. Deepening over the course of her career from the comic to the tragic, that comparison increasingly turns on the question of race in the most reductive sense of the word—the ways that Asians, like Jews before them, seem to be differentiating themselves from African Americans in the process of entering the so-called promised land. So doing, she moves in quite critical directions, exploring the complacencies as well as the contradictions of the model minority mythos. Much is gained in Jen's interrogation of these problems. But something is lost as well, perhaps by her concentration (like that of many of her peers) on the suburbanized, middle-class professional second and third generation of Asian Americans: a sense of the rawness, the complexity, and the affective challenges of moving into a U.S. cultural milieu, the problems faced by the less advantanged among these communities, and the new, critical culture being built by second- and third-generation Americans of Asian descent.

The fate of the Jewish example I have been tracing throughout this chapter in the new critical culture of contemporary Asian American letters is mixed. Jen's recent work, like Mukherjee's, has gone in different directions. Her most recent novel *The Love Wife*, for example, returns Jen to an überbourgie world very much like Scarshill, and to the complications of crossethnic desire that marks *Mona*; but here the relevant ethnic crossing is between Asians and WASPs, and very blonde WASPs at that. And younger writers by and large have moved on to different material. Just to name two of the more commercially successful, Susan Choi (herself Jewish Korean by birth) has published two accomplished novels juxtaposing Asian American and American narratives of decline and success, *The Foreign Student* (1996) and *American Woman* (2004), but in these works the Asian/Jewish paradigm that Jen explored has little or no purchase. Perhaps even more saliently, Christina Chiu's fascinating story cycle

Troublemaker disrupts the model minority paradigm in a number of ways; it represents an Asian American woman, for example, who, having shocked her mother by marrying an African American, comes up against the bulimia that marks her own driven personality when she confronts a young anorexic Asian girl whose disease ultimately proves fatal. Taking on the central icons of Asian American precursor texts—e.g., the mother-and-family fixation of *The Woman Warrior*, the centrality of cooking, food, and nourishment that recurs throughout Kingston's landmark work, or Amy Tan's more popular ones—Chiu proposes a model of Asian American transgressivity within the contours of model minority upward mobility culture that affiliates transgressing Asians with queer or African American others—but not with Jews.

There is one text among these, however, that deserves mention, before I continue on to what I think of as the most interesting revision of Asian American writerly engagement with Jews and Jewishness; a novel by Philippine-born, MacArthur Fellowship–winning playwright Han Ong, *Fixer Chao* (2001). The novel narrates the story of a gay male hustler turned unsuccessful author, William Paulinha, who is hired by an embittered, unsuccessful Jewish novelist named Shem to pose as a feng shui expert in order to con Shem's ex-wife, the daughter of a more prominent Jewish American novelist named Bill Hood and his circle of rich Park Avenue friends. After reading a few books, Paulhina reinvents himself as "Master Chao" and sets out to intervene in the lives of gullible New Yorkers eager for what they take to be sage Oriental wisdom. His pose grants him temporary fame—he is named Feng Shui master of the year—but collapses with a melodramatic murder of a blackmailer, after which he flees, penniless, to California. The masquerade ends with no one profiting from the scam but Shem, who has not only orchestrated Paulinha's impersonation but also his unmasking: Shem's exposé in *New York* magazine becomes a best-selling book, the success that he has been dreaming of for his entire second-rate career.

The novel is remarkable for its dyspeptic view of human nature across the board. But it is most remarkable for its angry engagement with complexities of ethnic identity—or, more accurately, the discourses about that identity—in nineties New York. The politics of ethnic identity it limns, however, are far from simple. Paulinha is an angry critic of the white racism he encounters, not only of the craze for feng shui or even in the inability of white New Yorkers to tell the difference between Chinese and

Filipinos, but of racist cultural representations as well: his best friend, an actress named Presiosa, appears in a Sondheim-like musical extravaganza called *Primitives* as a grunting savage, for example, before becoming a bit-player in the Fixer Chao masquerade—and robbing the houses that he has gained entry to in his guise as feng shui master. But the novel also includes a viciously satirical portrait of a young Asian American novelist on the make, Paul Toledo Lin, whose contribution to the field is to delineate the demasculinized condition in which Asian men discover themselves. Like Shem, Lin attempts to profit from his acquaintance with Chao, but his book bores his audience and Paulinha as much as it clearly does Ong.

The novel is remarkable as well for its treatment of white characters, particularly its Jewish ones, or rather, to be more accurate, its focus on the Jewishness of the white characters. Shem is introduced not merely as a novelist of Jewish descent; rather, we learn, "Shem C. was a Jew.... His name was given to him by his father. He told me it was the Yiddish word for name."* His daughter is known as a young "Jewess," her mother as "the sparkling Jewish princess" (24, 244). Similarly, Shem's father-in-law is given a withering portrait:

> a filthy, social-climbing human being if ever there was one—a man whose two or three good books were thought to be such contributions to American letters that they shielded the rest of his weak, watery (needlessly mournful) work from critical reproof—suggested pulling a few strings. A lizard slithering, that was it, long tongue licking its own lips in a ritual of self-satisfaction; frightening eyes magnified by psychotic black-framed glasses, always on the lookout for the next piece of ass and finding which, he would use his marquee value to oh so gently steer it toward his bed. (24)

Hood has, unforgivably for Shem, humiliated him by arranging a lucrative writing contract, in the face of which Shem falls into a protracted bout of writer's block. Shem's response to this "privilege transformed into hell"

---

*Shem, of course, is the name of Noah's eldest son, the progenitor, in the Hebrew Bible and subsequent commentary of both the Jewish and the Arab peoples. But he's also identified in a good deal of contemporary Bible commentary as the patriarch of East as well as West Asian nations—which is to say that his name is a crossroads where competing Orientalizations, that of the Semite and that of the East Asian, meet.

(26) is to seek revenge on those who offend him where it hurts them most, especially Hood, whom he coaches his daughter to accuse of an act of molestation Shem's ex-wife, who turns out to be Hood's lover and not his daughter, although she is young enough to be such, and a rich Asian American woman named Louise Yamada, who is Shem's former lover and who ends up as Hood's new one. And this endeavor at revenge is described in ethnically specific terms. On the last pages of the novel, Paulinha/Chao sums up the scam in which he has participated as follows: Shem "is a Jew who directed his animosity towards other Jews with a vindictiveness that verged on a calling. Bill Hood, the top Jew, was usurping a position that rightly belonged to him, to Shem. And he wanted, in a way that was devised on the spot, piecemeal, a plan . . . to move from the sidelines to the center" (329).

Complicating things further, the text's concerns with the dynamics of Asian identity and with those of Jewish identity are, from the first, interwoven. Not only his plot but also Shem's own book project involve him in Orientalism; the book that he proposes to write is one "with some ridiculous notion about Oriental motifs in recent American literature, an arcane—and what's more untrue—thing with no possible commercial appeal" that nevertheless garners him his sweetheart deal from his father-in-law's publisher after a perfunctory consideration (25). Of course, he is to a certain extent at one with the other whites who fill their house with Orientalia and listen to feng shui expert Chao with bated breath, especially the upwardly mobile Jews (including, to add another one to the gallery of caricatures, a repellent book editor named Cardie Karchoff with "a natural frizzy pompadour . . . sticking straight up the middle, so that the impression she gave was of the Bride of Frankenstein," a woman whose class standing Paulinha finds offensive ["Cardie. As in what her father, the cardiologist, did"] and whose consciousness of her Jewish history he finds contemptible: "Kerchpoff. Jews from Russia. She let you know as soon as you met her . . . as if she were the only Jew with a lineage traceable to Russia in the whole history of the world" [99]). But as such—as a writer attempting to profit, however unsuccessfully, from the public vogue for Asianness—Shem's not easily distinguished from Paul Chan Chuang Toledo Lin, whose magnum opus *Peking Man? Or Woman?* is as much an instance of that vogue as a critique of it, an attempt to fit gender complexity "into his patented, pet theme: Orientalism" as a way, or such is Paulinha's analysis, of disguising his sexual orientation from the world (or himself) (370).

Nor is Shem easily distinguished from the Asians he employs. This is true in the crudest sense, that of appearance; he seems to be one of those "Mongolian" Jews whose presence in the pre-1924 imaginary we noted in the previous chapter. When Paulinha first meets Shem, he records: "Shem C. was a Jew. His eyes sloped open at the sides, giving him a Far Eastern look, but his pupils were the cool gray of steel."* But as that latter ascription suggests, he's Jewish in the classic sense as a manipulator, a finagler—in a word, a *fixer*, the very identity (with its Malamudian overtones of sacrificial victim) that Paulinha takes on for himself. Not for nothing does a hustler who plays a role that brings him notoriety, fame, and fortune call Shem "Sham": both Paulinha and Shem are upwardly mobile hustlers, although one works the New York Port Authority and the other the salons of Park Avenue. What, after all, is Shem doing by marrying the daughter of a wealthy man other than making himself into a bought man? What, after all, does Paulinha do when he plays the role of Chao but seek revenge on the whites he encounters for their racism, their power, their privilege—revenge being, of course, the very wellspring of Shem's identity? (Cardie's abusive comments about her Asian servants, for example, cause Paulinha to alter her feng shui arrangements, with ironically disastrous effects on her life.) The only difference between the two, it would seem, is that the Jewish sham artist is a better conniver than the Asian he dupes.

For all its unpleasantness and borderline antisemitism (largely that of the first-person narrator, one assumes), *Fixer Chao* is a text that casts into perspective the Asian American engagement with the Jewish literary example. The book radiates with a paranoid version of the sense we've also seen communicated by *Publisher's Weekly* or by Jen's desire to pass muster with Cynthia Ozick—the sense that the New York publishing world is dominated by Jews and that their relations with each other—the bestowal of favors, book contracts, patronage—is fundamentally clannish, intraethnic, to the point of incestuousness (thematized in the book, through the recurrence of incestuous and neoincestuous desire among the novels' Jews). Paulinha's attempts to break into that world as

---

* So too is Bill Hood, whom Paulinha/Chao describes as follows: "He had salt-and-pepper hair, a pear-shaped face, a longish hook nose, pockmarked skin, thin lips that suggested a stingy nature, and dim eyes that had the curved silhouette of an umbrella, sloping down at both sides" (202). A conjunction of antisemitic and anti-Asian physical markers, Hood is a walking compendium of stereotypes.

a con man (and ultimately a writer, since the book is his version of the story Shem has sold), then, are to be read as a sign of the complex mix of ethnoracial envy and desire that informs aspirants to the cultural capital claimed for—and indeed achieved by—Jews. And his experiences there—including his ultimate failure as a writer—are to be read as informed by the set of understandings of the world that I mentioned in the previous chapter that distinguished the younger generation of Asian Americans from their immediate predecessors: a sense of the inadequacy of the model minority paradigm for dealing with the class reticulation of contemporary Asians, the supplementing of the discourse of race with that of gender and alternative sexualities, above all, a heightened sense of the exclusionary racism of white Americans, including white Americans who are Jewish.

I read Ong's text, then, as symptomatic of larger ambivalences that structure the Asian/Jewish writerly encounter. His work, crude and angry though it may be, represents one possible response to the imaginative priority of the Jew and the patterns of Jewish experience as a marker of ethnicity across the board as well as a compulsive continuation of that pattern through the very intensity of that response. Another, subtler, and more cogent response is that provided by the work of another writer—to my mind, one of the most accomplished writing today—Lan Samantha Chang. In her remarkable novella *Hunger* (1998) Chang takes up the most central questions posed by the Jewish example—the alienness of the immigrant; the thorny paths of assimilation or acculturation, particularly on the charged and difficult terrain of a masculinity tested by cultural or intellectual achievement—in such a way as to wrest them, subtly and magisterially, from the articulation given them by her Jewish precursors. My invocation here of Harold Bloom's terminology is, again, explicit, albeit inflected in a cultural direction; what she performs thereby is what Bloom might call an *apophrades*, a return of the dead—a reversal in which the text that comes after its precursor actually seems to come before it, to replace it ontologically. Or to put it another way, in taking up the central themes of Jewish American fiction and experience from an Asian perspective, she retells its narratives in such a way as to make the Asian, rather than the Jewish, the baseline for the experience of immigrant desire and acculturating loss. And in so doing, as Eric Liu might put it, she changes the inflection of the American question from Jewish to Asian.

That the Jewish example is not unknown to her is clear. Like Jen, Bharati Mukherjee, or Jhumpa Lahiri,* Chang has generously spoken of her debt to the previous generation of Jewish novelists, especially Bernard Malamud: "Overall, I found the post-World War II Jewish writers to be very inspirational.... When I was learning to write I was very personally affected by [Malamud's] early work: in its deep sorrow, its humanity and ruthlessness, its hints of the fabulous."[18] Her most accomplished work to date, *Hunger*, enters into direct dialogue with Malamud through a remarkable narrative trick. The story details traces the trajectory of Tian, son of doting middle-class Chinese family, who flees the Cultural Revolution to Taiwan, where he became a violin prodigy who then emigrates to America: having seen an Israeli musician performing with the San Francisco Symphony, he vows to succeed as a musician in New York, but ends up only a busboy in a Chinese restaurant. Specifically, the story traces the effects of his failure on his two daughters, one of whom—the talented one—he beats and the other—the one without talent—he neglects. In a stunning turn of the narrative screw, we realize near the end of the story that it has been told not by his wife but by her ghost, lingering to reckon the effects of Tian's physical and emotional violence on the daughters she has failed to protect. Chang's blending of Chinese folk belief with a Malamudian conjunction of the "fabulous" and "the sorrowful" suggests that Chang positions herself at the intersection of the Jewish and Asian American experiences. But she does so in a completely unique and original way.

---

*Lahiri has written an elegant and appreciative introduction to a recent edition of *The Magic Barrel*, first published in 1958, in which she claims Malamud as not just a powerful influence, but a career-altering one: "The experience of reading [*The Magic Barrel*] was akin to a rite of initiation: thrilling, inspiring, and accompanied by a sense that my appreciation for the art of fiction had been profoundly, permanently altered." She goes on to describe Malamud's appeal to her as an immigrant writer—and a human being—in ways that echo Chang's trope of hunger: "As the child of Bengali immigrants to the United States, I recognized, with particular affinity, many of the themes involved in Malamud's portrayal of Jewish immigrants.... But to deem this astonishing book 'immigrant fiction': would be both inaccurate and absurd. What Malamud locates about the immigrant experience—a sense of loss, of struggle, of wanting what we cannot have—constitutes the nuts and bolts of all dramatic fiction.... Malamud's characters ... are filled with regret, and, above all, with longing.... [They] want endlessly: they want better lives for their children, they want affordable housing, they want freedom, they want respect. None of these desires is exclusive to immigrants, of any one place or generation. All are central to the human condition" (x).

Unlike Jen, Chang looks at the tragic underside of that process of assimilation by culture that's crucial to the model-minority and assimilation narratives; unlike Malamud, she binds that tragedy specifically to the Chinese American experience.

Indeed, Chang's narrative works to turn the ones I have been describing above—both the cultural narratives of model minority success and the Jewish and Asian American texts that reflect on, refract, remake that process—inside out, in ways far more radical than those that Jen or Malamud employ. Thus, like Jen, her most immediate precursor (both as an Asian American woman highly lauded by the writing establishment and as a star student at the Iowa Writer's Workshop), she gives us a male protagonist who is a failure: as Min puts it, with a mixture of pain and ruefulness that is characteristic of her tone throughout the story, "some Chinese make their fortunes in America. Tian and I were not among them" (86). But Tian's lack of success is different in origins and implications than Ralph Chang's; whereas the representation of Ralph comports to the pattern of the immigrant-schlemiel, Tian's is tied to a wider variety of factors. He is a truly gifted musician, and the frustrations of his career have as much to do with institutional racism conjoined with cultural misprision as his own taciturn, driven personality and his not-unjustified pride. Unable to cope with the faculty politics at the conservatory where he lands (thanks to a recommendation from his Taiwanese teacher Ma), burdened by poor English and rigid teaching methods and shadowed by suspicions that result from cultural misunderstanding (he and Min find a valuable tuning fork after his recital, which they take as a sign of good luck; the colleague who has lost it thinks they are thieves), he is denied a permanent job and is unable to find another, having rejected out of pride the one chance he is given to continue his violin teaching at a girls' academy in the Midwest. To make ends meet, he is forced to take a job as a busboy and part-time kitchen help at the restaurant where he first met his wife and pours, with a maniacal energy born of his hunger for achievement, all of his musical genius into the training of his daughters, with the disastrous results of neglect and abuse I noted above. In short, by detailing Tian's course from promising young musician to horrific, violent father Chang shows how the project of social advancement by cultural achievement can lead to the reassertion of a violent masculinism as well as the gentle or sinister androgyny Frank Chin satirizes and Suzuki diagnoses.

And its revision of the immigrant/assimilation narrative itself is yet more extensive. For, while both of the daughters follow out the second-generation success story, they do so in such a way as to index its costs as well as its accomplishments. The most obvious of these is the elder daughter Ruth's rebellion; for it's clear that, while it follows out the rebellious-child-rejects-controlling-parent-in-order-to-Americanize paradigm that is familiar from so many immigrant novels, it adds an important twist to them. For Ruth is truly Tian's child, and in two senses: first, because she inherits his musical talent—indeed, she surpasses him, because, where he is driven by "bitterness," she can coax sweetness and mystery out of his violin(58). But, more than that, the essence of his being is reflected in hers—she is most like Tian (and unlike Min or her sister Anna) in being a creature of "hunger," "the willfulness, the intense desires, [that] ran in her blood" (67). And she follows out a Tian-like trajectory both in her departure from the house (although he goes East and she goes West, to San Francisco) and, abortively, her musical career. She is offered a chance to leave home and attend a conservatory by Tian's mentor/rival/boss Dr. Spaeth, to become, as it were, a more successful, because less conflicted, and perhaps most important, English-speaking and Americanized version of her father. This he cannot abide: in one of many acts of possessiveness and cruelty, he forbids her to leave, so that he can remain her teacher. When he beats her mercilessly, in sum, he is beating the ghost of his own talent—and testifying to the self-balking quality of the very desire he and Ruth both possess.

Their other daughter, Anna, bears the signs not so much of abuse as neglect; because she lacks Ruth's Tian-like genius, he treats her with a contempt that, oddly, becomes the ground of her salvation: unlike Ruth, she's able to go to college, have a successful career, and indeed remakes the apartment after her mother dies and entertains friends and occasional overnight guests. But it's clear that hers is an attenuated lot, that the imprinting of her family drama has left her unprepared for intimacy. "In the moments where some change in the mood might take place" with her lover, she shies away from him, stares at her hands. "Watching [Anna] I wonder this," says the fretful and guilty ghost of her mother, who knows that she should have protected her daughters but did not. "How long must we wait to outlast sorrow?" (100).

A lifetime, it seems—indeed, longer than a lifetime, an eternity—for the sorrow the daughters experience is itself matched by that of

Min's ghostly presence it calls into being. That sorrow is, to be sure, nothing original: it is, as we saw, the ground of her affinity with Malamud and an ironically distant echo of the weltschmerz that, as we saw in the previous chapter, defines the racial identity of the Oriental Jew in Yezierska, in Cahan, even in Hutchins Hapgood. But what Chang does is not only to deconstruct that desire but disarticulate it from the Jewish context to which it is inextricably bound. Seeing an Israeli violinist prodigy may have been what drew Tian from China to disaster in New York; but Chang suffuses the narrative he seeks to retrace with different ethnoracial resonances of longing and disaster. Tian's ghost, unlike Min's, returns to the ruined house of his cultured parents on the mainland, from which he had to flee during the Cultural Revolution—the place whose loss, Min tells us, gives him his sadness, his longing, his sense of displacement, but also his hunger for achievement, renown, genius. Tian's desire for success via cultural achievement may rhyme with that of the Jews, but it traces out its own itinerary of exile and return.

Were this all Chang does, it would, as some of us might say, have been enough. But the story also offers a countervision to that projected by upward mobility narratives, a vision not so much critical or affirmative as compassionate, and one that pushes beyond the ethnic specificity of the model minority mythos to something that aspires to be more primal: the terrain of imaginative desire that underlies the myth, gives it some larger meaning and deeper significance. Near the end of the novella, Min imagines the history that brought Tian to America:

> In Beijing, a boy takes music lessons from a German tutor who presents him with the gift of a violin. A slender-bellied instrument, with a rich,brown color and golden ribs that shimmer on its back. Later, a young man swims into the sea, holding a precious bundle in one hand above the darkened water. He gasps; he struggles onto a ship. As I imagine this ... I want him to get away, escape his life, even though I know he will not escape, cannot escape the punishment that inevitably comes to people who dare to dream such flagrant and extravagant designs. I cannot hide him. Even the ancient broken ship, the *Sonya*, with her vast indifference—how could she, I think, have failed to creak and shudder under the weight of this man's desire? The immen-

sity of such hunger, folded into his cloth shelter, waiting in the middle of the sea. (113)

In offering a vision of desire underlying this narrative of an immigrant's quest for freedom, autonomy, and legitimation through cultural experience, Chang simultaneously evokes and questions the emotion—the structure of feeling, to quote Raymond Williams—that has proved to be fundamental to both the Jewish and the Asian American experience even as the specifics of that experience have varied from the culturally hyperbolized model. Indeed, she does not so much critique or even comment on those emotional structures as reduce them to basic images—a man, a sea, a violin—and experiences—of escape from oppression, exile into loneliness, and the hunger for affirmation that devours that most hallowed icon of immigrant experience: family. The image of the violin, and the narrative of assimilation through (Western) cultural attainment that accompanies it, suggests that it is not just immigrant desire but also all the things that are privileged by the model minority discourse that lead to the disaster that is Tian's life in America. Yet it also suggests that there is a terrible beauty about them, as if the purity of the hunger were, like that of the music Tian makes, something to be as celebrated as it is at one and the same time condemned.

This push toward the archetypal does complex cultural work. On the one hand, it has a powerful ethnoracial salience despite—or more accurately because of—the claim to universalism that underlies it. Bernard Malamud, as I suggested in the last chapter, once famously observed that any man could be a Jew; but the impulse not only in his fiction but in that of his generation—Bellow is particularly important in this regard as well as Malamud—is to do the reverse: to make the Jewish into the baseline for the universal. The immigrant becomes, in *Augie March*, the Huck Finn or Tom Sawyer de nos jours; later in his career, second-generation Jew Moses Herzog is made into the archetypal modern man not only because he writes personal letters to Dostoevsky or Nietzsche but because he models the existential subject let loose in the contemporary world in all its glorious ludicrousness. In Malamud, as Mukherjee, Lahiri, and Chang all insist in their reverent readings, the sorrows but also the triumphs of the immigrant become a token of the rueful universal human condition itself. But, in her simultaneous and most un-Malamudian burst of eloquence and in her equally un-Bellovian imagistic concision, Chang proposes to install the Asian immigrant as the new benchmark of human experience. Replacing Bellow's rollicking picaresque or existential comedy with a narrative of immigrant tragedy, replacing Malamud's conjunction of "sorrow and ruthlessness" with a conjunction of sorrow and compassion, she supplants their vision with her own multiply invested one just as subtly and just as magisterially as she replaces the westering itinerary of the eastern European immigrant with the eastering trajectory of a Chinese one—or, more accurately, the progress of the European immigrant west to America with a shuttling back and forth between a China and a U.S. that negates the teleological narrative of the immigrant plot. If Chang succeeds where, I think, Mukherjee and Jen ultimately falter, it is in part because she has their example to fall back on (she is as generous in her acknowledgment to Jen as she is to Malamud) and in part because her imagination works by internalizing all her precursor texts, rather than wrestling with them via reinscription, parody, and play. She might best be figured, in other words, as a more successful version of her character Ruth, someone who can perform in the Western cultural sphere with sublime ease; but, like Ruth, she can only do so because Tian went before her.

To say that isn't, I think, to deny the power of Chang's recasting of the drama of immigrant desire; instead, I think, it is to enhance it in a specific social and historical context rather than the universal one (which, as powerful as it may be as a human impulse, ultimately pushes toward the bland). Chang's evocative images, her sense of the powers and fallibilities of immigrant desire, her demonstration that the high-cultural path to ethnic success in America often conduces to a violence that plays itself out over the generations, speak with special force to *both* Jewish American and Asian American communities as they each struggle with their own ascription as model minorities. Taking her vision seriously would mean that each group might be able to escape the dialectic of anxiety and envy founded in a common mythos of cultural aspiration with which we've seen Jewish and Asian writers struggling. Instead, Chang suggests, they might be permitted see themselves differently—not as success stories or antisuccess stories, as model minorities or as rebels against that status, as culture heroes or culture villains, but rather as peoples struggling at different times and with different means to surmount processes larger than themselves, as fellow wanderers, fellow exiles, fellow swimmers barely braving the waves of history.

Jews as the "New Asians": The Next Wave

The tides of history, however, continue to flow, and one of the most striking aspects of that tide has been the transformation of Jewish as well as Asian entry into the U.S. Particularly in the aftermath of the breakup of the former Soviet Union, new, poorer, usually secular Jews have emigrated to North America in large numbers, and they, too, have begun to enter the literary field. Such works as Gary Shteyngart's *The Russian Debutante's Handbook*, Lara Vapnyar's *There Are Jews in My House* and David Bezmozgis's *Natasha and Other Stories* register the experience of these new Jewish immigrants—and enact for their authors a version of the same upward-mobility-through-literary-achievement path we've been looking at throughout this chapter (thus all three have been published regularly in that arbiter of writerly success, the *New Yorker*, and have been reviewed favorably in the *Times*; Shteyngart has been profiled in the *New York Times Magazine*). What's most important about these writers and the experiences they represent, at least in the context of this chapter, is that all three comport more accurately to the model I've outlined for a certain strain of Asian American writing and experience than to the classic narratives of Jewish American experience. Like Jen, Ong, and Chang in particular, Shteyngart, Vapnyar, and Bezmozgis are quite astringently engaged with deconstructing the lineaments of the Jewish American success story, in portraying new Jewish immigrants as standing outside—if not subverting outright—the norms of that story. And, in doing so, they call our attention back to all the qualities repressed in the turn away from the construction of the Jew as Oriental—and toward an understanding of the Jewish experience in America that charts an eastering, not a westering, itinerary for the experience.

So, for example, Bezmozgis's *Natasha and Other Stories* subverts just about every dominant paradigm one might imagine for thinking about the experience of Jews in (North) America. Himself an immigrant to Toronto from Latvia, Bezmozgis dwells on the seedier aspects of the Russian experience in North America. Berman, the (autobiographical?) protagonist of his prize-winning, *New Yorker*-published short story, "Natasha," is, like David

Schearle or, for that matter, Alex Portnoy, a sensitive adolescent coming to terms with the complexities of adult desire; unlike these two, however, he finds himself initiated into sex by his fourteen-year-old cousin Natasha, who has emigrated from Russia Zina with her prostitute mother (who has entered into an arranged marriage with his sweet, studious, feckless uncle Fima) and is herself one step away from prostitution—Natasha has earned money in Russia by making porn films at a secluded dacha and ultimately leaves the besotted protagonist for his best friend, a drug dealer. Most forcefully, perhaps, the representation of contemporary Toronto youth—bored, stoned, alienated, with only Rufus the drug dealer encouraging Berman's cultural interests and aspirations—chimes with that of the Russia from which they have all escaped but to which Zina alone retains her ties, scamming Fima by keeping up her relation with her former husband, Natasha's father, with expensive phone calls she claims are to her mother. The dacha at which the porn movies are produced is the exact image of Rufus's suburban home—in both places drugs and/or sex are subsidiary to the pursuit of innocent leisure, a perpetual party; Moscow is as fully possessed by a capitalist ethos as the Canadian suburbs—its where Zina's scam originates and perhaps returns. The immigrant myth, in other words, is turned on its head: there's no difference between the Old World and the New except, perhaps, that the New World is full of naifs like Fima—and that, at the end of the story, Berman vows not to be one of them.

The story, like all of Bezmozgis's work, thus complicates the assimilation/acculturation narrative to the point of unrecognizability. The same enterprise is more comically pursued in Shteyngart's *The Russian Debutante's Handbook,* published to enormous acclaim in 2002. His protagonist, Vladimir Girshkin, comes from a fairly privileged but not unoppressed background in the former Soviet Union—he is a sickly but imaginative child of a Jewish family able to emigrate, via Jimmy Carter's ransoming of Soviet Jews, in 1979. Both Girshkin père and mère find material achievement in America—he as a doctor who runs Medicare scams, largely with recent immigrants; she as a businesswoman who, among other things, specializes in buying up assets of the bankrupt former Soviet Union. Like the Changs in *Mona,* they move to Scarsdale and invest in their son's educational success: Vladimir describes himself as "the coddled single child of Westchester parents who had once paid twenty-five thousand dollars a year to send him to a progressive Midwestern college."[19] The effect on both of the parents, however, is unsettlingly different. His father is as alienated from his work here as he was in Russia—he barely made his way through medical school in the former Soviet Union, and specializes in using recent Uzbeki immigrants to perpetrate his frauds while tending to his gardens in Scarsdale and Sag Harbor. His mother discovers her true calling in the dog-eat-dog world of American business; in her the American value of materialism intertwines monstrously with her Russian-born racism and homophobia, although she hasn't fully mastered the contemporary ways of concealing them: ("I have to fire someone in office," she tells Victor. "He is American African. I am nervous I will say something wrong.... You must teach me to be sensitive to Africans this weekend" [15]). As for Vladimir, he is stuck in a dead-end job at the Russia desk of the Emma Lazarus Immigrant Aid Society and in a dead-end relationship with a pudgy East Village dominatrix (the daughter of a Westchester orthodontist) named Challah. In short, he is beset with reminders of the Jewish immigrant experiences of the past, reminders that ring ironically against his own experience.

These experiences are represented in the text, as in Jen, very much through the mechanism of parody—here, specifically, parodies of the central narratives of the Jewish American experience. The narrative of mother love that resonates from *David Levinsky* (whose mother dies after attacking young Russian hooligans who have been harassing her beloved *boychick*) through *Call It Sleep* (that virtual paean to oedipality) through *Portnoy's Complaint* (ditto) gets redacted into Vladimir's nameless Mother, who protects her sickly child from antisemitic classmates in Russia with a fierceness reminiscent of Mrs. Levinsky. "He had always thought of himself as being the most thorough of Yids," muses Vladimir at one point, "small, stooped, sickly, and with a book regularly by his side. But how could anyone say that of Mother, who not only read Vladimir about the Battle of Stalingrad but looked ready to wage it all by herself" (175–176). Once in America, Mother extends the process by taking the lead in the effort to de-Jewify (or at least un-Yiddify) Vladimir, seeking to transform not only his love life and career but also his very bodily *hexis*: "Vladimir," she tells him, "you walk like a Jew . . . like an old Jew from the shtetl. Little Rebbe Girshkin" (44). Initially furious and humiliated, Vladimir, a reverse Portnoy, is so overcome by guilt and residual mother love that he allows her to teach him to "*walk like a gentile.* You had to keep your chin in the air. The spine straight." "He took his first baby steps," the narrator records, "to her delight" (46).

As in that passage, with its echoing of the tropes of Americanization as a new birth, the parodic focus of the book extends from mother love to other classic topoi of the immigrant novel. Its emphasis on the bodily refashioning of the immigrant, for example, reenacts the obsessive focus of Cahan's David Levinsky, who, as Donald Weber has wonderfully argued, understands his Americanization in terms of the disciplining of his immigrant Jewish body—of learning how to speak, eat, gesture like an American.[20] Classic cultural narratives, too, are clearly on Shteyngart's radar. Vladimir's loaded relation with his overpowering Jewish mother also spills into a revision of the model minority narrative, for she ceaselessly reminds him of his inability in America to conform to the pattern of Jewish intellectual success to which he has been raised:

> Vladimir . . . suffered under his mother's accusative wails as B-plus report cards were ceremoniously burned in the fireplace; as china was sent flying for chess-club prizes not won; as he once caught her in her study sobbing at three in the morning, cradling a photo of the three-year-old Vladimir playing with a toy abacus, so bright-eyed, so enterprising, so full of hope. (14)

The narratives of assimilation, acculturation, Americanization, and the specific narrative of triumph via the model minority pathway, in other words, get mocked by Shteyngart with a comic glee that reveals—and revels in—the physical and emotional pain that are the concomitants of these processes (Sander Gilman compares the early pages of this novel to *Oblomov*, but they read to me more like Gogol or Bulgakov).[21] And the comic note in the novel accelerates in its latter half in which Vladimir—fleeing a gay mob boss who tries to have sex with him in a Miami hotel room—ends up in "Stolovia," a mythical eastern European country where he gets involved with a group of gangsters whose father he had helped in America, so effectively that he ultimately becomes something of a crime czar himself. (In everything-goes Stolovia, Vladimir feels as though "his traditional outsider's place in the social hierarchy had been completely usurped" by Russian gangsters and Stolovian professors turned terrorists; there, in other words, he can—like his mother—move from "victim to victimizer" [380, 366].) In Stolovia, moreover, he falls in love with a beautiful American *shikse* named Morgan, who in turn gets involved with the aforementioned terrorists, and ends up shot by his gangster comrades in a comic-grotesque denouement that sends him back to the U.S to become Morgan's husband, an accountant "on the partnership track" in her father's firm and a father himself—the realization of many immigrants' desire, perhaps, but hardly the pot of gold at the end of the rainbow that stirs immigrant dreams (427).

In his own way, in other words, Shteyngart performs the same kind of revisionary maneuvers we're seen in contemporary Asian American fiction, and to something of the same end: a hollowing out of the hallowed narratives by which immigrant experience is rendered, a replacement of those narratives by ones stressing the physical and psychic costs of immigration and the absurdities, failures, and disjunctures of the model minority paradigm. "America, it seemed, was not entirely defenseless against the likes of Vladimir Girshkin," he muses as he prepares to depart for Stolovia. "There was a sorting mechanism at work by which the beta immigrant was discovered, branded by an invisible b on his forehead, and eventually rounded up and put on the next plane back to some dank Anatevka (the shtetl in *Fiddler on the Roof)*" (169). But more than this: America, in fact, seems in the first half of the book only a somewhat less sinister version of the Russia from which the Girshkins have emigrated, and, in the later stages of the book, is indistinguishable from the Stolovia in which he finds himself. To put it another way, while Vladimir may not be harassed by thugs and officials in the U.S., he's pursued by gangsters there, just as in his new Stolovian life. The one constant in all three of these places, in fact, is Victor's Russian Jewishness, which makes him an exoticized Other wherever he finds himself: a Yid in Russia (where it brings him nothing but grief), a Russian Jew in America (and hence an object of desire to Americans familiar only with the native kind—a "stinky Russian bear" who nevertheless seems to attract a bevy of American beauties), an American Jew in Stolovia (and hence credited with preternatural cunning by antisemitic Russian mobsters) (207).

But—and this ultimately leads to the second interesting contact point with the Asian American writers I have been describing—in so doing Shteyngart reinscribes Jewishness as a labile racial and ethnic category or, more accurately, uses Jewishness to index the inherent lability of racial and ethnic identities in a transnational context. Like Mukherjee's Alfie Judah (or for that matter Roth's Coleman Silk), for example, Vladimir is read in the racial encoding of the U.S. as Hispanic in ways that allow him to impersonate (as he disastrously does) the son of a crime boss:

> "As you can see" [says his friend, petty criminal Baobob Pirelli] "I'm as white as a sheet. You got that olive-skinned thing going, and with that facial hair you look like a young Yasir Arafat."
> "But I'm not quite . . . Jordi's what . . . Spanish?"
> "Don't ever call him Spanish. Jordi's *fiercely* Catalan."
>
> (133)

Though, of course, when Vladimir meets him, the Catalan Jordi looks not like Picasso but "a middle-aged Jew with a textile business" (135), which is to say that while Vladimir's Jewishness can be misread as another sort of ethnicity in the U.S, the same thing happens the other way around. The same *not quite*-ness (an echo of the *not-white*ness of the pre-1920s Jew?) is complemented by a host of other off- or not-yet-white Jews whom he encounters throughout the course of the novel. At a New York party appear the Libber sisters, whose father had "discovered the world's oldest dreidel . . . two pale, identical beauties with a slightly Asiatic cast" (73): the aura of incestuousness or at least uncanny similarity hangs over their doubleness, resonates in their Oriental/Jewish "Asiatic cast" (Sephardic tinge?). But the throwaway line about their father also reminds us of the origins of the dreidel itself, not as a kitschy Hannukah children's game but as a reminder of the Jewish exile throughout both the East and the West: its four faces represent, in one account, Babylonia, Egypt, Greece, and Rome, the four corners of the ancient world to which Jews wandered.

Most powerfully of all among these multiethnic figures is Mother, whose hair, we are told, was "darker than the exhaust hanging over [Leningrad] . . . they called her *Mongolka,* and she was, indeed, one-eighth Mongolian" (13). Indeed, via the dominating character of Mother, the leaching phenomenon between Jews and Asians noted in the previous chapter transpires: "Mongolka" links Jews and Asians—the two cynosures of the model minority mythos—together under the sign of a common unscrupulousness, the flip side of that mythos, the point at which anti-Jewish and anti-Asian constructions originally converged. Indeed, Mother's unique Russian/Mogolian/Jewish American synthesis is mimicked by that of the gangs her son encounters, composed of similar Tatar/Georgian/Russian criminals, to which Vladimir brings her distinctive brand of qualities and abilities. When he returns to an East that he has abandoned, Victor brings his mother's Jewish Americanized know-how to bear on eastern European criminal enterprise and shows he's not only his mother's son but a proper alpha—which is to say utterly unscrupulous—immigrant. Indeed, her unscrupulousness becomes the keynote to his success in eastern Europe, which he unites into a mini-international conglomerate of vice that marries Western corporate efficiencies with eastern European criminal enterprise. Not for nothing does Vladimir consult, as he plans the pyramid scheme that forms the basis of his criminal empire, with the internalized voice of Mother (who tells him: "take them for all they've got") as well as "Carlo Ponzi . . . the alpha immigrant from Parma, the little *gonif* that could" (188). Oscillating between eastern European and American inscriptions of ethnic identity and criminality, Shteyngart creates a blurring or dizzying effect in which these inscriptions are revealed to be mirror images of each other, different in specifics but similar in their divergence from the normalizing structures and patterns imposed on them in the U.S. imaginary.

Shteyngart's endeavor here, in other words, is to disarticulate the immigrant narrative in general and the Jewish narrative in particular as well as from the all-too-familiar associations they have come to accrue—as paradigmatic of the narratives of assimilation or acculturation, of model minorityness, suburbanization, success. Vladimir's destiny chimes more with that of Chang's Tian (in its downward spiral) or Ong's Paulinha/Chao (in its embrace of criminality) than it does with Levinsky's David Schearle's or even Alexander Portnoy's. His itinerary toward Americanization takes him East, not West, toward the undoing of the model minority model rather than the patient following out of its dictates. To be sure, he envisions, on the last page of the novel, a successful, safe, indeed quite boring assimilated identity for his and Morgan's son—"an American in America . . . growing up adrift in a private world of electronic goblins and quiet sexual urges . . . serious and a bit dull." But Vladimir's destiny in the West must run through and encompass "the fear and madness of . . . Eastern lands"—all the unassimilated, unassimilable elements of experience that Vladimir has had to encompass in Stolovia in order to survive in the U.S. (452). In the end, in other words, Vladimir's trajectory—like Shteyngart's, like those of the generation for which he speaks—must not only encompass but also embrace all that the Jewish American assimilation story left out of the picture, all that the Asian American writers of our generation have struggled to put back in.

CONCLUSION
The Klezmering of America

AS I WAS PUTTING the finishing touches on this book in the fall of 2006, I found myself entering into the academic's particular quadrant of the Twilight Zone. Whenever I opened the newspaper, surfed the net, went to the movies with friends—did any of the things that take me away from my writing, other than yelling at my kids—I kept encountering texts, events, and factoids that seemed uncannily to trump, complicate, or extend the arguments I had been laboriously putting together. Thus one fine morning I picked up the *New York Times* to learn that John Zorn, archrabbi of the radical Jewish culture movement, had been awarded the MacArthur "genius" award—clearly a sign that the conflation of the Jewish and the avant-garde he superintended has begun to meet the dire fate of all avant-garde movements: respectability. Soon thereafter, I received an email from the Jewish/Latino rap group the Hip-Hop Hoodios I mention in passing in chapter 1 announcing their next CD, an adaptation of "a Cuban traditional song [that is made to] deal with the subject of detainees, and how human rights and due process are still really nifty things to have around." And I just received in the mail from a friend a CD entitled *Jewface*, issued by a collective called Reboot Stereophonic, which includes remastered versions of original vaudeville songs presenting Jews in their most stereotypical guises, some written by Jews, others by gentiles. The Rebooters provided me with a fact that I had not previously known, though doubtless I should have: that the first few notes of a ditty from 1913 entitled "When Mose With His Nose Leads the Band," by Arthur Collins and Byron Harlan, formed the melodic basis for Irving Berlin's "God Bless America." It's also not irrelevant to the concerns of this book that Collins and Harlan were famous for their "coon" songs, songs written and performed in black dialect, including "That Funny Jas Band from Dixieland" (1916), a song that offers one of the first uses of the word *jazz* as a description of a kind of music rather than of that which the music accompanied in the bordellos of New Orleans.[1]

Meanwhile, on other cultural fronts, Min Jin Lee, the Korean American writer who told me, over lunch, of the link between her novel, *Free Food for Millionaires*, and Herman Wouk's *Marjorie Morningstar*, emailed to inform me that the novel had received a brief notice in *Publisher's Weekly*—the same journal that, as I observed in chapter 6, constructed Asian American writers of the 1980s in the model of the Jewish American writers of the 1950s and 1960s. And, sure enough, Lee's book was compared to Bellow, Roth, and Woody Allen—the last three being the first, according to *Publisher's Weekly*, to demolish the "model-minority stereotypes."[2] I then had another portion of my argument confirmed when I read Pearl Abraham's remarkable 2005 novel *The Seventh Beggar*, which, while verging on the tragic—in it, a young Hasidic scholar dies in a freak accident, only to find his spirit in some way transmogrified into his nephew, a computer scientist intent on making an AI golem—concludes with a scene set in a music festival in upstate New York, complete with klezmer performers who help redirect the novel's heartrending plot to an affirmative conclusion. Meanwhile, the *New York Times Book Review* informed me that Lara Vapnyar has published a new novel that continues the themes of literary achievement and ethnic self-construction, which, as I argued in chapter 7, are intertwined with each other in the progression from Jewish American to Asian American to Russian emigrant fiction making. Vapnyar's *Memoirs of a Muse* (2006) tells the story of a young Russian Jewish immigrant who idolizes Dostoevsky's mistress and muse, Appolonaria Suslova; she enacts these conjoined roles for an American Jewish novelist, Mark, who, with his combination of talentlessness and concern for his gorgeous New York apartment, resembles nothing so much as Han Ong's hideous Jewish novelist Shem.

And a more recent edition of the *New York Times Book Review* brought news that Gary Shteyngart's second novel, *Absurdistan*, has been named one of the ten notable books of the year. *Absurdistan* tracks the experience of an obese son of a Jewish Russsian millionaire, Misha, who, returning to Russia after earning his U.S. B.A. in multicultural studies (and finding himself deformed by a botched circumcision performed by American Hasids), is trapped in Russia by his father's criminality even after the father is assassinated by political enemies/business rivals (in contemporary Russia, of course, there is no difference). He attempts to return to the United States to rejoin his ghetto-authentic black girlfriend Rouenna (who has in the meantime taken up with her writing instructor at Hunter College, one

Gary Shteynfarb) by way of a former Soviet Republic named Absurdistan, in which a huge civil war breaks out that sends him fleeing to the enclave of the so-called Mountain Jews, those Jews of the Caucasus who may (or may not) be the descendents of the Khazars and who certainly are Turkic-Mongolic in appearance and identity. A more perfect illustration of many of the themes of this book—the persistence of the image of the queer Jew (in this case an obese Jewish man with a penis deformed by the very affirmation of his Jewishness), the coalescence between Jewish writerly self-expression and that of other minority groups struggling to tell their own stories, the mirror imaging of a multicultural U.S. by a post–Soviet Union Russia, the reckoning with the Asianness and exoticism of the far eastern European (or Western/Central Asian) Jew—I could not have asked for.

And to add just one more experience to the list: the number one movie in America in the fall of 2006 was *Borat: Cultural Learnings of America for Make Benefit Glorious Nation of Kazakhstan*, in which Sacha Baron Cohen, a Cambridge-educated British Jew, impersonates an antisemitic Kazakstani journalist, Borat Sagdiyev, who, on a previous tour of red state America, had led a barroom audience in a rousing rendition of a song containing the memorable lines: "Throw the Jew down the well / So that my people may be free," and in this one, confronts American audiences with a number of antisemitic, racist, and sexist slurs to which they respond with a mixture of puzzlement and enthusiasm. To round out the picture, the movie's success was followed by the obligatory David Brooks column denouncing Cohen for his condescension to red-state America (as well as news of lawsuits from the fraternity brothers whose drunken racist tirades were elicited by Borat/Cohen).

I could go on and on—to mention, for example, the arrival on my doorstep of the newest issue of *Heeb*, a magazine for twenty-something hipsters with attitude (the cover of the most recent issue, devoted to food, has a large and cute pig staring up at the reader), or to mention my discovery via MySpace, of Golem, a "6 piece Eastern European folk-punk band," or Zydepunks, who mix klezmer with Cajun, Breton, and Balkan folk musics. More important, I could and should mention here the theoretical articulations that underlie these developments, expressed not only by musician-intellectuals I discussed in the introduction like John Zorn or Marc Ribot but also by the collective responsible for *Jewface*, which includes academic Josh Kun, whose work on Mickey Katz and on Latino/Jewish musical intersections in the 1950s and 1960s I praised in the introduction. The collective proclaims itself as being dedicated as this book has been to resuscitating narratives of Jewishness from the past that incorporate "stories that have yet to be told: [of] hybrid identities, eclectic communities, racial dialogue, and pioneering ... style"—of projecting, through the act of recovery, such heterogeneous narratives into the stories we make of the present and future as well.[3]

All this wonderfully confirmed my sense that we are witnessing something important and new in the articulation of Jewish culture in America: a kind of renaissance that ushers into being new forms of Jewish cultural production by a generation that's free from much of the baggage weighing down their elders. As such, the new generation of Jewish culture makers are contesting the old sociological chestnut of "third generation return"— "the idea," as Adam Meyer puts it, "that grandsons will want to remember parts of their grandparents' lives that the fathers have wanted to forget, in this case their Jewishness."[4] For what marks the work of this generation is their ease of self-identification as Jews and its productive, though not complacent, relation to cognate programs underway among writers of other races and ethnicities. What marks it too is the willingness to let go of old metanarratives about Jews, most particularly the culturally dominant narrative of assimilation and/or acculturation and the leftist counterversion of uniform adaptation to whiteness. They may be returning to Jewishness, to be sure, but theirs is a Jewishness with an edgy difference.

This generation's "new language of a hybridized, flexible Jewish identity,"[5] to quote the Rebooters, does more than provide new histories or new perspectives; it might provide new opportunities for critical intervention. It's tremendously significant, it seems to me, that Sacha Baron Cohen, while an undergraduate at Cambridge, wrote his thesis on black/Jewish relations in the U.S. and that the first character he played was Ali G, a (British-) ghetto-authentic yob who, while transparently white, acted as if he were genuinely (or is it "genuinely"?) black, as he would wonderfully assert when responding to a hostile interlocutor in a tone of utter aggrievement: "Is it cuz I'm black?" Indeed, so successful was the put-on that Cohen, to his great delight, was greeted at one point with protesters with signs reading "No Al Jolson."[6] His career-long evolution—from a student of black/Jewish relations to a dead-pan performance of a white Jew doing a version of blackface to a performance as a Jew doing Central Asian-face—recapitulates, as it were, in reverse, the itinerary of Jewishness in the U.S., where he is now located, as well as the United Kingdom, where he began. But it does more than that: it uses that history to stage a wide-ranging cultural and political critique. When in his guise as Ali G he did blackface without blacking up, performing as black in his ownguise as white, Cohen reminded us of the investment of middle-class white British (and Americans) alike in the appropriation of black identities and cultural forms. But he didn't stop in this (somewhat familiar) place. Cohen proudly adopted this guise to speak truth to power, or at least (as Stephen Colbert might put it) to make power demonstrate its own truthiness: Ali G outrageously interviewed U.S. and world powermongers, from Newt Gingrich to Boutros Boutros-Ghali, and, by asking completely off-the-wall questions, forcing them to reveal themselves as bumbling, inadequate performers in the face of his brilliant impersonation.

Equally significant work is done by Cohen in Kazakhstani-face; for the success of this shtick, like that of many performances, is due to the complex response it elicits from its audience. The point of Borat's outrageous antisemitism is not, finally, to mimic or articulate the quite latent antisemitism that doubtless persists throughout much of the former Soviet Union. It is to force Americans to come to terms with their own weird feelings about Jews: the ease with which Borat can get a redneck bar cheerfully to sing an antisemitic song being matched by the quiet, almost sweet shock of people who try to correct him for his impolitic sentiments. As Cohen puts it:

> Borat essentially works as a tool. . . . By himself being anti-Semitic, he lets people lower their guard and expose their own prejudice, whether it's anti-Semitism or an acceptance of anti-Semitism. "Throw the Jew Down the Well" . . . was a very controversial sketch, and some members of the Jewish community thought that it was actually going to encourage anti-Semitism. But to me it revealed something about that bar in Tucson. And the question is: Did it reveal that they were anti-Semitic? Perhaps. But maybe it just revealed that they were indifferent to anti-Semitism.[7]

Some may find these words overstated. But in the light of the continuing power of the Christian Right in America, with its simultaneous embrace of the most extreme and nationalist form of Zionism and its denigration of the most expansive forms of Jewishness, they hardly seem an exaggeration. Certainly, in the face of the videogame *Left Behind* I mentioned in chapter 3, in which the player kills all the Jews, Muslims, and freethinkers he encounters in the course of a session, indifference to antisemitism has a greater salience and range than even Cohen might have imagined when he made the film.

At moments like these, the celebratory mode into which I find myself falling becomes necessarily more muted and complex. As the Left Behind series suggests, the problematic process by which ethnic otherness across the board has been defined by Jewishness—in both positive and negative guises—takes on renewed urgency. The recent passage of an antiaffirmative referendum in the economically depressed state of Michigan, for example, can serve to remind us just how powerfully the myth of upward mobility via education, bound so powerfully to the experience of twentieth-century Jews, can resonate to the detriment of other minority groups. And clearly an increasingly virulent anti-Arab agitation from the right has been articulated in terms virtually identical with those used in the past to denigrate Jews. Late in 2006 Representative Virgil Goode of Virginia elicited a storm of criticism (and some approbation) by claiming that immigration from "non-European" states should be limited in order to prevent the election of Muslims like Democrat Keith Ellison of Minnesota (a native-born convert—but whatever). Such restrictions are necessary, he argued, "to preserve the values and beliefs traditional to the United States of America. . . . If American citizens don't wake up and adopt the Virgil Goode position on immigration there will likely be many more Muslims elected to office and demanding the use of the Koran."[8] Substitute the Talmud, replace non-European with eastern European, and we're back with Telemachus Timayensis in the 1890s or with Henry Ford's *International Jew* in the 1930s—as some Jewish politicians were quick to note, to their credit, although the entire controversy was itself rather shamefully initiated by a Jewish right-wing talk show host, Dennis Prager.

Many of these examples will doubtless seem dated to the reader; by the time this book sees the light of day they will have been superseded by other epiphenomena that I can only hope (but don't expect) may prove to be less problematic. I'd like to conclude by foregrounding an event from the recent headlines that is already passing into historical memory, not only because it is fascinating its own right but also because it encapsulates so many of the themes of this book and transposes them into a new key. In August 2006 George Allen, Republican senator from Virginia, was struck by the appearance at one of his rallies in the rural part of the state by a young man of South Asian descent and, more important, appearance, S. R. Sidarth. Sidarth was there to videotape Allen's appearance for his opponent, James Webb. According to the *Washington Post*, Allen ad-libbed a response:

> "This fellow here, over here with the yellow shirt, macaca, or whatever his name is. He's with my opponent. He's following us around everywhere. And it's just great," Allen said, as his supporters began to laugh. After saying that Webb was raising money in California with a "bunch of Hollywood movie moguls," Allen said, "Let's give a welcome to macaca, here. Welcome to America and the real world of Virginia." Allen then began talking about the "war on terror."[9]

Allen, it should first be said, was using a classic nativist ploy, one tinged here as it has historically been with borderline antisemitism: the word *mogul* links Webb and Sidarth with the stereotype of all-powerful Jewish studio heads who have long ago receded into the historical past—and, as we may remember, that word also comprises one of the many links between Jews and Asians in the American imaginary, since it imparts the narrative of the kings of India of Mongol descent to the imperious rulers of Hollywood of Jewish descent. But it wasn't this word that most observers found striking but rather the term *macaca*. The word, as the *Post* was quick to observe, is descended from *macaque*, the French for a species of monkey frequently used by European racists as a term of abuse against Africans. Allen's feeble defense against the charge that he had uttered a racial slur was that he was using the word *Mohawk* to reference Sidarth's mullet hairstyle. I can think of no more ironic—almost comic—cascade of conflating prejudices spinning into one another: slurs against Jews, Africans, immigrants, Arabs (whom do we think the so-called war on so-called terror is aimed at?)[10] and Native Americans wheeling into a series of free-floating ethnic animadversions, each one more inappropriate to the bemused Sidarth (who recorded the whole event on video camera) than the last.

Comic as this incident may have seemed, events soon took a more serious turn. Former teammates and friends of Allen's came forward to claim that he had routinely used the word *nigger*, and not as a term of endearment; voters were rapidly reminded that as governor he had been a prominent advocate of the continued display of the Confederate flag. At the same time, some observers began to ask why he had used such a recondite term when there were so many more available, even acceptable terms of abuse (*foreigner, immigrant,* etc.—all of which would seem to be more obvious euphemisms for the nativist audience). Some noted publicly the North African ancestry of his mother, Hetty Lumbroso Allen—and of rumors that had long circulated about her Jewish origins (rumors that Allen, a favorite candidate of the Christian right, had always been quick to deny). A few days into the scandal, the *Jewish Daily Forward* published an article essentially "outing" the Allen family: Hetty was descended from a distinguished Sephardic family, the Lumbrosos, that had converted in Portugal in the fifteenth century under the threat of the Inquisition, then moved to Livorno, Italy, where they were able to reassert their status as Jews (the Medicis not sharing the prejudices of their Iberian counterparts).[11] One branch of the family moved to Tunis, where they prospered as traders, importers, and members of the local European elite (Allen's grandfather was the North African distributor of the Italian aperitif Cinzano); the other remained a powerful presence in Italy. A member of the Tunisian branch, Itzak Lumbroso, was grand rabbi of Tunis and a distinguished theologian; criminologist Cesare Lombroso belonged to the Italian branch; members of both fought with distinction in the resistance in World War II. The Lumbrosos were, in short, conversos who, like the unfortunate Alonso in fifteenth-century Mexico, had returned to their faith as quickly as they could—although with happier results. Moreover, Hetty, it appeared, had not fully concealed her family's past when she married George Allen Sr.—her openly Jewish father appeared at the wedding, which was held at her request in a Jewish friend's house rather than a Catholic church as her husband had wished—but she hadn't revealed it either. She had become, in essence—like Achy Obejas's character Enrique San José—someone who, having been brought up in a family that was once converso but had returned to Judaism, made up her mind to remarranize: to become a crypto-Jew by choice, not necessity. Despite the best efforts of all concerned at damage control, matters soon lurched out of control. Allen found himself publicly questioned about his heritage and reacted first with anger and then, when forced to acknowledge it, with a quip that would have been antisemitic if it weren't so transparently lame ("I still had a ham sandwich for lunch. And my mother made great pork chops"). These and other gaffes ultimately cost Allen the election and the Republican Party the Senate.

Compacted into this one incident are virtually all the phenomena that I have been foregrounding in this book; the only thing missing is a klezmer soundtrack to Allen's slow-motion political hara-kari. Thus, to pick one major concern from chapter 4, passing seems to have been in the Allen/ Lumbroso family blood, at least in America: Hetty's masquerade was matched by George himself, not so much as a Jew—his shock at discovering this part of his past seemed real enough—but as a racist Good Old Boy. For, as the voters of Virginia soon learned, while he affected a Southern accent, chewed tobacco and spat its juices (sometimes at the feet of people he didn't like), and posed as a defender of the Confederacy, Allen was born and raised in Southern California, only moving to Virginia to attend college. To be sure, his performance began on the other side of the country: according to press stories that emerged in the aftermath of the *macaca* incident, he had as a high school student pasted Confederate decals on his car and vandalized the school with slurs in an attempt to implicate black students in a racial incident. But it's clear the things in Allen's persona that appealed to his rural base—the things that he was seeking to call upon with his nativist ad lib—constituted a part he had so long been playing that it wasn't clear anymore where performance stopped and identity began. Just to indicate the flexibility to which such performances may also tend, Allen reversed racial fields by cosponsoring a bill offering a formal apology for slavery with Mary Landrieu, Democrat from Louisiana and member of a white political dynasty made famous by her father's decision to remove the Confederate flag from public buildings in New Orleans.

Allen's multiple ethnoracial performances rival in their vertiginousness even Coleman Silk's; indeed, they exceed Coleman's in their constant wheeling back into what can only be called compulsive spasms of self-hatred, from the use of the term *macaca* itself to the clumsy ham sandwich joke. They thus suggest, if nothing else, the continual power of Jewishness not only to inspire racial shifting—to define, enable, and perform racial equivocality—but to make people go completely crazy with the complexities of the terms it asks them to juggle: in Allen's case religion, family history, and, via ham sandwiches, culture. The story of George Allen also suggests the continuing power of seemingly buried or repressed narratives of Jewish identities lost and found, abandoned and returned to, particularly in the aftermath of the Expulsion from Spain and Portugal: indeed, somewhat melodramatically (but such is the way, as we have seen, of

Marrano and converso narratives), to reach out from the past and grab hold of destinies that seemed settled, secure.

There's one more way in which this incident speaks to the concerns of this book, and that's through the narrative of the object of Allen's abuse, Sidarth himself. For, it turns out, he was not, as Allen positioned him, an immigrant, or even much of an Other except in the crudest phenotypical sense. Indeed, not only is Sidarth an American citizen, but he was born in the Commonwealth of Virginia, making him far more authentic a citizen of the state than the man who was so sardonically "welcoming" him to it. And more: he is an authentic representative of the narrative that, as we have seen, bounces back and forth between Jews and Asians: the model minority narrative. According to a *Washington Post* profile that followed Allen's comments and aided his self-destruction, Sidarth is the son of a prosperous mortgage banker and the grandson of an adviser of Gandhi's; he was an honors student at Fairfax High School, graduating with a 4.1 grade point average (!) with special interest in chess, American politics, and history. According to the president of his local Hindu temple, he is the very model of a model Indian American, a synthesis of the values of both cultures: his parents have "instilled in him all the values that are important to a Hindu: being honest, working hard."[12] In attacking Sidarth, Allen—the crypto-Californian son of a crypto-Jew passing as a crypto-Southern nativist racist—was attacking nothing less than an embodiment of the American mythos itself—or at least a dark-skinned, ethnic version thereof.

The incident suggests how fully American culture and politics are undergoing a transformation as they wheel forward, it seems, into new ethnoracial combinations—the politics of the Commonwealth of Virginia have clearly been reshaped by success-oriented upper-middle-class ethnics like Sidarth as well as by the extraordinary growth in working-class Asians and Latinos that have moved in consequential numbers to the state. But it also reminds us of the continuing power of the model minority narrative; the salience of the narrative of ethnic passing; the role of racism American- (hatred of blacks) and European-style (the persistence from 1492 forward of an ethnicized racial hatred of Jews) as we wheel into the twenty-first century. It suggests, in short, that new itineraries of belonging and their fate in the nation at large will continue to be intertwined with older narratives and the social and imaginative structures they wrought—and as both remain, as they have since Oliver Wendell Holmes wandered into the pantomime house, fundamentally connected with Jews, Judaism, and/or Jewishness. Even as the ethnoracial future belongs to other Others, many of them in guises we can only begin to imagine, the narrative frames in which their alterity will be imagined, circumscribed, accommodated, the shapes into which they will revise those definitions and, in responding, trace new arcs of identity and culture for themselves and the nation at large—all these will continue to be shaped, for better or worse, by the discourses and experiences of those people who have historically served as the very emblem of otherness and whose greatest and most distinctive contribution to the national culture may well prove to have been to give that otherness a local habitation and a name.

NOTES

Introduction

1. Oliver Wendell Holmes, *Poetical Works of Oliver Wendell Holmes*, vol. 2 (Boston: Houghton Mifflin, 1949), pp. 210–213. I was led to this poem by Jacobson's remarkably encyclopedic *Whiteness of a Different Color: European Immigrants and the Alchemy of Race* (Cambridge: Harvard University Press, 2000). Although I take some issue with Jacobson's work, and even more so with his more recent *Roots Too* (Cambridge: Harvard, 2006), I have also learned an immense amount from the scope and trenchancy of both.

2. Robert Snyder, *Voice of the City: Vaudeville and Popular Culture in New York* (New York: Oxford University Press, 1989), p. 111; quoted in Jeffrey Melnick's fine *A Right to Sing the Blues* (Cambridge: Harvard University Press, 1999), p. 103.

3. Sir Walter Scott, *Ivanhoe* (Edinburgh: Edinburgh University Press, 1998), pp. 71–72.

4. There's a humongous—and frequently psychoanalytically inflected—literature on precisely this phenomenon; see, inter alia, S. B. Cohen, *Jewish Wry* (Detroit: Wayne State University Press, 1987); and Avner Ziv, *Jewish Humor* (New York: Transaction, 1998). But of course the ultimate comments on the Jewish joke as a socially and psychically compensatory mechanism belong to Freud himself; this is a recurring theme in *Jokes and Their Relation to the Unconscious* (1905).

5. Hasia Diner, *Lower East Side Memories* (Princeton: Princeton University Press, 2004).

6. Edna Nashon, "Israel Zangwill: Child of the Ghetto," in Israel Zangwill, *From the Ghetto to the Melting Pot: Israel Zangwill's Jewish Plays, Three Playscripts by Israel Zangwill*, ed. Edna Nashon (Detroit: Wayne State University Press, 2006), p. 21. Much of the material in my treatment of the term *ghetto* derives from Nashon's wonderfully informative introduction.

7. Deborah Dash Moore cites prominent lawyer, community leader, and politician Louis Marshall as decrying the effects of this particular scattering in precisely this language: "The ghetto of old had been the preserver of Judaism. . . . The gilded ghetto of today has no spiritual values." Moore, *At Home in America: Second-Generation New York City Jews* (New York: Columbia University Press, 1981), p. 69. I haven't found any earlier uses of the term *gilded ghetto,* but the tonalities of Marshall's comment (from the *Jewish Daily Bulletin*) suggest that the term was already broadly in circulation at that time. My son tells me that the current sense of the

term *ghetto,* at least among white suburbanites (as in: "that's so *ghetto*"), conjoins the connotations of authenticity, urban style, and blackness.

8. I am thinking here especially of the work of Milton Gordon, whose *Assimilation in American Life* (New York: Oxford University Press, 1968), while complicating Park and Burgess in a number of ways, also simplified their reciprocal notion of assimilation (Gordon by and large makes it unidirectional, as betokening a gradual disappearance of a sense of difference among the assimilators) and also renders it normative, the inevitable pattern that immigrant groups should and do follow. In addition, as we shall see in more detail in chapter 6, Gordon turns the argument to the psychology of the assimilator, picking up on Park and Burgess's notion of the "marginal man" (which they themselves derived from Simmel) and accentuating the alienation of such a figure in ways that make him into something of an existentialist *malgré lui.* With respect to all of these, Bauman makes the link to the Jewish experience in his extraordinary essay, "Exit Visas and Entry Tickets: The Paradoxes of Jewish Assimilation," *Telos* 77 (Fall 1988): 45–77. Jon Stratton engages with and substantively extends the argument in *Coming Out Jewish: On the Impossibility of Jewish Assimilation* (New York: Routledge, 2000). My thought here, especially with respect to sociological constructions of Jewishness, owes much to Bauman and Stratton.

9. Since Herder won't resurface in the argument below, let me take this opportunity to delineate some of his most interesting ambivalences with respect to Jews and Jewishness and their role in his theorizing of cultural difference at large. For, on the one hand, Herder saw the Jewish contribution to world civilizations as originating in their own distinctive language and national culture, to which he accorded a respect not always shown by his contemporaries. At the same time, he also sees Jews in the contemporary world as a parasitic race, contributing only their usurious practices to the Western civilization that has welcomed them. As such, the Jew's fate chimes with that of all the nations that Herder surveys—his account of national identity made through language, culture, and group affiliations is supplemented with a Viconian account of inevitable national decline. In this he not only begins the tradition of conflating what is going to be called race with what is going to be called ethnicity; he also uses the Jew (or, more properly, his ambivalence about the Jew) to shape his narrative of group identity across the board, in which such identity is both celebrated in ways that lead to later dogmas of cultural pluralism *and* bound into a narrative of the innate superiority of certain national cultures over others. For Herder, see, inter alia, *Outlines of a Philosophy of the History of Man,* trans. T. Churchill, vol. 2 (London: Johnson, 1803), pp. 355–356. For an argument celebrating Herder as the father of cultural pluralism, see Alain Finkielkraut, *The Defeat of the Mind,* trans. Judith Freidlander (New York: Columbia University Press, 1995). For a critique of Herder as the fount of protoracist German nationalism, see Paul Larence Rose, *Revolutionary Anti-Semitism in Germany from Kant to Wagner* (Princeton: Princeton University Press, 1990). For the argument with respect to Hegel, see *The Temple of Culture* (New York: Oxford University Press, 2001), pp. 39–41.

10. See Sander Gilman, "Jews and the Ethnic," in *Multiculturalism and the Jews* (London: Routledge, 2006), pp. 45–64.

11. See Victoria Hattam, "Ethnicity: An American Genealogy," in Nancy Foner and George Frederickson, eds. *Not Just Black and White: Contemporary Perspectives on Immigration, Race, and Ethnicity in the United States* (New York: Russell Sage Foundation, 2004), pp. 42–61.

12. Ann Powers, "Critic's Notebook: Latinos Give New Life to Neil Diamond Anthem," *Los Angeles Times*, May 9, 2006.

13. There has been a flood of recent books on the klezmer phenomenon, peaking around the year 2000. The ones I've learned the most from are (in alphabetical order) Seth Rogovoy, *The Essential Klezmer: A Music Lover's Guide to Jewish Roots and Soul Music, from the Old World to the Jazz Age to the Downtown Avant-Garde* (Chapel Hill: Algonquin, 2000); Henry Sapoznik, *Klezmer! Jewish Music from Old World to Our World* (New York: Schirmer, 1999); Mark Slobin, *Fiddler on the Move: Exploring the Klezmer World* (New York: Oxford, 2000), and *American Klezmer: Roots and Offshoots* (Berkeley: University of California Press, 2002); and Yale Strom, *The Book of Klezmer: The History, the Music, the Folklore* (Chicago: Chicago Review Press, 2002). For an insider's take on the birth and growth of the klezmer revival from one who helped make it happen, see Hankus Netsky, "An Overview of Klezmer Music and Its Development in the U.S.," *Judaism: A Quarterly Journal of Jewish Life and Thought* 47 (1998): 5–13; also useful is James Loeffler, "Klezmania," *New Republic* 218 (1998): 42. In that same special issue of *Judaism* as Netzsky's account can be found Kirschenblatt-Gimblett's field-establishing essay "Sounds of Sensibility"; its revised and reprinted version can be found in Slobin, pp. 129–173. The best source for current (as well as past) information on the klezmer phenomenon is a klezmershack, a Web site maintained by Ari Davidow (http://www.klezmershack.com). Davidow's words, from the site, exemplify the dynamic and creative moment of current postklezmer praxis that I'm focusing on in this book:

> The klezmer revival sparked a renaissance in Jewish music and culture. Nowadays, the revival is over—klezmer is a popular music form that is no longer exclusively Jewish, and other forms of Jewish music are also gaining in popularity. And no one questions the place of klezmer in both Jewish and popular cultures. Well, no one we care about. Meanwhile, the edges of musical and cultural boundaries continue to change, expand, and morph onward, fueled by the imperatives to explore new music on the one hand, and by the shifting sense of Jewish identity on another, not always related, hand.

14. See Mark Slobin, *Tenement Songs: The Popular Music of the Jewish Immigrants* (Urbana: University of Illinois Press, 1982), especially pp. 182–187. Slobin distinguishes two particular tonal patterns in Jewish music of eastern Europe: melodies built on scales that deploy an augmented second (an adaptation of the so-called Phrygian mode, often called *frygysh* by klezmer musicians, also called the *Ahabah rabah* liturgical mode) and those that use an augmented fourth. The

first in particular is identified by Jewish musicians as uniquely Jewish, despite broad evidence that these tonalities and the melodies built from them were shared with other cultures; the latter is associated with the "mournful" sound that marks eastern European Jewish music—and that of their gentile neighbors as well. Slobin extends his definitional consideration of the klezmer "sound" to consideration of ornament, pitch, *krechts* (the voicelike slides that distinguish the klezmer sound in violins and clarinets) in *Fiddler on the Move*, pp. 93–132. For an excellent review of Slobin's book, see MacDonald Moore, *American Jewish History* 89 (2001): 337–340. I take Moore's salutary skepticism about the phenomenon to heart in what follows; indeed, as he suggests, "legions of klezmer tourists" have "moved on"; and the term did, as he anticipated, become "tyranny" to a number of musicians, who have reinvented klezmer in the guise of radical Jewish culture. But such, in my view, is the diasporic nature of klezmer itself—or, as Moore says, channeling Kurt Vonnegut, "so it goes."

15. For examples of the former, see (or rather listen to) Leverett's CD, *Margot Leverett and the Klezmer Mountain Boys* (Traditional Crossroads 4318, 2003). Leverett—former lead clarinetist for the Klezmatics—stresses that her band

> isn't doing bluegrass versions of klezmer tunes or klezmer versions of bluegrass tunes. What it does do is pull off a seamless segue from one genre to another, say in the course of a four tune medley. The band will play Bill Monroe's "Lonesome Moonlight Waltz," in which Leverett, Kosek and Mitterhoff take solos, and in the course of three guitar notes the group shifts to a Russian Jewish waltz. This happens in a momentary pause in Leverett's clarinet lead and it takes listeners several seconds to realize the subtle shift in melody amounts to genre-hopping. Listening closely to Leverett playing bluegrass leads on her clarinet and you will acknowledge that it is indeed still bluegrass, but the rarity of the woodwind sound in bluegrass makes it almost sound like a whole new genre. "They just go together really well," Leverett said. "Both of these musics have really deep soul. They're fun, wonderful, joyous dance music, which is what I was attracted to at first." John Kalish, "Mixing Mountain Musics: How One Band Combines Klezmer and Bluegrass, *Jewish Daily Forward*, November 19, 2003.

For examples of the latter, see chapter 2.

16. See Tamar Barzel's splendid 2004 Michigan dissertation, "'Radical Jewish Culture': Composer/Improvisers on New York City's 1990s Downtown Scene."

17. As Don Byron put it in an interview with the *Wall Street Journal* at the height of the hubbub over the Mickey Katz project (which also saw him receive a long, adulatory profile in the *New York Times Magazine*): "I'm not doing Jewish music or doing classical music instead of doing black music. I play what I like and I don't feel the need to 'live' one genre of music like the young be-bop cats who only listen to be-bop and put down pop music." "A 'Cat' from the Bronx Makes His Mark on Klezmer," *Wall Street Journal*, September 19, 1991, p. A12.

18. John Zorn, liner notes to *Great Jewish Music: Burt Bacharach* (Tzadik, 1997).

19. For more on the Diaspora issue from the Jewish point of view, see Daniel and Jonathan Boyarin, *Powers of Diaspora: Two Essays on the Relevance of Jewish Culture* (Minneapolis: University of Minnesota Press, 2002). And for a series of case studies in Jewish diasporism itself—Diaspora viewed, that is, as a naturalized or even positive form of Jewish life—see Howard Wettstein, ed., *Diasporas and Exiles: Varieties of Jewish Identity* (Berkeley: University of California Press, 2002). For a recent attempt to read American Jewish literary culture in terms of diasporism,—the privileging of diasporic condition in explicit contradistinction to Zionist metanarratives of the Jewish experience—see Ronen Omer-Sherman, *Diaspora and Zionism in Jewish American Literature: Lazarus, Syrkin, Reznikoff, and Roth* (Dartmouth: University Press of New England/Brandeis University Press, 2002).

20. Eric Sundquist, *Strangers in the Land: Blacks, Jews, Post-Holocaust America* (Cambridge: Harvard University Press, 2005).

21. See Marlon Ross, *Manning the Race: Reforming Black Men in the Jim Crow Era* (New York: New York University Press, 2004); Tomás Almaguer, "Chicano Men: A Cartography of Homosexual Identity and Behavior," in *Social Perspectives in Lesbian and Gay Studies*, ed. Peter Nardi and Beth Schneider (New York: Routledge, 1998); and David Eng, *Racial Castration: Managing Masculinity in Asian America* (Durham: Duke University Press, 2001).

22. Leslie Fiedler, *The Jew in the American Novel* (New York: Herzl Society Pamphlet, 1959). As Fiedler quite eloquently puts it: "As the Jewish writer goes out in search of himself, he encounters the Gentile writer on a complementary quest to come to terms with the Jew, the stranger in his land. Collaborators or rivals, whether willingly or not, Jewish fictionist and Gentile engage in a common enterprise." (6) In this brilliant little book, he details how Jewish novelists had to come to terms with the images crafted of them not only by antisemitic writers like the nineteenth-century sensation novelists but also by figures like the fascinating Henry Harland, who, as "Sidney Luska," masqueraded as a Jew, and whose racy fictions set in the ghetto position him with the status, Fiedler wittily argues, of "the first Jewish-American novelist."

23. Gustavus Stadler, "Ejaculating Tongues: Poe, Mather and the Jewish Penis," in Tracy Fessenden, Nicholas Radel, and Magdalena Zaborowska, eds., *The Puritan Origins of American Sex: Religion, Sexuality, and National Identity in American Literature* (New York: Routledge, 2001), pp. 109–126; David Anthony, "Shylock on Wall Street; or, The Jessica Complex in Antebellum Sensationalism," unpublished MS; Julian Levinson, *Exiles on Main Street* (Bloomington: Indiana University Press, forthcoming); Maaera Schreiber; *Singing in a Strange Land: Towards a Jewish American Poetics* (Stanford: Stanford University Press, 2007); Daniel Itzkovitz, "Passing Like Me," *South Atlantic Quarterly* 98 (1999): 35–58, and "Secret Temples," in Boyarin and Boyarin, *Jews and Other Differences*, pp. 176–202; Rachel Rubenstein, "Nathanael West's Indian Commodities," *Shofar* 23 (2005): 98–120.

24. For major studies of Jews and African Americans, see E. Miller Budick, *Blacks and Jews in Literary Conversation* (New York: Cambridge University Press,

1998); Ethan Goffman, *Imagining Each Other: Blacks and Jews in Contemporary American Literature* (Albany: State University of New York Press, 2000); Adam Newton, *Facing Black and Jew: Literature as Public Space in Twentieth-Century America* (New York: Cambridge University Press,1999). For Jews and multiculturalism/ethnic studies, see Andrew Furman, *Contemporary Jewish American Writers and the Multicultural Dilemma: The Return of the Exiled* (Syracuse: Syracuse University Press, 2000); Dean Franco, *Ethnic American Writing: Comparing Chicano, Jewish, and African American Writing* (Charlottesville: University of Virginia Press, 2006).

For the question of gender, see, inter alia, Lillian Kremer, *Women's Holocaust Writing: Memory and Imagination* (Lincoln: University of Nebraska Press, 1999); Janet Burstein, *Writing Mothers, Writing Daughters: Tracing the Maternal in Stories by American Jewish Women* (Urbana: University of Illinois Press, 1996); Jay Halio, *Daughters of Valor: Contemporary Jewish American Women Writers* (Newark: University of Delaware Press, 1997); Lois Rubin, *Connections and Collisions: Identities in Contemporary Jewish-American Women's Writing* (Newark: University of Delaware Press, 2005). I should say a word here about contemporary fiction. Much of the enormous and substantive creative output of a new generation of Jewish fiction makers technically falls outside my concerns in the later chapters of this book, which are with the points of overlap and contestation between contemporary writers of color and Jewish American writers, not the quite powerful and consequential work of the likes of Pearl Abraham, Michael Chabon, Nathan Englander, Jonathan Safran Foer, Steve Stern, Aryeh Lev Stollman, which by and large remains focused on intra-Jewish concerns rather than extramural ones. But, as James Bloom has reminded me, a number of moments in Nathan Englander's stories are germane to this project, especially "The Wig" in *For the Relief of Unbearable Urges* (New York: Knopf, 1999), in which the protagonist Ruchma repeatedly leaves her Hasidic Brooklyn enclave for guilty encounters with Jamal, a Manhattan newsdealer who becomes her secret sharer (private communication to author).

25. For Roskies, see (among many works) *Against the Apocalypse: The Jewish Responses to Catastrophe in Modern Jewish Culture* (Syracuse: Syracuse University Press, 1999) and *The Jewish Search for a Usable Past* (Bloomington: Indiana University Press, 1999). In addition to Ruth Wisse's monumental (and monumentalizing) *The Modern Jewish Canon: A Journey Through Language and Culture* (New York: Simon and Schuster, 2003), I've learned an immense amount from Wisse's essay, "Language as Fate: Reflections on Jewish Literature in America," in Ezra Mendelsohn, ed., *Literary Strategies: Jewish Texts and Contexts* (New York Oxford University Press, 1996), pp. 129–148. For Anita Norich on Yiddish in America (to paraphrase Cynthia Ozick), see, inter alia, *"A Time for Every Purpose": Jewish Culture in America During the Holocaust* (Stanford: Stanford University Press, forthcoming), and "On the Yiddish Question," in Laurence Silberstein, ed., *Mapping Jewish Identities* (New York: New York University Press, 2000), pp. 145–158; Ilan Stavans; *The Inveterate Dreamer: Essays and Conversations on Jewish Culture* (Lincoln: University of Nebraska Press, 2000), and his anthology *The Scroll and*

the Cross: One Thousand Years of Jewish-Hispanic Literature (New York: Routledge, 2003). For Hana Wirth-Nesher (whom I single out from these other splendid examples because her book is closest in its focus to mine, although she goes into deep linguistic detail in ways that I don't), see *Call It English* (Princeton: Princeton University Press, 2005).

26. Josh Kun, *Audiotopia:Music, Race, and America* (Berkeley: University of California Press, 2005) pp. 48–85 and "Bagels, Bongos,and Yiddishe Mambos; or, The Other History of Jews in America," *Shofar* 23 (2005): 23–58; George Sanchez, "'What's Good for Boyle Heights Is Good for the Jews': Creating Multiracialism on the Eastside During the 1950s," *American Quarterly* 56 (2004): 633–661. For the term *not-yet-white*, see David Roediger, *Towards the Abolition of Whiteness: Essays on Race, Politics and Working Class History* (London: Verso, 1994), p. 143. Roediger frequently cites historian Barry Goldberg as the source of this phrase—as far as I can trace, to 1990, when Goldberg apparently used it in a talk at the New York Academy of Sciences. But Roediger also cites Goldberg as citing historian John Bukowczyk as the source of the term: see Roediger's essay "*Guineas, Wiggers*, and the Dramas of Racialized Culture" *ALH* 7 (1995): 654–668. I mention this not for the sake of pedantry, but to point to the broad dissemination of the phrase, equally evident in its uses by Jacobson and by a host of other historians of American white ethnics. I much prefer, I should say, the other term that jostles about in Roediger's work and that of his successors, "in-between peoples."

27. Michael Rogin, *Blackface, White Noise* (Berkeley: University of California Press, 1996), p. 101. For a powerful critique of Rogin from a Jewish studies point of view, see Joel Rosenberg, "Rogin's Noise: The Alleged Historical Crimes of the Jazz Singer," *Prooftexts* 22 (2002): 221–239. Rogin's work is flawed in a number of respects—he underestimates, for example, the degree of sympathy the African American press and public felt that the film displayed toward black people, as evidenced by enthusiastic reviews in the African American press (see Thomas Cripps, *Slow Fade to Black: The Negro in American Film*, 1900–1942 [New York: Oxford University Press, 1983], p. 222). But his reading is undeniably powerful, his conclusions dolefully inescapable—up to a point.

28. Isaac Goldberg, *George Gershwin: A Study in American Music* (New York: Ungar, 1931), p. 41. For MacDonald Moore, see *Yankee Blues: Musical Culture and American Identity* (Bloomington: Indiana University Press, 1985), pp. 98ff.

29. Michael Alexander, *Jazz Age Jews* (Princeton: Princeton University Press, 2001), p. 173.

30. William Dean Howells, "An East-Side Ramble" *Impressions and Experiences* (New York; Harper's, 1896), p. 107.

31. Roger Mitchell, "Recent Jewish Immigration to the United States," *Popular Science Monthly* (February, 1903), p. 340, quoted in Robert Singerman's excellent "The Jew as Racial Alien: The Genetic Component of American Anti-Semitism," in David Gerber, ed., *Anti-Semitism in American History* (Urbana: University of Illinois Press, 1986), pp. 109–110. This ascription of an essentially Oriental quality to the Jewish mind, of course, also possessed a philosemitic aspect; see, for example,

the descriptions of the mystical Mordecai in George Eliot's *Daniel Deronda* (1886). Indeed, the first encounter between "yellow"-faced Mordecai (sallow from consumption as well as from the coloring of the Near East) and Daniel is a test case of the Jewish/Oriental interplay I am attempting to describe here. For, in meeting Mordecai, Daniel—who does not yet know of his Jewish origins—is conflated syntactically and imagistically with that which he ostensibly opposes. At the very least, Eliot's mirroring of these two creates the possibility of the emergence of an "oriental" type within "the Latin races"—that admixture of East and West we might also call "the (assimilated) Jew":

> Opposite to him was a face not more distinctively oriental than many a type seen among what we call the Latin races; rich in youthful health, and with a forcible masculine gravity in its repose, that gave the value of judgment to the reverence with which he met the gaze of this mysterious son of poverty who claimed him as a long-expected friend. The more exquisite quality of Deronda's nature—that keenly perceptive sympathetic emotiveness which ran along with his speculative tendency—was never more thoroughly tested. He felt nothing that could be called belief in the validity of Mordecai's impressions concerning him or in the probability of any greatly effective issue: what he felt was a profound sensibility to a cry from the depths of another and accompanying that, the summons to be receptive instead of superciliously prejudging. Receptiveness is a rare and massive power, like fortitude; and this state of mind now gave Deronda's face its utmost expression of calm benignant force—an expression which nourished Mordecai's confidence and made an open way before him. Eliot, *Daniel Deronda* (London: Penguin, 1995) p. 492.

32. According to the *Hill*, a daily that chronicles the doings on Capitol Hill, anti-semitic charges were commonly made against Soros by Republican politicians, activists, or figures closely associated with the Republican party:

> "No other single person represents the symbol and the substance of globalism more than this Hungarian-born descendant of Shylock. He is the embodiment of the Merchant from Venice," wrote GOPAC, an organization that helps elect GOP candidates, on its website last year.
>
> In William Shakespeare's "Merchant of Venice," Shylock was the Jewish banker whose venality would not stop him from cutting human flesh to repay loans.
>
> Tony Blankley, the editorial-page editor of *The Washington Times* [and former press secretary for Newt Gingrich] said Soros is "a robber baron, he's a pirate capitalist, and he's a reckless man" in an interview on Fox News.

Jonathan Kaplan, "Soros Blasts Hastert Over Drug Allegation: Billionaire Demands Public Apology from the House Speaker," *Hill*, September 1, 2004.

33. Stephen Whitfield, "Why America Has Not Seemed Like Exile," in Sara Blair and Jonathan Freedman, eds., *Jewish in America* (Ann Arbor: University of Michigan Press, 2004), pp. 239–264.

1. Angels, Monsters, and Jews

1. The literature on antisemitism is, appropriately given its depressingly long-lasting history, extensive. The crucial text here remains Leon Poliakov's massive *Histoire de l'Antisemitisme* (Paris: Calmann-Lévy, 1955–1971), translated into English and published between 1974 and 1985 by Routledge and Kegan Paul. More recently, Albert Lindeman has attempted to counter Poliakov's argument—that antisemitism in modern sense owes its origins to the theological and economic antisemitisms of medieval and early modern Europe—with an argument that sees nineteenth-century antisemitism as a response to the increasing economic and political power of Jews; see *Esau's Tears: Modern Anti-Semitism and the Rise of the Jews* (New York: Cambridge University Press, 1997). I find his argument circular (relying on a quite restrictive definition of antisemitism, of course he finds its origins limited) and hence unconvincing. In addition to these, I've found most useful the following: Hannah Arendt, *The Origins of Totalitarianism* (New York: Harcourt, Brace, 1951); Nancy Harrowitz, *Antisemitism, Misogyny, and the Logic of Cultural Difference: Cesare Lombroso and Matilde Serao* (Lincoln: University of Nebraska Press, 1994); Gavin Langmuir, *Toward a Definition of Antisemitism* (Berkeley: University of California Press, 1990); Paul Rose, *Revolutionary Anti-Semitism in Germany from Kant to Wagner* (Princeton: Princeton University Press 1990); Rosemary Ruether, *Faith and Fratricide: The Theological Roots of Anti-Semitism* (New York: Seabury, 1974); Marc Shell, *Money, Language, and Thought: Literary and Philosophic Economies from the Medieval to the Modern Era* (Berkeley: University of California Press, 1982). A recent literature has arisen devoted to the rise of the so-called new antisemitism in Europe, largely in the context of young Muslims and/or skinheads, those left out of the economic and political order of modern Europe who turn to antisemitic acts (graveyard desecrations, beatings, and even murder) in response to their marginalization. Although it is perhaps the case that anti-Israeli sentiment fuels some of these acts, nevertheless what is most striking to me on a tropological level is the continuity between "new" and older antisemitisms, with Israel now serving as the synonym for "the Jew" in its most debased and horrific sense. For more on antisemitism and its ramifications in contemporary America, see chapter 5.

2. See Sander Gilman, *The Jew's Body* (London: Routledge, 1991) and *Freud, Race, and Gender* (Princeton: Princeton University Press, 1993).

3. As quoted in Marc Shell, *Money, Language, and Thought: Literary and Philosophic Economies from the Medieval to the Modern Era* (Baltimore: Johns Hopkins University Press, 1993), p. 51.

4. For a fuller treatment of the changes Proust rings on this interplay, and on the intersection between the discourse of Jewishness and that of homosexuality, see my essay, "Coming Out of the Jewish Closet with Marcel Proust," in Daniel Boyarin, Daniel Itzkovitz, and Anne Pelligrini, eds., *Queer Theory and the Jewish Question* (New York: Columbia University Press, 2004).

5. Tony Kushner, *Angels in America,* part 1: *Millennium Approaches* (New York: TCG, 1993), p. 21. Further citations in the text will refer to this edition and, when necessary, will be designated as *Millennium.*

6. Kushner, *Angels in America,* part 2: *Perestroika* (New York: TCG, 1995), p.114. Further citations in the text will refer to this edition and, when necessary, will be designated as *Perestroika.*

7. With respect to Cohn, I've learned the most from Nicholas Von Hoffman, *Citizen Cohn* (New York: Doubleday, 1988); and Michael Cadden's excellent essay, "Strange Angel: The Pinklisting of Roy Cohn," reprinted in Deborah R. Geis and Steven F. Kruger, eds., *Approaching the Millennium: Essays on Angels in America* (Ann Arbor: University of Michigan Press, 1997).

8. Arthur Lubow, "Tony Kushner's Paradise Lost," *New Yorker,* November 30, 1992, p. 60.

9. For an excellent account of the role of anti-Jewish thought in the period before the massive emigrations beginning in 1880, see Frederic Jaher, *A Scapegoat in the New Wilderness: The Origins and Rise of Anti-Semitism in America* (Cambridge: Harvard University Press, 1994). The use of the term *antisemitism* in this book strikes me as somewhat anachronistic; that term was coined late in the nineteenth century (by Moses Hess in Germany in 1868) and came quickly to reflect a racialized notion of Jewish difference. Nevertheless, Jaher shows that the other three pillars of American antisemitism—religious suspicion, economic anxiety, and an all-purpose fear of conspiracy—originate in the colonial period and persist throughout. These are well assayed by Aaron Gutfield and Robert Rockaway, "Demonic Images of the Jew in Nineteenth-Century United States," *American Jewish History* 89 (2001): 335–382.

10. See *The American Jew* (New York, 1888), collected in Michael Selzer, *Kike! A Documentary History of Anti-Semitism in America* (New York: World, 1972), p. 54. Further citations in the text will refer to this edition.

11. George Kibbe Turner, "Daughters of the Poor: A Plain Study of the Development of New York City as Leading Center of the White Slave Trade in the World, Under Tammany Hall," *McClure's* 34 (1909): 49.

12. Quoted in Robert Seitz Frey and Nancy Thomson-Frey, *The Silent and the Damned: The Murder of Mary Phagan and the Lynching of Leo Frank* (Madison: Lantham, 1987), p. 126; see also Leonard Dinnerstein, *The Leo Frank Case* (New York: Columbia University Press, 1968), p. 180. The best recent account of the Frank case, focusing more on its racial than its Jewish or queer subtexts, is Jeffrey Melnick, *Black-Jewish Relations on Trial: Leo Frank and Jim Conley in the New South* (Jackson: University of Mississippi Press, 2000).

13. Quoted in Dinnerstein, *Leo Frank Case,* p. 185.

14. Fellatio and Jewishness are explicitly linked elsewhere in the play; Harper attempts to win Joe back to her bed by telling him that "Mormons can give blowjobs." She learns how to do so not in her temple, however, but from "a little old Jewish lady with a German accent" on the radio (*Millennium*, 27).

15. David Savran, "Ambivalence, Utopia, and a Queer Sort of Materialism: How Angels in America Reconstructs the Nation," *Theater Journal* 47 (1995): 225.

16. Sacvan Bercovitch argues this most powerfully in *The American Jeremiad* (Madison: University of Wisconsin Press, 1978).

17. Tony Kushner, *Thinking About the Longstanding Problems of Virtue : Essays, a Play, Two Poems and a Prayer* (New York: Theater Communications Group, 1997), p. 5.

18. Walter Benjamin, "Theses on the Philosophy of History," in *Illuminations*, trans. Harry Zohn (New York: Schocken, 1969), pp. 257–58.

19. Naomi Seidman, "The Ghost of Queer Loves Past: Ansky's *Dybbuk* and the Sexual Transformation of Ashkenaz," in Daniel Boyarin, Daniel Itzkovitz, and Anne Pellegrini, *Queer Theory and the Jewish Question* (New York: Columbia University Press, 2003).

20. Alisa Solomon, *Redressing the Canon: Essays on Theater and Gender* (London: Routledge, 1997).

21. *The Dybbuk: A Play in Four Acts*, trans. Henry G. Ahlsberg and Winifred Katzin (New York: Liveright, 1926), p. 144.

22. Ibid.

23. Yale Strom, *The Book of Klezmer: The History, the Music, the Folklore* (Chicago: A Cappella, 2002), p. 241.

24. See Howard Pollack, *George Gershwin: His Life and Work* (Berkeley: University of California Press, 2007), pp. 461–464, for the most complete account of Gershwin's engagement with the *Dybbuk* material.

25. Amanda Vaill, *Somewhere: The Life of Jerome Robbins* (New York: Broadway, 2006), p. 33.

26. Ibid., p. 444.

27. Humphrey Burton, *Leonard Bernstein* (New York: Doubleday, 1994), p. 424.

28. Bernstein described this process at some length in an interview with Richard Shepard; see Richard Shepard, "Kaballah Numerology Inspires a Bernstein 'Dybbuk,'" *New York Times*, May 9, 1974, p. 57.

29. My perspective here differs from that of David Schiller, *Bloch, Schoenberg, Bernstein: Assimilating Jewish Music* (New York: Oxford University Press, 2003). For Schiller, Bernstein's musical expressions of his Jewishness represent an attempt to assimilate, or incorporate, the Jewish tradition in that of Western art music, as a powerful affirmation of his own Jewishness and of the survival of the Jewish people after the Holocaust. From my position, Bernstein's endeavor is to suggest how powerfully that presence is always already there and throughout the cultural field. So, for example, by including Hebrew verses in his *Chichester Psalms* (1965), he reminds us of the vital presence of Judaism in Christianity; and by his mixture of Broadway idioms in works like *Mass* (1971), Bernstein reminds us of the equally inexpugnable

presence of Jewishness in the cultures of the West despite their frequent attempts to marginalize, persecute, or exterminate Jews.

30. Quoted in Burton, *Leonard Bernstein*, p. 422.

31. Vaill, *Somewhere*, p. 443.

32. Sholem Aleichem, *Stempeniu*, in Marvin Zuckerman and Marian Herbst, eds., *The Three Great Classic Writers of Modern Yiddish Literature*, vol. 2: *Sholem Aleichem*, trans. Jaochim Neugroschel (Malibu: J. Simon, Pangloss, 1994), p. 101. Further citations in the text will refer to this edition. Because this is the only translation of the story I've seen that transliterates *Stempeniu* with an "i," I'll be silently correcting it to the more conventional "Stempenyu" in what follows. Neugroschel's innovative translation is known in Yiddish circles as the "jive "version of the text because of his decision to translate the passages written in *klezmerloshn* into an American hipster argot of the 1950s. For a similar analysis of the story, and of the klezmorim as marginal men, focusing more on its linguistic aspects, see Robert Rothstein, "Klezmer-loshn: The Language of Jewish Folk Musicians," in Mark Slobin, *American Klezmer: Its Roots and Offshoots* (Berkeley: University of California Press, 2002), pp. 24–34.

33. Women, it should be noted, were barred from klezmer bands but were bearers of the folk music traditions. Ansky, for example, collected many songs from female native informants.

34. See Anita Norich, "Portraits of the Artist: Sholem Aleichem's Artist Novels," *Prooftexts* 3 (1984): 237–251.

35. Henry Sapoznik, *Klezmer! Jewish Music from Old World to Our World* (New York: Schirmer, 1999), pp. 103–104.

36. The account of Brandwein that follows is drawn from the following sources: Sapoznik's excellent liner notes to the 1997 CD, *Naftule Brandwein; King of the Klezmer Clarinet* (Boston: Rounder 1127); Strom, *The Book of Klezmer*; Rogovoy, *The Essential Klezmer*; and an excellent dissertation by Joel Edward Rubin, "The Art of the Klezmer: Improvisation and Ornamentation in the Commercial Recordings of New York Clarinettists Naftule Branwein and Dave Tarras, 1922–1929" (London: City University of London Department of Music, 2001). Rubin is the source of the anecdote about Brandwein warning his son against klezmer I allude to above.

37. Walter Zev Feldman, "Bulgărească/Bulgarish/Bulgar: The Transformation of a Klezmer Dance Genre," in Slobin, *American Klezmer*, pp. 84–126.

38. Gary Giddins, *Visions of Jazz: The First Century* (New York: Oxford University Press), pp. 477–480.

39. To square the circle, the Klezmatics have recently contributed a klezmer score for a children's cartoon program, hosted by Rosie O'Donnell, accompanying the voice of shtickmeister Jackie Mason.

40. Anthony Coleman, *Sephardic Tinge* cover notes, Tzadik 7656.

41. As quoted on his website: http://www.robertojuanrodriguez.com/home.html.

42. Elliott Simon, "Roberto Juan Rodriguez," *All About Jazz*, January 25, 2003, http://www.allaboutjazz.com/php/article.php?id=54. The quotation from Rodriguez is also included in this article.

43. Mark Ribot, "Klezmer authenticity draft." Unpublished manifesto (c. 1995?). Courtesy Marc Ribot and Tamar Barzel.

44. Interview with Anthony Coleman, in *NewMusicBox: The Web Magazine from the American Music Center,* http://www.newmusicbox.org/page.nmbx?id=69hf01. Coleman makes his relation to both the klezmer revival and the radical Jewish culture scene clearer elsewhere in the interview:

> Klezmer—its gestures, its scales, its instrumentation—are the basis for the signification of Jewishness in nearly all the New Jewish Music. And that's why I'm uncomfortable with it. It's not that I haven't used it—you can surely hear it in my piece "Jevrejski by Night" (Disco by Night [Avant]). But the challenge for me has always been to figure out a way to use the tropes and signifiers in a more abstract way—Barnett Newman, Morton Feldman. That's my Radical Jewish Culture too! I'm looking for an image, an abstraction with traces of figuration—like DeKooning's women, Beckett's haunted landscapes, the dates and places in Celan (read Derrida's essay on Celan, "Shibboleth").

45. The currents of thought I am tracing here are quite divergent, and I conflate them only for the sake of necessary brevity: I mean only to be suggestive with respect to the theorization of postcoloniality, dealing here merely—and merely touching upon—the example of Bhabha on the one hand and the quite different take offered by Appiah. With respect to the first of these, it should be noted that, in addition to a number of side comments in his important essays, Bhabha has written quite interestingly on the subject of the Jew; see his forward to Bryan Cheyette and Laura Marcus, eds., *Modernity, Culture, and "the Jew"* (Cambridge: Polity, 1988). My own view is that, like Edward Said (who identified himself in one of his last essays with Adorno and other Frankfurt School theorists), Bhabha understands his own role as a postcolonial diasporic intellectual in terms that are inextricable from those used to assess Jews in the cultures of the West, a fact that causes some significant dis- and relocations in his thinking. In this he is very much like Fanon, who, as Bryan Cheyette has been powerfully arguing, finds his politics significantly shaped by a career-long identification of himself with/distancing of himself from both real, live Jews and the phantasmatic figure of "the Jew." For a treatment of postcoloniality and the Jewish question significantly in dialogue with Bhabha's, see Daniel Boyarin, *Unheroic Conduct: The Rise of Heterosexuality and the Invention of the Jewish Man* (Berkeley: University of California Press, 1997), especially pp. 305–308.

Appiah's deployment of the idiom of cosmopolitanism engages with many of the same questions, explicitly, however, framed in an attempt to construct a dialogue between Anglo-American ethics and the problematics of postcolonial identity formation. See *The Ethics of Identity* (Princeton: Princeton University Press, 2005). His lovely trope "rooted cosmopolitanism" suggests that the enterprise of affirming cosmopolitan identities doesn't invalidate the importance of the local—or vice versa; but there does seem to me to be some slight blitheness about his sense of historical process throughout Appiah's account of the mixing of cultures over time via conquest and imperialism as well as via trade and intellectual commerce. Ribot's trope works better for me in that it acknowledges the price paid in the service of making the cosmopolitan as well as, with the bitter humor of survivors, the antisemitic dimensions of the critique of the cosmopolitan's lack of connection to national, cultural, or linguistic tradition (one we find in T. S. Eliot, for example, as well as Hitler, Goebbels, or Stalin).

2. Arthur Miller, Marilyn Monroe, and the Making of Ethnic Masculinity

1. Sidney Stahl Weinberg, *World of Our Mothers: The Lives of Jewish Immigrant Women* (Chapel Hill: University of North Carolina Press, 1988).

2. To cite but one case: consider the "queer" moments in *The Rise of David Levinsky*—of Levinksy's youthful crush on a fellow yeshiva student in his home town of Antomir and then his transplantation of that crush to an American youth who introduces him to the Yiddish theater; for an excellent treatment, see Magdalena Zaborowska, "Americanization of a 'Queer Fellow': Performing Jewishness and Sexuality in Abraham Cahan's *The Rise of David Levinsky*, with a Footnote on the (Monica) Lewinsky'ed Nation," in Tracy Fessenden, Nicholas Radel, and Magdalena Zaborowska, eds., *The Puritan Origins of American Sex: Religion, Sexuality, and National Identity in American Literature* (New York: Routledge, 2001), pp. 213–234, and, more recently, Warren Hoffman, "The Rise and Fall of David Levinsky: Performing Jewish American Heterosexuality," *Modern Fiction Studies* 51 (2005): 393–415. Or one might follow the nexus between incest, sexual othering, and Jewishness traced by Sander Gilman into texts like *Call It Sleep*, in which the protagonist is understood to be culturally queer even as he is constructed as the paradigm of (sensitive) Jewish masculinity.

3. Arthur Miller, *Timebends: A Life* (New York: Penguin, 1995), pp. 130–131. Further citations in the text will refer to this edition.

4. See George L. Mosse, *Nationalism and Sexuality: Middle-Class Morality and Sexual Norms in Modern Europe* (Madison: University of Wisconsin Press, 1985); and, inter alia, Sander Gilman, *The Case of Sigmund Freud: Medicine and Identity at the Fin de Siècle* (Baltimore: Johns Hopkins University Press, 1993).

5. Daniel Boyarin, *Unheroic Conduct: The Rise of Heterosexuality and the Invention of the Jewish Man* (Berkeley: University of California Press, 1997), p. 151.

6. For the significance of Nordau's life and career, the best overview is provided by Daniel Pick, *Faces of Degeneration: A European Disorder, 1848–1918* (Cambridge: Cambridge University Press, 1993). In addition to Boyarin's, the best critique of the muscle Jew as a problematic reaction formation is Paul Breines's provocative *Tough Jews: Political Fantasies and the Moral Dilemmas of American Jewry* (New York: Basic, 1990).

7. Robert Park, Herbert Miller, and Kenneth Thompson, *Old World Traits Transplanted: The Early Sociology of Culture* (New York: Harper, 1921), p. 134.

8. Hutchins Hapgood, *The Spirit of the Ghetto* (Cambridge: Belknap, 1967), p. 17. Hapgood's "native informant," it should be observed, was none other than Abraham Cahan.

9. For more on the rise of the intellectual culture Jew, see Jonathan Freedman, *The Temple of Culture: Assimilation and Anti-Semitism, Literary Anglo-America* (New York: Oxford, 2000).

10. For these developments, see, inter alia, Albert Fried, *The Rise and. Fall of the Jewish Gangster in America* (New York: Holt, Rinehart, and Winston, 1980); Jenna Weisman Joselit, *Our Gang: Jewish Crime and the New York Jewish Community, 1900–1940* (Bloomington: Indiana University Press, 1983); Michael Alexander, *Jazz Age Jews* (Princeton: Princeton University Press, 2001).

11. See Matthew Roudané, ed., *Conversations with Arthur Miller* (Jackson: University of Mississippi Press, 1987), p. 109.

12. Robert Sylvester, "Brooklyn Boy Makes Good," *Saturday Evening Post* 222 (July 16, 1949): 26.

13. Philip Roth, *Portnoy's Complaint* (New York: Random House, 1969), p. 152. Further citations in the text will refer to this edition.

14. Anthony Summers, *Goddess: The Secret Lives of Marylin Monroe* (New York: Macmillan, 1985), p. 65.

15. S. Paige Baty, *Marilyn Monroe: The Making of a Body Politic* (Berkeley: University of California Press, 1995), p. 104. Baty gives Mailer's *Marilyn* as her source but I have been unable to find this quotation on the page she cites. The sentiments it expresses, however, are not at all inconsistent with what we know about Marilyn's attitude toward Lincoln or, for that matter, father figures.

16. Barbara Leaming, *Marilyn Monroe* (New York: Three Rivers, 1998), p. 243.

17. It may be appropriate to note in this context that this 1951 film presented a blonde mistress of a Washington politician educated—and in turn educating—an intellectual snob, and that the film's blonde bombshell—Judy Holliday née Julie Tumin—was not only groomed by the studios to be the next Marilyn Monroe but was a daughter of Upper West Side socialist intellectuals. But, to complete the chain of ironic associations involved here, she, unlike Miller, testified before the House Un-American Activities Committee in 1952 and was cleared by that body.

18. David Savran, *Communists, Cowboys, and Queers: The Politics of Masculinity in the Work of Arthur Miller and Tennessee Williams* (Minneapolis: University of Minnesota Press, 1992).

19. With respect to Rosten, I have largely relied on Martin Gottfried, *Arthur Miller: His Life and Work* (Cambridge: Da Capo, 2003), an account that is obviously biased toward Miller's point of view. My point here is not to take sides in this or any other quarrel—Rosten is not the only old friend of Miller's to have been charmed by Marilyn, and the charm (unlike Mailer's response) seems to have had as much to do with the sense of protectiveness that Marilyn called forth in Norman and his wife as anything else. But, as such, he no less than Bessie, Mailer, and Roth, found himself entering into competition with Miller not as a friend or a literary role model but as a *writer*.

20. Alvah Bessie, *The Symbol* (New York: Random House, 1967), p. 201. Further citations in the text will refer to this edition.

21. Norman Mailer, *Marilyn: A Biography* (New York: Grosset and Dunlap, 1973), pp. 19–20. Further citations in the text will refer to this edition.

22. Stefann Kanfer, "Two Myths Converge: NM Discovers MM," *Time* 102 (July 16, 1973): 60.

23. Richard Dyer: *Heavenly Bodies: Film Stars and Society* (New York: St. Martin's, 1986), pp. 42–44. As a sign of just how hegemonic Dyer's reading has become, consider the following passage from David Lubin's recent *Shooting Kennedy: JFK and the Culture of Images* (Berkeley: University of California Press, 1995):

> As the Mailer [description of Monroe's famous skirt-blowing scene in *The Seven-Year Itch*] indicates, the photos also celebrate the male gaze and women's corresponding self-objectification. Moreover, in subtle or not so subtle ways they suggest that only *whiteness* can transform the city from a jungle to a paradise. Hollywood's reigning blond sex goddess (*goddess* derives from the same root as *goodness*) symbolically modeled the universal worth of Caucasian hair color, skin pigmentation, and, ultimately, social identity. Soon after Marilyn famously flashed her white thighs and panties across America's movie screens in the summer of 1955, the Emmet Till murder case stunned the nation. (56)

24. See Matthew Frye Jacobson, *Roots Too* (Cambridge: Harvard, 2006) for a highly skeptical account of Kennedy's self-binding not only to his Irishness but also to his role in promulgating (and politically profiting from) the idea of a "nation of immigrants." I continue the dialogue with Jacobson below.

25. Nathan Glazer and Daniel Patrick Moynihan, *Beyond the Melting Pot: The Negroes, Puerto Ricans, Jews, Italians, and Irish of New York City* (Cambridge: MIT Press, 1963), p. 287. Further citations in the text will refer to this edition.

26. Emile Durkheim, *Suicide: A Study in Sociology*, trans. John Spaulding and George Simpson (Glencoe, IL: Free Press, 1951), p. 253.

27. I'm referring here to such works as C. Wright Mills, *White Collar: The American Middle Classes* (New York: Oxford University Press, 1951); William Whyte, *The Organisation Man* (New York: Doubleday, 1956); Sloan Wilson, *The Man in the Grey Flannel Suit* (New York: Simon and Schuster, 1955).The account of the late forties and early fifties culture goes somewhat against the grain of recent American studies scholarship, which has emphasized the extraordinary gender and racial ferment and the savage political repression evident throughout the seemingly complacent 1950s. This vision necessarily downplays the kinds of institutions and events I'm referring to here—the rise of the suburb, the birth of the Interstate Highway System, and the rise of mass college education, all of which conduced to the augmentation and depoliticization of the middle class. These views are in my opinion complementary.

3. Antisemitism Without Jews

1. Rachel Donadio, "Apocalypse, Nu? How New York Came to Embrace Mr. LaHaye Is Part Cosmic Irony, Part Business as Usual," *New York Observer*, September 27, 2004, p. 1.

2. Amy Johnson Frykholm, *Rapture Culture: Left Behind in Evangelical America* (New York: Oxford University Press, 2004). I am indebted to Fryckholm for much of the analysis in this paragraph.

3. Melani McAlister, "Prophecy, Politics, and the Popular: The *Left Behind* Series and Christian Fundamentalism's New World Order," *South Atlantic Quarterly* 102 (2003): 773–798. Further citations in the text refer to this edition.

4. For the role of the Left Behind series in cementing the powerful alliance between the Christian and the Israeli right, see Yaakov Ariel, "A Historical Discussion of Jewish-Christian Relations," in Bruce David Forbes and Jeanne Halgren Kilde, eds., *Rapture, Revelation and the End Times: Exploring the Left Behind Series* (New York: Palgrave Macmillan, 2004), pp. 131–166. More recently, Detroit-born Israeli journalist Ze'ev Chafets has authored a by-and-large sympathetic account of this conjunction in both the U.S. and Israel, *A Match Made in Heaven: American Jews, Christian Zionists, and One Man's Exploration of the Weird and Wonderful Judeo-Evangelical Alliance* (New York: HarperCollins, 2007). I wish the subtitle could be construed as completely ironic.

5. Timothy LaHaye and Jerry B. Jenkins, *Glorious Appearing: The End of Days* (Wheaton, IL.: Tyndale House, 2004), pp. 127, 151. Further citations in the text will refer to this edition. The question of the authorship of these books is somewhat complicated. Jenkins is the actual composer of the words on the page—he has a long and distinguished career as an author of adventure novels, children's books, and the Gil Thorp comic series. LaHaye sketches the plots and articulates the theology. He is a longtime Christian New Right activist, cofounder of the Moral Majority, as well as a prominent writer on (born-again) Christian ethics and marriage practices. I list LaHaye as the first among the authors of the series, which is also how libraries list them in their catalogues.

6. Bernard McGinn, *Antichrist: Two Thousand Years of the Human Fascination with Evil* (San Francisco: HarperSanFrancisco, 1994), pp. 255–256.

7. Timothy LaHaye and Jerry B. Jenkins, *The Remnant: On the Brink of Armageddon* (Wheaton, IL: Tyndale House, 2002), p. 81.

8. McGinn, *Antichrist*, pp. 74–75; and Joshua Trachtenberg, *The Devil and the Jews: The Medieval Conception of the Jew and Its Relation to Modern Antisemitism* (New Haven: Yale University Press, 1943).

9. Robert Fuller, *Naming the Antichrist: The History of an American Obsession* (New York: Oxford University Press, 1995), p. 143.

10. Timothy LaHaye and Jerry B. Jenkins, *Left Behind: A Novel of the Earth's Last Days* (Wheaton, IL: Tyndale House, 1995), p. 114. Further citations in the text will refer to this edition.

11. As Lara Trubowitz has reminded me, Dracula himself has often been interpreted as a version of the figure of the Wandering Jew. The presence of this, associating as it were underneath the identification of Carpathia with other forms of evil—soon to include Hitler as well as the Pope, as we shall see below—enacts the process whose dynamics I'm trying to stress here: the refitting of classic antisemitic structures to new uses.

12. Sander Gilman, *Smart Jews: The Construction of the Image of Jewish Superior Intelligence* (Lincoln: University of Nebraska Press, 1996).

13. Timothy LaHaye and Jerry B. Jenkins, *Desecration: Antichist Takes the Throne* (Wheaton, IL: Tyndale House, 2001), pp. 13–14.

14. Jeffrey Goldberg, "I Antichrist," *Slate*, November 5, 1999; http://slate.msn.com/id/45483.

15. Richard Hofstadter, *Anti-Intellectualism in American Life* (New York: Knopf, 1963). Rereading Hofstadter in the context of the current social and political scene is a fascinating experience. One is both impressed by the applicability of his analysis to our current moment and depressed by his evident faith that, for all of its currency in American life, anti-intellectualism was by and large a thing of the past.

16. Bryan Cheyette, *Constructions of "the Jew" in English Literature and Society: Racial Representations, 1875–1945* (Cambridge: Cambridge University Press, 1993); Jonathan Freedman, *The Temple of Culture: Assimilation and Anti-Semitism, Literary Anglo-America* (New York: Oxford, 2000).

17. Timothy LaHaye and Jerry B. Jenkins, *Nicolae:The Rise of Antichrist* (Wheaton, IL: Tyndale House, 1997), p. 129. Further citations in the text will refer to this edition.

18. See Thomas R. Ascher, *Light For Nations: A Short History of Jews in the Modern World* (N.p.: Vanguard News Network, 2005), p. 5.

19. See Laurence Goodwyn, *Democratic Promise: The Populist Moment in America* (New York: Oxford University Press, 1976), pp. 26ff. for the alliance and its role in sparking the Populist movement.

20. Neither of these is explicitly identified as a Jew. But their Old Testament first names associate them, at the very least, with Hebrew origins.

21. Michael Barkun, "Coxey's Army as a Milennial Movement," in Ronald Edsforth and Larry Bennett, eds., *Popular Culture and Political Change in Modern America* (Binghamton: State University of New York Press, 1991), p. 28. Further citations in the text will refer to this edition.

22. *Coxey's Sound Money*, April 7, 1896.

The question of the exact nature of antisemitism in the populist movement is an endlessly vexed one. Controversies were kicked off in the 1950s by (largely Jewish) historians and political theorists like Richard Hofstadter, Seymour Martin Lipset, and Daniel Bell, after Hofstadter ascribed to populism the "identification of the Jew with the usurer and the 'international gold ring' . . . the central theme of the American anti-Semitism of the age," and he went further by claiming "entirely verbal" antisemitism of the populists as "activat[ing] most of what we have of modern popular anti-Semitism in the United States"—a "persistent linkage between antisemitism and money and credit obsessions." Hofstadter, *The Age of Reform: From Bryan to F.D.R.* (New York: Knopf, 1955), pp. 78, 80–81. Bell and Lipset followed in such works as *The New American Right* (New York: Criterion, 1955) by linking populist energies to antisemitism, working-class reaction, and such formations as Father Coughlin and the McCarthyite right (and later, the John Birch Society).

In the 1960s, (mostly gentile) historians vigorously dissented. John Higham and C. Vann Woodward minimized the force of populist antisemitism in comparison with European variants or that of the American gentry elite, who, after all, unlike the populists, had the clout to get their views written into law. Norman Pollack pointed to the lack of overt antisemitic comments in the vast majority of populist tracts, letters, private papers, etc., and to the explicit warnings against antisemitism by the likes of Bryan, as signs that the occasional antisemitic comment or slogan was an exception to the rule. So, it should be added, does Michael Kazin, whose recent book on William Jennings Bryan includes a long exculpatory account of Bryan's tolerance for Jews, his refusal to engage in ad hominem antisemitic attacks, his insistence on liberal pluralism. See inter alia Norman Pollack, "Hofstadter on Populism," *Journal of Southern History* 26 (1960): 478–486, and "The Myth of Populist Anti-Semitism," *American Historical Review* 68 (1962): 78–88; C. Vann Woodward, "The Populist Heritage and the Intellectual," in *The Burden of Southern History*, 3d ed. (Baton Rouge: Louisiana State University Press, 1993), p. 155 (the essay was originally published in 1957 in *The American Scholar*); John Higham, "Anti-Semitism in the Gilded Age: A Reinterpretation," *Mississippi Valley Historical Review* 43 (March 1957): 559–578; and Michael Kazin, *A Godly Hero: The Life of William Jennings Bryan* (New York: Knopf, 2006), pp. 145–146.

These critics are by and large motivated by a desire to locate a positive, pre- or non-Marxist tradition of popular empowerment, with which I sympathize, and a sense that American antisemitism was less heinous than its European counterparts, which which I also agree. But it does lead to a kind of special pleading that I find troublesome. I thus incline more to the Hofstadter view, with a number of demurrals. There is ample evidence throughout the populist movement (and its successors) of the two main streams of antisemitism in the U.S.: the economic and the religious, and evidence, more importantly, of their problematic coalescence. Neither of these is, as the above suggest, as problematic as their European counterparts. Both, as Woodward suggests, are subsidiary to race as a problem in populist and populistlike movements. But the coalescence of these two remains one of the dirty little secrets of American life, persistently swept under the rug, marginalized, or just plain forgotten in accounts of American culture and political life, and, as I indicated at the outset of this chapter, I think they're far more prevalent and far more dangerous in the America that lies beyond the purview of most academics. At the very least, the fact that they each are powerful impulses in the best-selling books of our time should give us pause. Christian-inflected populism (understood as suspicion of elites, fear of economic forces larger than the individual community, anti-intellectualism, antiscientism, and a sense that true wisdom and virtue reside with the people) looks different now—it is not only a rural but increasingly a suburban phenomenon—but it has had real effects in the political sphere.

23. Leonard Dinnerstein, *Anti-Semitism in America* (New York: Oxford, 2001), p. 250.

24. Just to confirm LaHaye and Jenkins's promulgation of classically antisemitic fantasies under the guise of their Christianizing program, as I was completing this chapter, I learned that Tyndale House offered for sale a new video game, *Left Behind: Eternal Forces*, described by a hostile critic as follows:

> This game immerses children in present-day New York City—500 square blocks, stretching from Wall Street to Chinatown, Greenwich Village, the United Nations headquarters, and Harlem. . . . Imagine: you are a foot soldier in a paramilitary group whose purpose is to remake America as a Christian theocracy, and establish its worldly vision of the dominion of Christ over all aspects of life. You are issued high-tech military weaponry, and instructed to engage the infidel on the streets of New York City. You are on a mission—both a religious mission and a military mission—to convert or kill Catholics, Jews, Muslims, Buddhists, gays, and anyone who advocates the separation of church and state—especially moderate, mainstream Christians. Your mission is "to conduct physical and spiritual warfare"; all who resist must be taken out with extreme prejudice. You have never felt so powerful, so driven by a purpose: you are 13 years old.

See Jonathan Hutson, "The Purpose Driven Life Takers," www.talk2action.org/story/2006/5/29/195855/959.

4. The Human Stain of Race

1. Ross Posnock, "Purity and Danger: On Philip Roth," *Raritan* 21 (Fall 2001): 87.

2. See Jonathan Freedman, *The Temple of Culture: Assimilation and Anti-Semitism in Literary Anglo-America* (New York: Oxford University Press, 2000), pp. 220ff.

3. See Eric Sundquist, *Strangers in the Land: Blacks, Jews, Post-Holocaust America* (Cambridge: Harvard University Press), pp. 516–517; Sundquist is quoting from Anatole Broyard, "Portrait of the Inauthentic Negro" *Commentary* 10 (July 1950): 63.

4. James Weldon Johnson, *The Autobiography of an Ex-Coloured Man* (New York: Vintage, 1989), p. 211. Further citations in the text will refer to this edition.

5. Samira Kawash, *Dislocating the Color Line: Identity, Hybridity, and Singularity in African-American Narrative* (Stanford: Stanford University Press, 1997), pp. 135–155. Kawash's reading is infuriatingly irrefutable: the first-person narrator of the text stands outside constructions of racial identity, comes to know himself as "black" or "white" only through the interventions of others; therefore there's no

stable moment in the text at which his racial identity can be precisely named or known. I totally agree with her assessment that "we must take the narrator not for what the cultural logic of passing decrees him to be, a truly black man passing for white, but for what the narrative presents him as—unnameable" (155), and I too would want to emphasize the epistemological impasse that the texts seeks to create as it takes up the question of race as identity, but I would wish to press more on the return to racial identification under the sign of sentiment.

6. Philip Roth, *The Human Stain* (New York: Houghton Mifflin, 2000), p. 360. Further citations in the text will refer to this edition.

7. The literature on sentimentalism is immense. The classic works in the context of U.S. literary culture are, of course, Anne Douglas, *The Feminization of American Culture* (New York: Knopf, 1977); Jane Tompkins, "Sentimental Power," in *Sensational Designs: The Cultural Work of American Fiction* (New York: Oxford University Press, 1986); Mary Kelley, *Public Women, Private Stage: Literary Domesticity in Nineteenth-Century America* (New York: Oxford University Press, 1984); and Gillian Brown, *Domestic Individualism: Imagining Self in Nineteenth-Century America* (Berkeley: University of California Press, 1990). With respect to the crossover between sentimentalism and race, see (on the white side) Philip Fisher on Harriet Beecher Stowe in *Hard Facts: Setting and Form in the American Novel* (New York: Oxford University Press, 1986); and Karen Sanchez-Eppler, *Touching Liberty: Abolition, Feminism, and the Politics of the Body* (Berkeley: University of California Press, 1977); and on the side of African American writing, inter alia, Lora Romero, *Home Fronts: Nineteenth-Century Domesticity and Its Critics* (Durham: Duke University Press, 1997).

8. Cindy Weinstein, *Family, Kinship, and Sympathy in Nineteenth-Century American Literature* (Cambridge: Cambridge University Press, 2004).

9. For the script and a shot-by-shot analysis of Sirk's *Imitation of Life*, see Lucy Fischer, ed., *Imitation of Life*, Rutgers Films in Print (New Brunswick: Rutgers University Press, 1991). The scene I discuss is transcribed on pp. 140–141.

10. Philip Roth, "Zuckerman's Alter Brain" (interview with Charles McGrath), *New York Times Book Review* (May 7, 2000).

11. Brent Staples, "Back When Skin Color Was Destiny—Unless You Passed for White" *New York Times*, November 1, 2003.

12. Lauren Berlant, "National Brands/National Body," in Bruce Robbins, ed., *The Phantom Public Sphere* (Minneapolis: University of Minnesota Press, 1993).

13. See Mark Schechner, "Third Thoughts: Can't Get No Satisfaction," unpublished MS.

14. Roth, "Zuckerman's Alter Brain."

15. Jeffrey Melnick, *A Right to Sing the Blues: African Americans, Jews, and American Popular Song* (Cambridge: Harvard University Press, 1999).

16. Richard Crawford, *The American Musical Landscape: The Business of Musicianship from Billings to Gershwin, Updated with a New Preface* (Berkeley: University of California Press, 2000 [1993]), p. 233.

17. See Michael Rogin, *Blackface, White Noise* (Berkeley: University of California Press, 1996), p. 185.

18. A brief musicological note. The Shaw band to which Roth refers—the one that included Roy Eldridge—recorded "The Man I Love" in two versions in June, 1945. Neither of these was released by Victor, which used many other songs from these sessions (interestingly, they included seven other Gershwin songs), but the two versions have been made public in the intervening years. The one I refer to here is demonstrably more "Jewish"—i.e., the clarinet solo contains more klezmer motifs (mordents, *krechts,* glissando runs, etc.) than the other; I found it on *The Chronological Artie Shaw and His Orchestra* V.5 (Paris: Classics Records, 2002). The second version, in which Shaw's sole is less "klezmerical" but still not untouched by klezmer ornamentation, was included by Shaw in his own anthology, *Self-Portrait* (Bluebird, 2001), disc 3, cut 17; this version, too, was originally rejected by Victor but included in Shaw's LP *The Complete Artie Shaw.* (Eldridge's solo on both versions is almost identical.) The presence of dual takes; their rejection by Victor; the accentuated presence of klezmer motifs in the one Shaw chose not to rerelease: all these suggest the dynamics of veiling and passing I am trying to point to here. Shaw's Jewishness is there and not there, referenced and hidden at one and the same time throughout this session.

19. Rogovoy, *The Essential Klezmer*, p. 73.

20. Melnick, *A Right to Sing the Blues*, p. 137.

21. Richard Sudhalter, *Lost Chords: White Musicians and Their Contribution to Jazz, 1915–1945* (New York: Oxford University Press, 1999), p. 583. Further citations in the text refer to this edition.

22. The allusion here is quite complex. Russian folk music didn't merely enter into klezmer via the shared experience of Jews and Russians in the Pale of Settlement, but was itself shaped by the Jews who had lived among the Russians well before they were confined to that area (and vice versa). So in some sense, as Shaw klezmerizes the Russian folk song; reappropriating the Jewish element that is repressed or denied in aggressively Slavophilic iterations of Russian "folk" identity, in exactly the same way Roth seems to be claiming Eldridge's "black torch song" does with the African American elements in Gershwin's tune.

23. Artie Shaw, *The Trouble with Cinderella: An Outline of Identity* (New York: Farrar, Straus and Giroux, 1952), p. 92. Further citations will refer to this edition.

24. I was drawn to this passage by Ross Posnock, to whom thanks are due.

25. Judith Shulevitz, "The Book Club" (exchange with Brent Staples), *Slate*, April 27, 2000.

26. Contra this view, see the usually grouchy Stanley Crouch, who writes that in *The Human Stain* Roth "finally broke out of this ongoing segregation of American fiction.... You know—black people writing about black people over and over again, Jews writing about Jews. Brother Roth decided to climb the fence. It's a good sign not only for him but for American fiction." Quoted in Jennifer Senior, "Philip Roth Blows Up," *New York* 87 (May 1, 2000).

27. Matthew Frye Jacobson, *Whiteness of a Different Color: European Immigrants and the Alchemy of Race* (Cambridge: Harvard University Press, 1988), pp. 2–4, 172.

28. For Bauman's argument, see Zygmunt Bauman, *Modernity and Ambivalence* (Ithaca: Cornell University Press, 1991); to Bauman antisemitism is intimately tied to the project of modernity via the mechanism he calls proteophobia—fear of that which seems metamorphic, viscous, category challenging. As Daniel Itzkovitz has shown, precisely this sense of the Jew animated racist and antisemitic discourses in the U.S. during the period between 1880 and 1924. See Daniel Itzkovitz, "Passing Like Me: Jewish Chameleonism and the Politics of Race," in Maria Carla Sánchez and Linda Schlossberg, eds., *Passing: Identity and Interpretation in Sexuality, Race, and Religion* (New York: New York University Press, 2001), pp. 38–63. I've learned a good deal from Itzkovitz's work; particularly important to my thinking has been not only this essay but also his excellent "Secret Temples," in Jonathan Boyarin and Daniel Boyarin, eds., *Jews and Other Differences: The New Jewish Cultural Studies* (Minneapolis: University of Minnesota Press, 1997), pp. 176–202. A propos of Bauman's emphasis on the idea of the Jew as embodying fluidity, category-lessness, it might be added here that the discourse of this era persistently figured immigrants (and hence Russian-born Jews) in figures like *flood, tide,* or *wave.*

29. Walter Mosley, interview in *Newsday,* January 7, 2004. In another interview Mosley further nuances this claim: "Although Mosley saw his mother as white in 1950s America, he sees Jews as the 'Negroes of Europe.' Racial classifications are 'finally just cultural attitudes': his mother would not have been 'white' in 1930s Germany." See Maya Jaggi, "Socrates of the Streets," *Guardian,* September 6, 2003.

30. John Jackson, *Real Black: Adventures in Racial Sincerity* (Chicago: University of Chicago Press, 2005), p. 93. For Jackson's near encounter with his own "transnational" identity in the streets of Crown Heights or Flatbush, which seem closer to Kingston, Jamaica than Jamaica, Queens, see p. 92. I don't mean to fold his account of the Black Israelites into my treatment of African American and Jewish identities; they're a fascinating movement, or rather series of movements in and of themselves. And their paranoia has more than a little bit of reality behind it: it was a sect of Black Israelites who were firebombed by (African American mayor) Richard Goode in Philadelphia. For more on the varieties of Black Israelites and the literary ramifications of the MOVE catastrophe, see Sundquist, *Strangers in the Land,* especially pp. 464–473.

31. Richard Jerome, "Hidden Identities" *People* 60 (November 10, 2003): 121–122.

32. Don Byron, who is himself no mean shakes as a musicologist, has served, I might add parenthetically, as one of Ingrid Monson's informants, especially in her writing about the racial dynamics of allusion in jazz improvisation. And Monson herself, to complete the chain, was a klezmer performer alongside Byron at the New England Conservatory.

33. Richard Wagner, *Judaism in Music and Other Essays,* trans. William Ashton Ellis (Lincoln: University of Nebraska Press, 1995), pp. 96–99. Further citations in the text will refer to this edition.

34. Asim Memon, "Interview with Uri Caine," *All About Jazz* (December 2002), http://www.allaboutjazz.com/articles/asim1202.htm.

35. Ibid. Caine goes on to assert in the interview: "But then, there are many other aspects of that piece where I'm taking the harmonic form and giving jazz improvisors a chance to solo on it. And so, in a sense, there's a history of jazz that's embedded in the piece, too. Starting with the [Louis Armstrong's] Hot Six going to a much freer, open type of playing. There are references to all the other elements of Bach, like PDQ Bach, Switched On Bach, The Swingle Singers, Jacques Loussier, all these types of things that were part of Bach when we grew up. So, I'm just taking the cue 'variation' to make it the widest stylistic difference that I can find in two minute pieces, and see how long I can do that—that's the challenge in that piece." "Interview," Part Two.

36. Theodor Adorno, *Mahler: A Musical Physiognomy*, trans. Edmund Jephcott (Chicago: University of Chicago Press, 1992), p. 149. Further citations in the text will refer to this edition.

37. Norman Lebrecht, "The Variability of Mahler's Performances," *Musical Times* 131 (1990): 302–304. Lebrecht also reminds us that the first notes of the melody are shared by "If I Were a Rich Man" from *Fiddler on the Roof* (1969).

38. Hans F. Redlich, "The Creative Achievement of Gustav Mahler," *Musical Times* 101 (1960): 418–421.

5. Conversos, Marranos, and Crypto-Latinos

1. Quoted in Brigitte Sion, "Where Have All the Sephardim Gone?" online essay in http://www.sefarad.org/publication/lm/036/6.html; see also many of the essays collected in *Sephardic Identity: Essays on a Vanishing Culture* (Jefferson: NC: McFarland, 2005). It should be noted that for all the rhetoric of lament that has been circulating around the Sephardim in America—and for that matter the world—Sephardic culture has been staging a comeback in the U.S. in the past decades, led in part by the Society for Sephardic Identity, which sponsored the volume quoted in the last sentence. Part of this, as we shall see below, is due to a new influx of Cuban-born intellectuals, like Ruth Behar, Jose Kozer, and Achy Obejas, who reflect in their work on their multiple identities. A larger part, perhaps, is the rise of multiculturalism in the U.S. in the 1970s and 1980s, which led a number of Jews of Sephardic descent to discover their origins or to articulate a communal identity for themselves. See, for example, New York writer and critic Richard Kostelanetz, "Sephardic Culture and Me," in Sara Blair and Jonathan Freedman, eds., *Jewish in America* (Ann Arbor: University of Michigan Press, 2004), pp. 25–29. Or see also Guatemalan-born UCLA journalism professor Victor Perera's lovely *The Cross and the Pear Tree* (Berkeley: University of California Press, 1996). Ilan Stavans has been on a one-man mission to make the literature and experience of Sephardic Jews central to the canon of American literary studies, North and South; see his anthology *The Cross and the Scroll: A Jewish-Hispanic Reader* (New York: Routledge, 2000).

I should add that I make here a distinction between the Sephardim and the Mizrachim—Jews from the Near or Far East, despite the Sephardic origins of many of the latter and close ties between the great Jewish community of Baghdad before and after the period of the Expulsion. But many Mizrachim have emigrated in recent years from Iraq and Iran—so much so that Jewish life in Southern California is now split between traditional Jewish congregations, largely Ashkenazic in origin, and newer ones funded by relatively wealthy Jews of Persian descent.

2. For the dispersion of Jews throughout the Balkans and the Ottoman Empire in particular, see Esther Benbassa and Aron Rodrigue, *Sephardi Jewry: A History of the Judeo-Spanish Community: Fourteenth Through Twentieth Centuries* (Berkeley: University of California Press, 2000). The other swings of the Sephardic diaspora—toward the Low Countries and the Americas—are more important to my focus in this chapter, but it's important to recognize the near global sweep of the itinerary of exile it traced.

3. Jonathan Israel, *Diasporas Within a Diaspora: Jews, Crypto-Jews, and the World of Maritime Empires (1540–1740)* (Amsterdam: Brill, 2002). There were indeed Jewish slaveholders in the New World, as the Nation of Islam so polemically reminded us in the late 1980s with *The Secret Relationship Between Blacks and Jews* (Chicago: Nation of Islam, 1991), and the consequences of this charge have haunted scholars for the next decades. For a point-by-point refutation, see Eli Faber, *Jews, Slaves, and the Slave Trade: Setting the Record Straight* (New York: New York University Press, 1998). For a subtler view, emphasizing the ways in which Jewish slaveholders in the Caribbean sought to mainstream themselves in terms of race—as whites, or at least as participants in the privileged status of whiteness—even as they faced a world culture that had demonized them as religiously other, see Jonathan Schorsch's extraordinary, *Jews and Blacks in the Early Modern World* (Cambridge: Cambridge University Press, 2004).

4. The notion that Columbus was either a Marrano or a converso, or a descendent thereof, is frequently ascribed to the Spanish historian Salvadore Madariaga, *Christopher Columbus: Being the Life of the Very Magnificent Lord Don Cristóbal Colón* (London: Hodder and Stoughton, 1939); it has been toyed with by such distinguished Jewish writers as Cecil Roth, "Who Was Columbus? In the Light of New Discoveries," *Menorah Journal* 28 (1940): 21–51, and Simon Wiesenthal (no less), *Sails of Hope: The Secret Mission of Christopher Columbus*, trans. Richard and Clara Winston (New York: Macmillan, 1973). Throwing cold water on this speculation is one of America's leading scholars of crypto-Jewish history and practices, Todd Gitlitz. In his encyclopaedic survey of the available evidence, upon which I have relied heavily for my own knowledge of crypto-Jewishness, *Secrecy and Deceit: The Religion of Crypto-Jews* (New York: Jewish Publication Society of America, 1996), he reminds us that scholarship has provided no real evidence of Columbus's Marrano or even converso identity.

The question of Columbus's "Jewish" identity has been quite important for writers and scholars of color. For one Native American perspective, see Gerald Vizenor, "Christopher Columbus: Lost Havens in the Ruins of Representation," *American Indian Quarterly* 16.4 (Autumn 1992): 521–532: "Columbus the marrano . . . landed

500 years [late] in . . . historical studies. That a marrano would be celebrated as the discoverer of this nation, and the 'inventor of the American dream,' is an ironic weave of narrative histories; alas, the marrano must be an onerous signature to the anti-Semites."

5. Eva Alexandra Uchmany, "The Periodization of the History of New Christians and Crypto-Jews in Spanish America," in Yedida Stillman and George Zucker, eds., *New Horizons in Sephardic Studies* (Albany: State University of New York Press, 1993), p. 114. Further citations in the text will refer to this edition. Alonso has been credited by Seymour Liebman as being "the first Jew on the North-American continent"; see his article by that name in *Journal of Inter-American Studies* 5.2 (April 1963): 291–296.

6. Israel, *Diasporas Within a Diaspora*, p. 1.

7. Yirmiyahu Yovel, *Spinoza and Other Heretics: The Marrano of Reason* (Princeton: Princeton University Press, 1989).

8. Elaine Marks, *Marrano as Metaphor: The Jewish Presence in French Writing* (New York: Columbia University Press, 1996).

9. Jacques Derrida, *Aporias,* trans. Thomas Dutoit (Stanford: Stanford University Press, 1993), p. 81.

10. Geoffrey Bennington and Jacques Derrida, *Derrida* (Chicago: University of Chicago Press, 1991). I was led to this quotation by Robert Young's wonderful treatment of Derrida's status as a Jewish-born Algerian/French intellectual, and his tracing of Derrida's own tracing of the genesis of deconstruction as a critical practice to his own status inside/outside the culture in which he was an ambivalent participant. Particularly crucial here, Young suggests, was the Vichy government's 1940 revocation of the Cremieux edict of 1870, which granted full French citizenship to all Jews living in Algeria, and Derrida's expulsion from his lycée due to an overrepresentation of Jews following the imposition of quotas in that same year. Young addresses Derrida, then quotes him:

"This moment exists like a primal scene of *ressentiment* in your writing, the moment of not belonging, of being both inside and outside. . . . You felt doubly displaced."

> A paradoxical effect, perhaps, of this bludgeoning, was the desire to be integrated into the non-Jewish community, a fascinated but painful and distrustful desire, one with a nervous vigilance, a painstaking attitude to discern signs of racism in its most discreet formations or its loudest denials. Symmetrically, oftentimes, I have felt an impatient desire with regard to various Jewish communities, when I have the impression that they close in upon themselves . . . . From all of which comes a feeling of non-belonging which I have doubtless transposed.
>
> *Interviewer*: —in Philosophy?
> JD: Everywhere.

See Robert Young, *Postcolonialism: An Historical Introduction* (Oxford: Blackwell, 2001), pp. 424–425.

The crucial text for Derrida's own autobiographical identification as a Marrano—and his account of his sense of himself as a child as a "black Arab Jew"—can be found in his autobiographical meditation, *Circumconfession*, trans. Geoffrey Bennington (Chicago: University of Chicago Press, 1993); for an excellent overview of this theme in Derrida's thought, see Jill Robbins's review-essay "Circumcising Confession: Derrida, Autobiography, Judaism," *Diacritics* 25:4 (Winter 1995): 20–38.

11. Carl Gebhardt, *Schiften des Uriel da Costa* (Amsterdam, 1922), p. xix, as quoted by Daniel M. Swetschinski, *Reluctant Cosmpolitans: The Portugese Jews of Seventeenth-Century Amsterdam* (Oxford: Littman Library of Jewish Civilization, 2000), p. 315. The ligature I suggest below between the experience of conversos and Marranos and the making of ethnicity is also traced, in a dense and rich way, by Swetschinski in the account of Portugese Jews in the Low Countries. I've also learned much from Miriam Bodian, *Hebrews of the Portugese Nation: Conversos and Community in Early Modern Amsterdam* (Bloomington: Indiana University Press, 1997).

12. Tree-Poul See Yovel, *Spinoza and Other Heretics*, pp. 57–80.

13. This is the utopian vision proposed by the title, at least, of Maria Menocal, *The Ornament of the World: How Muslims, Jews, and Christians Created a Culture of Tolerance in Medieval Spain* (Boston: Little, Brown, 2002).

14. Jean-Paul Sartre, *Anti-Semite and Jew: An Exploration of the Etiology of Hate*, trans. George Becker (New York: Schocken, 1948), p. 37.

15. Benzion Netanyahu, *The Origins of the Inquisition in Fifteenth-Century Spain*, 2d ed. (New York: Random House, 1995), pp. 982–983.

16. Werner Sollors, "Preface" to *Theories of Ethnicity: A Classic Reader* (New York: New York University Press, 1996), p. xxxv.

17. For the multifaceted importance of Herder, see Paul Lawrence Rose, *Revolutionary Anti-Semitism in Germany from Kant to Wagner* (Princeton: Princeton University Press, 1993); and, on the opposite side of the coin, Alain Finkeilkraut, *The Defeat of the Mind*, trans. Judith Friedlander (New York: Columbia University Press, 1995).

18. Jacobson, *Roots Too* (Cambridge: Harvard University Press, 2006), p. 35.

19. Michael Omi and Howard Winant, *Racial Formation in the United States: From the 1960s to the 1980s* (New York: Routledge, 1996). As Dean Franco puts it, "It would be hard to overstate the influence of Omi and Winant's critique of ethnicity and championing of a race-based paradigm for literature study." And, with Franco, I would argue that the chief problem with their work, and its subsequent rise to near hegemonic status, has been the way that it not only "relies upon" but "reproduces stable concepts within the terms *white* and *American*." Dean Franco, *Ethnic American Literature: Comparing Chicano, Jewish, and African American Writing* (Charlottesville: University of Virginia Press, 2006), p. 17. The itinerary of

Jewishness I attempt to produce in this book is an implicit challenge to both of these procedures; it's different from Franco's comparative work, which in my view overemphasizes trauma and underemphasizes syncretism, but I hope in sympathetic dialogue with it.

20. Barbara Ferry and Debbie Nathan, "Mistaken Identity? The Case of New Mexico's 'Hidden Jews,'" *Atlantic Monthly* 283 (December 2000): 6–11. See also Michael Caroll, "The Debate Over a Crypto-Jewish Presence in New Mexico: The Role of Ethnographic Allegory and Orientalism," *Sociology of Religion* 54 (2002): 67–78.

21. Stanley Hordes, *To the End of the Earth: A History of the Crypto-Jews of New Mexico* (New York: Columbia University Press, 2005).

22. Janet Liebman Jacobs, *Hidden Heritage: The Legacy of the Crypto-Jews* (Berkeley: University of California Press, 2002), especially pp. 145–146. Jacobs's evidence is ambiguous: some of her informants do indeed identify as "white," while others use the ethical example of Judaism and the leftist traditions of American Jews to identify with the struggles of Latinos.

23. As described, with some sympathy and little of the animus of her *Atlantic* article, by none other than Debbie Nathan, "Cross Ways: Hispanics Search for the Origins of Their Unique Faith That Fuses Jewish Tradition with the Celebration of Christ," *Houston Press* 20 (January 17, 2002): x.

24. Wesley K. Sutton, Alec Knight, Peter A. Underhill, Judith S. Neulander, Todd R. Disotell, and Joanna L. Mountain, "Toward Resolution of the Debate Regarding Purported Crypto-Jews in a Spanish-American Population: Evidence from the Y Chromosome," *Annals of Human Biology* 33:1 (January-February 2006): 111.

25. Here's my logic: roughly sixty-seven thousand conversos survived the Inquisition, according to historians versed in census records (the actual number should be larger, given the fact that many conversos successfully veiled their Jewish origins). After ten generations, assuming that each generation produced three surviving children, the number of people of converso descent would equal 5.7 million out of a total population of roughly 40 million. Subtract for wars, pestilence, and the like, and you still have 10 percent of the population.

26. Especially in Portugal, where small Jewish communities in the remote area around Belmonte were discovered in the 1980s and received official apologies from the Portuguese government and the Catholic Church. For a good survey of these and other narratives of rediscovered crypto-Jewish communities, see Ruth Melammed, *A Question of Identity: Iberian Conversos in Historical Perspective* (New York: Oxford University Press, 2004) pp. 167–173.

27. Katherine Alcalá, "A Thread in the Tapestry—The Narros of Saltillo, Mexico, in History and Literature," *Halapid* 9 (Winter 2002), reprinted online by the Society for Crypto Jewish Studies, http://www.cryptojews.com/Alcala.htm. I want to thank Alcalá for her generous response to an earlier version of this chapter, from which the current version has benefited.

28. Katherine Alcalá, *Spirits of the Ordinary: A Tale of Casas Grandes* (New York: Harvest, 1997), p. 8. Further citations in the text will refer to this edition.

29. See José F. Aranda Jr., "Making the Case for New Chicano/a Studies," in José F. Aranda Jr., *When We Arrive: A New Literary History of Mexican America* (Tucson: University of Arizona Press, 2003), pp. 3–41.

30. Martha Menchaca, *Recovering History, Constructing Race: The Indian, Black, and White Roots of Mexican Americans* (Austin: University of Texas Press, 2001).

31. R. W. B. Lewis, *The American Adam: Innocence, Tragedy, and Tradition in the Nineteenth Century* (Chicago: University of Chicago Press, 1959).

32. Achy Obejas, *Days of Awe* (New York: Random House, 2001), p. 3. Further citations in the text will refer to this edition.

33. See Maurice Lamm, *The Jewish Way in Death and Mourning*, rev. ed. (Middle Village, N.Y.: David, 2000).

6. Transgressions of a Model Minority

1. For more on the affinity of Jews for Chinese restaurants, see Gaye Tuchman and Harry Gene Levine, "New York Jews and Chinese Food: The Social Construction of an Ethnic Pattern," in *A Reader on Regional and Ethnic Foods*, ed. Barbara Shortridge and James Shortridge (Lanham, MD: Rowman and Littlefield, 1998); and Hannah Miller, "Identity Takeout: How American Jews Made Chinese Food Their Ethnic Cuisine," *Journal of Popular Culture* 39:3 (June 2006): 430–465. This affinity has much to do with a number of factors—for example, that Chinese didn't observe the Christian Sabbath, for example; but one is the fact that Jews could experiment with *treyf* dishes—pork, shrimp, etc.—in a defamiliarized context. Eating in Chinese restaurants became a way of experimenting with not being Jewish, but, at the same time, not becoming Christian, either.

2. For an excellent account not just of the Jewish/Chinese restaurant conjunction, but of food as one of the major points of overlap between Jewish American and Chinese American fiction, see Judith Oster, *Crossing Cultures: Creating Identity in Chinese and Jewish-American Literature* (Columbia: University of Missouri Press, 2003). Oster's wide-ranging and smart study is the only sustained treatment I know of the overlap between Jewish and Chinese American writing; her model of the relation between them is Lacanian, in which the two not only mirror each other, but enact the mirroring process of coming-to-ethnic identity at large. My model here, and in the following chapter, is more historicist and agonistic: for me, what matters is the ways in which Jews and Asians, constructed via many of the same processes, responded to their construction in ways that have led both to a sense of affinity and to one of resentment.

3. Hasia Diner, *Lower East Side Memories* (Princeton: Princeton University Press, 2002), pp. 42, 44.

4. Michael Gold, *Jews Without Money* (New York: Liveright, 1930), pp. 177–178.

5. Luc Sante, *Low Life: Lures and Snares of Old New York* (New York: Farrar, Straus and Giroux, 1991).

6. This information comes from Jeffrey McIllwain, *Organizing Crime in Chinatown: Race and Racketeering in New York City* (Jefferson, NC: McFarland, 2004), pp. 87–88. I was led to this book by Jeffrey Melnick.

7. Henry Roth, *Call It Sleep* (New York: Penguin, 1977), pp. 171–172.

8. Jacob Riis, *How the Other Half Lives: Studies Among the Tenements of New York* (Cambridge: Belknap, 1970 (reprint of the 1890 edition), p. 70. Further citations in the text will refer to this edition.

9. Hutchins Hapgood, *The Spirit of the Ghetto* (New York: Funk and Wagnalls, 1902), p. 261.

10. As quoted by Matthew Frye Jacobson, *Whiteness of a Different Color*, p. 164.

11. "The Russian Jew in New York," *Atlantic Monthly* 82 (July, 1898), p. 283.

12. Quoted in Jacobson, *Whiteness of a Different Color*, p. 184.

13. Anzia Yezierska, *Salomé of the Tenements* (Urbana: University of Illinois Press, 1995), p. 132. Further citations in the text will refer to this edition.

14. Abraham Cahan, *The Rise of David Levinsky* (New York: Harper, 1917), p. 4.

15. Roger Mitchell, "Recent Jewish Immigration to the United States," *Popular Science Monthly* (February 1903), p. 340, quoted in Robert Singerman's excellent "The Jew as Racial Alien: The Genetic Component of American Anti-Semitism," in David Gerber, ed., *Anti-Semitism in American History* (Urbana: University of Illinois Press, 1986), pp. 109–110. This ascription of essentially "Oriental" qualities to the Jewish mind of course also possessed a philosemitic aspect; see, for example, the descriptions of the mystical Mordecai in George Eliot's *Daniel Deronda* (1886). Indeed, the first encounter between "yellow"-faced Mordecai (sallow from consumption as well as from the coloring of the East) and Daniel is a test case of the Jewish/Oriental interplay I am attempting to describe here. For, in meeting Mordecai, Daniel—who does not yet know of his Jewish origins—is conflated syntactically and imagistically with that which he ostensibly opposes. At the very least, Eliot's mirroring of these two creates the possibility of an "Oriental" type within "the Latin races"—that admixture of East and West we might also call "the (assimilated) Jew":

> Opposite to him was a face not more distinctively oriental than many a type seen among what we call the Latin races; rich in youthful health, and with a forcible masculine gravity in its repose, that gave the value of judgment to the reverence with which he met the gaze of this mysterious son of poverty who claimed him as a long-expected friend. The more exquisite quality of Deronda's nature—that keenly perceptive sympathetic emotiveness which ran along with his speculative tendency—was never more thoroughly tested. He felt nothing that could be called belief in the validity of Mordecai's impressions concerning him or in the probability of any greatly effective issue: what he felt was a profound sensibility to a cry from the depths of another and accompanying that, the summons to be receptive in-

stead of superciliously prejudging. Receptiveness is a rare and massive power, like fortitude; and this state of mind now gave Deronda's face its utmost expression of calm benignant force—an expression which nourished Mordecai's confidence and made an open way before him.

George Eliot, *Daniel Deronda* (London: Penguin, 1995), p. 492.

16. As quoted in Irving Howe, *World of Our Fathers* (New York: Simon and Schuster, 1976), p. 378.

17. Goerge Kibbe Turner, "Daughters of the Poor: A Plain Study of the Development of New York City as Leading Center of the White Slave Trade in the World, Under Tammany Hall," *McClure's* 34 (1909): 45. The point about the Orientalism of the naming of the pimp as *kaftan* is also made by Mara Keire, "The Vice Trust: A Reinterpretation of the White Slavery Scare in the United States, 1907–1917," *Journal of Social History* 35 (2001): 5–46. Keire is alert to the ways in which Progressive-era reformers pinned "white slavery" on the figure of the Jew (in this case, the stereotype of the Orientalized wandering Jew) and is attentive as well to the ways in which their understanding of that figure turned to a critique of the market economy. But she doesn't go the next step and see how coimplicated these two moves are, Jews, of course, being associated with malignant economic forces both traditionally and with greater power in the 1920s.

18. Henry Ford, *The International Jew: The World's Foremost Problem* (Dearborn, MI: Dearborn 1920–22), p. 96; *My Life and Work* (New York: Doubleday, 1922), pp. 250–51.

19. Michael Rogin, who is after other game, mentions this connection *en passant* in *Blackface/White Noise* (Berkeley: University of California Press, 1996), pp. 128–136. I should say here that the process of thought that led to this chapter was sparked by Rogin's provoking and powerful intervention as well as Jacobson's impressive book. In both cases, I felt, these splendid cultural historians described the Orientalization of the Jew but passed it over in favor of the more pressing black/Jewish context. My own sense is that we're now at a moment when that master narrative (crucial as it no doubt has been) has crumbled, and other narratives, no less involved with the making of whiteness but more complexly so, can be told. This work is the beginning of an effort to do just that.

20. Stewart Creighton Miller, *Unwelcome Immigrant: The American Image of Chinese, 1785–1882* (Berkeley: University of California Press, 1969), p. 193.

21. A point made by Ronald Takaki; see *Strangers from a Different Shore* (Boston: Back Bay, 1998), p. 76. Or consider the following statement, made in the midst of the usual assortment of racist denunciations of the Chinese on the Senate floor by Edgar Cowan of Pennsylvania in 1868, in support of the Trumbull bill that would grant citizenship to Asians as well as Gypsies and other others: "Nobody," Cowan argued, distinguishing the Chinese from the problematic Gypsy, "should doubt the superior industry, skill and pertinacity of the yellow race"—and, indeed, one suspects that it is this lingering sense of the superiority, or at least the competitiveness, of the "yellow race" that motivated much of the anti-Asian sentiment of the time. Quoted in Najia

Aarim-Heriot, *Chinese Immigrants, African Americans, and Racial Anxiety in the United States, 1848–82* (Urbana: University of Illinois Press, 2003), p. 89.

I might add here (as I suggested briefly in the introduction) that the trope of the "stranger" is adopted explicitly by Takaki from the German Jewish sociologist Georg Simmel, for whom it obviously had ethnocultural racial resonances (Simmel's example of the perpetually alienated stranger, for example, is the Jew who must pay taxes but is not granted the full rights of citizenship). Takaki's point in so doing, of course, is that these strangers come from a *different* location, in every sense, from Europe; but the paradigm he relies upon—that of the eternal stranger—comes directly out of the experience of the "others within" the European context, Jews.

22. "The Future of the Chinese People," *Atlantic Monthly* 85 (January 1900): 80.

23. Jay Geller, quoting (and translating) Herder in his astonishing essay "*'Judenzopf/Chinesenzopf'*: Of Jews and Queues," *positions* 2.3 (Winter 1994): 509–510. Geller quotes from a wide array of sources in the German and English traditions to suggest that the conflation of Chinese and Jews is widespread in the eighteenth and nineteenth centuries, extending from philosophers like Hegel and Herder to popular writers like Karl May and even to the cartoons of *Punch;* throughout, it's the commercialism and sense of themselves as a distinct people that allow these groups to be conflated in the Western imaginary. American writers like Riis, in other words, are continuing and extending this tradition, not beginning a new one.

24. John Kuo Wei Tchen, *New York Before Chinatown: Orientalism and the Shaping of American Culture, 1776–1882* (Baltimore: Johns Hopkins University Press, 2001), pp. 214–218. Note how the very characterization of Chinese as "rats" anticipates the fin de siècle ravings of Henry Adams, much less those of Drumont et al. in France and ultimately the Nazi understanding of Jews as vermin to be exterminated. Fantasies of extermination of the Chinese were not unknown to Americans; see Jack London's horrifying 1910 story, *The Unparalleled Invasion*, in which the entire Chinese people is wiped out by a biological attack sponsored by the rest of the world.

25. Singerman, "The Jew as Racial Alien," pp. 118–119; Singerman's point here is that the notion of the Jew as an Asian (or Khazar/Mongol) Other recedes in the 1930s in the favor of economic antisemitism à la Father Coughlin.

26. Maurice Fishberg, *The Jews: A Study of Race and Environment* (New York: Walter Scott, 1911). Fishberg's book is a cogent argument against the claim that Jews constitute a distinct race; he sees the multiplicity of Jewish appearances as growing out of a constant, and varying, process of intermarriage with the peoples among whom Jews lived. Especially given the eugenicist tenor of the times, in other words, it is a progressive document, anticipating the arguments of anthropologists cum antiracists of the 1940s and 1950s like Ashley Montagu (née Israel Ehrenberg, by the way). As such, as we have seen in the introduction, Fishberg has been identified along with a number of other Jewish writers of the 1920s as a prime mover in the construction of the discourse of ethnicity—and an accomplice in the encoding of

the very notion of race in the midst of ethnicity. My own view, to recapitulate, is that the confusion of the idiom of race and ethnicity is built into the terms of each—and has been since the very origins of the discourse systems in the nineteenth century.

27. See Ira Nadel, *Joyce and the Jews: Culture and Texts* (Iowa City: University of Iowa Press, 1989), p. 162.

28. Here are two such: www.jewwatch.com and www.radioislam.org/koestler/index.htm. Both link to or cite Koestler's book as "proof" that Ashkenazic Jews are not related to biblical Jews of the Near East. These arguments would seem to be undercut by recent genetic testing that has established continuities between the descendents of the priests of the high temple (the cohanim) and contemporary Ashkenazic Jews who claim that status. But such tests also reveal the constant admixture of blood from other peoples among Jews of the world, which is to say that the argument from race into which these discussions tend to devolve is fraught with historicist and essentialist traps.

29. *Puck* 8 (December 14, 1881); I was led to this piece by John Appel, "Jews in American Caricature: 1820–1914," in *Jewish American History* 71 (September 1981): 103–133.

30. Willa Cather, *Youth and the Bright Medusa* (Boston: Houghton Mifflin, 1937), pp. 181–182. Kitty Ayreshire recurs as a character through many stories of this collection, as do representations of the Jew, most prominently in the short story "The Diamond Mine." The two phenomena, I am arguing, are not unrelated.

31. Ken Hanke, *Charlie Chan at the Movies: History, Filmography, Criticism* (Jefferson, NC: McFarland, 2004), p. 1.

32. Sax Rohmer, *The Insidious Fu Manchu* (New York: Pyramid, 1997), p. 84.

33. Sander Gilman, *Smart Jews: The Construction of the Image of Jewish Superior Intelligence* (Lincoln: University of Nebraska Press, 1996), p. 178.

34. Barbara Kirshenblatt-Gimblett, "Spaces of Dispersal," *Cultural Anthropology* 9 (1994): 341–342. Her quotation is from Milton Gordon, *Assimilation in American Life: The Role of Race, Religion and National Origins* (New York: Oxford University Press, 1964), p. 56.

35. See William Wu, *The Yellow Peril: Chinese Americans in American Fiction, 1850–1940* (Hamden: Archon, 1982), pp. 108, 164–182. I've also learned a good deal from Tina Chen's excellent "Dissecting the Devil Doctor: Stereotype and Sensation in Sax Rohmer's Fu Manchu," in Josephine Lee, Imogine L. Lim, and Yuko Matsukawa, eds., *Recollecting Early Asian America: Essays in Cultural History* (Philadelphia: Temple University Press, 2002), pp. 218–237.

36. For the rise of theories of superior Asian intelligence, see Barry Sautman, "Theories of East Asian Superiority," in Russell Jacoby and Naomi Glauberman, eds., *The Bell Curve Debate: History, Documents, Opinions* (New York: Random House, 1995), pp. 100–106: Sautman explicates in particular the theories of Richard Lynn, who hypothesizes that, since the ice age was more severe in North Asia, early Asians needed to develop their intellects in order to survive. J. Phillipe Rushton (supported by the notorious Pioneer Fund) has developed this thesis

even farther, commenting on the superior intellectual skills of Asians (and on their alleged smaller penis size, as David Palumbo-Liu dryly points out); Rushton continues the tendency to belittle Asian intelligence even while celebrating it in his claim that the "relatively strong visuospatial and weak verbal abilities of Oriental Americans may result in a tendency to do well in professions like science, architecture, and engineering and less well in law." Quoted in Palumbo-Liu, *Asian/American: Historical Crossings of a Racial Frontier* (Stanford: Stanford University Press, 1999), p. 154.

37. Charles Murray and Richard J. Herrnstein, *The Bell Curve* (New York: Simon and Schuster, 1994), p. 275.

38. Frank Chin, "Confessions of a Chinatown Cowboy," in *Bulletproof Buddhists and Other Essays* (Honolulu: University of Hawaii Press, 1998), pp. 95–96. The essay was originally published in 1972.

39. David Eng, *Racial Castration: Managing Masculinity in Asian America* (Durham: Duke University Press, 2001), p. 199, quoting Suzuki, "Education and Socialization of Asian Americans: A Revisionist Analysis of the 'Model Minority' Thesis," *AmerAsia* 4 (1977): 23–51.

40. Robert G. Lee, *Orientals: Asian Americans in Popular Culture* (Philadelphia: Temple University Press, 1999), p. 227. Lee is discussing here the symmetry of language used to describe Chinese and South Asian American immigrants.

41. While the Asians-as-new-Jews argument was commonplace in the writing on ethnic success in the 1980s (see, for example, Thomas Sowell, *Ethnic America: A History* [New York: Basic, 1991]; Sowell develops at great length the thesis that Asian Americans follow the Jewish model of entrepreneurial bootstrapping and success by educational achievement), it was broadcast with the greatest of enthusiasm in Martin Peretz's *New Republic*, a journal strongly identified with the largely Jewish neoconservative movement (although somewhat to the left of *Commentary*) and one not uncoincidentally strongly opposed to affirmative action in higher education. See, for example, David Bell's cover story from 1985 (illustrated with an Asian American face on the Statue of Liberty), "The Triumph of Asian Americans: America's Greatest Success Story," *New Republic* 193 (1985): 24–26; not only does the story contain a number of comparisons between Jewish and Asian success stories and their problems vis-à-vis university admissions (e.g., Walter Lippman, himself a Jew, worrying about the effects of a Jewish presence of over 15 percent at Harvard) but also a sidebar enumerating the relations and lack thereof between these two groups. For the most effective refutation of the Sowell thesis, with particular reference to its applications to Jews and Asians, see Steinberg, *The Ethnic Myth: Race, Ethnicity and Class in America* (Boston: Beacon, 2001), especially 263–275, part of an afterword nicely entitled "Ethnic Heroes and Racial Villains."

42. Deborah Woo, *Glass Ceilings and Asian Americans: The New Face of Workplace Barriers* (Walnut Creek, CA: AltaMira, 2000).

43. Vivian Louie, *Born to Excel, Immigration, Education, and Opportunity among Chinese Americans* (Stanford: Stanford University Press, 2004).

NOTES 367

44. See Nazli Kibria, *Becoming Asian American: Second Generation Chinese and Korean American Identities* (Baltimore: Johns Hopkins University Press, 2002), especially pp. 157–158.

45. As quoted in David Roediger, *Working Toward Whiteness: How America's Immigrants Became White: The Strange Journey from Ellis Island to the Suburbs* (New York: Basic, 2005), p. 49.

46. For a good account of these, see Andrew Muchin, "Sephardic Music Comes Out of the Shadows: Lilting Tunes of the 'Other Exile' Rock On," *Jewish Daily Forward* 88 (March 7, 2003): 67. As Muchin puts it, "Sephardic music combines lilting melodies in minor keys played on stringed instruments, usually guitar or oud, along with hand drums and flute. Its more Arabic stylings exude a feeling of floating. The older Spanish style feels more rooted.... 'It's an excellent music,' [performer Bill] Goodman said. 'It's Mediterranean; it's Eastern. It has as many qualities of the Eastern, Oriental music as it does of Western music. That gives it a different quality. Its holiness aspect is profound. Also, there's a kind of quiet, yearning quality, a touch of sadness.'"

47. Lawrence Lasher, ed., *Conversations with Bernard Malamud* (Jackson: University Press of Mississippi, 1991), p. 30.

7. Asians and Jews in Theory and Practice

1. Eric Liu, "The New Jews," in *The Accidental Asian* (New York: Random House, pp. 171–172.

2. Michael Omi, review of *The Accidental Asian*, *Civil Rights Journal* 18 (1998): 76.

3. David Leiwei Li, "On Ascriptive and Acquisitional Americanness: *The Accidental Asian* and the Illogic of Assimilation," *Contemporary Literature* 45 (Spring 2004): 130.

4. Gayle Feldman, "Spring's Five Fictional Encounters of the Chinese American Kind: Chinese American Authors," *Publisher's Weekly* 238 (February 9, 1991), p. 25.

5. I draw the term from Jonathan Dollimore's classic *Sexual Dissidence: Augustine to Wilde: Freud to Foucault* (Oxford: Clarendon/New York: Oxford University Press, 1991).

6. This and the subsequent quotations from Mukherjee are from Alison Carb, "An Interview with Bharati Mukherjee," *Massachusetts Review* 29 (1988): 645–654.

7. Here, for example, is Anindyo Roy's comment on the same passages I have quoted above: "With the authority to sustain [a] form of cosmopolitan aesthetics, Bharati Mukherjee not only suppresses the complex realities of economic, political and historical exigencies of immigration, but also 'forgets' the implications of the post-colonial subject's authorizing of such aesthetics.... By subsuming her post-coloniality in [a] Euro-centered aesthetic rite of passage, Mukherjee seeks to legitimize her own romantic 'epic' imagination, seamlessly weaving it into the archetypal

European immigrant experience in the New World." Anindyo Roy, "The Aesthetics of an (Un)willing Immigrant: Bharati Mukherjee's *Days and Nights in Calcutta* and *Jasmine*," in Emmanuel Nelson, ed., *Bharati Mukherjee: Critical Perspectives* (New York York: Garland, 1993), p. 130.

8. Bharati Mukherjee, "The Middleman," in Bharati Mukherjee, *The Middleman and Other Stories* (New York: Grove, 1988), p. 3. Further citations in the text will refer to this edition.

9. Jonathan Raban makes a version of this point in his perceptive *New York Times Book Review* response to *The Middleman:* "Her characters have a good deal in common with their Jewish counterparts: they're heroes to themselves, a size larger than life. And they see the surfaces of American life with the bug-eyed clarity of the greenhorn afloat in a gaudy new world. Yet they are not tired, huddled, or even poor: they own motels, work scams, teach in college, breeze through on private funds. Their diaspora is a haphazard, pepperpot dispersal. With no Lower East Side to keep the manners and morals of the old world alive, they're on their own and on the make. How the introspective and overmothered sons of the ghetto, from David Levinsky to Alexander Portnoy, would have envied Ms. Mukherjee's new Americans, their guiltlessness, bounce, sexual freedom, their easy money. Unlike their Jewish literary ancestors, Ms. Mukherjee's people are no more troubled by conscience than butterflies." *New York Times Book Review* 93 (June 19, 1988): 22. My own view is that what's important about Mukherjee's work in the Jewish American context is that she might allow us to remember just how much of this conscienceless, scam-perpetrating, sexually free behavior circulated throughout Lower East Side culture and why these writers had to repress that side of their own experience or encode it in rascally, usually non-Jewish "reality instructors."

10. I have just begun here to scratch the surface of the interplay between Mukherjee and Jewish American fiction; for an excellent and extensive treatement of it, see James Bloom, "For the Yankee Dead: Roth, Mukherjee and the Diasporan Seizure of New England," *Studies in American Jewish Literature* 17 (1998): 40–47.

11. Feldman, "Spring's Five Fictional Encounters"; Gish Jen, interview in powells.com, January 2001.

12. Rachel Lee, *The Americas of Asian-American Literature: Gendered Fictions of Nation and Transnation* (Princeton: Princeton University Press, 1999), p. 44.

13. An "emphasis on intensity," Wisse writes, "is one of the basic components of the schlemiel-character in American fiction and indicates his main point of departure from European sources. . . . He is an expression of heart, of intense passionate feelings in surroundings that stamp out individuality and equate emotion with unreason. The schlemiel is used as a cultural reaction to the prevailing Anglo-Saxon model of restraint, inaction, thought and speech. . . . The American schlemiel declares his humanity by loving and suffering in defiance of the forces of depersonalization and the ethic of enlightened stoicism." Ruth R. Wisse, *The Schlemiel as Modern Hero* (University of Chicago Press, 1979), p. 82.

14. Gish Jen, interview in powells.com, January 2001.

15. Gish Jen, *Mona in the Promised Land* (New York: Vintage, 1996), p. 44. Further citations in the text will refer to this edition.

16. Philip Deloria, *Playing Indian* (New Haven: Yale University Press, 1999).

17. Gish Jen, *Who's Irish?* (New York: Vintage, 1999), p. 30.

18. Lan Samantha Chang, "A Conversation with Lan Samantha Chang," in the aftermatter to Lan Samantha Chang, *Hunger: A Novella and Stories* (New York: Penguin, 1998), p. 9. Further citations in the text will refer to this edition.

19. Gary Sheyngart, *The Russian Debutante's Handbook* (New York: Riverhead, 2002). Further citations in the text will refer to this edition.

20. Donald Weber, *Haunted in the New World: Jewish-American Culture from Cahan to the Goldbergs* (Bloomington: Indiana University Press, 2005).

21. Sander Gilman, "'We're Not Jews': Imagining Jewish History and Jewish Bodies in Contemporary Multicultural Literature," *Modern Judaism* 23 (2003): 126–155.

Conclusion

1. Liner notes to *Jewface* (Reboot Stereophonic, 2006). As for "That Funny Jas Band," issued by Edison records in 1916, the recording can be accessed online via an opensource Web site: http://www.archive.org/details/fjasband1916.

2. Michael Sharf, "Notes from the Book Room: The Bellow-Roth Equation," www.publishersweekly.com/blogger//2681html&. This association—which we saw in the previous chapter surfacing as early as 1991—seems to be a *Publisher's Weekly* speciality: their interview with Indian writer Abha Desawar is entitled "The Philip Roth of India?" and begins with this question, "By writing so frankly about sex and ethnicity, are you doing for Indian fiction what Philip Roth and Saul Bellow did for Jewish fiction in the '50s and '60s?" www.publishersweekly.com/article/CA6323189html.

3. Liner notes to *Jewface*.

4. Adam Meyer, "Putting the 'Jewish' Back in "Jewish American Fiction": A Look at Jewish American Fiction from 1977 to 2002 and an Allegorical Reading of Nathan Englander's 'The Gilgul of Park Avenue,'" *Shofar* 22 (2004): 104.

5. Irving Field, *Bagels and Bongos*, Reboot Stereophonic 2006.

6. Rich Cohen, "HELLO! IT'S SEXY TIME!" *Vanity Fair*, December 2006, pp. 262.

7. Neil Strauss, "The Man Behind the Mustache (Sacha Baron Cohen—The Real Borat—Finally Speaks)," *Rolling Stone* 1014 (November 30, 2006), p. 33.

8. Zachary Goldfarb, "Va. Lawmaker's Remarks on Muslims Criticized" *Washington Post*, December 21, 2006, p. A11.

9. Michael D. Shear and Tim Craig, "Allen Quip Provokes Outrage, Apology," *Washington Post*, August 15, 2006, p. A01.

10. I take the phrase, and the point, from Brian Edwards.

11. E. J. Kessler, "Alleged Slur Casts Light on Senator's (Jewish ?) Roots," *Jewish Daily Forward*, August 25, 2006, p 1. For other details on Allen, see Ryan Lizza, "George Allen's Jewish Question," *New Republic* (online edition), August 25, 2006; and John Campanelli, "Preppy Allen Has a Problem with His Jewish Heritage," August 27, 2006, www.dailykos.com.

12. Frederick Kunkle, "Fairfax Native Says Allen's Words Stung," *Washington Post*, August 25, 2006, p. B01. Further citations in the text refer to this story.

INDEX

Abe Gubenko's Radio Novelty Orchestra, 187
Absalom, Absalom! (Faulkner), 167
Absurdistan (Shtyengart), 323
The Accidental Asian (Liu), 283
Adam, *see* American Adam
Adorno, Theodor, 201–2, 205
The Adventures of Augie March (Bellow), 292, 313
African Americans: discrimination against, 301; experiences of, 23–24; jazz and, 88, 181; Jewish relations with, 87–88; passing for white, 167, 213; prejudice against, 169; racial identification of, 302; *see also* Blackness
afromestizo, 234
Afro-Semitic Experience, 87
AIDS virus, 45, 52, 54
Alcalá, Kathleen, 216, 227–39, 237–38
Alexie, Sherman, 227
Ali, Rashid, 199
Allen, George: antisemitism of, 327–28; Jewish origins of, 328–30
Allen, Woody, 44, 96, 111, 273, 274, 323
Almanac of the Dead (Silko), 232
Alonso, Hernando, 211, 212
America: Alcalá and, 237–38; antisemitism in, 45–46, 159–60, 290; Catholicism as religion in, 131, 135; ethnicity in, 11, 221; identity of, 129; as immigrant nation, 139; Jewish immigration to, 7, 7*n*–8*n*; Kushner and, 58; Mexican-American identity in, 233–34; Oriental Jews and, 263; populism in, 161–62, 161*n*–162*n*; racialism in, 220–21
"America" (Diamond): blackface and, 15; Latinos on, 13–14
American Adam: Alcalá, 237–38; Lewis and, 238
American Eve, Obejas and, 239–40
The American Jew (Timayensis), 45; Jewish sexual deviance in, 46
American Jews: ethical sensitivity of, 193; prostitution, alleged control by, 47; security of, 37
American Pastoral (Roth, Philip), racial conflict in, 166
American Utopia: Bercovitch on, 58; Kushner on, 58–59
American Woman (Choi), 303
Angels in America (Kushner), 42–60, 90, 93, 124, 233, 239; Christ in, 56; Cohn, Roy, in, 42, 48, 49–50, 53–54; gay male identity in, 42, 45, 50, 55, 64, 66–67; Jewish ambivalence in, 54–55; Prior Walter in, 42, 43, 55–59; race in, 42; right-wing culture theme in, 42, 48, 52; Savran on, 57
Angelus Novus (Klee), 52
Animal Dreams (Kingsolver), 232
Annals of Human Biology, 224
Annie Hall (Allen, Woody), 44
Ansky, S. (Rappaport, Shloyme-Zanvel), 41–42, 91, 93
Antichrist, 149, 163; Carpathia as, 149; Fuller on, 149; Jew as, 149
Anti-Semite and Jew (Sartre), 218

INDEX

Antisemitism, 58n, 340n32, 341n1; of Allen, George, 328–30; in America, 45–46, 159–60, 290; Carpathia and, 149, 350n11; in Christianity, 159; of Coughlin, 140–41, 162; of Coxey's Army, 158–59, 350n22–352n22; Dinnerstein on, 162; of Ford, 140; Frank case of, 47–48; for Jewish writers, 337n22; without Jews, 140–63; by LaHaye/Jenkins, 156; in *Left Behind* series, 146, 150–51, 154, 159–60, 327; in *Millennium*, 44; Netanyahu on, 218; populist, 162–63; propaganda, 40, 48; renovation of, 142, 162–63; Rosenzweig and, 150–51; Rothschild family and, 158; slurs as, 328–29; of Gerald L. K. Smith, 141, 162; terrorism and, 141
Anzaldúa, Gloria, 234
Aporias (Derrida), 214
Appiah, Anthony, on cosmopolitanism, 92, 345n45–346n45
Aramaic, 52n
Aranda, José, 234
"Are You Sticking," klezmer solo in, 188n
Arendt, Hannah, 10
Armstrong, Louis, 84, 187, 200; Brandwein v., 84–85; stop-time and, 85, 85n
Arshawsky, Abraham Isaac, née Shaw, Artie, 186
Arshawsky, Arthur, aka Shaw, Artie, 186
Asch, Gregor, aka DJ Olive, 203n
Ashkenazic Jewish culture, 70, 209–10, 223, 365n28; conflicts within, 61–62; see also Sephardic Jews
Asian Americans, 251–82, 366n41; as model minority, 252; as "new Jews," 12; Singerman on, 267; as writers, 283–315, 321
Asians: contributions of, 284; demasculinization of, 275; as economic players, 265; as intellectual, 274; Jews v., 265–67, 269, 279, 306; as model minority, 267; as outcasts, 276; psychological toll of, 275–76; racial identification of, 302; as "rats," 364n24; superiority of, 274–75, 278, 363n21–364n21, 365n36–366n36; values of, 277–78; as villainous, 271–73; WASPs and, 303; whiteness of, 285; see also Asian Americans
Assimilation: anxiety of, 35; Jewish masculinity and, 98–99; of Jews, 29, 96, 99–100, 136, 165, 184, 213, 285, 334n8; Kennedy, John/Robert, and, 129–30; Lei on, 284; of Liu, 284–85; of Miller, Arthur, 105, 110; of past generations, 282
Assimilation in American Life (Gordon), 273–74
Atlantic magazine, 223, 263
Authenticity: of race, 170, 170n; Ribot on, 90–91
Autobiography of an Ex-Coloured Man (Johnson), 167; Kawash on, 168; on race alterity, 168–69
Ayler, Albert, 201
Ayrshire, Kitty, Orientalism of, 270–71

Bach, Johann Sebastian, 199, 201
Bacharach, Burt, 20, 21
Bailen, Isadore (Irving Berlin), 255
Balanchine, George, 67
Barzel, Tamar, 17, 19, 90
Baseball, immigrants and, 128–29
Bauman, Zygmunt, 9, 194
Bechet, Sidney, 84, 86
Beck, Louis, 253n
Beethoven, Ludwig, 199
The Bell Curve (Murray), 275
Bell, Daniel, 6, 11, 136
Bellow, Saul, 6, 27, 288, 292, 294, 313, 323; Jen v., 292–93; narratives of, 293
Belmont, Augustus, 158
Benjamin, Walter, 59–60
Bennington, Geoff, 214
Bensoussan, Aaron, 280; Caine and, 203

Bercovitch, Sacvan, 56n; on American utopia, 58
Berlant, Lauren, 177
Berlin, Irving, 6; aka Bailen, Isadore, 255
Bernard, Calvin (as character in *The Symbol*): Miller, Arthur, and, 113–14
Bernstein, Leonard, 6, 67, 72, 204n, 343n29–344n29; and *Dybbuk*, 67–71; on Mahler, 204n, 205
Bessie, Alvah, 114; Miller, Arthur, and, 112
Beyond Ethnicity: Consent and Descent in American Culture (Sollors), 9n–10n
Beyond the Melting Pot (Moynihan), 130, 136
Bezmozgis, David, 315–16
Bhabha, Homi, on cosmopolitanism, 92, 345n45–346n45
"Birthmates" (Jen), 300
Black Atlantic (Gilroy), 22–23
Black Legend, 223n
Blackface, 14, 15, 183–84; Rogin on, 183
Blackface, White Noise (Rogin), 28, 30
Blackness: Jacobson on, 184; Jewishness and, 23; Melnick on, 184; rejection of, 29; Rogin on, 184; Sundquist/Gilroy on, 24
Bloom, Harold, 22, 135, 291, 308
Borat: Cultural Learning of America for Make Benefit Glorious Nation of Kazakhstan (movie), 324
Boyarin, Daniel, 26, 98, 277, 280
Brandwein, Naftule, 80–82, 81, 86, 89, 91; Armstrong v., 84–85; Gonsalves v., 85; klezmer and, 82–84; musical talent of, 82–83; recording structure of, 84; Rodriguez, Roberto Juan, and, 89
Brodkin, Karen, 28
Broken Glass (Miller, Arthur), 103
Bronfman, Yefim, 180, 181
Brown v. Board of Education, 177
Browne, Carl, 159, 161
Broyard, Anatole, 167
Bryan, William Jennings, 159

Bug Music (Byron), 87, 199
Burgess, E. W., 9, 10
Business, Jewish masculinity and, 95, 102
Byrd, Donald, 87
Byron, Don, 20, 86, 336n17, 355n32; Caine and, 198, 199, 201, 203

Cahan, Abraham, 6, 168n, 258
Caine, Uri, 34, 87, 165, 198–208, 280; Bach music and, 201; background of, 199; Bensoussan and, 203; Byron and, 198, 199, 201, 203; Jewishness and, 199–200; Mahler and, 201–2, 207; on Mahler's Jewishness, 205n; Wagner music and, 199–200
Call It English, 28
Call It Sleep (Roth, Henry), 255, 287, 317
Cantor, Eddie, 255
Caroline, or Change (Kushner), 72
Carpathia, Nicholae: antisemitic description of, 149, 350n11; "Jewish" power of, 153–54, 155; as *Left Behind* character, 143–46, 148; universal currency and, 157–58
Carroll, Michael, 223
Casas Grandes, 232, 236
Castro, Fidel, 245, 246
Cather, Willa, 232, 270, 271
Catholicism: America and, 131, 136; Cuban culture, 248; Marranos and, 229, 236
Chang, Lan Samantha, 286, 308–14, 315; Chinese folk belief and, 309–10; Jen and, 310, 314; new immigrant narrative of, 303–15
Charlie Chan: model minority narrative and, 274; Oland and, 272
Charlie Chan at the Ringside, 272
The Cheat (De Mille), 254
Cheech and Chong, 14, 15
"Cherokee" (Parker), 182, 184
Cheyette, Bryan, on ambivalence, 153
Chicano studies, Aranda on, 234

Children of the Ghetto (Zangwill), 8
Chin, Frank, 275, 310
Chinatown, 253–55, 267
Chinese Exclusion Act of 1882, 263
Chiu, Christina, 286, 303–4
Choi, Susan Malka, 286, 303
Chonen, as character in *A Dybbuk*, 62–64
Christ: in American populism, 158–61; in *Angels in America*, 56; in *Left Behind* sequence, 146, 148, 149
Christian New Right, 31, 163; Falwell/Robertson and, 162; LaHaye/Jenkins and, 161
Christian Science Monitor, 272
Christian Zionism, McAlister on, 147
Christianity, 31–32, 269; antisemitism in, 159; Identity movement of, 161; Jews and, 4–5, 12, 56n; philosemitism and, 142–43
Civil Rights Act, 177
Civil War, 234
Clarissa (Richardson), 172
Clark, Kenneth, 9
Coates, Helen, 70
Cohen, Sacha Baron, as character in *Borat*, 325–26
Cohn, Harry, 106
Cohn, Roy, 65, 102; blessings/cursings of, 53; death of in *Perestroika*, 52; as Jewish character in *Angels in America*, 42, 43, 45, 48, 49–50, 53–54; octopus image of, 49–50
Coleman, Anthony: on Jewish pride, 91–92; on radical Jewish culture/klezmer revival, 345n44
Coleman, Ornette, 86
Collier's Magazine, 272
Collins, Arthur, 322
Coltrane, Alice, 187
Coltrane, John, 85–86
Columbus, Christopher, Marranos and, 211–12
Commentary, 167

Common Ground: Reimagining American History (Okihiro), 276
Communism, 191
Conversos (New Christians): Netanyahu on, 218; Sephardic Jews as, 210–12; Yerushalmi on, 211n
Copland, Aaron, 107
Cosmopolitanism, 93; Appiah/Bhabha on, 92, 345n45–346n45
Coughlin, Charles, 156; antisemitism of, 140–41, 162; terrorism and, 140–41
Count Basie, 181
The Counterlife (Roth, Philip), 166, 193
Coxey's Army, 160, *160*; antisemitism and, 158–59, 350n22–352n22
Crawford, Richard, 182
Creation, negative view of, 65
Crypto-Jews: Iglesia de Dios Israelita and, 224; *see also* Marranos
Cuba, Obejas and, 240–42
Culture: black/white interrelation in, 165; ethnicity and, 11n–12n; imagination, Jews influence on, 2–3, 16–17
Currency, universal: Carpathia and, 157–58; criticism of, 158

Dark Flame (Caine), 202, 204n
Darriau, Matt, 87, 89
Dawison, Magnus, 205n–206n
Day of Atonement (Raphelson), blackface of, 15
Days of Awe (Obejas), 216, 239–50; cubanidad in, 243–45; marranism in, 248–49; multiple affiliations in, 242, 248; passing for Gentile in, 242, 243; San José, Alejandra, as narrator in, 240
De Mille, Cecil B., 254
de Prado, Juan (Daniel), 215
"De Shtiler Bulgar" (Elman, Ziggy), 186
Dearborn Independent (Ford), 46, 140, 261
Death of a Salesman (Miller, Arthur), 95, 116, 119, 300
Depression, Jewish masculinity and, 100

Iberian Jews, 215–16; Diaspora of, 225; racism and, 217
Iglesia de Dios Israelita (Israelite Church of God): Crypto-Jews and, 224; Seventh Day Adventist roots of, 224
The Imaginary Jew (Finkielkraut), 39
Imitation of Life (Hurst), 173n–174n
Imitation of Life (Sirk), 165, 167, 173, 176–79; Berlant on, 177; racial identity in, 177
Immigrant Acts (Lowe), 276
Immigrants: acculturation of, 279–80; allegiances of, 278; baseball and, 128–29; complaints about, 14; Lower East Side and, 8; narratives of, 287, 291, 294, 309–15; "New" v. "Old," 13–14, 277; representation of, 277–78
Immigration Restriction Act of 1924, 2
Inquisition, survivors of, 360n25
Intermarriage, Jewish identity and, 35
The International Jew (Ford), 45, 140, 156, 261–62, 278
Iola Leroy (Harper), 167
Irish-Americans, 7n–8n, 103, 129–31
Israel, in *Left Behind* series, 146–47
Israel, Jonathan, 211, 212
Israelite Church of God; see Iglesia de Dios Israelita
Italian Americans: Ferraro on, 7n; Orientalization of, 30n
Itzkovitz, Daniel, 194; *Imitation of Life* and, 174n
Ivanhoe (Scott, Walter), 3

Jackson, John, 196
Jacobs, Janet Liebman, 223–24
Jacobson, Matthew Frye, 28, 29, 32, 130, 137, 184; on race, 220
James, Henry, 164, 175
James, William, 100
Jazz, 356n35; African American and, 88, 181; Caine on, 200–201; Coltrane and, 85–86; klezmer v., 84, 85–86, 87–88; musicians, racial-ethnic dynamic of, 198; radical Jewish culture and, 86–87; *Rhythm* changes in, 182; riffing on Gershwin melodies in, 182
The Jazz Singer, 13, 14, 14n, 30, 233, 280, 281; blackface in, 15, 184; sexual ambiguity in, 32, 32n, 33
Jen, Gish, 9n, 251, 278, 286, 288, 292–302, 307, 309, 315, 317; Bellow v., 292–93; Chang and, 310, 314; inspiration for, 292; narratives of, 293, 294–95, 303; Paley and, 301
Jenkins, Jerry; see LaHaye, Timothy
Jewish American theater, gay diasporic vision of, 66–67
Jewish American writers: and antisemitism, 337n22; Asian perspective of, 308–9; inspiration of, 286, 292; on model minority, 304, 310, 321
"The Jewish Cemetery in Newport" (Longfellow), 5n
Jewish culture: authenticity of, 90–91, 195–96; fiction and, 286; hybridity and, 92; klezmer and, 18; problematic past of, 35; return of, 325; see also Radical Jewish Culture
Jewish Ethnographic Expedition, 61
Jewish identity: formation of, 29; as intellectual, 100, 151, 153, 273; intermarriage and, 35; klezmer and, 21; Kushner and, 41; as perverse, 124; as pimp, 261; queerness, compared to, 39–41; self-construction of, 279, 281; as sinister, 150; and tough guy, 101
"The Jewish Jazz Singer Finds His Voice" (Rogin), 32n
Jewish masculinity, 94, 345n2; American constructions of, 100; assimilation and, 98–99; business and, 95, 102; Depression and, 100; disembodied respectability/embodied assertiveness as, 100; double construction of, 97; gentile culture and, 98, 105, 122;

INDEX

Goodman, Benny, 180, 181, 186, 188n; Elman and, 186
Gordon, Milton, 6, 136, 273–74, 276
Gordon, Rebecca Walker, 195
The Grand Gennaro (Lapolla), 7n
Grand Synagogue, of Amsterdam, 209
The Great American Novel (Roth, Philip), 164
Great Jewish Music (Zorn), 20
Gubenko, Julius, 187
Guinzberg, Vladimir Horace, 61
Gustav Mahler in Toblach (Caine), 202, 204n
Guthrie, Woody, 19n

Halevy, Judah, 217
Hancock, Herbie, 199
Hapgood, Hutchins, 8, 99, 258–59
Harlan, Byron, 322
Harlow, Larry, Salsa music and, 88
Harper, Frances, 167
Harris, Phil, 106
Haskalah, as Jewish enlightenment, 62n
Hattam, Victoria, 11
Hawthorne, Nathaniel, 167
Haymes, Dick, 180
"My Heart Belongs to Daddy" (Shaw), 188
Hebrew, v. Yiddish as Jewish language, 62
Hegel, race/ethnicity idiom and, 10
Heifitz, Jascha, 259
Heinlein, Robert, 144
Henry Box Brown (Kushner), 72
Herberg, Will, 136
Herder, Johann Gottfried: on Jews, 334n9; race/ethnicity idiom and, 10
Herzog (Bellow), 293, 294
Hitchcock, Alfred, 170n
Hitler, Adolf, 103, 251
Hofstadter, Richard, 152–53
The Holder of the World (Mukherjee), 288
Holiday, Billie, 183

Holliday, Judy, 110
Hollywood moguls, 262
Holmes, Oliver Wendell, 1, 2, 5, 6, 12, 16, 25, 258, 331–32; on Jewish characteristics, 3–4
Holocaust, 289; ethnicity ideas shaped by, 11
The Holocaust of Texts (Hungerford), 170n
Homophobia, 54
Hoover, J. Edgar, 107
Hordes, Stanley, 222–23
House Un-American Activities Committee (HUAC), 112, 119; Miller, Arthur and, 108; Shaw and, 190–91
How the Jews Became White Folks (Brodkin), 28
How the Other Half Lives (Riis), 257, 263–64
Howe, Irving, 94, 184n, 193
Howells, William Dean, on Lower East Side, 31
HUAC; *see* House Un-American Activities Committee
Hughes, Langston, 9
The Human Stain (Roth, Philip), 164–92, 196; Coleman as character in, 168–69, 171, 180, 191; Ernestine as character in, 170, 171; Jewish musical references in, 180–81; racial identity in, 166–67, 170–71; Staples on, 192; whiteness discourse in, 197; Zuckerman as character in, 166, 170, 171, 180
Humboldt's Gift (Bellow), 293
Hunger (Chang), 308–14; immigrant/ assimilation narrative of, 311–14; synopsis of, 309
Hungerford, Amy, 170n
Hurst, Fannie, 173n–174n

"I Got Rhythm" (Gershwin): Crawford on, 182; Parker and, 182
I Married a Communist (Roth, Philip), 119, 165, 166, 191

Falwell, Jerry, 149, 162
Family, virtues of, 127–28
Fanfare for the Common Man (Copland), 107
Fante, John, 7n
Farmer, Frances, 106
Farrell, James, 8n
Faye, Alice, 106
Feeling Italian: The Art of Ethnicity in America, 7n
Feldman, Walter Zev, 83
Female exploitation, allegedly undertaken by Jews, 47
Ferraro, Thomas, 7n
Ferry, Barbara, 223
Finkelman, Harry, née Elman, Ziggy, 186
Finkielkraut, Alain, 39
First Symphony (Mahler), 206–7; Caine version of, 205
Fishberg, Maurice, 11, 267–68
Fisher, Eddie, 106
Fitzgerald, Scott, 101
Fixer Chao (Ong), 306, 307; cultural representations of, 305, 305n; human nature and, 304–5; narrative of, 304–5
Focus (Miller, Arthur), 104
Ford, Henry, 45, 103, 140, 156, 261–62, 278, 290; antisemitism of, 140
The Foreign Student (Choi), 303
Frailach (klezmer dance), 206–7
Frank, Leo: antisemitism and case of, 47–48; Watson and, 47
Frank, Waldo, 221
Franklin, Benjamin, 292
Free Food for Millionaires (Lee, Min Jin), 251, 323
"Frère Jacques," 205, 206
Freud, Sigmund, 15, 40, 133, 136, 152
Freydl, as character in *Stempenyu: A Yiddish Romance*, 76
Frisell, Bill, 20
Frykholm, Amy Johnson, 145–46
Fu Manchu, 271, 272–73, 275

Fuchs, Lawrence, 131–33, 136
Fuller, Robert, on Antichrist, 149

Gaebelein, Arno, 149
Gainsbourgh, Serge, 20, 21
Gardner, Ava, 190
Gates, Henry Louis Jr., on Broyard, 167
Gay male identity, as *Angels in America* theme, 42, 45, 50, 55, 64, 66–67
Gaye, Marvin, 199
Gehrig, Lou, 128; DiMaggio and, 129
Geller, Jay, 265
Gender difference, 15; Klezmatics on, 20
Gentile culture, Jewish masculinity and, 98, 105, 122
German Romantic philosophy, in Hegel/Herder, 10
Gershwin, George, 6, 66, 85, 180–81, 185, 186n, 192, 201, 253, 359; Klezmer and, 186; Melnick on, 182; Parker riffing on songs of, 182, 197; Shaw/Eldridge riffing on songs of, 182–83
Ghetto, 333n7–334n7; historical use of, 9; Jewish quarters as, 8; literature, 7n
The Ghetto (Wirth), 8–9
The Ghost Writer (Roth, Philip), 166
Gibbs, Terry, née Gubenko, Julius, 187
Gilded Age, 7n
Gilman, Sander, 10, 26, 40, 151, 273, 277; on physical characteristics of Jews, 48–49
Gilroy, Paul, 22–23; on Jewishness/blackness, 24
Girshkin, Vladimir, 316–17
Glazer, Nathan, 11, 136
Gold, Michael, 254
Goldberg, Jeffrey, 151–52
The Goldberg Variations (Caine), 199, 201
Goldstein, Eric, 28, 29
Gonsalves, Paul, Brandwein v., 85
Goodbye, Columbus (Roth, Philip), 166
Goode, Virgil, 327

Derrida, Jacques: Bennington and, 214; on Marranos, 214, 249, 358*n*10–359*n*10
Dershowitz, Alan, 35
The Diabelli Variations (Caine), 199
Diamond, Neil, 13–14, 14*n*
Diaspora, 20, 22, 250; dybbuk narrative and, 66; Jewish, 90, 368*n*; Kushner on, 42; Spanish, 262*n*; *see also* Sephardic Diaspora
Diasporic vision, of Jewish American theater, 66–67
Diasporism, queer, 80, 80*n*, 90, 92, 207
Dickens, Charles, 40, 172
Dieu Protège Israel (Doré), 49
"The Difference Between Them," 264
The Difference Between Them, 265
DiMaggio, Joe, 97, 110, 128; Gehrig and, 129; Monroe and, 107, 126
Diner, Hasia, 8
Dinnerstein, Leonard, 162
Dollimore, Jonathan, 286
Don Byron Plays Mickey Katz!, 87
Doré, Gustave, 49
Dorsey, Tommy, 180
"Dr. Livingstone I Presume?" (Shaw): klezmer solo in, 187; Sapoznik on, 187
Draschler, Julius, 11
Drew, Charles, 171
Drumont, Eduoard, 49
Du Maurier, George, 49, 153, 272
DuBois, W. E. B., 178
Dukakis, Michael, 137
Duke Ellington Orchestra, 188*n*
Durkheim, Émile, 133–34; anomic suicide and, 133, 134
Dutiful Daughters (Mukherjee), 290
The Dybbuk (Ansky), 41–42, 60, 93; Seidman on, 63; translation of, 61; *zivug* in, 64
A Dybbuk (Kushner), 41–42, 60–65, 71; sexual transgressivity of, 63; transcendence in, 64–65; *zivug* in, 64

Dybbuk (Robbins/Bernstein), 67–68, 68, 69, 71*n*; Bernstein's agenda for, 69–70, 343*n*29–344*n*29; Coates on, 70; New York City Ballet and, 67; Robbins's agenda for, 68–69
Dybbuk narrative: diaspora and, 66; queer genealogy and, 65–66, 67
The Dybbuk Variations (Robbins), 71
Dyer, Richard, on whiteness, 126
The Dying Animal (Roth, Philip), 164

Ebest, Ron, 7*n*–8*n*
Einstein, Albert, 151
Eldridge, Roy, 165, 181, 191, 192; riffing of Gershwin's songs by, 182–83; Roth and, 185; songs by, 354*n*18
Eliot, T. S., 290
Ellington, Duke, 200
Ellis, Mary, 66
Ellison, Keith, 327
Elman, Mischa, 259
Elman, Ziggy: Goodman and, 186; née Finkelman, Harry, 186; Rogovoy on, 186
Emerson, Ralph Waldo, 64
Eng, David, 257, 275
Epistle to the Hebrews (Lazarus), 259
Epstein, Jacob, 258–59
Ethnic masculinity, making of, 94–139
Ethnicity, 295–98; in *Days of Awe*, 249; European context/American adaptation of, 11; Fuchs on, 131–33; Gilman on, 10; Hattam on, 11; Holocaust and, 11; Jewish construction of, 12, 137; Jewish experience and, 9; Moynihan and, 130–33, 136; production by Holocaust, 11; race/culture and, 11*n*–12*n*, 222; Sollors on, 9–10, 9*n*–10*n*
Europe, ethnicity and, 11
Eve; *see* American Eve
Ex-Coloured Man (Johnson), 168
Expulsion of Jews, from Spain, 216–17, 219*n*, 223*n*, 330

Jewish intelligence and, 273–74; Mailer and, 118; Miller, Arthur, as ideal type of, 95–96, 123; Miller/Monroe encounter and, 119, 122; Monroe and, 125–26; negative view on, 105; Nordau and, 99; personae of, 102; as pervert/feminized, 97; Roth, Philip, and, 123; traditional models of, 99

"Jewish science," Durkheim and, 134, 134n–135n

The Jewish Spirit in Music (Wagner), 200

Jewishness, 15, 193–94; blackness and, 23; Caine invocation of, 199–200; Indians and, 238; of Mahler, 204n; of Miller, Arthur, 103; multiplicity of, 194; of new generations, 325; notions of, 34–35; Radical Jewish Culture and, 22; role of, 136–37; Roth, Philip, on, 179; Shteyngart on, 319; Sundquist/Gilroy on, 24

Jews, 266; adolescent rebellion and, 99, 101; African American relations with, 87–88; as aliens, 42–43; antisemitism without, 140–63; Asians v., 265–67, 269, 279, 306; assimilation of, 29, 96, 99–100, 136, 165, 184, 213, 285, 334n8; blackness mask of, 184; characteristics of, 3–4; Chinese food and, 361n1, 361n2; Christian conversion of, 147, 148, 149–50; Christianity and, 4–5, 12, 56n; class structures of, 138; contributions of, 284, 286–87; as economic player, 265; emigration of, 315; ethnicity and, 9, 12; exclusion of, 138; as exiles, 5n; expulsion of, 10; female exploitation, allegedly, by, 46; Fishberg on, 267–68; Herder on, 334n9; Holmes on, 3–4, 5n; Holy Land return of, 147–48; imaginative production by, 6; literary/cultural imagination influence of, 2–3, 16–17, 292, 300–302, 307–9, 313–15; mascu-linity of, 25–26, 38; media and, 16; mind control by, 154–55; as model minority, 12, 252–82; multiplicity of, 364n26–365n26; Native Americans and, 36, 36n; Orientalism of, 30n, 34, 259, 260, 261–62, 266–67, 272–73, 279–80, 281–82, 362n15–363n15; physical characteristics of, 47, 48–49, 307, 307n; pride of, 91–92; properties of, 39; queer contiguity with, 44–45, 57, 66, 71; radical/religious persecution of, 148; representation of, 6, 153, 283; secular representation of, 152; sexual deviance of, 40–41, 45, 46; sexual dissidence of, 25; slave trade and, 211; U.S. immigration of, 7, 7n–8n; in U.S. theater, 5; as victims, 4n; as villainous, 271–73; WASP discourse about, 260–61; white slavery and, 261, 271, 363n17; Yiddish/Hebrew as language of, 62; *see also* American Jews; Asian Americans; Iberian Jews; Marranos; Mizrachi Jews; Oriental Jew; Sephardic Jews; Spanish Jews

There are Jews in My House (Vapnyar), 315

Jews Without Money (Gold), 254

"Jewtown," 254; *see also* Lower East Side

John F. Kennedy and American Catholicism (Fuchs), 131

Johnson, James Weldon, 167, 168

Jolson, Al, 184, 255

Jones, Philly Joe, 199

Joyce, James, 97

Judah, Alfie: assimilation of, 289–90; as The Middleman character, 288, 290

Kaddish, 52–53, 247–48

Kaftan (pimp), 261

Kallen, Horace, 6, 11, 27, 221

Kamen, Henry, 219n

Karchoff, Cardie, 306

Katz, Mickey, 20, 187, 324

Kawash, Samira, 168
Kazan, Elia, 106
Kennedy, John, 97, 131; assimilation and, 129–30; Monroe and, 126
Kennedy, Robert, 97; assimilation and, 129–30; Monroe and, 126
Khazars, identity of, 268, 268n, 324
Kibria, Nazli, 278
Kingdom Come: The Final Victory (LaHaye/Jenkins), 145
Kingsolver, Barbara, 232
Kirschenblatt-Gimblett, Barbara, 17–18, 274
Klee, Paul, 59
Klein, Manny, 187
Klezmatics, 19n, 42, 73, 87, 280, 336n15, 344n39; on gender differences, 20; musical innovation by, 19; on New/Old Left politics, 19–20
Klezmer: Brandwein and, 82–84; components of, 18–19, 75; diasporic queerness within, 80; *frailach*, 206–7; history of, 17, 74, 74n; jazz v., 84, 85–86, 87–88; Jewish culture and, 18, 75–76; Jewish identity and, 21; as "Jewish Jazz," 186; Kirschenblatt-Gimblett on, 17–18; Kushner on, 73; Latin music and, 88n; Lower East Side and, 17; Mahler and, 205–7; New England Conservatory of Music and, 17; non-Jewish musicians and, 20; radical Jewish culture and, 86–87; revisionism of, 18; revival of, 17–18, 21, 42, 80, 83–84, 90, 93, 280, 335n13, 345n44; Russian folk music and, 354n22; Shaw and, 187–88; tonal patterns of, 335n14–336n14; tune of "De Shtiler Bulgar," 186
Klezmer Conservatory Band, 20, 198
Klezmer Madness! (Krakauer), 199
Klezmer musicians, 79; *Stempenyu: A Yiddish Romance* on, 76–79; women as, 344n33

Klezmer, New York (Krakauer), on Brandwein/Becht, 86
Klezmorim: cultural hybridity and, 74–76; weddings and, 74–75
Koestler, Arthur, 268
Korean American history, ethnocentric teaching of, 251
Krakauer, David, 83, 86, 89, 199
Kristeva, Julia, on passing for white, 175–76
Kun, Josh, 28, 324
Kushner, Tony, 6, 34, 42–60, 65, 71–72, 90, 91, 93, 124, 233, 239, 280; on American utopia, 58–59; on Jew/queer contiguity, 44–45, 57, 66; on klezmer, 73; themes of, 72–73

LaHaye, Timothy, 140–63; antisemitism and, 156; Christian New Right and, 161; on Jewish mind, 151–52; Jewish power fears of, 156–57; Jewish representation by, 153; political involvement of, 162
Lahiri, Jumpha, 286, 309, 309n, 313
Lambert, Joshua, 252n
Landrieu, Mary, 330
Langmuir, Gavin, 56n
Lapolla, Garibaldi M., 7n
Larsen, Nella, 167
Latin music, klezmer and, 88–89, 88n
"Latinos Give New Life to Neil Diamond Anthem," 13
Latinos: in America, 196–97; on "America," 13–14
Lawford, Peter, 136
Lazarus, Emma, 7, 27, 210, 259
Lazzarri, Tony, 129
Leah, as character in *A Dybbuk*, 62–64, 66
Leaming, Barbara, on Monroe, 108–10
Lebrecht, Norman, 205
Lee, Chang-Rae, 286
Lee, Don, 286
Lee, Min Jin, 251, 323

Lee, Rachel, 292, 299
Left Behind (LaHaye/Jenkins), 140–63; antisemitic expression in, 146, 150–51, 154, 159–60, 327; Carpathia as character in, 143–46, 148; character's descriptions as coded antisemitic, 149, 350*n*11; character's internal struggles in, 146; Christ in, 146, 148, 149; Israel in, 146–47; Jewish control in, 155–56; McAlister on, 163; philosemitism in, 146; political strategy of, 159–60; Rosenzweig as character in, 143–45, 147; success of, 145; synopsis of, 143–45; videogame of, 326–27, 352*n*24
Lei, David, 284
Lennon, Julian, 20
Letting Go (Roth, Philip), 166
Levine, Sammy "Red," 101
Lewis, R. W. B., 238
Li, Robert G., 275, 366*n*40
Light for Nations, on capitalism, 156
Limpieza de sangre (purity of blood), 219*n*, 225; Netanyahu on, 217–18, 225; Sollors on, 218
Lin, Paul Toledo, 305, 306
Lincoln, Abraham, Monroe and, 107
Lipset, Seymour Martin, 6, 11, 136
Literary imagination, Jews influence on, 2–3, 16–17
The Little Drummer Boy (Bernstein), 204*n*
"The Little Drummer Boy," Caine version of, 203, 204, 206
Liu, Eric, 308; assimilation and, 284–85; as model minority, 283, 283*n*
Locke, Alain, 27
Lohengrin (Wagner), 205*n*
Loman, Willy, 120, 121
Lombroso, Cesare, 40, 329
London, Frank, 89
"The Long Distance Runner" (Paley): racial discrimination in, 300, 302; synopsis of, 300
Longfellow, Henry, 5*n*

Los Angeles Times, 13
Lost Boundaries (Preminger), 165; racial conflict in, 167
Lott, Eric, 192
Louie, David Wong, 286
The Love Wife (Jen), 303
Low, Benjamin, 260
Lowe, Lisa, 276
Lower East Side, 7, 67, 259–60, 281; Chinatown and, 253–55; Chinese communities in, 253; Howells on, 31; immigrants and, 8, 253–54; "Jew Town," 254; klezmer and, 17; nature/properties of, 8; Oriental Jew in, 262; Riis on, 261
Lunt, Paul, 11

Mahler, Gustav, 180, 181, 205–7; Adorno on, 201–2, 205; background of, 201; Bernstein on, 204*n*; Caine and, 199–200, 201, 207; Jewishness of, 204*n*, 205, 205*n*
Mailer, Norman: Jewish masculinity and, 118; on Miller, Arthur, 116; Miller, Arthur, competition with, 114–19; on Monroe, 114–15, *118*
Makino, Kazu, 20
Malamud, Bernard, 6, 310, 313; Mukherjee and, 287–88
"Mammy" (Jolson), 184
"The Man I Love" (Gershwin), 180–81, 188, 207; Holiday and, 183; klezmer in, 192
Marilyn: A Life (Mailer), 114
Marjorie Morningstar (Wouk), 252; Lambert on, 252*n*
Marks, Elaine, 213–14
Marranos (Crypto-Jews), 210, 360*n*26; Alcalá on, 233–34, 236–37, 239; in America, 216–17; Catholic identity of, 215–16; Columbus and, 211–12, 357*n*4–358*n*4; concealment of, 214–15; Derrida on, 214, 249, 358*n*10–359*n*10; ethnicity and, 248;

Marranos (*continued*)
  genetic testing and, 224–25; Hordes on, 222; identity of, 213; Jacobs on, 223–24; Marks on, 213–14; Netenyahu on, 221; Neulander on, 222–23; in New Mexico, 222–27, 223*n*; Obejas on, 240, 243–45; Sollors on, 221; study of, 222–23; suppression of, 235; Yerushalmi on, 211*n*
Marsalis, Wynton, 200
Martin, Dean, 135
Masculinity: of Asian Jews, 257; Boyarin on, 98; ideals of, 98; of Jews, 25–26, 38; traditional models for, 37; *see also* Jewish masculinity
McAlister, Melani, 146, 163; Christian Zionism and, 147
McBride, James, 195
McCafferey, Anne, 120
McCarthy, Joseph, 45, 48, 102
McClure's Magazine, 260
McCord, Alice, aka Coltrane, Alice, 187
McGinn, Benard, 147–48; on Antichrist, 149
McVeigh, Timothy, 37
Media, Jews and, 16
Melnick, Jeffrey, 28, 30, 32, 182, 184, 187, 197
Melville, Herman, 167
Memoirs of a Muse (Vapnyar), 323
Menchaca, Martha, 234–35; effaces Spanish Jews, 235; on *mestizo/afromestizo,* 234
Mercer, Johnny, 186
The Merchant of Venice (Shakespeare), 55
mestizo, 234
The Metamorphosis, The Breast (Roth, Philip), 164
Mexican-American identity, 233–35; Alcalá on, 237; Aranda on, 234
Mexicanness: Alcalá and, 233–35; Menchaca on, 234–35

Meyer, Adam, 325
Meyerbeer, Giacomo, 200
Meyerson, Martin, 136
Mezzrow, Mezz, passing as black of, 186
Michaels, Walter, 11*n*–12*n*, 221
Mickey Katz album (Byron), 199
The Middleman (Mukherjee), Judah as character in, 288, 290
Millennium Approaches: of *Angels in America,* 43; antisemitism in, 44
Miller, Arthur, 94, 126, 273, 300; assimilation and, 105, 110; career of, 115–16; family superiority of, 102–3; HUAC and, 108; as ideal of Jewish masculinity, 95–96, 123; Jewishness of, 103, 116; Mailer competition with, 114–18; Monroe and, 96, 96*n*, 105, 106–11, *109*; novel about, 119–21; Portnoy and, 119–20; representation of, 103–4; resentment of, 95, 102; Rosten and, 111–12; sexual inadequacy of, alleged by Mailer, 116; transformation of, 110–11
Miller, Herbert, 99
Mingus, Charles, 200
Mizrachi Jews, 262*n*
Mobley, Hank, 199
Model minority, 252–82, 331; Jewish American writers on, 304, 310, 321; Jews as, 12; Liu as, 283, 283*n*
Mofaz, Shaul, 262*n*
Mona in the Promised Land (Jen), 9*n*, 251, 292, 301; on ethnicity, 295–98; racial conflicts in, 298–99, 298*n*, 302
Monk, Thelonius, 199
Monroe, Marilyn: blonde hair and, 127; career of, 117, 117*n*; dating life of, 132; dating patterns of, 125–26; death of, 133*n*; desires of, 125–26, 133; DiMaggio and, 107, 126; ethnic assimilation of, 135; family virtues of, 127–28, 134; Jewish masculinity and, 125–26; as Judaic convert, 135; Kennedy, Robert/John, and, 126;

INDEX

Lincoln and, 107; Mailer on, 114–15, *118*; Miller, Arthur, and, 96, 96*n*, 105, 106–11, *109*; novel about, 121; Rosten and, 112, 347*n*19; as social hermeneutic, 134–35; transformation of, 111; white ethnics and, 126, 138; whiteness of, 96–97, 126–27, 139
Monson, Ingrid, 198
"More Life" (Kushner), 59
Morgan, J. P., 158
Morton, Jelly Roll, 85
Mosley, Walter, 195, 196*n*, 355*n*29
Moynihan, Daniel Patrick, 11, 130; ethnicity and, 136; on Kennedy, John, 130–31
Mukherjee, Bharati, 286–91, 300, 303, 309, 313, 319; Jewish American narrative and, 288–89; Malamud and, 287–88; writing ambitions of, 287–91, 291*n*
Multiracial, Gordon/McBride/Mosley as, 195
Munich (Kushner), 72
Murder Incorporated, as Jewish-dominated enterprise, 101
Murray, Charles, 275
"My Heart Belongs to Daddy" (Shaw), 188
Myrdal, Gunnar, 9

The Naked and the Dead (Mailer), 115, 116
Nashon, Edna, 9
Natasha and Other Stories (Bezmozgis), 315
Nathan, Debbie, 223
A Nation of Immigrants (Kennedy, John), 130
Native Americans, Jews and, 36, 36*n*
Nelson, Joshua, 87
Netanyahu, Benzion, 217–18
Netsky, Hankus, 198
Neugroschel, Joachim, 64, 91

Neulander, Judith, 222–23, 224
New England Conservatory of Music, 198; klezmer and, 17
New Left politics, Klezmatics and, 19–20
New Mexico, Crypto-Jews in, 222–27, 223*n*, 248
New York Chinatown (Beck), 253*n*
New York Post, 136; on Monroe/Miller, Arthur, marriage, 108
New York Times, 70, 322
Nichols, Terry, 141
Nordau, Max, 40, 99
Norich, Anita, 28

Obejas, Achy, 216, 239–40
Odets, Clifford, 106
Okihiro, Gary, 276
Oland, Warner, 271–72
Old Left politics, Klezmatics on, 19–20
Olive, DJ, 203; aka Asch, Gregor, 203*n*
Omi, Michael, 221, 359*n*19–360*n*19; on Liu, 284
Ong, Han, 304, 306, 308, 315
Oresme, Nicholas, 40
Oriental Jew, 30, 262*n*, 271*n*, 339*n*31–349*n*31; attention, lack of, 34; exoticism, 259; as hysterical Jew, 260; in Lower East Side, 262; Rogin on, 34; sexual ambiguities of, 31–32
Orientalism: Asians and, 261–63; Ayrshire and, 270–71; in *Fixer Chao*, 306; Jews and, 30*n*, 34, 259, 260, 261–62, 266–67, 272–73, 279–80, 281–82, 362*n*15–363*n*15; language of, 263; Said on, 257
"Orient-eyed" (Holmes), 258
The Original Mr. Jacobs (Drumont), 49
Our America (Michaels), 221
Our Gang (Roth, Philip), 166
Ozick, Cynthia, 292

Pace, Amedeo, 20
Pace, Simone, 20
Paley, Grace, 6, 300; Jen and, 301

Pamela (Richardson), 172
At the Pantomime (Holmes), 1, 2; theology of, 4–5
Park, Robert, 9, 10, 11, 99
Parker, Charlie, 182, 184, 197; riffing of Gershwin's songs by, 182–83
Passing (Larsen), 167
Passing for white, 168–70, 196–97; African Americans as, 167, 213; Kristeva and, 175–76; maternal loss and, 173–75; Staples on, 175
The Past Through Tomorrow (Heinlein), 144
Paul Whiteman band, Klein and, 187
"Pelagian-Arminian culture," 134; inadequacy of, 138
"Peppino" (Venture), 7n
Perestroika: of *Angels of America*, 43; Cohn's, Roy, death in, 52
Peretz, Amir, 262n
Philosemitism: Christianity and, 142–43; in *Left Behind* series, 146
Pinky (Preminger), 165; political correctness of, 167
Pitt, Joe, as Mormon character in *Angels in America*, 43, 44
Podhoretz, Norman, 35
Porgy and Bess (1935) (Gershwin), 66
Portnoy, Alexander, 190, 288, 316, 321; Miller, Arthur, and, 119–20; sexuality of, 123
Portnoy's Complaint (Roth, Philip), 317; on Miller, Arthur, 119–21
Posnock, Ross, on Roth, Philip, 164
Pound, Ezra, 290
Powers, Ann, 13
Prager, Dennis, 327
The Prague Orgy (Roth, Philip), 164
Preminger, Otto, 165, 167
Private Histories: The Writing of Irish Americans (Ebest), 7n–8n
The Professor's House (Cather), 232
Prostitution, American Jews alleged control of, 47

The Protocols of the Elders of Zion (Timayenhsis), 46, 49, 140, 150, 156
Proust, Marcel, 40–41, 44, 97
Publisher's Weekly, 307, 323
Puck (magazine), 265, 267, 269

Race: authenticity of, 170, 170n; ethnicity and, 11n–12n, 222; "hue" of, 29; human identity and, 168; Jacobson on, 220; Netenyahu on, 221; passing for white of, 168–70, 173–76; racialization and, 165, 184; Rogin on, 34; Roth, Philip, on, 179, 193; Sirk on, 179; Sollors on, 221; thinking, history of, 218–19
Rachel, as character in *Stempenyu: A Yiddish Romance*, 76–78
Racial alterity, 15, 168–69
Racial castration, Eng on, 257
Racial Formation in the United States (Omi/Winant), 221
Racial identity: Jackson on, 196; Johnson and, 168
Racism, Silk, Coleman, and, 169
Radical Jewish Culture, 34, 86–93, 124, 280; authenticity and, 90–91; Coleman, Anthony, on, 345n44; Jewishness and, 22; klezmer/jazz and, 86–87; music and, 87–89; Zorn on, 22
Raphelson, Samson, 15
Rappaport, Shloyme-Zanvel; see Ansky, S.
Rapture Culture (Frykholm), 145–46
Real Black: Adventures in Racial Sincerity (Jackson), 196
The Real Mr. Jacobs (Timayensis), 45
Recovering History, Constructing Race: The Indian, Black, and White Roots of Mexican Americans (Menchaca), 234
Reynolds, Debbie, 106
Rhapsody in Blue (Gershwin), 182, 186, 201; klezmer effects in, 186n
Rhythm changes, in jazz, Parker and, 182
Ribot, Marc, 89, 90n; on authenticity, 90–91

INDEX

Ricardo, David, 210
Richardson, Samuel, 172
The Right to Sing the Blues (Melnick), 28
Right-wing culture, 191; as *Angels in America* theme, 42, 48, 52
Riis, Jacob, 254, 258, 261, 263–65
The Rise of David Levinsky (Cahan), 168n, 259–60
The Rise of Fu Manchu (Rohmer), 272
Rise Up! (Klezmatics), 19
Rivers, Sam, 199
Rizzuto, Phil, 129
Robbins, Jerome, 67, 71, 72; sexual identity of, 68–69
Robertson, Pat, 162
Rodriguez, Roberto Juan, 88–89
Roediger, David, 28, 29, 30n
Rogin, Michael, 28, 30, 32, 32n, 34, 184, 192, 197; on blackface minstrelsy, 183
Rogovoy, Seth, 186
Rohmer, Sax, 272
Roosevelt, Franklin Delano, 140
Rose, Paul, 56n
Rosenzweig, Chaim: as antisemitic caricature, 150–51; conversion of, 152; as *Left Behind* character, 143–45, 147; as "smart" Jew, 151
Roskies, David, 28
Rosten, Norman: Miller, Arthur, and, 111–12; Monroe and, 112, 347n19
Roth, Henry, 6, 8n, 27, 255, 287, 317
Roth, Philip, 6, 96, 106, 111, 119, 164–92, 273, 287, 288, 323, 354n26; black/white conflict and, 166, 168; critiques of, 166; Jewish masculinity and, 123; on passing, 192; Posnock on, 164; racial identity and, 170; as sentimental novelist, 175–76, 180; Shulevitz on, 192–93; writing style of, 164, 165
Rothschild family, antisemitism and, 158
Rothschild, Mayer, caricature of, 49
Rothstein, Arnold, 101

A Russian Debutante's Guide (Shteyngart), 315, 316; immigrants and, 316–21
Russian folk music, klezmer and, 354n22
"The Russian Jew in America" (Cahan), 258

Said, Edward, 30, 257
Salammbô (Flaubert), 352
Salomé of the Tenements (Yezierska), 259
Salsa music, Harlow and, 88
Salter, "Nigger Mike," 255
San José, Alejandra: as *Days of Awe* narrator, 240; as Marrano, 244–46
San José, Enrique: Catholic Cuban culture and, 248; as *Days of Awe* character, 240; as Marrano, 247
Sanchez, George, 28
Sapoznik, Henry, 17, 187; on Brandwein, 80–81
Saturday Evening Post, on Miller, Arthur, 104–5
Savran, David, on *Angels in America*, 57
Scandal (Cather): Ayrshire as character in, 270–71; Stein as character in, 270
Schearle, David, 288, 316, 321; as *Call It Sleep* character, 255
Schorch, Jonathan, 220
Scott, Raymond, 87
Scott, Walter (Sir), 3
Seidman, Naomi, 62, 63
Seligman, Joseph, 2, 258
Selzer, Michael, 49
Selznick, David, 189
Sentimental Journey (Sterne), 172
Sentimental melodramas: of 1950s, 165; Roth, Philip, and, 180
Sentimentalism: family and, 172–73, 176–77; in *The Human Stain*, 172, 175–76; in literature, 172–73; Sirk and, 178; Weinstein on, 173
Sephardic Diaspora, 211n, 216, 219; Derrida of, 214; from Spain, 209
Sephardic Home for the Aged, 210

Sephardic Jews, 90, 209–10, 249, 262*n*, 356*n*1–357*n*1; Carroll on, 223; as conversos, 210–12; Ferry on, 223; music of, 367*n*46; Nathan on, 223; race/ethnicity of, 219–20; Schorch on, 220; U.S. immigration of, 210; whiteness and, 220
Seth, Vikram, 286, 296
Seventh-Day Adventism, 223; Neulander on, 224
Sex and Character (Weininger), 97
Sexual ambiguity: in *The Jazz Singer*, 32, 32*n*, 33; of Orientalized Jew, 31–32
Sexual deviance: of Jews, 40–41; Kushner and, 41–42
Sexual dissidence, 15; of Jews, 25
Sexual transgressivity, 63, 80, 124
Shakespeare, William, 40, 55, 253, 296
Shaw, Artie, 6, 180, 181, 182–83, 185, 188, 194, 197–98, 200; aka Arshawsky, Arthur, 184; autobiography of, 188–89; Gardner and, 190; high culture and, 190; HUAC and, 190–91; née Arshawsky, Abraham Isaac, 186, 188–89; passing as Gentile by, 186, 188–90, 208; as Roth character, 190; Sudhalter on, 187, 189; Winsor and, 190
Sholem Aliechem, 74–75, 76, 91
Shore, Billy, 300
Shtetl culture, 61*n*; complexity of, 66; sexual desire within, 62, 63
Shteyngart, Gary, 34, 315, 323; assimilation narrative and, 318–19; immigration narrative and, 320–21; on Jewishness, 319
Shulevitz, Judith, 192–93
Sidarth, S. R., 328, 331
Siegel, Bugsy, 101
Silk, Coleman, 330; death of, 178; as *The Human Stain* character, 168–69, 171, 191; impersonation by, 170; passing as white of, 170, 175–76, 183; racism and, 169

Silk, Ernestine: as *The Human Stain* character, 170, 171; sentimentalism and, 172
Silko, Leslie, 232
Simmel, Georg, 10
Sinatra, Frank, 135, 180
Singerman, Robert, 267
Sirk, Douglas, 165, 167, 173, 176–79, 198; on racial identity, 177; sentimentalism, of family/race, 178
Skeffingon, Frank, 131
Slobin, Mark, 17
Smith, Gerald L. K., 156; antisemitism of, 141, 162
Smith, Willie "the Lion," as jazzman, 187
Society for the Study of Crypto-Jews and Anusim, 222
Sollors, Werner, on ethnicity, 9–10, 9*n*–10*n*, 218
Solomon, Alisa, 63
"Sometimes I Feel Like a Motherless Child" (Gershwin), 184
Sorrows of Young Werther (Goethe), 172
Southworth, E. D. E. N., 172
Spanish Inquisition, 215–16, 218*n*, 223*n*
Spanish Jews, 217
Spinoza, 210, 215; as Marrano, 213; Yovel on, 213
The Spirit of the Ghetto (Hapgood), Jewish masculinity and, 99
Spirits of the Ordinary (Alcalá), 216, 227–39; Marrano narrative in, 229–30; Mexican narrative in, 232–38
Staples, Brent, 175, 192
Stavans, Ilan, 28
Steffens, Lincoln, 8
Stein, Sigmund, as *Scandal* character, 270
Stempenyu: A Yiddish Romance (Aleichem), 74–75; on klezmer musicians, 76–79; on marriage, 77–78; sexual promiscuity in, 76, 79–80

Stempenyu, as character in *Stempenyu: A Yiddish Romance*, 76–78
Sterne, Laurence, 172
Sternowitz, as *Call It Sleep* character, 255–56
The Stranger (Simmel), 10
Strangers from a Difference Shore (Takaki), 10
Strangers in the Land (Sundquist), 23
Stratton, Jon, 9
Strom, Yale, 66
Sudhalter, Richard, 187
A Suite of Dances (Robbins), on Jew/queer contiguity, 71
"Summertime" (Gershwin), 184
Sundquist, Eric, 23, 24, 167; on Jewishness/blackness, 24
Suzuki, Bob, 275–76, 310
Swann (Proust), 42
Swingle Singers, 201
The Symbol (Bessie), 114; Bernard as character in, 113–14; on Monroe, 112

Takahashi, Maki, 20
Takaki, Ronald, 10
Tarras, Dave, 82
Taylor, Elizabeth, 106
Tenth Symphony (Mahler), Adorno on, 203–4
Terrorism, 37; Coughlin and, 140–41
Terry Gibbs Plays Jewish Melodies in Jazztime, 187
"Theses on the Philosophy of History" (Benjamin), 59
Third Symphony (Mahler), 180
The Thirteenth Tribe (Koestler), 268
Thompson, Ahmir, 199
Timayensis, Telemechus, 45–46
Timebends (Miller, Arthur), 94, 103, 112
Timlin, David, 203
Tin Pan Alley, 17, 182, 281
Todd, Mike, 106
Touro Synagogue, Sephardic Jews and, 209

Trilby (Du Maurier), 49, 153, 272
Trilling, Lionel, 195n–196n, 196
The Trouble with Cinderella (Shaw), 188–89
Troublemaker (Chiu), 303–4
"Turkish-Bulgarish" (Brandwein): Rodriguez version of, 89; *see also* Vedado Street Mix
Turkishe Yalle Vey Uve (Brandwein), 84, 85
Turner, George Kibbe, 260–61
Twelfth Night (Shakespeare), 55
Typical American (Jen), 292, 296, 299

Universal currency; *see* Currency, universal
Updike, John, 300
Uris, Leon, 104

Vaill, Amanda, 68
Vapnyar, Lara, 315, 323
Veblen, Thorsten, 11
Vedado Street Mix (Rodriguez), 89; *see also* "Turkish-Bulgarish"
Venture, Luigi, 7n
Vienna Opera, 201
Vienna Philharmonic, 201, 204n

Wagner e Venezia (Caine), 200
Walter Prior, 64; as Gentile character in *Angels in America*, 42, 43, 55–59
Ward, Arthur Henry, 272
Warner, Susan, 172
Warner, W. Lloyd, 11
Washington, Grover, 199
WASPs, 260–61; American identity and, 129; Asians and, 303
Watson, Tom, Frank and, 47
Webb, James, 328
Weber, Donald, 318
Weber, Max, 10
Weddings, klezmorim and, 74–75
Weinberg, Sidney Stahl, 94
Weininger, Otto, 97, 118

Weinstein, Cindy, on sentimental fiction/family, 173
Weschler, James, 136
West, Nathanael, 27
"When the Angels Sing" (Mercer), 186
White Heat, 165
White slavery, Jews and, 261, 271, 363*n*17
Whiteness: of Asians, 285; blonde hair and, 126, 127, 347*n*17; Dyer on, 126; magic status of, 127; of Miller, Arthur, 96–97; of Monroe, 96–97, 126–27, 139; Sephardic Jews and, 220
Whiteness of a Different Color (Jacobson), 28, 192
Whitfield, Stephen, 37
Winant, Howard, 221, 284, 359*n*19–360*n*19
Winsor, Kathleen, 190
Wirth, Lewis, 8–9
Wirth-Nesher, Hana, 28
Wisse, Ruth, 28
Women, as klezmer musicians, 344*n*33
Woo, Deborah, 277
Woody Herman orchestra, 199
World of Our Mothers (Weinberg), 94
Wouk, Herman, 104, 252

Yerushalmi, Yosef, 211*n*
Yezierska, Anzia, 6, 259
Yiddish, as Jewish language, 62
Yovel, Yirmiyahu, 213, 214, 215

Zangwill, Israel, 8
Zionist Occupational Government (ZOG), 141
ZOG; *see* Zionist Occupational Government
Zorn, John, 6, 20, 86, 88, 322, 324; on Radical Jewish Culture, 22
Zuckerman, Nathan, 193; as *The Human Stain* character, 166, 170, 171, 180

GPSR Authorized Representative: Easy Access System Europe, Mustamäe tee 50, 10621 Tallinn, Estonia, gpsr.requests@easproject.com

www.ingramcontent.com/pod-product-compliance
Lightning Source LLC
Chambersburg PA
CBHW032147010526
44111CB00035B/1237